NARRATING THE SELF

Fictions of Japanese Modernity

Narrating the Self

Fictions of Japanese Modernity

TOMI SUZUKI

STANFORD UNIVERSITY PRESS

Stanford, California

Stanford University Press
Stanford, California

© 1996 by the Board of Trustees of the
Leland Stanford Junior University

Printed in the United States of America

CIP data are at the end of the book

The costs of publishing this book have been supported in part by an
award from the Hiromi Arisawa Memorial Fund (named in honor of the
renowned economist and the first chair of the Board of the University of
Tokyo Press) and financed by the generosity of Japanese citizens and
Japanese corporations to recognize excellence in scholarship on Japan.

For Kuniichi and Keiko Suzuki

Acknowledgments

I owe a great debt of gratitude to many teachers, friends, and family members, not all of whom I can mention here. First and foremost, I thank Edwin McClellan, my dissertation advisor at Yale University, who has been a source of inspiration over these many years. His detailed comments on the early drafts as well as his enthusiasm for this project were truly invaluable. I am also grateful to Shōichi Saeki, my teacher at the University of Tokyo, who first encouraged me to consider the problem of narration and the self in modern Japanese literature. His readings of a wide range of narratives had an immense influence on my formative years. I also acknowledge Sukehiro Hirakawa, Tōru Haga, Mark Morris, Georges May, Peter Brooks, and Shoshana Felman for their guidance and encouragement during my graduate days at the University of Tokyo and Yale University.

I also thank those individuals who offered valuable comments on the manuscript: Janet Walker, Phyllis Lyons, William Sibley, Marston Anderson, Paul Anderer, Mary Elizabeth Berry, and Kazuko Ōuchi. I am especially grateful to Janet Walker for her advice, which proved critical in the revision of the manuscript. The astute comments of the two anonymous readers for Stanford University Press helped to clarify the focus of this study. I express my deep appreciation for the intellectual and moral support of my colleagues Joel Lidov and Susan Spectorsky. Kazuko Ōuchi, Mihoko Suzuki, Sawako Shirahase, Jahar and Sunita Bhattacharya, and Gen and Sakae Shirane provided continuous encouragement. I feel especially privileged to have worked with John Ziemer, a thoughtful and exemplary editor at Stanford University Press. I must also mention Helen Tartar at Stanford University Press, who first took an interest in publishing this project. Generous funding from the Japan Foundation enabled me to conduct research in Tokyo, and successive grants from The City University of New York PSC-CUNY Research Award Program helped me prepare the manuscript.

Last but not least, I give my deepest thanks to Haruo Shirane, who contributed beyond words in shaping this book and who enabled me to complete what turned out to be a long and complex undertaking, and to our son Seiji, who showed great patience as he grew up with this project. I am grateful to my parents, Kuniichi and Keiko Suzuki, who gave me warm support whenever I needed it and wherever I lived.

T.S.
New York City

Contents

    Tanizaki Jun'ichirō's *Fool's Love*   151

    Epilogue: Tanizaki's Speaking Subject and
    Creation of Tradition   175

Reference Matter

NARRATING THE SELF

Fictions of Japanese Modernity

Narratives of Japanese Modernity

In the final analysis, the basis of all art lies in the self [*watakushi*]. It follows that the form that expresses the "self" directly and frankly, without pretense and disguise, that is to say, the I-novel, should become the main path, the basis, and the essence of the art of prose.

—Kume Masao

The problem of the I-novel is never limited to questions of literature. Instead, it is related to the nature of the modernity [*kindai*] of our country.

—Takeuchi Ryōchi

Literary critics both in Japan and in the West have characterized the Japanese "I-novel," the *watakushi shōsetsu* or *shi-shōsetsu*, as the most salient and unique form of modern Japanese literature.[1] *Shi-shōsetsu* generally designates an autobiographical narrative in which the author is thought to recount faithfully the details of his or her personal life in a thin guise of fiction. Literary historians usually trace the origins of this autobiographical genre to the works of Japanese Naturalist writers, specifically Tayama Katai's *Futon* (The quilt; 1907). A passage from Donald Keene's history of modern Japanese literature reflects the standard Japanese view.

As many critics have pointed out, Japanese Naturalism developed along quite different lines from any European example. European Naturalism arose largely as a reaction to the excessive emphasis on the individual in Romantic literature, but in Japan the most salient feature of Naturalist writing was the search for the individual. This search was intensified after the brief flowering of a specifically Romantic literature had passed and achieved its ultimate expression in the I-novel (*watakushi shōsetsu*), which were attempts in the form of novels to establish the individuality of the authors. The Naturalism of Zola or Maupassant came to be interpreted not as a method of examining human beings with scientific detachment, but as an absolutely faithful reproduction of real events, without admixture of fiction or even of imagination.[2]

According to the standard view, the mature form of Japanese Naturalism, which flourished from 1906 through the early 1910's, emphasized the search for the individual self through the faithful, objective reproduction of the author's personal life in his novels. In this version of literary history, Tayama Katai (1871–1930) is considered a Naturalist and the founder of the I-novel, and Shiga Naoya (1883–1971) is the writer who brought this form to its peak.

Despite the established position of the I-novel in literary historiography and the wide circulation of the term, the notion of the I-novel remains extremely elusive and difficult to grasp. The term *watakushi shōsetsu*, which emerged in the early to mid-1920's, initially referred to certain contemporary autobiographical sketches whose authors appeared to write directly about their personal lives for a closed circle of fellow writers. It soon grew into a broader, more nebulous concept. A number of literary historians and critics have tried to define the I-novel in terms of the author's intention, as a direct and faithful transcription or confession of his or her personal life, or in terms of the text's referential accuracy or faithfulness with regard to the facts of the author's "real life." Others have tried to define the I-novel thematically. It is impossible, however, to reach a comprehensive definition of the I-novel by examining only those texts designated as I-novels.

As Part I of this study reveals, the term *watakushi shōsetsu* circulated as a powerful and uncanny signifier without a fixed, identifiable signified, generating a critical discourse that informed not only the nature of literature but also views of Japanese selfhood, society, and tradition. This critical discourse, which I refer to as "I-novel discourse" or the "I-novel meta-narrative," is not a descriptive representation of a particular body of pre-existing texts. Rather, the characteristics of the so-called I-novel texts were largely defined by and within this I-novel meta-narrative and then projected back on certain texts. A genealogy and corpus of I-novels were retroactively constructed within this larger discourse and generated by it. I shall argue that the uncanny ability of *watakushi shōsetsu* as a signifier to generate such a powerful literary and cultural meta-narrative derived from the special mystique of the notion of *watakushi*, the "I" or "self," and from the privileged status of the novel, both of which emerged under the cultural hegemony of Western modernity. Given its special position in modern Japanese literary and cultural discourse, *watakushi shōsetsu* may best be rendered in English by "I-novel," a word used not as a descriptive or normative term, but as an evocative, ambiguous, and unique signifier.

I-novel discourse extended far beyond a closed literary circle to a wide and disparate community of writers, critics, social theorists, journalists, and historians. Why has the I-novel been so widely discussed since its emergence in the mid-1920's? What salient features did this I-novel meta-narrative have? What impact did I-novel discourse have, and how did it affect our present perception of Japanese literary texts? As I shall argue, although I-novel discourse evolved from the 1920's through the 1960's, it maintained certain significant structural features. First, the notion of the I-novel was always formulated on a polar axis that contrasted the Western novel with its Japanese counterpart. As we shall see, the I-novel meta-narrative was premised on a binary, polar opposition between the Western novel, which was seen as a fictional, imaginative construct, and the Japanese I-novel, which was characterized as a factual, direct expression of the author's lived experience. Second, from the time of the term's appearance in the early 1920's, "I-novel" was always a value-laden concept: the binary contrast was never neutral or simply descriptive; instead, it implied a hierarchical opposition that always raised the question of which pole was the "truer" novel. The I-novel was, for example, alternately celebrated for its veracity and reviled for its immaturity. Third, the evaluation of the I-novel extended not only to the author's "self" and "life" but also to Japanese society—one writer, for example, said: "The deformed I-novel was the product of a deformed society"[3]—and to the nature of Japan's modernity (*kindai*) as well as of its history and tradition.

From the 1920's the I-novel meta-narrative not only defined the modern Japanese novel as a form that directly transcribed the author's lived experience but also emphasized the confessional, self-exploratory, autobiographical nature of the "indigenous" Japanese literary tradition, describing classical literature with such highly Western, romantic terms and phrases as "immediacy," "directness," "lyricism," "spiritual search for the self," "unity with nature."[4] Both detractors and eulogizers of the I-novel, who unwittingly collaborated in characterizing the I-novel as direct, immediate, and factual as opposed to fictional, projected these same notions of directness and factuality on the so-called indigenous tradition and emphasized its continuity with the I-novel. I-novel critical discourse, in short, became from the mid-1920's the dominant paradigm and meta-narrative by which almost all literary works, including classical texts, were described, judged, and interpreted, regulating the reception and production of modern literary texts and governing contemporary views of the Japanese literary and cultural tradition.

Since the late 1960's, Western critics have attacked the assumption of the "self" or "subject" as an a priori, self-sufficient entity. Lévi-Strauss, Barthes, Foucault, Lacan, Derrida, and others have questioned the notion of the subject as a controlling consciousness and as the ultimate origin of meaning. The subject has been presented instead as a process and effect constituted by

and resulting from the interplay of historically conditioned institutional, political, and discursive systems of differences. There has also been a growing
awareness in the West of the historicity of Western modernity, spurred on in
particular by the debate in the 1980's on post-modernism. One result is that
the I-novel issue no longer seems to haunt Japanese writers and readers with
the same intensity. But although the I-novel issue may have lost some of its
earlier urgency, the I-novel as a meta-narrative still affects our perception of
Japanese literary texts—both the language of those texts and the "reality"
represented in them—as well as our perception of the so-called Japanese
literary, cultural, and linguistic tradition.

For example, in a recent major study of the I-novel, *The Rhetoric of
Confession: Shishōsetsu in Early Twentieth-Century Japanese Fiction* (1988), Edward Fowler emphasizes its "intrinsic" narratological features, features he
claims are rooted in an "indigenous linguistic and epistemological tradition"
that values only "immediate, lived experience." "In a culture that views
'reality' only as immediate experience of the natural world, literature not
surprisingly becomes a chronicling or transcribing of that experience rather
than an imaginative reconstruction of it."[5] The continuity that Fowler emphasizes between the *shi-shōsetsu* and the "indigenous tradition," however, is
the direct result as well as a sophisticated reinforcement of what I call I-novel
discourse, the explanatory and analytical narrative schema that retroactively
constructed the "indigenous" tradition according to the I-novel paradigm.
Fowler's portrait of this tradition is in fact based on a 1949 article ("From
Carnal Literature to Carnal Politics") by the intellectual historian Maruyama
Masao, who characterized the Western intellectual tradition as one that valued fiction or "mediated reality." Maruyama argued that the quintessence of
Western modernity is the "notion of fiction as an intellectual construct of the
individual mind freed from a predetermined social order" and contrasted this
Western tradition with the "Japanese tradition" which, in his view, values
only "immediate reality" and in which "man's intellectual and spiritual side is
neither differentiated nor independent from perceived nature."[6] Maruyama
consequently placed contemporary, postwar Japanese society at the same
stage as medieval European society and urged Japanese society to modernize
by developing a proper notion of fiction.

Maruyama's argument was in fact part of the larger I-novel discourse,
particularly that aspect developed by Kobayashi Hideo in 1935, which was in
turn reinforced by Nakamura Mitsuo in 1950.[7] In his *Essays on the Novel of
Manners* (*Fūzoku shōsetsu ron*; 1950) Nakamura condemned the I-novel for
"distorting the proper development of the genuine modern realistic novel" as
well as for developing a "deformed I" instead of the "socialized I or true
modern individual" found in the modern European novel. Nakamura argues

that this "mistaken path" occurred because early twentieth-century Japanese Naturalist writers—who became the first I-novelists—blindly acted out the role of Western fictional protagonists without really understanding how Western authors treated or created fictional characters. Nakamura criticized Japanese Naturalist writers for not properly understanding fictionality and for confusing fiction and facts. Nakamura was one of the few I-novel critics who analyzed the texts themselves instead of vaguely discussing the author's "life" or the relationship of the "work" to the author's "life" (which was in fact an amalgam of "documentary data" taken from the works themselves). But even Nakamura often confused the authors of the I-novel with their fictional protagonists, who, as we shall see, cannot automatically be identified with their authors.

The I-novel was considered a single-voiced, faithful record and reproduction of the author's lived, personal experience, but many of the texts defined by I-novel discourse as typical I-novels—such as Katai's *Futon*, Tōson's *Haru* (Spring; 1908), and Shiga Naoya's *An'ya kōro* (A dark night's passing; 1921–37)—are actually narrated in the third person. Contrary to what is generally believed, the voice and perspective of the protagonist do not necessarily overlap with those of the narrator, who does not have to be identified with the author. The referential context has also been altered. The fact that certain words or expressions earlier taken as direct references to the extra-textual "reality" of the author's "life" now appear to be part of a larger web of verbal signs reveals the textual nature of what were formerly believed to be "extra-textual realities" and "lives." This applies even to overtly autobiographical works such as Shiga Naoya's *Wakai* (Reconciliation; 1917), which have often been thought to make little sense when read outside the framework of the author's life story.[8] In short, when these texts are read apart from an established context or a meta-narrative of the author's "life story," these so-called I-novels can no longer be identified as such on purely formal grounds.

In his influential study of autobiography as a genre, Philippe Lejeune argues that an indispensable criterion for an autobiography is the presence of an "autobiographical contract," a textual affirmation of the identity of the author, the narrator, and the protagonist, an identity that ultimately refers to the name of the author on the cover of the book.[9]

> When we look for something to distinguish fiction from autobiography, to serve as a basis for the referent of "I" in first-person narratives, there is no need to appeal to an impossible region "outside-the-text": the text itself provides, on its outer edge, this final term, the proper name of the author, which is at once textual and indubitably referential. This referentiality is indubitable because it is based on two social situations: the legal identity of the individual (a convention

which is internalized by each of us from early childhood) and the publisher's contract; there is hence no reason to doubt the author's identity.[10]

Lejeune's most fruitful contribution to the study of autobiography and to the study of narrative in general lies in his definition of autobiography as a contractual genre. For Lejeune, the "meaning" of a text depends on how it is read. Ultimately, however, Lejeune stresses the author's initiative in establishing this mutual contract. This apparent contradiction does not damage Lejeune's argument since his examples are drawn from European literature written from the end of the eighteenth century to the 1970's. According to Lejeune, the contemporary Western notion of autobiography was codified in Europe around 1770. A contract ("autobiographical" versus "fictional") is mutually established between an author and a reader who share certain assumptions about the nature of literary genres, particularly the distinction between "fictional" and "referential" narratives in relationship to the value of proper names and individual identity.

Modern Japanese literature, however, did not have the kind of codified epistemological and literary consensus (such as the distinction between fiction and autobiography) that Lejeune finds in modern European literature. The referential, autobiographical reading of these texts was not necessarily the result of a contract proposed by the author. In the case of the I-novel, it is ultimately the reader who assumes a "hidden contract" in the text. Such a reader sees the referential "faithfulness" of the text *or* a specific formal characteristic (such as a single-voiced narrative presenting a single consciousness and following the chronological order of the "author's" life), or both, as signs of the author's I-novel intentions. Contrary to the arguments of previous studies, the so-called I-novel is not a genre that can be defined by certain referential, thematic, or formal characteristics. Instead, as I shall argue, the reader's expectations concerning, and belief in, the single identity of the protagonist, the narrator, and the author of a given text ultimately make a text an I-novel. The I-novel is best defined as a mode of reading that assumes that the I-novel is a single-voiced, "direct" expression of the author's "self" and that its written language is "transparent"—characteristics hitherto regarded as "intrinsic" features of the I-novel. The I-novel, instead of being a particular literary form or genre, was a literary and ideological paradigm by which a vast majority of literary works were judged and described. Any text can become an I-novel if read in this mode. Indeed, the so-called characteristics of the I-novel often reveal more about the particular ideology and epistemological paradigm that dominated the period from the 1920's to the 1960's than about the intrinsic nature of these particular texts. As we shall see, I-novel critical discourse retroactively created a corpus or canon of I-novels.

The establishment of an interpretive tradition or reading paradigm based on these assumptions eventually led to what can be called the "self-conscious I-novel" and the "self-conscious anti-I-novel." In the "self-conscious I-novel" the author presupposes these autobiographical assumptions on the part of the reader. The "self-conscious anti-I-novel," by contrast, works against, and yet still within, these expectations. Toward the end of the Taishō period (1912–26), the notion of the I-novel had acquired wide currency among writers and the reading public, and the I-novel reading mode had become firmly established. This new I-novel critical discourse designated Kasai Zenzō (1887–1928), who had been writing autobiographical pieces under the heavy influence of Japanese Naturalism, as the most representative contemporary I-novelist.[11] A group of younger writers—Kamura Isota (1897–1933), Makino Shin'ichi (1896–1936), Ozaki Kazuo (1899–1983), Kawasaki Chōtarō (1901–85), Kanbayashi Akatsuki (1902–80), among others—subsequently emerged as "self-conscious I-novelists"; that is, they became novelists after the notion of the I-novel had been established, and they presupposed and internalized the I-novel reading mode. The novels of Kasai and these younger writers share certain thematic similarities: the depiction of the sordid, daily life of a novelist or artist locked in a painful struggle to write while suffering from difficulties with his wife or other women as well as from poverty, sickness, loneliness, and an awareness of a lack of creativity. Indeed, available biographical information about these self-conscious I-novelists leads to the strong suspicion that they were caught in a vicious circle of "art" and "life." Although it is generally believed that these I-novelists faithfully depicted their daily lives, their I-novels, it appears, often influenced their own lives, and their actions were frequently governed by the needs and demands of self-portraiture. In fact, the interrelations between life and art, one of the main concerns of I-novel critical discourse, became one of the themes of these self-conscious I-novels.

The problem of the I-novel, however, is not limited to these self-conscious I-novelists. As we shall see, the I-novel reading paradigm influenced both the production and the reception of texts written during the period of its dominance as well as retroactively the interpretation of almost all earlier texts. The I-novel reading mode was part of a larger historical process (generally referred to as Japan's modernization) involving fundamental changes in assumptions about literature, the novel (*shōsetsu*), language, representation, and views of the "self." I-novel discourse emerged at a time when literary work was thought, above all, to be a process by which the author faithfully reveals his or her "genuine self." It is no coincidence that the Japanese I-novel became a topic of critical discourse in the mid- to late Taishō period, in the

1920's, after the liberal, humanistic movement called Taishō Democracy had swept through Japan. The concern for the "modern, individual self," which came to the fore from the early 1890's and lay behind Taishō Democracy, was reinforced on a wide scale by this liberal humanistic movement. By the latter half of the Taishō period, the ideal of the individual self as an independent social and moral entity was widely considered a fundamental premise of life, literature, and art. In fact, many intellectuals of the time were drawn to Marxism, which questioned the naïveté of humanistic individualism and which grew influential after the mid-1920's, out of their larger concern for the "true" and "genuine" self.

I-novel discourse emerged at a time not only when literary work was thought to be an expression of the author's empirical or "genuine" self but when the language of the novel was regarded as a transparent medium that could directly represent the author's "self." By the mid-1920's, when the concept and practice of *genbun-itchi* (unification of the spoken and written languages) were standardized and widely institutionalized, language was generally assumed to be a transparent medium capable of directly transcribing both external and internal realities. Paradoxically, the introduction in the 1920's of European modernism, which emphasized the materiality and autonomy of written language, reinforced the view that *genbun-itchi* language existed *a priori* as a transparent medium and was not a recent construct. The Japanese superimposed the European modernist criticism of the "established, old realism"—an attack on realism for its view of language only as a referential tool—on what had now come to be regarded as I-novels, a body of texts thought to transcribe the "facts" of the author's lived experience in a "transparent" *genbun-itchi* language.

Some scholars (Fowler and some Japanese critics) argue that the I-novel was the cultural product of a guild-like, small, closed society, the *bundan* (literary circle), in which writers, readers, and publishers knew each other personally and developed a referential mode of reading and writing, and that this cultural phenomenon ended in the mid-1920's because of the emergence of the aesthetically oriented Neo-Perceptionists and of the more socially conscious Proletarian writers as well as because of the massive expansion of journalism. The growing role of journalism in an expanding industrialized mass society after the mid-1920's, however, actually spread and institutionalized I-novel critical discourse, making it the dominant paradigm of historical and cultural analysis.

Readers today are more conscious that both the production and the reception of texts are culturally and socio-historically conditioned. Critics are similarly more self-conscious of their "subject position," of their historical and ideological stance toward the text. Two recent well-researched book-length studies in Western languages on the I-novel—Iremela Hijiya-Kirschnereit's *Selbstenblössungsrituale* (1981) and Edward Fowler's *Rhetoric of Confession* (1988) are products of such critical consciousness. Hijiya-Kirschnereit, who criticizes Japanese scholarship for lacking a critical norm for the I-novel and warns Western critics against imposing the expectations developed in the context of the European novel on the I-novel, attempts to define the genre by constructing an Ideal Type, a comprehensive structural model based on a reconstruction and synthesis of earlier Japanese definitions and evaluations of the I-novel. Drawing on Hans Robert Jauss's notion of the horizon of collective expectations, Hijiya-Kirschnereit attempts to construct a comprehensive model of the I-novel based on an "equal treatment" of a vast number of secondary sources on the topic of the I-novel (written from the 1920's through 1980). In creating this model, Hijiya-Kirschnereit combines two fundamental principles: (1) "factuality" (*Faktizität*), mutual understanding between the author and the reader about the referential fidelity of the author's lived experience, and (2) "focus figure" (*Fokusfigur*), a single perspective common to protagonist, narrator, and author. Although Hijiya-Kirschnereit considers the I-novel a contextual genre realized when the reader adopts these two principles, she ultimately regards them as inscribed in the text itself—an inscription she traces to a horizon of expectations that she believes to be deeply rooted in a traditional Japanese aesthetics—the "*makoto* principle," which values "fact," "truth," or "sincerity" as opposed to "fabrication," "non-truth," or "lie."[12]

Hijiya-Kirschnereit's sociological approach, which attempts to study the I-novel as a mode of social and cultural communication, and Fowler's textual approach, which tries to reveal the "powerfully persuasive rhetorical apparatus" that "sustains the myth of sincerity," converge in that both ultimately regard the I-novel as an inherent literary genre with identifiable textual features and an essential meaning that can be correctly decoded and interpreted. Their emphasis on the continuity between the "intrinsic features of the *shishōsetsu*" and the "indigenous cultural—literary, aesthetic, linguistic, epistemological—tradition," particularly the "value on the experiential truth," provides them with a kind of analytical meta-narrative that legitimizes their particular interpretations of modern Japanese texts. As I have noted, however, the characterization of such an indigenous tradition as well as the emphasis on its continuity are in large part a modern construction of the I-novel meta-narrative. What Hijiya-Kirschnereit refers to as the "traditional *haiku* theory of *shasei*, 'sketch or snapshot of *shinkyō* ("state of mind"),'" for example, is none other than a modern, Western-based notion, first proposed by a modern *haiku/tanka* poet Masaoka Shiki (1867–1902), retroactively projected back on the "tradition."[13]

My study, which began independently of those by Hijiya-Kirschnereit and Fowler, takes a different critical approach. My purpose is not to reconstruct a comprehensive model of the I-novel or to identify and describe its "intrinsic" textual features. In this sense, my study is not about the I-novel per se. As I have stated, instead of taking the I-novel as naturally given, objectively identifiable texts to be described and interpreted "correctly," I consider the I-novel issue ultimately as a historically constructed dominant reading and interpretive paradigm—which soon became a generative cultural discourse. Instead of simply examining the thematic and formal features of what standard literary histories narrowly categorize as I-novels, my study emphasizes the historical formation of a discursive field in which the corpus of the I-novel was retroactively created and defined and from which the standard literary histories emerged. My study attempts to place this dynamic "I-novel discourse" in the perspective of the broader historical context of Japan's modernization, which has hitherto been described by this I-novel discourse.

Parts I and II of this study focus on the changing discursive position of the *shōsetsu* as a cultural trope between the 1880's and the 1950's, on Christianity and Japanese Naturalism from the 1890's through the 1910's, on the Humanist ideals of the Shirakaba group and Taishō Democracy in the 1910's and 1920's, on the *genbun-itchi* movement from the mid-1880's and the creation of a standardized national language, and on the introduction of modernism in the late 1920's—all of which significantly shaped the larger literary and epistemological paradigms of the modern period. These two parts attempt to reveal how I-novel discourse was inextricably related to the interaction among certain fundamental assumptions—about literature, the *shōsetsu*, literary language, representation, the "self," and the problems of history and tradition—that were constructed and naturalized between the 1880's and the 1920's and that persist to the present. In the process, this study explores in depth the significance of the modern Japanese concern for, and preoccupation with, Western notions of love, sexuality, nature, and "truth," which, as I will show, constituted a major axis of I-novel discourse and radiated from the privileged signifier of modernity, the "self." This study reveals that I-novel discourse cannot be reduced to the so-called liberal-humanist or romantic view of the self and language—the self viewed as an autonomous entity and the source of its own language—but always involves the (hi)story of Japan's cultural identity and tradition.

These various arguments inform and are developed in Parts II and III through a linked series of close readings of selected texts categorized by later literary historians either as I-novels—for example, Tayama Katai's *Futon* and Shiga Naoya's "autobiographical novels"—or as "anti-I-novels"—such as Tanizaki Jun'ichirō's *Chijin no ai* (A fool's love; translated into English as *Naomi*) and Nagai Kafū's *Bokutō kidan* (A strange tale from east of the river). As we shall see in Part II, many early twentieth-century Japanese writers such as Katai and Shiga became preoccupied with the notion of the "self" as an enigmatic, yet essential, new reality. It was this reality, which they thought they had discovered through their encounter with Western novels, that they attempted to develop and achieve through their novel writing. These Japanese writers also aspired to create a new written language that could directly represent this new reality just as the language of Western novels appeared to do. But although these writers advocated and promoted the view of language as a direct and transparent vehicle to transcribe objective reality, they in fact often wrote narratives—later regarded as I-novels—that dramatized and problematized the historical processes by which the new paradigms of reality were adapted through the mediation and ideologically charged authority of Western literature and taken for granted as *a priori* reality or "fact." By the mid-1920's, however, when the notion of the I-novel had emerged, these narrative texts were regarded as autobiographical I-novels, as direct transcriptions of the author's lived experience, and the multiple and often conflicting voices informing these texts had been reduced to the author's "self" (or "non-self"). Although critics of the I-novel spoke of the immaturity or absence of a modern self in the Japanese novel, they assumed that the ultimate meaning of these texts resided in their "origin," the author's "self." At the same time, my discussion of narrative fiction by Kafū and Tanizaki in Part III reveals that although their texts moved beyond the so-called I-novel by defamiliarizing the established assumptions of the I-novel, these texts nevertheless returned to the powerful obsessions that inspired and nourished I-novel discourse in the continuing dialogue about the self, modernity, tradition, and writing.

In this study I use the term "discourse" with three overlapping implications. First, as developed by the Russian formalists and the French structuralists, especially by Gérard Genette, discourse (*récit*) refers to the narrative plane, actualized through the particular manner and way of narrating, as opposed to its content plane or "story" (*histoire*).[14] Second, the notion of discourse as developed by the linguist Emile Benveniste in his analysis of two distinct and complementary narrative systems or planes of utterance—"discourse" (*discours*) and "history" / "historical utterance" (*histoire*)—in which discourse involves a reference to the act of enunciation, implying a sender / speaker and a receiver / hearer, and establishes a link between the statement and the context in which the enunciation occurs. In history, by contrast, events are presented without reference to the speaker in the narration.[15] Third, the notion of discourse as developed by Michel Foucault refers to a way or practice of speaking (in a broad sense) situated in social, historical, and institutional (and thus political and economic) conditions, the emphasis being on the social practices and institutions that, both as an instrument and an effect of power, shape and condition the production and reception of verbal and other statements.[16] In this study, I use the term "discourse" primarily in this third sense, but activate the first and second implications to analyze the act of enunciation in relationship to the shaping of narrative in various broader contexts. Focusing in particular on the problem of narration and language and on the issue of reading and interpretation, this study reveals that while the narrative texts discussed here are related to, and in many cases contributed to, the historical formation of the fundamental ideological assumptions that inform I-novel discourse, they often problematize, question, and subvert these very I-novel reading assumptions. In the process, they place not only the I-novel discursive field, itself increasingly oblivious of its historicity, but also the various fictions of Japanese modernity in a relative, ironical, and historical perspective.

PART I

The Novel and the Self as Master Signifiers

᠊᠊᠊᠊᠊᠊᠊᠊

CHAPTER I

The Position of the 'Shōsetsu': Paradigm Change and New Literary Discourse

In an article written in 1950, Terada Tōru (1915–), a critic and scholar of French literature, astutely noted that "*watakushi/shi-shōsetsu* is no more than a formal designation in that we can never tell what is contained in it. . . . The term forces the reader to confront a word whose resonance is much greater than what it designates, the meaning of which is only vaguely understood in common usage."[1] As we shall see, the term functioned and circulated as a powerful signifier (*signifiant*) without a fixed, identifiable signified (*signifié*), generating a critical discourse that not only affected the reception of particular texts but formed the center of the dominant ideological, aesthetic, and epistemological paradigms of the modern period. The uncanny and mystifying power of the I-novel as a privileged signifier is epitomized in the following passage, written in 1925 by Kume Masao, an early eulogizer of *watakushi shōsetsu*.

> I consider the I-novel to be the true path and essence of prose art. . . . What I call the I-novel is not a translation of the German *Ich-Roman*. Instead, it refers to another sort of *shōsetsu*, the "autobiographical" *shōsetsu* [*jijo shōsetsu*]; it signifies a *shōsetsu* in which the author reveals his self directly. The I-novel, however, does not signify "autobiography" [*jijoden*] or "confession" [*kokuhaku*]. Above all, it must be a *shōsetsu*; that is to say, it must be art [*geijutsu*].[2]

This strong reliance on the privileged status of the notion of the *shōsetsu* as well as that of the *watakushi* are characteristic of I-novel critical discourse from the 1920's through the 1960's, which will be examined in Chapter 3.[3] Indeed the term *watakushi shōsetsu* became a powerful master signifier in large part as a result of the special mystique of the notion of the *watakushi*, the "I" or "self," as well as the new notion of the *shōsetsu*, both of which resulted from Japan's encounter with the West in the latter half of the nineteenth century. I-novel discourse emerged in the mid-1920's, but one must turn to the notions of *watakushi* (I, self) and the *shōsetsu*, which acquired a special mystique much earlier, to understand the full implications of I-novel discourse. How, then, did the notions of the *shōsetsu* and the "self" come to assume such special positions and under what historical circumstances? How were they related to other discursive formations? How did they lead to the formation of I-novel discourse? This chapter will examine in a larger historical context the transformation of the discursive position of the *shōsetsu* as a cultural trope.

Premodern Notions of the Shōsetsu

Today the word *shōsetsu* is used to refer to Japanese and Western prose fiction of any length, including Western novels, short stories, the *roman*, and the *nouvelle*. The word itself derives from the Chinese *hsiao-shuo* (literally, "small talk"), a term that Pan Ku (A.D. 32–92) used in his "Treatise on Literature" in the *History of the Han Dynasty* (1st c.) to refer to "not-so-valuable street talk collected by minor officials."[4] Although *shōsetsu* is now applied to a variety of premodern Japanese narrative genres, including medieval tales, the word appeared in Japan only after the late seventeenth century, when Japanese Confucian scholars (such as Ogyū Sorai and Itō Tōgai), in studying Ming period Chinese phonology and linguistics, generated popular interest in Ming vernacular fiction. These scholars, who lectured on Chinese vernacular fiction, were called *shōsetsuka*, "scholars of *shōsetsu*."[5]

Until the 1880's, *shōsetsu* primarily referred to Ming and Ch'ing Chinese vernacular *hsiao-shuo*, such as *The Water Margin* (*Shui-hu chuan*), *The Journey to the West* (*Hsi-yu chi*), *The Three Kingdoms* (*San-kuo yen-i*), *Chin P'ing Mei*, and *The Dream of the Red Chamber* (*Hung-lou meng*), which were widely read in Japan in annotated versions, translations, or adaptations. It also referred to the popular Japanese historical narratives called *yomihon* (literally, "reading books," as opposed to *kusa-zōshi*, "illustrated books"), which were to a great extent adaptations or imitations of the Ming and Ch'ing vernacular *hsiao-shuo* and which were widely enjoyed not only by women and children, as commonly believed, but by a wide range of intellectuals, samurai, and wealthy townsmen well versed in both the Chinese and the Japanese classics.[6] Although the *yomihon*, often referred to as *shōsetsu*, incorporated features of earlier literary genres—*kabuki*, *bunraku*, medieval epics, Buddhist tales—they remained within the sphere of Ming-Ch'ing critical discourse, including the use of the vernacular.[7]

In the Chinese tradition, *hsiao-shuo*, often referred to as *pai-shih* (unoffi cial history) or *yu-shih* (supplemental, leftover history), stood in a subsidiary relationship to orthodox historiography, which occupied a central position in the Chinese narrative tradition. In the Tokugawa period, the word *shōsetsu* was similarly interchangeable with the term *haishi* (vulgar, unorthodox history) as opposed to *seishi* (official, orthodox history). *Shōsetsu* and *haishi* in fact sometimes appeared together as a compound word *haishi-shōsetsu* or *shōsetsu-haishi*. The following comments by Kyokutei (Takizawa) Bakin (1767–1848) and Shikitei Sanba (1776–1822), respectively, on their own works are typical of the Tokugawa attitude toward the *shōsetsu*.

> According to the ancients, *haishi-shōsetsu* attempt to explicate what appears in the *seishi* (official histories) and make their contents widely available to the general public. *Bōkan-yashi* (vulgar histories), by contrast, follow the wind and seize the shadows, thereby deluding the public. There is no doubt which of the two—*haihen-shōsetsu* [otherwise called *haishi-shōsetsu*] or *bōkan-yashi*—is erroneous and groundless, and which causes people confusion. Although this book, *Yumiharizuki*, is a *shōsetsu*, it draws on historical records and is completely faithful to the official histories. It never fabricates unsubstantiated events. Every word is carefully considered. Thus it does not confuse or mislead. The book is based on authentic sources that can be documented. As a consequence, its popularity will not be ephemeral and people will rely on it forever.[8]

> To educate and raise children, we use both bitter medicine and sweet candy. When it comes to books, the three Chinese classical histories and the five Confucian classics are bitter medicine, while narrative fiction [*haikan-yashi*, "unorthodox, vulgar history"] is sweet candy. Although there are many manuals for the education of women, such books as *Onna daigaku* and *Imagawa* are so bitter that women and girls can hardly appreciate them. This *shōsetsu* about a bathhouse for women may appear to be no more than light entertainment, but it is as easy to appreciate as sweet candy and the ways of good, evil, and righteousness can be learned without effort.[9]

The *shōsetsu*, which were referred to as "defective or dubious historical writings," were thought to be inferior yet more entertaining than "official historical writings," and their authors were content to call them "playthings" or "amusements" (*nagusamimono* or *gesaku*). Under the pretense of being "playthings," *shōsetsu* in fact could deviate from the official histories (*seishi*) and satirize orthodox social values. They were so potentially subversive that beginning in the late eighteenth century successive governments frequently banned them. When the *shōsetsu* attempted to justify itself, however, it always did so by claiming a close relationship to *seishi*, the "official histories." Even when the *shōsetsu* differentiated itself from the "official histories," it did so by claiming to be a more effective vehicle for popularizing and transmitting Confucian moral values than the "official histories" themselves. (The clichés in Sanba's statement, which are presented with humor and irony, cheapen, while clarifying, the standard attitude toward canonical writing.)

Modern literary histories have tended to overemphasize the low position of the *shōsetsu* in the Tokugawa period vis-à-vis the highly regarded histories. The contrast between "vulgar history / *shōsetsu*" and "official history," however, was not necessarily a distinction between fiction and facts, or between imagination and lived experience, as a number of modern scholars believe.[10] The concern for "history" expressed by Bakin is not a matter of actual "facts" but of earlier historical sources, of documentability within the corpus of authoritative "official histories," the ultimate model of which was, as Sanba's comment suggests, the three Chinese classical histories—Ssu-ma Ch'ien's *Historical Records* (*Shih chi*), Pan Ku's *History of the Han Dynasty* (*Han shu*), and the *History of the Later Han Dynasty* (*Hou Han shu*).[11]

This notion of the *shōsetsu* or *haishi* (unofficial, vulgar history) carried over into the early Meiji period. The *seiji shōsetsu*, or political *shōsetsu*, which became popular at the height of the Freedom and People's Rights movement (Jiyū minken undō), inherited the same critical framework. From around 1880, the advocates of this movement, who were educated in the Chinese tradition and later in Western languages, attempted to popularize their political ideals of equality, universal suffrage, and representational government through the *shōsetsu*, in the form of the *yomihon*, which they considered the most effective means of instructing and enlightening a wide range of people. They called for a new *shōsetsu* to "free people from evil customs" by "disseminating the ideals of freedom and equality," a new *shōsetsu* to replace the traditional *shōsetsu*, which, "as a product of traditional society, had advocated the traditional moral doctrine of Confucian filiality and obedience."[12] This need for "reform" of the *shōsetsu* became an urgent issue in 1883 among activists of the People's Rights movement, when the government, in an attempt to suppress the movement, stiffened its restrictions on the publication of newspapers and public gatherings. Inspired by politically influential Western writers such as Victor Hugo and Benjamin Disraeli, these ambitious young activists began writing *seiji shōsetsu*, which were loose, free adaptations of late eighteenth- and early nineteenth-century European historical romances such as Alexandre Dumas's *Mémoires d'un médecin* (which referred to the French Revolution and to Rousseau's *Contrat social*). Written in the *yomihon* narrative style, these political *shōsetsu* followed the basic plot pattern of the Ming and Ch'ing historical hero-centered *hsiao-shuo* or of the *ts'ai-tzu chia-jen hsiao-shuo* (J. *saishi-kajin shōsetsu*), a type of *shōsetsu* based on a romance between a "young talented hero" (*saishi*) and "beautiful women" (*kajin*).[13]

The *seiji shōsetsu* were allegorical stories that attempted to popularize parliamentary and constitutional ideals, including such Enlightenment notions as equality and freedom thought to provide the necessary basis for an "advanced nation." The critical posture of their authors toward the *shōsetsu* remained essentially the same, however, as that of Bakin and other Tokugawa *yomihon* writers. In his preface to *Keikoku bidan* (Commendable anecdotes on creating a nation: young politicians of Thebes; 1883–84), one of the most influential and popular *seiji shōsetsu*, Yano Ryūkei (1850–1931), a Freedom and People's Rights activist, alternated between defining his *shōsetsu* as "mere amusement" and as a "supplement to history." He stated, no doubt to protect himself against government censorship, that "the work should be regarded as no more than a *haishi-shōsetsu*, a plaything [*yūge no gu*] that allows people to wander in a world of fantasy."[14] At the same time, however, he emphasized that this work—about the rise of democratic Thebes in ancient Greece—was based on "true" documented "history."

> My original intention in writing this book was to write an orthodox history [*seishi*]. Therefore I will not distort historical facts or confuse the just and the unjust, good and evil, like the ordinary *shōsetsu*. I will only add a little color to the framework of historical facts. . . . In order to give the reader the pleasure of reading a *shōsetsu* and the benefit of reading orthodox history, to let the reader know that this book is based entirely on orthodox history, the author will cite all historical sources.[15]

In the fashion of Tokugawa *yomihon* writers, Ryūkei justified his *seiji shōsetsu*—which follows the basic plot pattern of the *Water Margin*—in terms of "orthodox history" and meticulously cited Western histories throughout.[16] Although the model for orthodox histories was shifting from the Confucian classics to Western sources, the need to justify the *shōsetsu* in terms of those "orthodox histories" remained essentially the same. This stance is also evident in *Kajin no kigū* (Chance meetings with beautiful women; 1885–97), a *seiji shōsetsu* by Tōkai Sanshi enthusiastically received in the late 1880's. Its characters are drawn from various countries (such as Spain, Ireland, China, Japan). Each of them is fighting for the national independence of his or her country, but the narrative constantly refers to events in the classical Chinese histories regardless of the nationality of the character.[17]

Paradigm Change: Tsubouchi Shōyō and Futabatei Shimei

The significance of the term *shōsetsu* changed radically in the mid-1880's, when Tsubouchi Shōyō, in his influential *Shōsetsu shinzui* (The essence of the novel; 1885–86), referred to the Western novel as the "true *shōsetsu*" (*makoto no shōsetsu*). In contrast to *seiji shōsetsu* writers, for whom the *shōsetsu* was ultimately a vehicle for popularizing their political ideals, Shōyō advocated the "autonomous value of the true *shōsetsu*," whose mission was to "concretely represent the invisible and mysterious mechanism of human life."[18] Shōyō argued that, "as the most advanced literary art," the *shōsetsu* must not be a slave of didacticism, whether it be the traditional Confucian morality found in the *yomihon* or the new political ideals of the *seiji shōsetsu*. Shōyō's *Shōsetsu shinzui* should be understood as part of the larger movement in the 1880's to promote the rapid development and westernization of Japan as a modern nation-state. The following passage reveals his motives.

> If the *shōsetsu* has such values, it behooves us to reform and improve our immature *shōsetsu-haishi* to perfect them so that they surpass the Western *shōsetsu*, thereby making our *shōsetsu* the greatest art, the flower of our nation [*kokka no hana*]. If we really desire to achieve this goal, we should first investigate why and how advanced civilizations obtained their strength while avoiding their past mistakes. Unless we study and follow the superior ways of the West, thereby creating the basis for a superior *haishi*, our Eastern *shōsetsu-haishi* will remain at the stage of the Western romance and never have the opportunity to progress.[19]

Using the framework of Herbert Spencer's theory of Social Darwinism, which lay behind many Meiji period notions of modernization and westernization, Shōyō placed all existing Japanese prose fiction within the category of *shōsetsu*, whose most advanced form, in his eyes, was the Western novel, the "true *shōsetsu*." The title *Shōsetsu shinzui*, usually translated as "the essence of the novel," can also mean "the (Western) novel as the essence of the *shōsetsu*."

Shōyō was the first to use the term *shōsetsu* systematically as a generic term for prose fiction in general. In the Tokugawa period, prose fiction was referred to by a variety of terms based on content—such as *ukiyo-zōshi* (books on the floating world), *sharebon* (books on the refined manners of the licensed quarters), and *ninjōbon* (books on human feelings)—or on physical appearance—such as *akahon* (red books, mainly illustrated books for children), *kurohon* (black books, historical fiction), *kibyōshi* (yellow books, illustrated humor and satire for adults)—or on the mode of presentation—such as *yomihon* (reading books) and *kusa-zōshi* (grass books, or illustrated books).[20] By placing this amalgam of prose genres alongside the Western romance and Western novel and calling all of them *shōsetsu*, Shōyō established a common ground for evaluating all existing Japanese prose fiction according to an "universal" standard, along a nineteenth-century Western, evolutionary axis in which the earlier Japanese *shōsetsu* (represented by Bakin's *yomihon*) was placed at the stage of the Western romance and prior to the stage of the Western novel, the "true *shōsetsu*."[21]

In his effort to "reform the Japanese *shōsetsu*," Shōyō emphasized the "imitation" or "mimetic depiction" (*mosha* or *mogi*) of "human feelings" (*ninjō*) as the key to making the novel the "most advanced form of literary art."[22] Influenced by Victorian literary discourse (represented by Matthew Arnold),[23] Shōyō argued that the essential value of art, particularly that of the novel, is to "amuse and elevate the human mind," to offer a "criticism of life" that forces the reader to reconsider human life in terms of both human feelings (*ninjō*) and socio-historical circumstances (*setai*).[24]

In *Shōsetsu shinzui*, *ninjō* refers broadly to "human feelings" or "human psychology," one of whose main forms is "affection or love [*airen*] between man and woman."[25] According to Shōyō, "affection" should be the "central topic of the true novel [*makoto no shōsetsu*] because it dramatically reveals human psychology [*shinri*]."[26] Shōyō's *ninjō*, however, also had a narrower, specifically negative dimension, denoting "vulgar, obscene desires."[27] Indeed, for Shōyō the word *ninjō* was most closely associated with the late Tokugawa period writer of popular fiction Tamenaga Shunsui's *ninjōbon*, which he regarded as low-class entertainment, far inferior to Bakin's *yomihon* (*shōsetsu*) because of its "vulgarity, frivolity, and obscenity."[28] At the same time, Shōyō praised Tamenaga Shunsui's *ninjōbon* for being free of Neo-Confucian didacticism and for "mimetically depicting" "human feelings" (*ninjō*) in a "contemporary setting" using more vernacular language. But he severely criticized Shunsui for depicting *ninjō* only in the limited negative sense, as "vulgar, obscene desires." The "true *shōsetsu*," Shōyō argued, should depict *ninjō* in a wider sense, incorporating both negative and positive aspects of *ninjō* and treating the "conflict between vulgar, obscene desires *and* reason or morality."[29]

Shōyō's prescription for a "true *shōsetsu*" was to use the "well-structured" *yomihon* form but to "improve" it by replacing its "didacticism and absurdity" with the "mimetic depiction" of *ninjō* in contemporary society—a *ninjō* "more advanced and complex" than that depicted in the *ninjōbon* written by Shunsui and his imitators. Influenced by the evolutionist psychology of Alexander Bain and Herbert Spencer, Shōyō argued that "novelists [*shōsetsuka*] were like psychologists: they should create characters based on the principles of psychology." "As civilization develops and the human mind advances to higher stages, human feelings [*ninjō*] are also transformed and inevitably become more complex." According to Shōyō, only the "true shōsetsu," using a suitable new written style, could represent or mimetically depict the "complex and refined human feelings held by the people of advanced, civilized countries" and make the reader "discover and experience such advanced *ninjō*."[30]

Following publication of *Shōsetsu shinzui*, Shōyō continued to advocate the "mimetic depiction of *ninjō*" by elevating Shunsui's *ninjōbon* even further. In an article published in 1886, Shōyō compared Shunsui's works to Samuel Richardson's and praised Shunsui for having excelled, as Richardson had, in depicting the personalities and emotions of various female characters.[31] While criticizing Shunsui for "confusing pure love [*renjō*], the most important form of *ninjō*, with animalistic lust [*jūjō, jūyoku*]," Shōyō praised him for being a "realist who represents actual incidents and actual people." Shōyō here used the English word "realist" for the first time along with the neologism *shujitsu haishika*, which he created to translate that English word.[32] In 1886, Shōyō also started to use another new key word, *shinri*, or "truth," which the "true *shōsetsu*" was required to depict. In an article published in August 1886, Shōyō wrote: "What matters is the power of writing to depict human truth [*ningen no shinri*]. . . . A *shōsetsu* should depict the formless, invisible truth [*shinri*] and give it life."[33] Incorporating the notion of *shinri* into his earlier argument in *Shōsetsu shinzui*, he defined *shinri* as "exquisite ideas [*myōsō*] that cannot be visualized in paintings" and as "the essence of human feelings" (*shinzuitaru ninjō*) as opposed to external appearances.[34]

Shōyō's younger contemporary Futabatei Shimei (1864–1909), who was more deeply involved with the Western literary tradition as a result of his extensive study of nineteenth-century Russian literature and who had a firmer grasp of European poetics and metaphysics, was largely responsible for Shōyō's shift from the "depiction of human feeling" to the "realistic depiction of the truth of human feeling."[35] Futabatei's theoretical essay, "Shōsetsu sōron" (General theory of the novel; April 1886), written and published at Shōyō's encouragement, presents Futabatei's view of the novel and of realism, based on his reading of the early works of Russian literary critic V. G. Belinsky (1811–48).[36] In this concise essay, Futabatei explained the relationship between "form" (*katachi, fōmu*), a "contingent and variable phenomenon," and "idea" (*i, aidia*), an "invariable, universal essence, which is usually hidden or deformed in contingent form." Futabatei argued that art (*bijutsu*), through inspiration (*kandō, insupirēshon*), grasps the "idea concealed in form" and gives it appropriate form so that people can appreciate these "ideas" easily. Only the "mimetic, or realistic novel" (*mosha shōsetsu*) based on "realism" (*shujitsushugi, riarizumu*) is the "true novel" that can accomplish this task. Referring to Shōyō's advocacy of *mosha* in a slightly ironical tone, Futabatei stated, "We can not simply intone *mosha, mosha*: we must define it in order to advocate it." "What is called *mosha* represents invisible ideas [*kyosō*] through the use of concrete forms (*jissō*)."[37]

Around the same period, in 1886, Futabatei translated two essays on aesthetics by Belinsky and M. N. Katkov, both of whom had a profound impact on Futabatei's own view of art and the novel.[38] In both translations, the word *shinri* (truth) is used to define what "art" should be. "Art is the direct observation of truth; in other words, art is cognition through Form or Image [*keishō*]."[39] Futabatei has replaced the term *i* (idea), which he used in "Shōsetsu sōron," with the term *shinri*.[40] In an introductory article "Introduction to Katkov's Aesthetics" ("Katokofu-shi bijutsu zokkai"), which was written in a less metaphysical manner, Futabatei again stressed *shinri*.

> What should be sought from art is above all truth [*shinri*]. What should be sought from exquisite thoughts or art [*bimyō no shisō*] is the pursuit of the essential relations among various phenomena and an understanding and revelation of the mysterious world of life. . . . We should believe in the revelation of truth and should expect the artist, like the philosopher, to devote himself entirely to the service of truth.[41]

Although the word *shinri* had existed as a Buddhist term meaning "true principles" or "eternal laws,"[42] it was only after the mid-1880's that progressive intellectuals began using it as a key term. Futabatei's notes in 1889 refer to *Shinri ippan* (Aspects of truth, 1884), written by the Protestant leader Uemura Masahisa (1857–1925), to Christianity, to Spencer's "First Principle," to Buddhism, and to Confucianism, all in relationship to the question of *shinri*.[43] Although Futabatei expressed skepticism about Christianity, the "truth of God" (*kami no shinri*), and other religious or philosophical claims for an absolute truth, he continued to be concerned with the notion of *shinri* as an "universal principle or the true essence of the world."[44] In contrast to Shōyō, who saw the "mimetic novel" (*mosha shōsetsu*) as the "most advanced literary form in the West" in a Spencerian evolutionist context, Futabatei valued the "realistic novel" because of its special power to reveal "reality" (*riaritii*), "the truth that takes shape in the phenomenal world."[45] Although Futabatei's early treatises on the *shōsetsu* did not attract much public attention until considerably later, in 1928, when "Shōsetsu sōron" was reprinted, Futabatei's key terms—"truth," "reality," and "realism"—became, through Shōyō, part of the dominant discourse on the *shōsetsu*.

Dissemination of the New Critical Idiom

The new notion of the *shōsetsu*, which incorporated Futabatei's Western metaphysical discourse, assumed that the *shōsetsu* was the ultimate means of revealing the "truth" (*shinri*) of life and the universe through the "realistic representation" (*mosha*) of "human feelings" or "human nature" (*ninjō*). This new notion spread rapidly among Meiji intellectuals, and by the late 1880's it had been widely disseminated by such journals as *Kokumin no tomo* (1887–99), *Shin shōsetsu* (1889–90), *Miyako no hana* (1888–93), and *Jogaku zasshi* (1885–1904).[46] In the second issue (November 1889) of *Shigarami zōshi*, a journal of literary criticism established by Mori Ōgai (1862–1922),[47] Saganoya Omuro (1863–1947) wrote in an article entitled "Mission of a Novelist" ("Shōsetuska no sekinin"):

> The revelation of truth [*shinri no hakki*], the explanation of life [*jinsei no setsu-mei*], and the criticism of society [*shakai no hihyō*] are the duties of the *shōsetsu* writer. A *shōsetsu* writer is thus an observer of universal phenomena, a pursuer of truth, an acquirer of truth, a student of mankind, a master of human beings, a leader of men, an observer of society, a master of society, a social reformer. . . . In what way should a *shōsetsu* writer reveal the truth? A *shōsetsu* writer reveals the truth through human feelings [*jō*]; a *shōsetsu* writer reveals the ultimate, which is formless, by means of familiar forms. . . . Only philosophers and *shōsetsu* writers reveal the ultimate and the road to progress.[48]

In the same issue, Ōgai published an article entitled "Reading Contemporary Japanese Essays on the Novel" ("Gendai shoka no shōsetsuron o yomu") in which he developed his own argument (against Shōyō and others) on aesthetic idealism and the theory of the novel, drawing on Rudolf von Gottschall's *Poetik* and Paul Heyse's "Introduction" to *Deutscher Novellenschatz*.[49] In criticizing Shōyō, however, Ōgai nevertheless incorporated and consolidated the critical idiom initiated by Shōyō.

The subsequent development of Japanese critical discourse occurred in various heterogeneous, often divergent contexts, as demonstrated by the famous 1891–92 "Debate over Non-ideals" (*Botsu risō ronsō*) between Tsubouchi Shōyō and Mori Ōgai. Shōyō believed that literary criticism should be free of preconceived "ideals" in approaching complex works such as Shakespeare's plays. In contrast, Ōgai argued that it should grasp and analyze the "aesthetic ideas and ideals that constitute the essence of art." Shōyō characterized Shakespeare's plays as texts "as vast and as deep as nature / the universe [*shizen*] itself," as great texts that could absorb all possible ideals and interpretations and that differed significantly from the "didacticism" (*kanchō*) of Edo *yomihon* (represented by Bakin).[50]

Ōgai, however, superimposed Shōyō's notions of "nature" and "realism" on Emile Zola's naturalism, of which Shōyō and his contemporaries were still unaware. He then attacked Shōyō—actually Zola—from an anti-naturalist point of view—the aesthetic idealist standpoint derived from the German anti-naturalist critic Gottschall, whose works Ōgai had read during his stay in Germany in 1884–88.[51] Following the German philosopher Eduard von Hartmann, Ōgai emphasized that the function of art was to grasp and analyze the *Idee*, the "absolute reality of the universe," and to make that *Idee* concrete.[52] The opposition between Ōgai and Shōyō cannot be reduced to a polar, Western-based opposition between idealism and realism/naturalism. Rather, the debate reveals the heterogeneous ground of the new critical idiom, which was rapidly being westernized and homogenized. Despite the gap between the two positions, this debate between two respected intellectual leaders strengthened the authority of such new terms as *bungaku* (literature), *shinri* (truth), *risō* (ideal), *shizen* (nature), and *bi* (beauty), all of which, while having different connotations for individual users, formed the core vocabulary of the new critical discourse.[53]

Although the new notion of the *shōsetsu* as a privileged medium that could reveal the "truth" through the "realistic representation of human nature" was widely accepted, there was little consensus as to what this "reality" or "truth" referred to. There was agreement on the importance of the leading signifiers—mimetic representation, realism, truth, and human feeling—but the signifieds remained fluid and ambiguous. A succession of debates in the 1890's reveals the discrepancy between the apparent homogeneity of the dominant critical idiom and the heterogeneity of the concrete perceptions, which had nonetheless started to reshape existing texts through the lens of the new discourse. A revealing example is the so-called *Bungaku gokusui ronsō*, a debate in 1889–90 whether literature was declining or prospering. The debate spilled over into public discussion about the relative merits of a *seiji shōsetsu* by Yano Ryūkei called *Fujō monogatari* (Tale of the floating castle; 1890). Those who stressed the decline of literature complained that the contemporary *ninjō shōsetsu* depicted the silly passions (*chijō chiwa*) of male and female students and consequently narrowed the range of the *shōsetsu*, whose "true form" should depict the "great ideals of the universe" and the "true feelings of great individuals in order to enlighten people's spirits."[54] A number of those critics—such as Ozaki Yukio (1858–1954) and Tokutomi Sohō (1863–1957)—who lamented the decline of literature celebrated the publication of Yano's work, praising it as a nineteenth-century *Water Margin*.[55] The opponents of this view argued that the mission of the *shōsetsu*, whose most advanced form was the realistic novel, was to "reveal the truth of life [*jinsei no shinri*] aesthetically by depicting contemporary *ninjō*" and criticized *Fujō monogatari* for having puppet-like characters and for not "delving into the inner workings of human life and not revealing the formless truth beyond visible facts." One writer criticized *Fujō monogatari* for "confusing large-scale plot with the greatness of art."[56]

This debate can be regarded as a confrontation between older *shōsetsu* or *yomihon*—based on Ming-Ch'ing fiction with its large-scale plot, its entertaining elements, and its Confucian didacticism—and the newer, "mimetic" *shōsetsu*, with its focus on the "psychological aspects of contemporary life," at a time when the former was being surpassed but had not been completely superseded by the latter.[57] More noteworthy, however, is the striking similarity in the language of both sides of the debate. Despite the apparent differences, such words as *dai* (greatness), *tenchi* or *uchū* (universe), and *shinri* were used to characterize the ideal *bungaku* (literature) represented by the *shōsetsu*, whose privileged position is already taken for granted by both sides.[58] The sudden elevation of the lowly regarded Shunsui and the revival of the long-forgotten Genroku writer Ihara Saikaku (1642–93) as "realistic novelists" also occurred in the late 1880's, as part of an attempt to find concrete examples of the depiction of *ninjō* and "realism," two terms that had begun to circulate as powerful and privileged signifiers.[59]

The New Shōsetsu *and the Freedom and People's Rights Movement*

The rapid formation and dissemination of the new notion of the *shōsetsu* was closely related to sociopolitical conditions in the 1880's and 1890's. In a diary entry for 1889, Futabatei wrote:

> If we can, by means of the pen, reveal the character, the mores, and the orientation of citizens [*kokumin*], depict the general condition of the nation [*kokka*], and describe the condition of human life, and if we can explore truth in a realm that is beyond the perception of either the scholar or the moralist, and if we can thereby find our own spiritual peace as well as provide aid for other people to live in this world, that should be worthwhile. Writing *shōsetsu* cannot be a trivial activity.[60]

Futabatei's desire to reveal the "truth" by means of the *shōsetsu* was closely bound to his concern for the welfare of "citizens" and the "nation." This no doubt reflected a Confucian concern for society, represented in the traditional terms *keikoku saimin*, or *keisei saimin* (administrating the nation and saving the people), but his use of the terms *kokumin* (literally, "people of the nation") and *kokka* (nation-state) reveals that this concern was specifically rooted in his exposure to the Freedom and People's Rights movement (mid-1870's to the mid-1880's), which developed and disseminated the notions of national independence and individual independence—notions thought to be two complementary sides of the same modern ideal.

The Freedom and People's Rights movement began in 1874 when Itagaki Taisuke, who had resigned from the government the previous year, presented the government his famous "Petition for the Establishment of a Representative Parliament." At the time, Itagaki and his followers established the Patriotic Public Party (Aikoku kōtō), which advocated the modern notion of "patriotism" or "love of the nation" (*aikoku*)—as opposed to the more dispersed and localized feudal loyalties—and emphasized freedom, individual independence, and equal rights as the basis for the nation's prosperity.[61] Progressive intellectuals, who had been exposed to similar ideals in Fukuzawa Yukichi's *Seiyō jijō* (Affairs of the West; 1866–70) and John Stewart Mill's *On Liberty* (translated in 1872), enthusiastically embraced the People's Rights movement, which also attracted discontented former samurai (who had been deprived of their social privileges and had encountered financial difficulties under the new Meiji regime) and middle-to-large propertied farmers, who sought local representation.[62] Despite the increasing intervention of the government, the movement spread rapidly, encompassing various classes and reaching a peak in 1880, when over 240,000 people signed a petition calling for the establishment of a parliament.[63]

The rapid spread of the People's Rights movement until the early 1880's was made possible by the fact that a wide range of people had already become acquainted, during the early 1870's, with the Western Enlightenment ideal of an independent, enterprising individual free of the restraints imposed by traditional society who can serve as the basis for a vigorous and prosperous nation. Leaders of the new Meiji regime, both within and outside the government, used this idea to restructure the rigid Tokugawa social system into a centralized, modern nation-state and to promote modernization and industrialization in the face of Western military and economic pressure. Following the "abolition of local clans and the establishment of prefectures" (*haihan chiken*) in 1871 and the "abolition of the four-class system" (*shimin byōdō*) in 1870–71, the government attempted to centralize and control the nation through three new systems: compulsory education (established in 1872), national conscription (ordered in 1872–73), and tax reform (proclaimed in 1872). All of these promoted the homogenization of citizens (*kokumin*) and the establishment of a centralized nation-state (*kokka*). Indeed, the Meiji government embraced Western Enlightenment notions of natural rights, freedom, and individual equality in order to introduce and justify the new systems of centralization, which emphasized the duty of citizens to their nation.[64] Such works as Samuel Smiles's *Self-help* (translated in 1870–71 as *Saigoku risshi-hen* by Nakamura Keiu) and Fukuzawa Yukichi's *Gakumon no susume* (Encouragement of Learning; 1872–76), which opens with the celebrated phrase "Heaven did not create man above another nor under another," were adopted as compulsory textbooks for elementary schools (*Gakumon no susume* in 1872, *Saigoku risshi-hen* in 1877) and had an enormous influence on the dissolution of the four-class system and the dissemination of new social ideals.[65]

As the People's Rights movement spread, however, the government altered its progressive, egalitarian educational policy of the 1870's to one that
emphasized loyalty to the emperor and traditional ethics that excluded liberal
political ideals. In 1880, textbooks "interfering with national peace" (*kokuan
o bōgaisu*) were prohibited, and in 1880–81 Fukuzawa's *Gakumon no susume*
and Nakamura's *Saigoku risshi-hen*, both of which advocated the independence of the enterprising individual, were excluded from the government list
of school textbooks.[66] While stiffening its controls on the populist People's
Rights movement, the government incorporated and absorbed that movement into what Benedict Anderson calls "official nationalism," particularly by
following the model of Hohenzollern Prussia-Germany, in which Bismarck
established a modern dynastic nation-state after and in reaction to the popular
national movements that proliferated in Europe in the 1820's.[67] By the late
1880's the Meiji government had effectively suppressed these political activities.[68]

The rise of the new notion of the *shōsetsu* was directly related to the rise
and decline of the Freedom and People's Rights movement and the consolidation of governmental power in the late 1880's and early 1890's. The notion
of the "true *shōsetsu*" began to attract Western-educated students who in their
earlier years had been educated in the Confucian classics (which emphasized
social commitment) and who had later witnessed the sudden rise and decline
of the People's Rights movement. The *seiji shōsetsu* (political novel), which
emerged in the early 1880's, attracted a wide range of young, ambitious,
intellectuals who developed an acute awareness of the complementary ideals
of national and individual independence.[69] Tsubouchi Shōyō's social and
intellectual background were similar to those of the *seiji shōsetsu* writers active
in the early 1880's who had directly participated in the People's Rights movement,[70] but Shōyō differed from these writers, who had primarily been political activists rather than writers, in that he was the first university graduate to
become a "professional" *shōsetsu* writer. In the following passage, Uchida
Roan (1868–1929) looked back on the impact of Shōyō's writings and his
decision to become a professional writer—unprecedented for a university
graduate—on his generation.

> The *shōsetsu* jumped, in one bound, from a low position, as a form of amuse-
> ment, to become an integral and contributing element of civilization as well as
> an activity that a respectable scholar could proudly turn into a life's pursuit.
> Aspiring young men of the time, who had hitherto considered politics the only
> way to realize their ambitions, discovered a new world and rushed into literature
> as if they had suddenly been awakened.[71]

From the late 1880's and the early 1890's, when their political options were rapidly closed off by the Meiji government, a number of young students who had been politically awakened by the People's Rights movement—Futabatei Shimei, Kitamura Tōkoku (1868–94), Yamaji Aizan (1864–1917), Masaoka Shiki (1867–1902), Tokutomi Roka (1868–1927), Kinoshita Naoe (1869–1937), Uchida Roan—decided to devote themselves to literature and to the newly defined *shōsetsu* in particular.

Futabatei entered the Russian department in the Tokyo University of Foreign Languages in 1881 out of a patriotic desire to defend his country against Russia, one of the great military threats to Japan at the time. He subsequently became a devoted student of Russian literature, which, in his view, "tackled the human and social problems caused by oppressive governments." Futabatei sympathized with those Russian writers who "pursued the problems of life with their body and soul, with the thought of awakening the people [*kokumin*] with their pens rather than with swords and bombs."[72] When the government restructured the entire educational system, "despotically" (in Futabatei's words) abolishing his university and causing him to leave, he turned to writing.[73] Influenced by Shōyō, whom he met in January 1886, Futabatei began to write the *shōsetsu* that was to become *Ukigumo* (Drifting clouds; 1887–89). Although Futabatei's understanding of Russian literature was rare, his sociopolitical motivation for writing was shared by those young students who decided to pursue the path of literature in the late 1880's and the early 1890's.

Another dramatic example of the transition from politics to literature is Kitamura Tōkoku, who actively participated in the Freedom and People's Rights movement from 1883 to 1885 and later became a central figure in Bungakukai, a group of young literati who introduced Western romanticism to Japan and advocated the ideal of self-affirmation and self-expression in the 1890's. In a letter written in August 1887, Tōkoku attempted to recount the "various stages of his ambitions," explaining that in 1881 (at the age of thirteen), at the height of the Freedom and People's Rights movement, he was obsessed by a "burning ambition to become a politician who fights for the cause of freedom."[74] Tōkoku then recounted the next stage of his "ambition," which occurred in 1884, at the age of sixteen.

> This ambition was completely different from my earlier ambitions: the desire to achieve fame and fortune had completely vanished. Instead, I fervently hoped to become a great politician who could save the declining fortunes of the pathetic East and who would be willing to sacrifice himself to benefit all people. I wanted to exert myself in the political sphere as Christ had done in the religious sphere.[75]

After briefly mentioning the disillusionment he experienced in 1885 that led to the end of his political activities, Tōkoku expressed a strong, but still uncertain, aspiration to become a *shōsetsu* writer.

> Finally, I desired to be a *shōsetsu* writer, although at the time I still did not attempt to become a literary artist [*bijutsuka*]. I hoped to carry out political change, using the power of a sharp pen, in the manner of France's Victor Hugo. That year I traveled to various places and became an aficionado of landscapes [*fūkei*] and a student of human nature [*ninjō*] by cultivating various acquaintances.[76]

Although Tōkoku initially hoped to become a *seiji shōsetsu* writer, using the *shōsetsu* for political objectives, he soon aspired to become a "literary artist" (*bijutsuka*) and a "student of human nature" (*ninjō no kenkyūka*), a *shōsetsu* writer as defined by Shōyō in *Shōsetsu shinzui*.

Despite the rapid formation and spread of the new notion of the *shōsetsu*, there was as yet little consensus as to its actual content, form, and language. Even Futabatei Shimei, who had believed that the *shōsetsu* could "represent universal ideas" and "truth" through "concrete forms and verbal expressions" and whose translations (1888–89) of Turgenev's novels and whose *Ukigumo* had a profound impact upon later *shōsetsu* writers,[77] felt deeply frustrated and inadequate in his attempts to create the language and "concrete form" of such a *shōsetsu*. After finishing the third part of *Ukigumo*, Futabatei wrote in a diary entry for June 24, 1889:

> If I am to continue to live by writing *shōsetsu*, I have no choice but to learn to master styles. . . . The books that I have to read for this purpose, however, are useless books casually written by those who led leisurely lives claiming to be connoisseurs of life. The vexation of spending my entire life straining to read such books and wasting my life! Yet this is the life of a petty rhetorician [*bunshō-ka*]. *Shōsetsu* writers must have more substance to pursue. If, by means of the pen, we can reveal the character, the mores, and the orientation of citizens, depict the general condition of the nation, and describe the condition of human life, and if we can explore truth in a realm that is beyond the perception of either the scholar or the moralist, and if we can thereby find our own spiritual peace as well as help other people live in this world, that should be worthwhile. Writing *shōsetsu* cannot be a trivial activity.[78]

In *Shōsetsu shinzui*, Tsubouchi Shōyō urged the creation of a new literary language for the *shōsetsu*, a new hybrid of traditional written and vernacular (more colloquial) styles, that could offer, as the Western novel appeared to do, a "mimetic depiction of the new reality." Various conventional styles—separated by function and occasion—existed at the time: *kanbun* (based on Chinese) or *kanbun-kundoku* style (Japanese conventions for reading classical Chinese), which was used in the official and public domain; classical Japanese (employed in *waka* poetry and in the *gabun* neo-classical, or neo-Heian, prose style developed by Edo scholars of National Learning); and the various hybrid narrative styles, which, under the influence of Ming and Ch'ing vernacular fiction, mixed these written styles (*kanbun* and classical Japanese) with more vernacular, colloquial styles. Shōyō believed that the written styles used at the time were too conventionalized and archaic to allow the new *shōsetsu* to depict contemporary life and society vividly, in the manner of Western novels. On the other hand, the pre-existing spoken languages, which had already been used for dialogue in Edo *gesaku* popular fiction, were too closely associated with particular socio-geographical groups (e.g., Edo townsmen, Edo courtesans) to be used for descriptive prose (*ji no bun*), which, in Shōyō's opinion, should impartially and objectively represent modern man and society, as Western novels appeared to do.[79] Shōyō's proposal for a new literary language was part of a larger movement that sought to establish a modern vernacular written language, commonly referred to as the *genbun-itchi* (unification of spoken and written languages) movement, which was inextricably related to the formation of the modern nation-state and the development of the modern Japanese *shōsetsu*.

Futabatei's *Ukigumo*, which was soon considered the first successful product of the *genbun-itchi* movement and which, from the late 1900's, was regarded as Japan's first modern novel, reveals the experimental process by which Futabatei groped for and created a new written language that could realize his new literary "ideas" and perceptions of "reality," which were shaped by those Russian authors (such as Dostoyevsky, Turgenev, and Gogol) he had read in the original.[80] In contrast to Shōyō, for whom the "new written language" was a matter of achieving a new mixture of "elegant" and "vulgar" styles, following Bakin's stylistic principles,[81] and who, despite his new ideals and views of literary language, remained within the paradigms of the traditional writing system, Futabatei (who claimed that he was "not good at writing sentences")[82] felt a certain uneasiness and dissatisfaction with the pre-existing written styles and encountered great difficulty in finding the appropriate "concrete form" and language for his new *shōsetsu*. *Ukigumo*, particularly in Part I, retains much of the style of Edo *gesaku* popular fiction, using conventional wordplay (*kakekotoba*, *engo*), the traditional seven/five syllabic rhythm, and sentences generated and linked by traditional word associations. The language of *Ukigumo* was in fact an amalgam of Edo literary styles derived from popular narrative fiction, the local Tokyo Fukagawa dialect, oral-storytelling features (inspired by printed transcriptions of Enchō's *rakugo*), *kanbun* syntax, classical literary diction, and Western borrowings. Although the styles of Parts II and III now appear to be relatively close to contemporary speech, in Futabatei's time there was still no established vernacular prose style nor a standard spoken language. *Ukigumo* did not transcribe contemporary speech. On the contrary, the standard vernacular writing style and the standard spoken language as they exist today are the product of a *genbun-itchi* movement deeply influenced by Futabatei's literary language (developed both in *Ukigumo* and in his translations of Russian literature).

It was during the 1900's that certain new paradigms of reality as well as the notion of immediate representation emerged in and through the newly constructed vernacular literary language, which was rapidly becoming standardized. During this period the so-called Naturalist writers—Shimazaki Tōson, Kunikida Doppo, Tayama Katai, Iwano Hōmei, Tokuda Shūsei, and the like, many of whom were later regarded as I-novelists—began to write *shōsetsu* in the belief that it was the ultimate medium for directly representing "true reality" and out of a desire to realize a new language free from traditional rhetoric that could directly transcribe this true reality. As we shall see, this aspiration for an immediate and transparent written language was inextricably related to the ideology of *genbun-itchi*, which stood in an intimate relationship to the new notions of the *shōsetsu*, realism, representation, truth, and the self, a key concern from the 1890's in almost all fields.

~✒

CHAPTER 2

Self, Christianity, and Language: 'Genbun-itchi' and Concern for the Self

The notion of an independent, individual "self" emerged first and foremost in the political arena. As noted earlier, the new Meiji regime advocated the Enlightenment ideal of free and equal citizens as part of its effort to construct a centralized, modern nation-state. The People's Rights movement, while opposing the government's monopoly on power, helped to reinforce and disseminate in the late 1870's and early 1880's this new ideal of a free and equal citizen (*kokumin*), of a political subject with the right to act for the nation (*kokka*). From the early 1880's the central government began to transform this popular nationalism into an "official nationalism," establishing a national constitution (promulgated in 1889) that legally defined all individuals as "equal subjects" (*subjectus*) of the emperor, whose mythical "sacred" power was legalized and used to unify the nation-state.[1] The notion of the individual self as an independent ethical and moral subject (*subjectum*), a notion that played a key role in the transformation of the larger literary and cultural discourse, emerged in the late 1880's–early 1890's in reaction to this newly defined, limited political subject—a reaction aided by the spread of Christianity, and, in particular, Protestantism.[2]

Christianity and Concern for the Self

A number of young people who had actively participated in the People's Rights movement converted to Protestantism when the People's Rights movement declined following its suppression.[3] In a January 1888 letter sent to Ishizaka Mina, his future wife, whose father (a leading activist in the People's

Rights movement) had been imprisoned for political activities, Kitamura
Tōkoku wrote:

> What is the point of conquering violence with violence? To subjugate violence
> one must confront it with arms, but these arms should not be destructive
> swords. They must be spears of truth [*shinri*]. We must fight with truth, not with
> real swords and spears. We must not fight these battles by ourselves. We must
> fight with the aid of God. . . . My enthusiastic desire to serve society and save
> people has suddenly returned. This desire is not a chivalrous spirit that enjoys
> personal power but a patriotic spirit that hopes to be a soldier of truth [*shinri no
> heisotsu*].[4]

Tōkoku's recent conversion to Christianity resulted in a dramatic fusion of
the spheres of politics and religion, which Tōkoku had kept separate in a
previous letter. In personal notes written at the end of August 1887, Tōkoku
recorded two intense experiences: "spiritual love" (*rabu*) with Ishizaka Mina
and a revelation that he must become a "loyal subject" (*chūginaru shinka*) of
the Christian God.[5] Tōkoku's aspiration to "save the nation and the people by
grasping and then revealing the truth through writing" resembles Futabatei's,
but for Tōkoku truth is associated with the truth of a Christian God. In a
similar fashion, many of the young literati surrounding Tōkoku in the 1890's
—Hoshino Tenchi (1862–1950), Shimazaki Tōson (1872–1943), Kunikida
Doppo (1871–1908), Hirata Tokuboku (1873–1943), and Iwano Hōmei
(1873–1920), and others—turned to Christianity in the late 1880's in their
high school or college years.

Christianity had been prohibited during the Tokugawa period, but under pressure from the West, the Meiji government quietly removed the ban in
1873.[6] During the period of the People's Rights movement, Christianity,
which shared with that movement the basic ideal of individual equality,
gradually spread.[7] It was not, however, until the mid- to late 1880's, with the
second generation of Meiji Christians (including Tōkoku and his literary
colleagues), that Christianity suddenly expanded.[8] As Yamaji Aizan, Tōkoku's contemporary, pointed out in his *Gendai Nihon kyōkai shi ron* (History of
the modern Japanese church; 1905), those Japanese who became Christians
during the late 1860's were sons of supporters or retainers of the former
Tokugawa shogunate denied political opportunity within the new Meiji government.[9] The critic Karatani Kōjin argues that Christianity spread rapidly
among the sons of supporters of the former Tokugawa shogunate precisely
because Christianity—a monotheism that derived from the West but that
transcended the individual nations of the West—allowed these young Meiji
intellectuals to relativize and disregard the recently constructed monarchic
authority of the Meiji government (led by former lower-ranking samurai

from the Western provinces of Chōshū and Satsuma). It also enabled them to "transcend" conceptually the difficulties imposed on Japan by Western nations. Christianity satisfied, in an ironically inverted form, the "will to power" of those young people who felt both powerless and resentful.[10]

The ambitious but disillusioned activists who converted to Christianity in the late 1880's, when their political options suddenly diminished, came from a similar socio-historical background. Aizan, whose history of first-generation Christians can be interpreted as a form of self-projection and self-assessment, was the son of a retainer of the Tokugawa shogunate whose family suffered after the Meiji Restoration. He started to study English in 1883 and became a Christian (Methodist) in 1886. Tōkoku's background was similar. From the time of his conversion to Christianity in the late 1880's, Tōkoku repeatedly called himself "the general of a vanquished army" (*haigun no shō*) and defined poets as "lofty soldiers" (*kōdai naru senshi*) who fight with a "spiritual sword" (*rei no tsurugi*) or the "spear of truth" in order to "save the nation and its people."[11]

These metaphors had both a figurative and a literal significance for many young Christians of Tōkoku's generation, for whom the "spirituality" of their Christian faith was inextricably related to their political and nationalistic concerns and to their "will to power." In 1892–93 Tōkoku advocated "spiritual freedom" (*seishin no jiyū*) and "spiritual independence" (*seishin no dokuritsu*), distinguishing these two concepts from "political freedom" and "political independence," which, he claimed, had not yet been achieved in Japan. Tōkoku defined the Meiji Restoration as "a revolution that attempted to distribute to the public the spiritual freedom of the individual by turning samurai and commoners into 'people,' all of whom became equal."[12] Tōkoku, who redefined the People's Rights movement as the "sudden rise of the individual spirit," claimed that one must pursue spiritual freedom independently of political restraints since the "spirit" or "inner life" exists "independently of contingent material conditions" and because this "inner life" "corresponds to the spirit of the other world," to "the spirit of the universe," which is called God.[13] Although Tōkoku separated spiritual freedom and spiritual independence from the political sphere, his stance remained highly political and "patriotic" in that he aspired to "serve society and save people" by presenting an alternative, more universal value system, which could systematically place the contemporary political and social situation in a relative and critical perspective.

For these young people, Christianity was also closely associated with their attraction to Western literature and culture, knowledge of which seemed to lead to success in Meiji society.[14] Young Tōkoku's account of his "spiritual progress" itself was inspired by his reading of Disraeli's novel *Contarini Fleming*,[15] and his metaphors of battles and soldiers initially came, as Tōkoku himself revealed, from such Western texts as Patrick Henry's "Liberty Speech" (1775). Early Meiji Christian leaders such as Uemura Masahisa and Uchimura Kanzō introduced not only the Bible but Western literature to young Japanese.[16] It was also no coincidence that most of the major Western romantic poets and thinkers—Byron, Shelley, Wordsworth, Carlyle, and Emerson—to whom the newly converted Christian youths were drawn, were themselves patriotic, political activists who saw continuity rather than conflict between their literary and social commitments. For these Western-educated youths, who turned to Christianity in the late 1880's and early 1890's, Christianity was inextricably linked to the Enlightenment, liberal political ideals of freedom and independence—both individual and national—and to Western romanticism.

Tōkoku and other young Christians such as Hoshino Tenchi and Shimazaki Tōson were contributors to *Jogaku zasshi*, a Christian humanist journal. In 1893 they established the literary journal *Bungakukai*, which originally started as the literary branch of *Jogaku zasshi* but soon became an independent journal. In *Bungakukai*, Tōkoku declared that their mission was to be poets in a broad sense and defined the "lofty enterprise of poets and philosophers" as "saying" (in an Emersonian sense) "an invisible inner life," as giving expression to "an essential life [*konpon no seimei*] created by God."[17] According to Tōkoku, "literary art" (*bungei*) consists of "ideas" (*shisō*) and "art" (*bijutsu*), and its specific mission is to "convey the invisible inner life" by "observing Various Manifestations [Tōkoku's English] of human life and human nature [*jinsei ninjō*]" and by "grasping the spirit of the universe or the Absolute Idea [Tōkoku's English]," which is God, and by "giving concrete form in phenomenal reality to the Idea or the Great Reality of the ideal world [*sōsekai no dai-dai-dai no riaritii*]."[18] This view of literature followed the new discourse on the *shōsetsu*, but Tōkoku and *Bungakukai* introduced a distinctly new element: the "truth" that literature was to grasp and present was specifically connected to the "individual self," which Tōkoku believed was endowed with a universal truth derived from God. In the dominant critical discourse prior to Tōkoku, "truth" or "truth of human nature" was formulated not in purely metaphysical terms but was posited, in the evolutionist perspective, as an imagined reality, whose model was thought to exist in the West but had yet to be achieved in Japan. Tōkoku's Protestant and Emersonian perspective enabled him and his followers to universalize and naturalize this "truth" or "truth of human nature" and allowed them to posit it within all of them. According to Tōkoku, the "inner life" resided not only inside man but corresponded to the "spirit of the universe," which could be attained when one overcame one's "selfish ego" (*jiko no ware*).[19]

Although most of the *Bungakukai* participants eventually renounced Christianity, it left a deep imprint not only upon them but on the larger literary and intellectual field, which soon forgot its origins. Christianity not only enhanced the validity and authority of literature by providing a firm belief in a universal truth, it also shaped the perception of reality, particularly the value of the inner self and spiritual freedom, thus enabling them to transcend social and historical constraints. Indeed, it was precisely in the name of pursuing spiritual freedom and spiritual independence—the very notions acquired from Christianity—that Tōson and other literati in the Bungakukai group renounced Christianity by the mid-1890's. (Tōkoku killed himself in 1894.) As we shall see in the chapters on Tayama Katai and Shiga Naoya, the notion of "sacred love," which Tōkoku saw as a key to realizing spiritual freedom and the "true self," had a profound impact on Tōkoku's younger contemporaries and on later generations. Most important, it created a conflict between a longing for the "spirituality of love" and an incessant awareness of "carnal desires," a polarity induced by Christianity that made them feel the restraints of Christianity itself. From the mid-1890's, *Bungakukai* turned away from Christianity and celebrated the pagan tradition, particularly the European Renaissance and classical Greece and Rome, looking to love and art as the ultimate means of realizing one's true self. For example, in 1894, Togawa Shūkotsu (1870–1939) wrote in *Bungakukai*: "Love is the primary essence of life. . . . That which negates love is that which negates the essence of man; that which negates the essence of man is that which negates human life; that which negates human life is that which negates the life of the universe and the God of the universe."[20] Shūkotsu essentially replaced what Christians, including himself, had called God with the notion of life, thereby negating Christianity in the name of life. In this article Shūkotsu criticized those Japanese Christians who "had proudly but imprudently imported the rigid disciplinary Christianity of the United States," which Shūkotsu regarded as "an animalistic civilization."[21] In anticipation of the Sino-Japanese War (1894–95), Shūkotsu defined the present as "a time of revolutionary chaos when a new spirit should arise, when life should emerge so that the people of this nation can truly become themselves, an objective that the Meiji Restoration had not yet achieved." Shūkotsu proudly asserted that "this revolution should arise from the spiritual sphere of religion and art."[22]

Both the stagnation of Christianity from the mid-1890's and the growing concern for the notion of the self (*jiga*) were closely related to the surge of

nationalism resulting from the Sino-Japanese War (1894–95), which consolidated the collective sense of the nation, and by the subsequent Triple Intervention, which impressed upon the Japanese the power of Western imperial-
ist nations. Following the war, Takayama Chogyū (1871–1902), a young but
influential critic, proudly celebrated the collective sense of the nation by
arguing that the modern nation-state was a "form necessitated by mankind's
evolution," which "had overcome the religious dominance of the medieval
period," and that this modern nation-state "aimed at the greatest happiness of
the nation's people."[23] In this article written in 1895, Chogyū stressed the
"nation's spirit of independence," the "founding spirit of the nation," which
he characterized as the "oneness of the emperor and his subjects," and the
"life of the nation" with which the people were conceived as one. Indeed,
Chogyū soon began to celebrate the "individualism" of Walt Whitman, "a
poet of life who valued natural desire, a people's poet who celebrated the
greatness of man by resisting all formalism, a poet who uncovered the secret
truth of man by removing all masks, and finally a poet who, as an individual
American, expressed the national character [kokuminsei] of the United States
most clearly and faithfully."[24] Chogyū's attraction to Whitman's "individualism" was strongly related to his nationalistic concerns: he praised Whitman
for "criticizing the hypocrisy of those who have power and wealth in the
United States, those who, while advocating freedom and equality, practice
imperialism and persecute other races in the name of religion."[25]

In 1901 Chogyū advocated what he called the "pure individualism"
(junsuinaru kojinshugi) of Friedrich Nietzsche, "a great poet and Kulturkriti-
ker" who "rebelled against almost all aspects of nineteenth-century Western
civilization," particularly the "oppressive weight of History" (representing
the Western tradition), a History "that had negated subjectivity, oppressed
man's nature, ignored natural instinct, hindered the development of individual freedom, made all of mankind equal and banal, and cursed all geniuses."[26]
Chogyū, whose knowledge of Nietzsche was second-hand, was apparently
attracted to Nietzsche because he was, for Chogyū, the "most advanced" and
"most influential" Western thinker to have persuasively criticized contemporary nineteenth-century Western civilization. Nietzsche enabled Chogyū to
condemn and ignore the actual historical conditions and power of Western
nations as well as to celebrate the "emancipation of individual life," which he
saw as the most advanced universal truth. (According to Chogyū, it is impossible to differentiate the nation and the individual.) Chogyū celebrated
"Nietzsche's negation of History," particularly his negation of Christianity,
and ahistorically superimposed "History," that is, the Western tradition, upon
the historical conditions of Japan at the time. The fact that some progressive

intellectuals—such as the members of Bungakukai—had been involved in and were leaving Christianity probably made this superimposition appear convincing and natural.

Christianity, which progressive intellectuals had regarded as the essence of Western civilization, gave these intellectuals a conceptual, "universal" standpoint by which to transcend their historical conditions both inside and outside the nation. Christianity now started to become—through Nietzsche's condemnation of Christianity—the institution that they needed to overcome in order to achieve individual freedom. Although Chogyū was not a Christian, the concluding passage of his influential article "Discussing the Aesthetic Life" ("Biteki seikatsu o ronzu"; August 1901) reveals the degree to which he and his contemporaries had unknowingly absorbed Christian terminology in speaking about the "more advanced" or "more awakened" stage of life.

> Those whom we should really pity are not the starving but those who have no provisions other than bread. When natural human desires are satisfied, there is, even in the life of a beggar, a paradise [*rakuchi*] that a king would envy. Those who should grieve are not the poor but those who recognize no value other than that of wealth. The life of those who die without understanding love has no value. . . . In these days life has become increasingly busy and people have no time to ponder. Yet, poor people, don't grieve! Those who have lost hope, don't deplore! The true kingdom always exists in your heart. And that which lets you understand this gospel is the Aesthetic Life [*biteki seikatsu*].[27]

Much like Shūkotsu, Chogyū singled out love (*ren'ai*) and art (*geijutsu*) as exemplary ways of the "aesthetic life," claimed that the ultimate purpose of life was "to satisfy the natural human instincts of the self," and stressed the absolute value of such a pursuit by calling it the "aesthetic life."[28]

By the turn of the century, the celebration of life and the self had become a driving force in the literary and intellectual world.[29] In 1900, Yosano Tekkan (1873–1935) started a movement to reform *waka*, the classical poetic form, by establishing a new literary journal called *Myōjō*, which published the *waka* of a group of young poets earlier influenced by *Bungakukai*. In the group's manifesto, Tekkan, who had revealed his nationalistic ardor by going to Korea immediately after the Sino-Japanese War, proclaimed that their poetry would be the "new national poetry [*kokushi*] of the Meiji period"; it would "give full play to the poetry of the self [*jiga no shi*] without imitating the poetry of the past."[30]

As Chogyū's celebration of "life" and "freedom of the self" suggest, the notion of the nation (the collective "national spirit") and that of the individual were not clearly differentiated in this alluring notion of the self, which was posited as a universal, unquestioned reality. Chogyū urged literary writers to

awaken to their "lofty and privileged mission" "as exemplified by the poet
Nietzsche, whose somewhat intangible individualism [*kojinshugi*] proved to
be the dynamic force of the civilization of one nation." For that purpose,
"literary writers should appreciate and study the masterpieces of recent Western poets and novelists."[31] It was in this intellectual climate that ambitious
young intellectuals became involved in literature, particularly *shōsetsu*, and
that they pursued the enigmatic "self" by interacting with Western literature.
In 1908 Futabatei Shimei, one of the first Meiji intellectuals to believe in the
value of the *shōsetsu* as a means of serving the nation and the people through
the exploration of truth, offered this warning to those with blind faith in the
authority of literature.

> Unless we question the value of literature and philosophy, how can we under-
> stand their true value? As for the development of Japanese literature, has there
> ever been such a moment of questioning? Surely, there has not. Under Western
> influence, those presently involved in literature are suddenly heralding literature
> as something with an *a priori* privileged status. This attitude reveals that they are
> still lacking in understanding. In any case, you must destroy, at least once, the
> atmosphere in which literature is blindly worshipped. The new attitude that will
> be established on those ruins will be one that realizes that "after all, literature is
> not so bad."[32]

As this self-critical comment suggests, by the late 1900's, literature had acquired an unquestioned and privileged status in progressive cultural discourse,
the relative historical context and ideological nature of which Futabatei probably was still aware. As we shall see, this strong reliance on the authority of
literature, particularly that of the *shōsetsu*, in relationship to the enigmatic self
would become a basic premise of modern Japanese literature.

Language and the Self

Like the notion of the *shōsetsu*, that of the "self"—referred to by a cluster
of terms such as *jiga, jiko, jibun, kojin,* and *watakushi*—became a privileged,
master signifier whose signifieds remained vague and fluid. For those Meiji
writers who aspired to "represent" the new "reality" of the self in "concrete
form," there were still no established assumptions about what the individual
self might represent. Tōkoku's depiction of the "imprisoned self" in two long
poems, "Soshū no shi" (1889) and "Hōraikyoku" (1891), and in "Waga
rōgoku" (My jail; 1892), a short *shōsetsu*, was directly inspired by Byron's
"Prisoner of Chillon" and "Manfred"; and Kunikida Doppo's depiction of
the self contemplating the "external nature" of Musashino in "Musashino"
(1898) and of Hokkaidō in "Sorachi-gawa no kishibe" (1902), was deeply

influenced by Wordsworth and Futabatei's translations of Turgenev's novels. In other words, the new paradigms of reality based on an enigmatic self took shape through the assimilation and naturalization of literary representation in Western literature. In the following passage (from 1909), Shimazaki Tōson commented on the profound impact of Rousseau's *Confessions* on him when he first read it in English translation in 1894, at the age of twenty-two.

> In those days I was suffering from various difficulties, and I was depressed when I encountered Rousseau. As I became involved in the book, I felt as if it brought out a self [*jibun*] that I had not been hitherto aware of. . . . I felt that through this book I was beginning to understand, though vaguely, modern man's way of thinking and how to view nature directly.[33]

Tōson here believes that the literary representation found in Rousseau's text led him to "discover" the same universal self in himself, which is here regarded as a reality that is made visible and knowable through the "authentic" language of Rousseau, whom Tōson considered to be the "forerunner of the modern self" and "the father of free thinkers."[34]

This kind of reflection on the interdependent nature of self and language also appeared earlier, in the premodern period. For example, Hattori Nankaku (1683–1759), a mid-Tokugawa Confucian scholar-poet, provides a revealing contrast.

> The diction in my poems was used by the people of the past, and the emotions expressed there were also fully expressed by the people of the past. When I recite my poem side by side with the poems of the past, the two are so similar that I cannot distinguish between them. This is not because I imitate poems of the past. On the contrary, the poems of the past construct my self [*ware*].[35]

Nankaku posits his self not as an absolute entity that exists *a priori* but as a construct that takes shape in and through the acquisition of the language of the past. This view of language is strikingly similar to the post-modern view of language and subjectivity. But Nankaku's view differs in that he presupposes an ultimate and absolute prototype of the self in classical poetry and language. For Nankaku, that model was T'ang poetry, which he and his mentor, the great Confucian scholar Ogyū Sorai, believed most fully expressed the human emotions suggested in the Confucian canon, particularly the *Shih ching*, the *Book of Songs*.

In contrast to Nankaku, Tōson believed that he had "discovered" and understood his potential or true self through Rousseau's language, which Tōson thought could directly reveal "modern man's true self." Tōson did not posit the self as an absolute entity that exists independently of any particular language. Instead, he regarded it as something that has yet to be fully discovered, something that will be revealed through his encounter with the authentic language of the true modern self. At the same time, Rousseau's language, the medium that would reveal Tōson's yet undiscovered self, was thought to be a transparent vehicle that could directly represent its source, Rousseau, the true modern self.

In the 1904 preface to an anthology of his collected poems, Tōson wrote, "Life is power. Power is voice. Voice is language. New language is new life."[36] Whereas Hattori Nankaku and other Tokugawa scholar-poets tried to master the language of the past through *kanshi*, or Chinese poetry, which represented the intellectual orthodoxy of the time, Meiji writers aspired to represent or discover a new reality and a new self by experimenting with a new language, by gradually breaking away from the traditional rhetorical fabric and by creating a language containing what they believed to be the essential characteristics of the Western languages they admired as the source of truth and power. In the 1890's Tōson and other young literati associated with *Bungakukai* devoted themselves to writing lyrical poetry that, while maintaining the traditional form of *waka*, was deeply influenced by European romantic poets. It is significant that Tōson's declaration "New language is new life" was made in 1904, three or four years after he had shifted from poetry to prose in the pursuit of a new colloquial language. From the early 1900's, the so-called Japanese Naturalist writers—Shimazaki Tōson, Kunikida Doppo, Tayama Katai, Iwano Hōmei, Tokuda Shūsei (1871–1943), among others—many of whom were later considered I-novelists, believed that the *shōsetsu* was the best and ultimate medium for directly representing the true reality of life, and they aspired to realize a new language that could directly transcribe that reality. This preoccupation with a direct and transparent written language was also closely related to the larger *genbun-itchi* movement, which began in the mid-1880's and became inextricably related to the new notion of the *shōsetsu* and its languages.

The Genbun-itchi *Movement*

The term *genbun-itchi* was first used in 1885 by Kanda Kōhei (1830–98), a scholar of Western (Dutch) learning who worked as an institutional planner for the new Meiji government: "If we wish to unite the spoken and written languages, we should have a written language that can be immediately understood when rendered orally. For that purpose, we have no choice but to use the language of everyday speech. To write in such a style is to unify the spoken and written languages."[37] The proposal for a new vernacular written language was initiated at the end of the Tokugawa period by scholars of

Western learning who noticed that modern Western languages did not ex-
hibit the disjunction that existed in Japan between the written languages
(especially those based on classical Chinese) and the spoken languages. After
the Meiji Restoration, such intellectuals as Fukuzawa Yukichi, Katō Hiro-
yuki, Nishi Amane, and Kanda Kōhei, all of whom considered the enlightenment of people through universal education the first priority in establishing a
strong modern nation, promoted the creation of a new, colloquial written
language. Although a proposal to establish a standardized vernacular language
was advanced in 1873–74, it died out as the government's educational policy
turned reactionary in the face of the Freedom and People's Rights movement. It was not until the mid-1880's, during the so-called Rokumeikan
period, a time of radical westernization, that the *genbun-itchi* movement became an urgent national concern.[38]

The Kana-no-kai (Society for the Promotion of the Kana Syllabary),
established in 1883, and the Rōmaji-kai (Society for the Promotion of Ro-
manization), created in 1885, were the center of this new movement. As their
names suggest, the *genbun-itchi* movement was based on a belief in, and an
aspiration to, the "directness, immediacy, efficiency, and impartiality" of the
phonogram—which was perceived to be an essential feature of Western civilization. Mozume Takami, a professor at Tokyo Imperial University and a
central figure in the Kana-no-kai, wrote an influential book entitled *Genbun-
itchi* (Unification of spoken and written languages; 1886), in which he stated:

> What emerges from one's own heart [*hara*] is alive since it is natural, but what
> derives from others is dead since it is not genuine. . . . I consequently believe that
> it is most desirable that we abolish the parrot-like, nonfunctional, conven-
> tionalized, written language, and that we directly transcribe the vigorous, living
> discourse that spontaneously and naturally flows from our mouths. To those
> people, including myself, who have become accustomed to the traditional,
> written language, that writing style will still appear superior. But this is only the
> effect of habit, which can be transformed.[39]

Mozume, who argued for a transcription of contemporary speech because of
its "naturalness" and "immediacy," admitted that even in his eyes the traditional writing style, based heavily on Chinese ideograms, still appeared more
appropriate and superior. But he urged the Japanese to break away from this
practice and its conventionalized perceptions and to adopt a more "spontaneous," "living language" that "directly transmits one's thoughts and feelings."
The *genbun-itchi* written language that Mozume proposed, however, was not
a direct transcription of the language actually spoken at the time. Instead,
Mozume advocated the creation of an "efficient, neutral" language based on
the writing style found in diaries and notes—styles that, while close to the

living "voice," were neutral in the sense that they were relatively free from the complex honorific system used in daily conversation.[40] The *genbun-itchi* movement, in short, was not simply an attempt to turn the spoken language into a written form; it was a conceptual transformation of the written language.

When Shōyō urged the creation of a new literary language for the purpose of "mimetic depiction" in *Shōsetsu shinzui*, the key issue was the creation of a new descriptive prose that he believed should be neutral and impartial. In the late 1880's, new *shōsetsu* writers such as Futabatei, Yamada Bimyō (1868–1910), and Saganoya Omuro (1863–1947), all of whom devoted themselves to the ideal of the "realistic representation of truth," experimented with various new vernacular writing styles, adopting Western writing conventions such as periods, commas, paragraphs, and clearly delineated subject-predicate sentences. They made a particular effort to create descriptive or declarative sentences that, while based on the vernacular, employed sentence endings that appeared neutral, free of the honorific or humble indicators found in all spoken languages. In 1889 Yamada Bimyō published an article, "Outline of *Genbun-itchi* Theory" ("Genbun-itchi ron gairyaku"), in which he distinguished between two groups, one that advocated *futsūbun* (standard written language) and was trying to bring the spoken language (*gen*) closer to the written language (*bun*), and another that advocated *genbun-itchi* (unification of spoken and written) and was attempting to bring the written language (*bun*) closer to the spoken language (*gen*).[41] Although Bimyō clearly considered himself an advocate of the *genbun-itchi* group, his written style was characterized by rhetorical features adopted from Western literature: personification, passive voice, inversion, ellipsis, different grammatical persons, Western notions of tense, and other hitherto unfamiliar tropes. Bimyō's written style was in fact far from the spoken languages of the time.

Despite the influence in the 1880's of Bimyō's *genbun-itchi* written style, which became popular for its Western flavor, and the profound impact of Futabatei's *genbun-itchi* style on later generations, by the early 1890's the movement had stagnated as the Japanese reacted against the excessive westernization of the Rokumeikan period. There was in fact no standard spoken language, and it became apparent that the so-called *genbun-itchi* written languages created in the late 1880's were no more than experimental literary languages. But instead of simply retreating to the established traditional literary languages, writers in the 1890's continued to experiment with various new literary styles, the most memorable being Ozaki Kōyō's (1868–1903) new amalgam of "elegant" and "vulgar" (in the manner of the long-forgotten Ihara Saikaku), Mori Ōgai's high-toned hybrid style of *kanbun*, classical Japanese, and Western syntax (developed in his early novellas "Maihime" [Dancing girl; 1890], "Utakatanoki" [Foam on the waves; 1890], and "Fumizukai" [The courier; 1891]), and the *waka* poet Ochiai Naobumi's (1861–1903) "new national literary language" (*shin kokubun*), which attempted to reform the classical literary style.

Ozaki Kōyō, who opposed *genbun-itchi* in the late 1880's, explored (from the early 1890's) the sentence-ending *de aru*, used since the end of the Tokugawa period as a literal translation of the Western verb "to be." Influenced by Kōyō's popular *shōsetsu* (*Aobudō* [Green grapes] and *Tajō takon* [Passions and resentments; both 1895]), which successfully used the *de aru* style, a number of *shōsetsu* writers began to use this style. Since it had not existed in the spoken language, it seemed more neutral and objective (having no honorific or interpersonal connotations) compared to other vernacular sentence endings such as *da* and *desu*, which *genbun-itchi* writers had experimented with earlier. From the late 1890's onward, the *de aru* style rapidly became the dominant "vernacular" style for the *shōsetsu*.[42]

This sudden transformation was not a purely literary phenomenon; rather, it was closely related to the institutional promotion of a "national language" after the Sino-Japanese War (1894–95). According to Yamamoto Masahide, a modern scholar who has extensively studied the historical development of writing styles from the end of the Tokugawa period on, the *genbun-itchi* movement gained momentum after the Sino-Japanese War, which convinced the Japanese of the decline of Chinese civilization and led to a devaluation of the authority of a Chinese-based writing system. In 1895 Ueda Kazutoshi, a linguist who had just returned from Germany where he had witnessed the promotion of a standardized national language by the Deutscher Sprachverein (established in 1885), argued that the establishment of a standard national language (*hyōjungo, kokugo*) was the foremost priority of a modern nation-state. In 1900 the government began promoting the establishment of national, standardized vernacular language.[43] Ueda and other intellectuals who had become involved in this project urged writers to explore and establish a polished *genbun-itchi* written style not only to establish a new standard written language but also to create a national standardized spoken language. Although the *genbun-itchi* style continued to evolve as a *written* language, incorporating various translation styles and neologisms, it gradually came to be viewed as a transcription of the living voice. The national standardized spoken language, which the *genbun-itchi* movement had constructed, was presented as the "origin" of the *genbun-itchi* written style.[44]

It was in such a climate that Kunikida Doppo and later Naturalist *shōsetsu* writers (such as Tōson and Katai), influenced by Futabatei's translations of

Turgenev, started to practice the "nature sketch" (*shizen no suketchi*) in which they explored various new colloquial *genbun-itchi* styles.[45] It was also in 1900 that the *tanka/haiku* innovator Masaoka Shiki (1867–1902) and his group—which included Takahama Kyoshi (1874–1959), Natsume Sōseki (1867–1916), Terada Torahiko (1878–1935), Nagatsuka Takashi (1879–1915), Itō Sachio (1864–1913), Suzuki Miekichi (1882–1936), and others—started the *shaseibun* (literary sketch, literary *dessin*) movement, involving not only poets and writers but schoolteachers and other amateur writers.[46] Inspired by his friend Nakamura Fusetsu (1866–1943), who had studied Western-style painting under the Italian landscape painter Antonio Fontanesi, Shiki advocated the "direct transcription of things as observed, without verbal embellishment or rhetorical exaggeration." Shiki suggested that a plain type of *genbun-itchi* style that avoided difficult or discordant Chinese loanwords would be appropriate for *shaseibun*.[47] Takahama Kyoshi, Shiki's collaborator and the leader of the movement after Shiki's early death in 1902, also advocated *genbun-itchi*, urging writers to become aware of their mission with regard to the future of the "national language."[48]

Both the *shaseibun* writers and the Naturalists sought a direct transcription of observed reality in the *genbun-itchi* style. In 1906, Kunikida Doppo, who had, through his collections of short *shōsetsu*—*Musashino* (1901), *Doppo shū* (1905), and *Unmei* (1906)—become known as a pioneering writer, wrote, apparently in answer to a question of how to describe nature:

> I have never thought about what kind of writing style was suited for describing nature. . . . One thing that we should consider is that those who write too well, that is to say, those who have read too many classical travel accounts and who can freely use Chinese characters, may be more susceptible to distorting nature as a result of being carried away by those writing styles. In order to see and describe nature, you have to write exactly as you see it and feel it. . . . The written styles of my nature sketches must be chaotic in terms of style. I do not intend to write well. I represent in unsophisticated language what I see and feel as faithfully as possible. And if I can make others feel what I have felt in this fashion, I think that is good enough. My work "Musashino," for example, might be written in a poor style, but I transcribed exactly what I felt. I faithfully described the nature that filled my mind at Musashino and that presented itself so clearly that I could not erase it even if I tried. Since it was exactly what I received from nature, I can also say that I transcribed my mind through nature. It is a lyrical poem that conveys through nature what I felt about nature.[49]

Doppo wrote confidently about the spontaneity and transparency of his written language and believed that, due to his "poorness" and "unsophistication" in the use of traditional writing conventions, he was able to "faithfully describe nature" as he saw it. Doppo also revealed a deep concern for expressing his self: the "faithful description of nature" is ultimately discussed in terms of a faithful transcription of his mind.

In an important, path-breaking study, *Origins of Modern Japanese Literature* (*Nihon kindai bungaku no kigen*; 1980), Karatani Kōjin argues that both "interiority" and the homogeneous exterior "landscape" came about simultaneously around 1900 through the internalization of the phonocentrism of the *genbun-itchi* conception of language.[50] He also argues that Doppo was the first "modern" Japanese writer to "discover" and embody such "interiority." Karatani rightly stresses the profound rupture caused in the signifying system by *genbun-itchi*, which he defines as an institutionalization of a phonocentric conception of language. The so-called transparency and immediacy of *genbun-itchi* language, however, had yet to be achieved in the early 1900's (or so it was believed); nor did it emerge suddenly. Although Doppo emphasized the immediacy and directness of his description of nature in "Musashino" (1901), his first work in a colloquial *genbun-itchi* style, the text itself reveals (by citing passages that had impressed Doppo) how it was mediated and informed by various written languages, especially those of Wordsworth, Carlyle, and Turgenev (particularly the descriptions of nature found in Futabatei's Japanese translations of Turgenev).

As we shall see in Chapter 4, Japanese Naturalists advocated a direct transcription of objective reality and promoted the view of language as a transparent vehicle. However, many of their texts—which came to be regarded as I-novels—in fact dramatize the process by which certain paradigms of reality came into existence not merely as a matter of personal experience or perception but as a result of a historical process in which an ideologically charged reality—which emerged through the mediation of, and interaction with, representations in Western literature—was constructed through language and then soon came to be taken for granted as an *a priori* reality. By the middle of the 1920's, when the notion of the I-novel emerged, these historically constructed and ideologically charged realities and new languages had become naturalized and their origins had been forgotten. The Japanese Naturalist texts and other modern *shōsetsu* regarded as autobiographical began to be received and read as a direct transcription of the author's lived experience and of his "self," which was considered to exist *a priori* and independently of language, itself now regarded as a transparent vehicle for expressing the self.

CHAPTER 3

~A

The Furor over the I-Novel: The Question of Authenticity

Watakushi shōsetsu, or the I-novel, formed the center of one of the dominant interpretive and cultural paradigms in the period after the mid-1920's
largely as a result of the powerful aura surrounding the notions of the *watakushi* and the *shōsetsu*, which we have examined in the previous two chapters.
These interrelated yet separate notions, however, did not automatically pro-
duce the notion of the I-novel or I-novel discourse per se, which is the topic
of this chapter. Part II will examine the period following that covered in
Chapter 2, that of Japanese Naturalism, which flourished in the first two
decades of the twentieth century and which had a decisive impact on the
formation of modern Japanese literature, including I-novel discourse. Before
turning to Japanese Naturalism, however, we will examine the series of critical debates that surrounded the I-novel from the mid-1920's through the
1950's.

Standard literary histories trace the origin of the I-novel to the confessional novels of the Naturalist (*shizenshugi*) writers and to the writings of the
Shirakaba group. Tayama Katai's *Futon* (The quilt; 1907), which became
closely associated with Japanese Naturalism, and Mushakōji Saneatsu's *Omedetaki hito* (A blessed person; 1911), a product of the Shirakaba group, are
usually referred to as the first I-novels. The genealogy of the I-novel, however, was created retroactively, after the mid-1920's. Not only did the term
watakushi-shōsetsu, or I-novel, not appear until 1920–21,[1] but the I-novel did
not become a serious issue in literary circles until 1924. It was even later,
between 1925 and 1935, that *Futon* and *Omedetaki hito* were retrospectively
selected by critics as the "origins" of the I-novel.

The Authentic Novel Versus the I-Novel

The I-novel debate was triggered by the journalist Nakamura Murao's (1886–1949) "The Authentic Novel and the State-of-Mind Novel" ("Honkaku shōsetsu to shinkyō shōsetsu to"), an article published in the literary magazine *Shin shōsetsu* (The new novel) in January 1924.

> What I call the authentic novel [*honkaku shōsetsu*] is, in form, a third-person novel as opposed to a first-person novel. This authentic novel is written in a strictly objective manner as opposed to a subjective manner. This sort of novel does not directly express the author's state of mind or feelings but instead represents his attitude toward life [*jinseikan*] through the depiction of certain characters and their lives. . . . It is a novel in which the "author" is completely hidden behind "what is being presented or depicted." The interest and significance of this sort of novel does not lie in who wrote it but in "what is written."[2]

Nakamura contrasted this "authentic novel"—of which the works of Turgenev, Tolstoy, Chekhov, and other Russian novelists are given as examples—with the *shinkyō shōsetsu*, the "state-of-mind novel."

> The state-of-mind novel is just the opposite of the authentic novel. The author appears directly in the state-of-mind novel. The author speaks directly in the work, or rather, the novel appears to present the author's direct speech. . . . The main focus is not on what is written but rather on the person who wrote it.[3]

Nakamura stated that he could not recall a European example of the state-of-mind novel. It is, he observed, "a peculiar novelistic form that has recently acquired influence among Japanese writers."[4] As examples, Nakamura listed Satō Haruo (1892–1964), Kasai Zenzō (1887–1928), Nagai Kafū (1879–1959), Masamune Hakuchō (1879–1962), Murō Saisei (1889–1962), Hirotsu Kazuo (1891–1968), Shiga Naoya (1883–1971), and Uno Kōji (1891–1961), that is to say, many of the recognized writers of the time. Nakamura criticized the current trend in which writers wrote only about themselves, about the "workings of their minds rather than about people or life," and advocated the authentic novel, modeled on the nineteenth-century European novel, the most representative of which was, in Nakamura's opinion, Tolstoy's *Anna Karenina*.

This kind of criticism began appearing in the mid-1910's, before the word "I-novel" came into use in the 1920's. In 1916, for example, Chikamatsu Shūkō, whom standard literary histories now regard as one of the founders of the I-novel, wrote: "I have become sick of confessional novels that describe the author's personal experiences. . . . I am not interested in those works in which the first-person character/narrator is identified with the author."[5] Similar complaints were made, using such terms as the "auto-biographical novel" (*jijoden shōsetsu*), the "confessional novel" (*kokuhaku shō-setsu*), the "self novel" (*jiko shōsetsu*), and the "first-person novel" (*ichi-ninshō shōsetsu*).[6] Nakamura articulated and synthesized these hitherto scattered lit-erary views in a more systematic fashion than his predecessors had, and his binary opposition between the authentic novel and the state-of-mind novel was adopted by subsequent critics, who often replaced "state-of-mind novel" with *watakushi shōsetsu* or "I-novel." Whichever term was chosen, a binary opposition between the I-novel / state-of-mind novel and the authentic novel was always implied, an opposition that inevitably raised the question of which was the truer novel.

Nakamura based his opposition on the question of form: the third-person, "objective" prose narrative found in the authentic novel versus the first-person, "subjective" state-of-mind novel. Subsequent critics, however, defined the I-novel / state-of-mind novel as an autobiographical novel writ-ten either in the first or the third person. In an article titled "The I-Novel and the State-of-Mind Novel" ("Watakushi shōsetsu to shinkyō shōsetsu"; January–February 1925), often regarded as the first public eulogy of the I-novel, the novelist and critic Kume Masao (1891–1952) defined the I-novel by differentiating it from the *Ich-Roman*, which, in Kume's view, is a first-person novel only in form: "I do not use the term 'I-novel' as a translation of the German term *Ich-Roman*. Instead it refers to another sort of novel, which should be called the autobiographical novel [*jijo shōsetsu*] and which signifies a novel in which the author reveals himself most directly."[7]

This definition of the I-novel as an autobiographical novel—as opposed to a novel narrated in the first person—was soon widely accepted by the reading public. In "My Personal View of the 'I-Novel'" (" 'Watakushi shō-setsu' shiken"; October 1925), one of the earliest essays to defend the I-novel, Uno Kōji (1891–1961) pointed out that the first-person novels by Shirakaba writers, particularly those by Mushakōji Saneatsu, are presented in such a manner that the first-person narrator/protagonist is easily identified with the author,[8] in contrast to earlier first-person novels, in which there was an obvious distance between the first-person narrator/character and the author. Uno, who sought the origins of the I-novel in Mushakōji's works, however, emphasized that "I-novel" did not refer only to recent first-person novels: "I would like to make it clear to unknowing readers that, despite its name, the I-novel is not necessarily a novel written in the first-person. Instead, it should be considered an autobiographical novel."[9]

While sympathizing with Nakamura's view of the "monotony" of the

I-novel (in which "novelists write only about their personal lives") and of the I-novel's dependency on context, Uno argued that no novel could be absolutely autonomous and context-free. In contrast to Nakamura, Uno regarded the authentic novel and the state-of-mind novel as two different, equally valuable, modes of self-expression, and believed that most literary works, including those of Shakespeare and Balzac (for him, the ideal of the authentic novel), could ultimately be considered expressions of the writer's "self." Most important, for Uno, the Western novels—the model of the authentic novel—was the most natural form for Western writers to express this "self," whereas the I-novel, created out of the "deepest self" (*mottomo fukai watakushi*), was the most natural form for Japanese writers.[10] This view, later expanded by Itō Sei in *Method of the Novel* (*Shōsetsu no hōhō*; 1948), remains one of the most widely accepted characterizations of the I-novel.

Despite appearing to oppose Nakamura's position, Uno's viewpoint represents a logical extension of it. If the function of the novel is to express the author's view of life, why not express it directly as the I-novel does rather than indirectly in the fashion of the authentic novel? Nakamura's condemnation of the state-of-mind novel was based on a spatial metaphor: the wide and comprehensive authentic novel versus the narrow and partial state-of-mind novel. Uno, by contrast, used a vertical metaphor and praised the I-novel for its "depth" in searching for the "self," replacing Nakamura's key phrase "view of life" (*jinsei-kan*) with the words "self" and "I" (*watakushi*). Uno saw the "depth" of the search for the "self" not only as a quintessential feature of the modern I-novel but as a salient characteristic of the works of Matsuo Bashō, the seventeenth-century *haikai* poet, thereby creating a historical continuity between the I-novel and the "indigenous Japanese tradition" that would become an integral part of subsequent I-novel discourse.[11]

Kume Masao took Uno's argument one step further by completely inverting Nakamura's hierarchical opposition.

> In the final analysis, the basis of all art lies in the self [*watakushi*]. It follows that the form that expresses this "self" directly and frankly, without pretense and disguise, that is to say, the I-novel, should become the main path, the basis and essence of the art of prose. To use others as a means of expressing the self is, after all, to reduce art to the commonplace [*tsūzoku*].[12]

The self is seen here as the basis of art, and art in turn is celebrated as the means of expressing the self. Kume did not have a high regard for nineteenth-century European novels—Tolstoy's *War and Peace*, Dostoyevsky's *Crime and Punishment*, and Flaubert's *Madame Bovary*—which Nakamura considered typical models of the authentic novel. Kume found them "commonplace, popular novels" (*tsūzoku shōsetsu*) and criticized them as "fabrications" (*tsuku-*

rimono). In Kume's words, the primary function of the *shōsetsu* is to express and depict faithfully the "true self" (*honmono no watakushi*) "no matter how mediocre that individual is."[13]

Taishō Democracy and I-Novel Discourse

The emergence of I-novel critical discourse in the mid-1920s was closely related to the social-liberal movement of the late 1910's and early 1920's known as Taishō Democracy, which sought to expand the franchise. Japan's industrialization, which accelerated after the Sino-Japanese War (1894–95) and developed even further after the Russo-Japanese War (1904–5), expanded significantly during World War I (1914–18), increasing the population of the urban working class, which provided the social base for the Taishō Democracy movement. The immediate driving force behind the movement was the notion of "popular polity" (*minpon-shugi*) advocated by the liberal-socialist Yoshino Sakuzō (1878–1933), who emphasized the "development of individual personality" for the populace and "humanistic consideration and reflection" for the upper class.[14] In related views, Abe Jirō (1883–1959) advocated Personalism (*jinkaku-shugi*), the development and achievement of the individual self as the basis for all social reform,[15] and the Shirakaba group espoused Humanism (*jindō-shugi*), the pursuit and development of the individual self as the ultimate goal of life. Both Personalism and Humanism became influential ideals by the middle of the Taishō period (1912–26) and formed the intellectual ground for Taishō Democracy.

In "A Personal Recollection of Myself in Those Days" ("Ano koro no jibun no koto"; 1919), Akutagawa Ryūnosuke (1892–1927)—who, together with Kume Masao, published a literary magazine called *Shinshichō* (1914–16) during his college years—recalled the enormous impact that Mushakōji Saneatsu's (1885–1976) humanistic individualism had on the younger generation, on himself and his friends, "despite their dissatisfaction with Mushakōji's artistic imperfection."[16] Mushakōji, a vocal spokesman for the Shirakaba group, argued that the goal of life was to pursue, to develop, and to express one's self. In "Work Done with My Own Pen" ("Jibun no fude de suru shigoto"; March 1911), an essay published in the *Shirakaba* journal, Mushakōji proudly declared:

> I intend to make writing my life's pursuit. But that is a means, not a goal. I would like to create a work that will possess great life; but for me, who was not born an artist, that is not my ultimate goal.... What is of utmost importance is my Self [*jiga*], the development of my Self, the growth of my Self, the fulfillment of the life of my Self [*jiko*] in the true sense of the word. I chose writing for this purpose.... I love Beauty, I love Power, I love Life, I love Thought. But that is

all because I love my Self, because I want to develop my Self, and want to give life to my Self.... I will not sacrifice my Self for anything. Instead, I am willing to sacrifice everything for my Self. I believe, however, that what is the Self is probably much greater and deeper than is usually assumed. I haven't truly discovered the Self yet.[17]

Mushakōji continued to express his optimism in the efficacy of self-assertion, in the notion of exploring and developing the Self through Work, which, for the Shirakaba group, meant Art—a process they believed led directly to true Humanity. For Mushakōji and the Shirakaba group, there were no Japanese: there existed only Humanity (*ningen*), or Mankind (*jinrui*), together with such universals as Love, Art, Nature, Justice, Beauty, and Life. All of these were defined in relation to Humanity, a universal reality directly represented by each of their individual selves. This absolute acceptance of Western discourse, the uncritical universalism and internationalism, and the notion of cultivating the individual self reflected the general intellectual atmosphere of the 1910's[18]—a time when the sense of national crisis had dissipated in the aftermath of the Russo-Japanese War but when political activity was tightly controlled by the government. In 1910–11, in the Imperial Treason incident (Taigyaku jiken), for example, socialists and anarchists were arrested and executed for an alleged attempt to assassinate the emperor. Mushakōji and Abe Jirō, however, saw no disjunction or contradiction between their highly abstract, idealistic individualism—with its supposed unbound potential for self-cultivation—and the sociopolitical realities of the day. In 1918 Mushakōji established an utopian, egalitarian farming community called New Village (Atarashiki mura) where, according to Mushakōji's vision, "workers would be gentlemen, and gentlemen would be workers, commoners would be aristocrats, and aristocrats would be commoners."[19] In 1921 Abe Jirō, proudly declaring his Personalism as the basis for all social and economic reform, criticized the "materialism of both capitalism and emerging Marxism" and urged both capitalists and workers to avoid it and strive for "spiritual creation."[20]

The Russian Revolution of 1917, however, brought an awareness of class struggle, and questions began to surface about the validity of idealistic humanism and individualistic spiritualism. (In fact, Mushakōji's New Village and Abe's Personalism emerged in this climate.) This was reflected in Japan in the formation in December 1920 of the Socialist Confederation of Japan (Nihon shakaishugi dōmei), which brought together Marxists, anarchists, labor unionists, students, and young writers. In 1922 Arishima Takeo (1878–1923), a member of the Shirakaba group skeptical of Mushakōji's New Village, published an essay called "One Declaration" ("Sengen hitotsu") in which he criticized the self-complacent and self-righteous identification of the "third class," the bourgeoisie to which intellectuals and writers belonged, with the "fourth class," or the proletariat.[21] Arishima's "One Declaration" led to debates about the relationship between art (*geijutsu*) and social class, between art and life (*jisseikatsu*), and between prose fiction and social reality.[22] The growing consciousness by intellectuals of the industrial working class and the vast expansion of journalism and the reading public in the late Taishō period, particularly after the Great Kantō Earthquake in 1923, raised the question of "popular literature" or "popular art" (*minshū geijutsu*) versus "bourgeois literature," and later of "proletarian literature" versus "bourgeois literature," or the "popular novel" (*tsūzoku shōsetsu*) versus the "artistic novel" (*geijutsuteki shōsetsu*).[23]

It was in this literary and sociocultural climate that the I-novel debate emerged. In "The I-Novel and the State-of-Mind Novel," Kume Masao referred to a statement made in 1920 by his friend Kikuchi Kan (1888–1948), a writer and the founder of the journal *Bungei shunjū*, that anyone, however mediocre, could become a writer as long as that person could describe his or her own mediocre life faithfully and vividly. While sympathizing with Kikuchi Kan's views, Kume distinguished his position by stressing the notion of art, particularly the privileged status of the novel and specifically that of the "artistic" *shōsetsu*.

> Everyone has the material for an I-novel. . . . However, only those who can truly grasp the self within them and who can represent this self through words can be called artists and can create I-novels. "To represent truly" never means to depict the material as it is. There must be condensation. One should condense the self [*watakushi*]—unite it, filter it, concentrate it, stir it, and then reproduce it entire.[24]

While emphasizing the direct and faithful expression of the self, Kume attempted to differentiate the I-novel from the autobiography (*jijoden*) and the confession (*kokuhaku*).[25] According to Kume, although Tolstoy's *My Confession* has some artistic elements, it cannot be considered an I-novel. Nor can Rousseau's *Confessions*, "even though there are a number of novelistic scenes." Kume admired Sōseki's *Garasudo no uchi* (Inside the glass door; 1915) because "its author is revealed directly," but, he added, "unfortunately, *Garasudo no uchi* is not a novel."[26] Kume, whose genre classifications are bewildering, asserted that the I-novel is distinguished from a "bare confession" or an autobiography by the presence of *shinkyō*, a "firm attitude toward life, whether derived from one's view of life [*jinseikan*] or from one's social view [*shakaikan*], as advocated by recent proletarian literature."[27]

Kume's vagueness and abstraction are typical of subsequent discussions of the I-novel, a term that inevitably calls for a definition of "I" or "self" in relationship to the *shōsetsu*. Despite Kume's mystifying genre classifications, it is clear that he ardently espoused the essential connection between the "self" and art, particularly the *shōsetsu*. In Kume's view, a "firm attitude toward life"—which echoes the cultivation of individual personality advocated by Mushakōji, Abe, and others—is not merely a prerequisite for the "true" I-novel, it can only be manifested through a "true I-novel." At a time when the Japanese were beginning to question the value and function of art vis-à-vis social engagement, Kume's argument stood as a defense of art in the name of the self, a defense that was persuasive because of the power that the notion of the self exercised at the time over readers of diverse social and political inclinations.

Kume's defense of art soon came under criticism from his fellow writer Akutagawa Ryūnosuke, who argued that in itself autobiographical referentiality in a novel had nothing to do with the intrinsic value of art.[28] However, Kume's axiom that the "basis of all art lies in the self [*watakushi*]" outlived this particular debate and soon became a widely held perception, supported and spread by the expanding media. Some scholars (including Fowler) argue that the I-novel was the product of a small, closed literary circle (*bundan*) in which writers and readers knew each other socially and read the texts on an autobiographical, referential level, and that this socio-literary structure faded away after the late Taishō period because of the expanded role of journalism and the impact of new literary forces such as Proletarian literature and the modernist Neo-Perceptionist school. The fact of the matter is, however, that I-novel discourse emerged in the mid-1920's not so much as a description or explanation of a particular body of literary works created within a small *bundan* but rather as a result of a new literary consensus created by contemporary writers and critics (opposed to radical Marxism), a consensus institutionalized by the expanded mass media[29] about a particular mode of reading and about the newly perceived social function of the novelist (in a growing industrialized, mass society) as the "earnest martyr and representative of human life," to quote Satō Haruo.[30] In a radio program broadcast to the general public in 1926, Satō announced that the "true I-novel" was not a trivial account of personal experience but an "honest and earnest record of the author's struggle with his fate," which the reader should identify with and view with sympathy.[31]

The Mid-1930's: Yokomitsu Riichi and Kobayashi Hideo

Generally speaking, there were three periods when the I-novel became the subject of intense literary and intellectual discussion: the late Taishō period (mid-1920s), around 1935, and immediately after World War II (late 1940's and early 1950's). In the late Taishō period, the general consensus formed that the I-novel was a uniquely Japanese form of the autobiographical novel in which the author revealed his "genuine self" most directly. Around 1935 the I-novel again became the focus of attention, following the publication of Yokomitsu Riichi's "Essay on the Pure Novel" ("Junsui shōsetsu ron"; April 1935), Kobayashi Hideo's influential "Discussion of the I-Novel" ("Watakushi shōsetsu ron"; May–August 1935), and Nakamura Mitsuo's "On the I-Novel" ("Watakushi shōsetsu ni tsuite"; September 1935). All of these condemned the I-novel for its narrow perspective and "simplistic realism" (*soboku jitsuzai ron*), to use Yokomitsu's words.

In "Essay on the Pure Novel," Yokomitsu Riichi (1898–1947) argued that the I-novel, which had been widely recognized as "genuine literature" (*junbungaku*), had led the Japanese novel into a cul-de-sac, a deformed, abstract world. According to Yokomitsu, the "pure novel"—a term no doubt inspired by André Gide's *le roman pur*—was the highest form of the novel but had yet to appear in Japan. The pure novel overlaps with the *tsūzoku shōsetsu* (popular novel, commonplace novel) in that "contingency" (*gūzensei*) plays a critical role in the development of the plot, just as in real human relationships. As examples of great "pure novels," Yokomitsu cited Dostoyevsky's *Crime and Punishment*, Tolstoy's *War and Peace*, and the novels of Stendhal and Balzac.[32] His praise of these European novels is an obvious attempt to refute Kume, who had called these same works "*tsūzoku shōsetsu*" (commonplace novels). But Yokomitsu did more than simply reverse Kume's argument or return to the ideal of Nakamura Murao's authentic novel. He argued that the modern novel should ultimately deal with "self-consciousness" (*jiishiki*) or the "self that sees itself" in a modern age that had "destroyed the hitherto accepted notions of the psyche, the intellect, and the emotions" and that had consequently created a "new realism." According to Yokomitsu, future writers of the "pure novel" should cultivate this "new realism" by employing a "fourth-person" technique that reveals the complex interrelationship among multiple "self-consciousnesses."[33]

Kobayashi Hideo's (1902–83) "Discussion of the I-Novel," which was written in response to Yokomitsu's "Essay on the Pure Novel," is one of the most influential essays on the Japanese I-novel and on modern Japanese literature in general. Kobayashi began by citing the opening passage of Rousseau's *Confessions*, which he refers to as "the first European I-novel." When Rousseau declared in *Confessions* that he would undertake the unprecedented task of exposing his self to society, he was not, according to Kobayashi, concerned only with depicting his personal life. Instead, he wanted to question the position and significance of the individual in society. Kobayashi argued that the recent European I-novel, as exemplified by the works of André Gide, Marcel Proust, and James Joyce, appeared after European naturalism (as represented by Zola and his followers) had become an established and oppressive institution. Writers such as Gide attempted to "restore the humanity [*ningensei*] that had collapsed under the overwhelming ideological pressure of nineteenth-century naturalism and positivism." Kobayashi's central view of the "European I-novel"—which includes works by "romantic I-novelists" (such as Rousseau, Goethe, and Constant) as well as by Flaubert and Maupassant—is summarized in the famous remark: "The reason why they did not make mistakes in studying the 'I' is because their 'I' [*watakushi*] was an 'I' that had already been fully socialized."[34]

Kobayashi argued that although Japanese I-novels appeared when the Japanese Naturalist movement had reached its height (while Gide and others were writing I-novels), Japanese novelists merely imported the techniques of the European naturalist novels without understanding the social forces that had led to their creation. (For Kobayashi, in Japan all modern novelists beginning with the Naturalists, with the sole exception of Ōgai and Sōseki, were I-novelists.) Kobayashi pointed out that Japanese I-novelists naively believed that their daily personal life could supply the dreams and material for artistic activity: "For Katai to believe in the 'I' meant to believe in the unquestionable validity of his own personal life and that of the I-novel, whereas for Gide, to believe in the 'I' meant to believe only in the experimental studio inside the 'I' and nothing else." Kobayashi not only attacks the tradition of eulogizing the I-novel, as exemplified by Kume, he implicitly criticizes Yokomitsu's advocacy of the "pure novel," which, according to Kobayashi, reduces the significance of André Gide's "I-novels" and "his intense pursuit of the self" to the level of literary technique.[35]

Two major events between the late Taishō period and 1935 stimulated and renewed the debate on the I-novel: first, the introduction and intellectual dominance of Marxism, which forced Japanese intellectuals to reflect critically on and reconsider the notion of the individualistic self that lay behind Taishō Democracy, and second, the importation and translation of contemporary autobiographical novels by André Gide, Marcel Proust, and James Joyce. From the end of the Taishō period, particularly from 1926 until the beginning of 1930's, Marxism attracted a wide range of intellectuals, including literary writers. The major force in this movement was Fukumoto Kazuo (1894–1983), the theoretical leader in the late 1920's, who emphasized the "self-reflective" and "self-determining" and "active" role of the individual subject in adopting Marxist principles. The communist movement, however,

was quickly suppressed by the government from the end of the 1920's, and
many Marxist "proletarian writers" (*proretaria sakka*) abandoned communism
following their party leaders' public renunciation of "foreign communism" in
1933.[36] The fact that these former proletarian writers began writing confessional novels about their renunciation of communism made the public aware
of the persistence of the I-novel tradition.

According to Kobayashi Hideo, the introduction of Marxism destroyed
the belief in the *a priori* value of daily life as an object of literary representation
and forced Japanese writers to confront an "overwhelming social ideology":
the question of how to view society as a whole. Furthermore, the deliberate
abandonment of refined novelistic techniques by proletarian writers seriously
damaged the Japanese I-novel. Kobayashi suggested that the present socio-
historical and intellectual environment bore a close similarity to that surrounding the European I-novelists. Because Japanese contemporary writers
had been confronted with the overwhelming ideological institution of Marxism, they had the potential to create a "true I-novel," as Flaubert, Maupassant,
and Gide had done under the ideological pressures of naturalism and positivism. Kobayashi's advocacy of a "true individualistic literature" (*shin no kojinshugi bungaku*), in short, reveals his desire to protect and redress the notion
of the "true self" or "true individual" challenged by Marxist ideology. Although Kobayashi criticized the Japanese I-novel, beginning with Katai's
Futon, he ultimately wanted the Japanese to interrogate the "self" properly
and to develop a "true I-novel" along the lines of Gide's novels.

Kobayashi's criticism of the Japanese I-novel had a significant influence
on the hitherto fragmentary advocacy of the authentic novel, the model for
which was sought in the nineteenth-century European novel. The authentic
novel had been praised as the "true" novel because its prototype was thought
to reside in Europe. Kobayashi, however, argued that the European modern
novel was superior to the Japanese novel not because it was European but
because of the manner in which it treated and problematized the self. At the
same time, Kobayashi here seems to imply that the Japanese intellectuals and
writers now shared contemporary European concerns as well as the potential
of their European counterparts.[37]

Postwar Clamor: Itō Sei, Hirano Ken, and Nakamura Mitsuo

The I-novel again became a serious topic of criticism after Japan's defeat
in World War II. Indeed, after the war anyone who claimed to be a serious
literary critic apparently had to confront the problem of the I-novel. The
devastating defeat caused the Japanese to re-examine and reflect critically on

the various systems and ideologies in place prior to the war, including litera-ture. Of the numerous critical essays on the I-novel written during this period, Itō Sei's *Method of the Novel* (*Shōsetsu no hōhō*; 1948), Nakamura Mitsuo's *Essays on the Novel of Manners* (*Fūzoku shōsetsu ron*; 1950), and Hirano Ken's "Antinomy of the I-Novel" ("Watakushi shōsetsu no niritsu haihan"; 1951) were the most influential.[38]

One characteristic of these essays is the attempt to establish a larger historical perspective and comparative typology. As Itō Sei (1905–65), a nov-elist and critic, notes in *Method of the Novel*: "Contrary to the belief held by the Japanese literary community that the I-novel is a uniquely Japanese prob-lem, when it comes to the novel, the question of the author's self [*watakushi*] is the most essential problem in modern world literature, or literature in gen-eral."[39] Stimulated by Albert Thibaudet's remark that the modern novel emerged as a literary form produced in an isolated room and then was read in printed form in an closed room, Itō argued that the modern novel generally has at its core the "author's inner voice" (*uchinaru koe*). Based on this central premise, Itō constructed, in a manner reminiscent of Uno Kōji's 1925 article, a typology of the novel based on the manner by which the author expresses his or her "inner voice." The European novelists required "fiction" (*kyokō*) as a "mask" in order to extract and explore the "pure essence" of their "inner self"; the more sincerely these European novelists attempted to confess, the more they concealed themselves in fiction. By contrast, the Japanese authors revealed their natural selves directly without any "extraction or abstraction" (pp. 50–54, 65–70).

In contrast to Uno, who created a similar typology based on an inherent cultural tendency toward one type or another, Itō's typology is grounded on his view of the novelist's position vis-à-vis society. European novelists were respectable, socialized individuals, initially as gentlemen in high society and aristocratic salons and then later as citizens in a broader society. They tried to examine the relationship between the individual and his social environment, observing manners, ethics, human relationships, and other factors that condi-tioned and restricted the individual. For European novelists, fiction was an indispensable, protective disguise that allowed the novelist to express and explore fully his or her own individual self or ego, which was essentially "ugly" (*shūaku*) (pp. 53–55, 64, 124, 132). By contrast, modern Japanese writers since the early twentieth century—who developed, in the name of Naturalism, an autobiographical literary form called the I-novel—abandoned society and lived in a small, isolated *bundan girudo* ("literary circle-guild"), in which they relentlessly pursued and fearlessly expressed their "ugly and prim-itive inner selves" (*uchinaru ware*) without concealment or distortion. Unlike

European novelists, whom Itō called "masqueraders," the Japanese I-novelists were "fugitives," without fear of or concern for their social respectability as secular individuals (pp. 65–70).

According to Itō, the "literary circle-guild" was an isolated and, in some regards, fictional, closed world, in which the novelists abandoned real society—the outer feudal, reactionary world—and entered into a dream-like world. There they could become free individuals relieved of the burden of social and political responsibility and action, which the government had severely restricted from the end of the Meiji era. Itō contributed to the construction of the "origins" of the I-novel genealogy by arguing that the Buddhist and Shintoist eremitic tradition lay behind the I-novels created in the literary circle-guild, which, in his view, resembled the closed world of the recluse.

Itō contrasted European and Japanese novels ultimately in order to contextualize and evaluate the modern Japanese I-novel, which he equated with modern Japanese literature in general. Itō, who shared the negative view presented by Kobayashi Hideo in his 1935 article, recognized the I-novel's narrow perspective and its lack of a social dimension. He also criticized what he saw as the elitist, self-complacent pride and blindness of those I-novel writers who believed in the uniqueness of their own experiences as well as of themselves as "confessors" of these experiences. Itō argued that this narcissistic belief in uniqueness prevented the I-novel writers both from thinking philosophically or theoretically and from creating representative, contemporary human characters in their novels. Itō, however, also emphasized the positive aspect of this narrowness, asserting that modern Japanese writers, by not attempting to represent or engage society at large, had succeeded in "extracting and creating certain kinds of genuine human relationships" as well as in "developing the writer's genuine self, which relentlessly observed its own natural, primitive, asocial self from a detached, objective point of view" (pp. 104–10). Significantly, Itō's positive view of the I-novel is based on the premise that the essential core of the human self, whether it be that of a Japanese or an European, is "ugliness" (shūaku).

As a novelist whose writings were strongly influenced by James Joyce (whom he introduced to Japan in the early 1930's), Itō argued that the conventional use of fiction as a means of self-projection or protective disguise for European novelists had lost its meaning for contemporary European experimentalists—such as Proust, Joyce, Gide—as it had for Japanese I-novelists. Itō, however, also emphasized the difference between the two. In Japan "the author's actual life is regarded as identical with art, and the ethical value of that life is regarded as identical with the value of his art" (p. 153). Here Itō's criticism of the Japanese standard literary view was directed toward both writers and critics/readers, particularly the latter.

> The value of those works by recent European novelists is never based on the actual value of the author's social action. Instead, it is understood as the necessary outcome of their methodological experiments and as the site of their thinking. In contrast to Japan, critics and readers never regard the author as identical with the protagonist; they never criticize the author's personal life based on the protagonist's thoughts and deeds. Literary works are evaluated as the concrete manifestation of the author's philosophy. (p. 194)

Reflecting the standard view of the I-novel since the mid-1920's, Itō defined it as a first-person narrative—whether or not written in the first or third person—that does not fully explain the protagonist's personal situation or background on the assumption that the reader already has a knowledge of the protagonist/author's career and background (pp. 65–66).

> Iwano Hōmei's protagonist resembles—indeed closely resembles—Don Quixote. The tragedy of Hōmei's protagonist, however, is one-dimensional. The protagonist is not objectified by the author in relationship to society. The work becomes a tragedy or comedy only when the reader contextualizes the work. The reader thus constructs the work himself or herself by supplying the information about the author. This is the standard way of the Japanese novel. (p. 141)

Itō astutely pointed out that in these context-dependent texts, the reader plays a major role in completing the work as well as in forming the standard view of the I-novel, which Itō was trying to redress. In fact, although he criticizes I-novel writers for not objectifying the protagonist (the novelist himself) in relationship to society, Itō also emphasized the experimental nature of Japanese I-novelists, which he claims has been overlooked by the Japanese reader.

The typology of the I-novel that Itō presented (later developed by Hirano Ken in a slightly different direction) was based on the "experimental" nature of I-novel writers that Itō praised. "The I-novel writers were themselves experiments of modern thought. . . . They described their experimental selves" (p. 106). Itō distinguished the "observed self, or the acting subject" (*kōisuru jiga*), from the "observing self, or the writing subject" (*nagameru, egaku jiko*), arguing that "part of the newness of the modern Japanese writers' artistic methods lies in the fact that they experimented with their lives by constructing their selves so that they would be worthy of being described by themselves" (p. 110). According to Itō, "the self as the subject" (*shukakunaru jiko*) was split between the self that observes his own self and the self that constructs his self as an ideal human being." By the early 1930's, two types of writers emerged: one type, such as Kamura Isota, made his own "writer's egotistical self" the object of his writing; the other, such as the Marxist writer Kobayashi Takiji (1903–33), tried to make himself an ideal person worthy of being described by himself. Itō categorizes Tokuda Shūsei, Iwano Hōmei, and Masamune Hakuchō as the former type, and Shimazaki Tōson and the early Shōwa period (late 1920's–early 1930's) Marxist writers as the latter type. According to Itō, the early Shōwa Marxist writers were essentially no different from the other non-Marxist, aesthetically oriented I-novel writers since both groups "created a special place for their activities inside this backward society and reported those activities in their literary works" (pp. 134–35). Significantly, Itō never applied this distinction between the "observed self, or the acting subject" and the "observing self, or the writing subject" to the analysis of individual texts. Instead, he categorized all past writers (and their works) as one type or the other, thereby continuing to follow the standard I-novel reading that superimposes the protagonist on the author.[40]

In "Antinomy of the I-Novel," Hirano Ken (1907–78), elaborating on a distinction made earlier by Itō, called the state-of-mind novel a "harmonious type" (*chōwa-gata*) as opposed to the "I-novel," which he labeled a "destructive type" (*hametsu-gata*).

> If we define the I-novel as destructive literature, the state-of-mind novel can be characterized as the literature of salvation. If the I-novel can be described as the disclosure of an unresolvable crisis, the state-of-mind novel is nothing but the concluding remarks of a surmounted crisis. If the I-novel is rooted in a sense of conflict between the self [*jiga*] and the outside world, the state-of-mind novel is an attempt to achieve a sense of harmony between the two. In one, there is a life crisis, deriving from a sense of helpless stupidity and sinfulness; in the other, there is a purified sense of fate that emerges from having overcome such a crisis. The I-novel tries to seek salvation in art; and the state-of-mind novel seeks salvation in real life. The difference derives from the fact that the former originates in the Naturalist school, which espoused a non-ideal and a non-solution, while the state-of-mind novel derives from the idealistic Shirakaba group. In other words, the I-novel is a literature of the "defeated" [*hametsu-sha*], of those who have abandoned the world, whereas the state-of-mind novel is the literature of those who are in possession of this world. There are two identifiable streams: one that runs from Chikamatsu Shūkō through Kamura Isota and reaches Dazai Osamu and another that runs from Shiga Naoya through Takii Kōsaku and reaches Ozaki Kazuo.[41]

Hirano's distinction between the "destructive" I-novel and the "harmonious" state-of-mind novel was based on two different criteria: an intratextual/thematic aspect and an intertextual/biographical dimension, which are not clearly differentiated. According to Hirano, the destructive I–novel depicts a crisis caused by sinful, perverse, or shameful behavior, without presenting an explicit solution or salvation. The harmonious state-of-mind novel, by contrast, expresses an elevated state of mind acquired as a result of overcoming a crisis. The former represents a pessimistic, fatalistic attitude toward life; the latter an optimistic, idealistic attitude. The distinction between the two types was also based on the relationship between the author's "real life" and his "artistic activity." An author of an I-novel seeks salvation or a resolution of his personal crisis through his art, whereas an author of a state-of-mind novel seeks a solution to his personal crisis or salvation in his real life. The former is a person who sacrifices and abandons his personal life to create art; the latter is a person for whom his personal life is the main priority and a work of art is a secondary product, a result of overcoming a personal crisis.

In defining the "destructive" I-novel and the "harmonious" state-of-mind novel, Hirano distinguished two biographical types, according to events in a novelist's personal life before and after the writing of a particular novel. The thematic aspect of the novel becomes significant only in light of the author's "life," which functions as the central frame of reference. As the title of his book *Art and Real Life* (*Geijutsu to jisseikatsu*) suggests, Hirano Ken attempted to clarify the relationship between a novelist's "real life" (*jisseikatsu*) and his writings, particularly the personal motives for writing novels and the effects that novel writing had on the author's life. By the end of World War II, so-called I-novelists such as Kasai Zenzō and Kamura Isota were dead, and in 1948 Dazai Osamu killed himself, leaving behind *No Longer Human* (*Ningen shikkaku*), which was soon recognized as a representative "self-destructive" I-novel. The deaths of these novelists invited readers and critics such as Hirano to reflect on the novelists' lives and the relationship between their works and their lives. As Hirano noted, "I try to gain an overview of the works of a particular author in order to learn how he lived his life. The crucial point in learning how he lived his life is finding out how that writer overcame or failed to overcome the crises of his life."[42]

In contrast to Itō Sei, who was both critical and sympathetic toward the I-novel largely because of his own stance as a novelist, Nakamura Mitsuo (1911–88) fiercely attacked the I-novel tradition as the epitome of the larger problem of realism, literature, and modernity (or their distortion or lack) in Japan. In Nakamura's view, the I-novel tradition since Tayama Katai's *Futon* "naively described the author's socially isolated, daily life . . . without ever analyzing or objectifying his personal experiences or sensibility in relationship to society."[43] In several articles written in 1935, including "On the

I-Novel," Nakamura, under the strong influence of Kobayashi Hideo, defined the Japanese Proletarian literary movement, which had recently collapsed after several years (1928–31) of intellectual domination, as the "first truly romantic movement" in Japan. According to Nakamura, it had "irreversibly destroyed the primitive harmony of the homogeneous feudal ethics" underlying the earlier I-novel tradition, and was a movement that had forced writers and intellectuals to confront the notion of society and to awaken to the inevitable confrontation between the individual and society.[44] At the same time Nakamura attacked Proletarian literature, arguing that Proletarian realism was no more than a mechanical repetition of earlier I-novel techniques (in which author and protagonist share the same vision) except that it prohibited a focus on the writer's inner self and categorically denied the human individual—as opposed to the proletariat as a collective hero.[45] Nakamura also argued that although the Proletarian literary movement had destroyed the form of the traditional I-novel, the "spirit" of the I-novel unfortunately survived, and as a consequence writers needed to develop "true modern realism."

The fifteen years that separate Nakamura's "On the I-Novel" (1935) and his *Essays on the Novel of Manners* (1950) made him keenly aware of the "further deterioration" of the contemporary Japanese novel: in his view, the "distorted realism" of the I-novel tradition continued to thrive in a mechanical and empty form long after the literary ideal and authority of the I-novel had died. Nakamura's immediate motive for writing *Essays on the Novel of Manners*, which represents the full development of his views on modern Japanese literature, was to criticize the contemporary *fūzoku shōsetsu* (novel of manners), the journalistic popular narratives that, in Nakamura's view, superficially depicted contemporary social manners without critically examining the individual or society. Nakamura argued that the *fūzoku shōsetsu*, which had developed since the prewar period in reaction to the I-novel tradition, not only revealed the shortcomings of Japan's modern literature but "destroyed modern literature."[46] The postwar state of the novel, in short, was a twofold "distortion [*yugami*] of genuine modern literary realism."

In Nakamura's view, the "distortion" of the Japanese novel could be traced to Naturalist novels in which writers superficially adopted the techniques of the nineteenth-century European novel without understanding the social and ideological struggles in which these novelists were engaged. Nakamura severely criticized the I-novel for developing a "deformed I" in contrast to the "socialized I" (Kobayashi's term) found in the modern European novel. According to Nakamura, the modern Japanese novel started with Futabatei's monumental novel *Ukigumo* (Drifting clouds; 1887–89) and reached its first

apex with Shimazaki Tōson's *Hakai* (The broken commandment; 1906), a
novel in which Tōson—like such European novelists as Balzac, Flaubert, and
Zola—successfully pursued "the author's individualistic struggle against traditional society" through a fictional character.[47] The publication in the following year (1907) of Katai's *Futon* (The quilt) distorted this "healthy" development toward "true realism." The success of *Futon*, which Nakamura (along
with Kobayashi Hideo) regarded as the start of the I-novel tradition, over-
shadowed the achievements of *Hakai* as "a genuine modern novel of realism."
As a consequence, even Tōson, following Katai's example, began writing
autobiographical I-novels: *Haru* (Spring) in 1908, *Ie* (The family) in 1910–11,
and *Shinsei* (New life) in 1918–19. The easy success of *Futon*, in Nakamura's
view, distorted the notions of both "realism" and "literature."

Nakamura differed from his predecessors in that he carefully analyzed
texts rather than concentrating on biographical material, but in the process,
he reinforced what became orthodox literary history—the Japanese modern
novel, in attempting to follow the "true" realism of Europe produced a
"uniquely Japanese" form called the I-novel, which was deeply rooted in
Japanese society and "tradition." This genealogy of the I-novel was created in
the late Taishō period, was fully developed by Kobayashi Hideo, Itō Sei, and
Nakamura Mitsuo, and then subsequently adopted by all literary histories in
one form or another.

This genealogy, which supplied the main narrative for the "history of
modern Japanese literature," also represented an autobiographical moment
in which the Japanese literary and cultural tradition was retroactively constructed in the intense debate over the meaning of modernity, westernization,
Japanese identity, and the self. There is no transcendental position to frame
this I-novel discourse, which still persists. Part II of this study, however, will
attempt to defamiliarize this I-novel discourse—which has become oblivious
of its figurative and historical nature—by re-reading those narrative texts that
participated in its formation yet were not completely subsumed by it. Chapter 4 examines Tayama Katai's *Futon* and Japanese Naturalism, both considered the "origin" of the I-novel; and Chapter 5 analyzes Shiga Naoya's
oeuvre, thought to represent the apex of the I-novel tradition. The objective is not so much to correct past misreadings as to examine those various
elements and issues that they problematized before they were retroactively
shaped by I-novel discourse. Indeed, the two opposing yet complementary
vectors implied in any historical description—the generative historical processes marked by heterogeneity and contingency, and the teleological, causal
shaping of events—lie at the heart of my analysis of the body of texts related to
Katai and Shiga.

PART II

Rereading the I-Novel

CHAPTER 4

⁓

Love, Sexuality, and Nature: Tayama Katai's *'Quilt'* and Japanese Naturalism

I-novel discourse as it evolved from the mid-1920's generally considered Tayama Katai's *Futon* (The quilt; 1907) the first overtly autobiographical Japanese I-novel, that is to say, the first modern Japanese novel to depict faithfully the "facts" of the author's life. This view was clearly articulated by Kobayashi Hideo and then solidified by Nakamura Mitsuo's highly influential *Essays on the Novel of Manners*, which traced the origin of "distorted realism" in the modern Japanese novel to *Futon*. Nakamura argued that *Futon* was a narcissistic monologue by a protagonist/author who remains completely unaware of the superficiality of his understanding of the imported notions of love and literature. In Nakamura's view, Tayama Katai played out the role of Johannes, the protagonist of *Lonely People*, a play by the German naturalist writer Gerhart Hauptmann, without understanding the playwright's intentions.

> Compared to the protagonist of Oguri Fūyō's *Seishun* [Youth] or that of Shima-zaki Tōson's *Hakai* [The broken commandment], Takenaka Tokio is both more lively and comical. . . . Unfortunately, however, the author is not aware of the protagonist's comical dimension, and as a consequence, the irony that should exist between the author and the protagonist emerges between the work and the reader, who is forced to grin at the character/author instead of feeling sympathy for him. The best description in *Futon* probably occurs when Tokio, having realized that the lover of his beloved student has come to Tokyo, decides to visit the place where Yoshiko is temporarily residing. In the scene in which Tokio lies on the shrine ground, weeping and covered with mud, there is one sentence—"Tears fell in torrents down Tokio's whiskered face"—in which the author almost appears to have recognized the comical nature of the protagonist. But in this monologic, hero-dominated novel, even the phrase "Tears fell in torrents down Tokio's whiskered face" does not induce the author's laughter.

Instead, Tokio's self-indulgent self-consciousness, which is epitomized by this one sentence, remains unchanged, untouched by anyone. The inherent comedy of this situation completely escapes the eyes of the author, and the comic material is forced to become a tragic monologue. This is the birthplace of the Japanese I-novel.[1]

For Nakamura, no critical distance exists between the protagonist Takenaka Tokio and the author Tayama Katai. As I shall argue, however, the interest of *Futon* lies not only in the ironic and critical perspectives that the text develops vis-à-vis the protagonist but also in the historical process by which this critical distance was eventually erased.

Narrative Voice and Ironic Perspective

Katai's contemporary readers were in fact aware of the ironical presentation of the protagonist, with whom they felt a certain affinity and sympathy. Perhaps the most famous comment on *Futon* is Shimamura Hōgetsu's (1871– 1918), "This work is a bold and outspoken confession of a man of flesh,"[2] which Nakamura Mitsuo cited as evidence of this work's reception as a "confession." The manner in which *Futon*'s contemporary readers interpreted this "confession" or the "expression of the self," however, differs significantly from Nakamura's view. Some contemporary readers were drawn to *Futon* out of sympathy for the protagonist;[3] some spoke of the "models" for the work;[4] others read *Futon* as an autobiography written in the third-person. For example, Katagami Tengen (1884–1928) wrote a critical review entitled "Mr. Tayama Katai's Naturalism" in which, drawing on Hōgetsu's famous phrase, he referred to *Futon* as a "bold and outspoken confession of fleshly agony by a self-conscious, modern man."[5]

> For the first time, this author has attained a state of self-consciousness that attempts to objectify and criticize even himself. The author, beginning to feel the pull of nature, has transcended the stage of merely expressing his deep feelings toward the power of nature and has finally attained the critical awareness that this power of nature is deep within himself.[6]

Whereas Tengen stressed the critical distance between Tokio, the "objectified self," and Katai, the "objectifying self," Sōma Gyofū (1883–1950), a Naturalist critic who participated in a joint review of *Futon* with Hōgetsu, Tengen, and others in *Waseda bungaku* (October 1907), emphasized the work's self-consciousness.

> Today many people confuse Naturalism with Realism and assume that detached and objective description is the quintessential characteristic of Naturalism. I am

overjoyed to find that this work has, in this literary context, presented the true character of Naturalism—which is to be intellectually detached and emotionally involved. In dealing with objective matters, this work has superseded the distinction between the subject and the object and has maintained an attitude of self-consciousness [*jiishiki*] rather than one of observation [*kansatsu*]. This is the true character of Neo-Naturalism, which is fully realized in this work. Here the self [*ware*] is merged with nature, and on top of this is imprinted an arduous self-consciousness. I believe that the freshness of this work derives from the layer of self-consciousness that lies on top of the literary style, which, when observed from another angle, appears emotional, sentimental, or lyrical.[7]

In Gyofū's view, the self-consciousness found in *Futon*, which makes this work a "remarkable achievement of true Naturalism," cannot be reduced to either that of the protagonist or that of the author. Instead of considering *Futon* a single-voiced, direct monologue by the author/protagonist, as later critics did, contemporary readers such as Gyofū and Tengen saw layers of self-consciousness not only in the protagonist but in the differentiation between the "objectifying" author and his "objectified" self (Tokio). In contrast to Nakamura Mitsuo, who criticized *Futon* for being a confession without "self-criticism," its first readers regarded *Futon* as a "confession" precisely because they observed the author's self-criticism and self-condemnation in his portrayal of the protagonist.

Although standard literary histories characterize *Futon* as a personal monologue by the protagonist/author, *Futon* is basically narrated in the third person. One stylistic innovation of Japanese Naturalist writers such as Shimazaki Tōson and Katai in their attempt to adopt the languages of Western novels, which subsequently had an enormous impact on the standard *genbun-itchi* style, was the overt indication of the grammatical subject. *Futon* systematically uses the third-person pronoun "he" (*kare*) or the proper noun "Tokio."[8] Nevertheless, many sentences in *Futon* have no overt grammatical subject even though the implied grammatical subject can be clearly identified in most cases.[9] This lack of subject indicators, combined with the nature of the sentence endings—in which past or perfect tense indicators can coexist with non-past sentences within the same diegetic plane—blurs the distinctions between first and third person narrations, between indirect and direct discourses. In fact, as the presentation of Tokio turns inward, the grammatical person often shifts, before one notices, from the third-person *kare* to the quasi-first person *jibun* (one's self, I), creating the impression that the protagonist's feelings are being articulated directly through his own voice.[10] But although *Futon*'s narrative voice often creates the effect of a first-person personal monologue, *Futon* is not a confessional monologue. Instead, it resembles what Roland Barthes has called the "personal narrational system."

There are narratives, or at least narrative episodes, which, though written in the third person, nevertheless have as their true instance the first person. How can we tell? It suffices to rewrite the narrative (or the passage) from he to I: so long as the rewriting entails no alteration of the discourse other than this change of the grammatical pronouns, we can be sure that we are dealing with a personal system.[11]

In *Futon* "he" can frequently be replaced with "I" without a significant change. A number of passages, which can only be translated into English in the free indirect style (using a third-person, past-tense narration in which the reported enunciation is integrated into the narration without introductory markers such as "he thought"), have an even greater sense of directness in the original Japanese and resemble an interior monologue in the first person, thus intensifying what Barthes calls the "personal narrational system." And yet the narrative voice of *Futon*, which often appears to speak for the protagonist and occasionally to merge completely with the protagonist's own voice, discreetly provides, either through the dialogue among the characters or through the omniscient narration, perspectives not shared by or not accessible to the protagonist. An example is the following scene—cited by Nakamura—in which Tokio lies down on the shrine grounds.

> He was sad, truly deeply sad. His sadness was not the sadness of florid youth, nor simply the sadness of lovers. It was a more profound and greater sadness, a sadness inherent in the innermost reaches of human life. The flow of water, the withering of blossoms—when one encounters that irresistible force that is deep within nature, there is nothing as wretched or as transient as man.
> Tears fell in torrents down Tokio's whiskered face.   (chap. 4, pp. 146, 55)[12]

Although the English translation demands a third-person "he" and a past-tense narration, the Japanese sentences in the first paragraph contain no overt grammatical subject, nor are they in the past tense. As a consequence, Tokio's thoughts and emotions emerge with a greater sense of directness. The English translation also obscures the fact that it is Tokio himself who considers his loneliness and sadness "profound" and "inherent in the innermost reaches of human life." In the last sentence the highly formal adverb *ōzen* (in torrents) is unexpectedly combined, in a manner reminiscent of *haikai*, with a vulgar, unpoetic word *higezura* (whiskered face), thereby making ironical, if not entirely comical, Tokio's sentimental self-pity. The narrative voice of *Futon* thus reveals Tokio's blindness, the gap between his narrow perception of the world (and of himself) *and* those events that occur around him (and in himself) of which he remains unaware.

Futon basically follows the temporal unfolding of events from Tokio's discovery of Yoshiko's relationship with Tanaka, a young student at a Christian college, to her return to her hometown in the provinces. In chapters 2 and 3, however, the narrator reviews the preceding three years of Tokio's life, revealing his attraction to Yoshiko, the nature of their relationship, and Tokio's anger and despair at discovering Yoshiko's new relationship. The narrator describes the loneliness and sense of stagnation that led Tokio to become attached to Yoshiko as follows: "This anguish in fact was the sort that any man in his mid-thirties experiences. In the final analysis, many men of this age flirt with lower-class women to cure this loneliness. And many of those who divorce their wives are of this age" (chap. 2, pp. 128, *38*). This statement, presented by the narrator immediately after the interior monologue in which Tokio superimposes his anguish on that of Johannes, creates an ironical perspective.

.Although Tokio espouses new ideals taken from Western literature and cannot tolerate the traditional, "old-fashioned" morality and life-style (represented in his eyes by his wife and sister-in-law), he also feels an unbridgeable gap between himself and the "modern" (*shinpa*) younger generation represented by Yoshiko and Tanaka. Tokio is aware that even as he longs for the kind of love inspired by Western literature, he is also concerned for his social status as a teacher and married man. Thus, his "secret love" for Yoshiko, whom he cherishes as a source of artistic rebirth, is simultaneously a disreputable matter, to be concealed "deep" within himself. Although Tokio is conscious of being caught between these opposing forces, the third-person, omniscient narration reveals the nature of his attachment to Yoshiko, his unconscious hypocrisy, and his fundamental lack of self-knowledge. *Futon* in fact ironically juxtaposes Tokio's inner world with the perspective of the "old-fashioned" people— Tokio's wife, his sister-in-law, and Yoshiko's father—who do not share his "literary vision." Although Tokio considers the fundamental problem of Meiji society to be the conflict between "old-fashioned people" (*kyūha*) and enlightened "modern individuals" such as himself, these old-fashioned people, who ostensibly have no understanding of his problems, reveal the limitations of the protagonist's vision as well as his excessive narcissism.[13]

Occasionally, the narrator also provides an omniscient viewpoint that ironically transcends those of the characters. For example, Yoshiko, the "fashionable" modern student whom Tokio superimposes on Anna (in *Lonely People*) and who is herself moved by Elena, the tragic heroine of Turgenev's *On the Eve*, is not portrayed solely from Tokio's perspective. In the following passage from chapter 2, the narrator relates how Yoshiko became an "educated modern woman."

> After finishing the local primary school, Yoshiko had gone straight to Kōbe and entered Kōbe Women's Academy, where she had led the life of a fashionable

student. Compared to other girls' schools, the Christian schools were open-minded when it came to literature. At that particular time there was a stipulation forbidding the reading of such works as *The Devil Wind, the Love Wind* [by Kosugi Tengai; 1903], and *The Golden Demon* [by Ozaki Kōyō; 1897–1902], but before this stipulation by the Ministry of Education went into effect [in 1905–6] there had been no problem with reading such books as long as it did not occur in the classroom. In the church at school, Yoshiko had learned the value of prayer, the pleasure of Christmas, and the significance of cultivating ideals, and had become a member of a group that concealed mankind's vulgar side while celebrating the beauty of mankind. At the beginning she had missed her home and mother and had been greatly upset, but eventually she had forgotten all that and had come to appreciate above all else the life of a female student at a boarding school. Once you have joined a troop of female students who tease the dormitory cook by placing soy sauce on the rice to demonstrate their dissatisfaction at not being served a tasty pumpkin, or who trim their words when speaking face to face with a crotchety old dormitory mistress but talk freely behind her back, how can you be expected to view things simplistically, as would a girl raised in the home? Beauty, ideals, and vanity—these Yoshiko now acquired, and thus she had all the traits, good and bad, of a Meiji-era female student.   (pp. 130, *41*)

Whereas Tokio is enraptured by the notion of having a modern disciple and potential lover who can share his literary world and his ideals of love, the omniscient perspective reveals Yoshiko's still childish frivolity, to which Tokio is completely blind, and depicts life at a girls' mission school with considerable detachment and humor.

Ideology of Love

As the passage quoted above suggests, the omniscient narrator reveals a larger context in which Christianity, love, literature, and the "new woman" are intimately interrelated. In *Futon* Tokio pejoratively refers to Yoshiko's relationship with Tanaka as *ren'ai*, or "sacred love" (*shinseinaru ren'ai*), while calling his own love for Yoshiko *koi*. The word *ren'ai*, which Yoshiko and Tanaka use to try to convince Tokio that their relationship is sacred and spiritual, is emphatically marked in the text. *Ren'ai*, which is now so naturalized that almost no one is aware of its historical origin, was a neologism adopted in the late 1880's to translate the English "love" and the French "amour."[14] In contrast to the traditional word *koi*, *ren'ai* signified the newly imported notion of love, understood to mean a more spiritual, deeper, and more highly valued mutual affection between man and woman. The notion was propounded from the late 1880's through the 1890's by *Jogaku zasshi* (1885–1904), a literary journal organized by the Christian educator/critic Iwamoto Yoshiharu (1863–1943). Although *Jogaku zasshi* was a Christian, humanistic journal that aimed to enlighten and liberate women from so-called feudalistic subordination, its contributors and readers included a number of young intellectual men. The young Methodist journalist and critic Yamaji Aizan wrote the following in an article entitled "The Philosophy of Love" ("Ren'ai no tetsugaku") in the November 1890 issue of *Jogaku zasshi*.

> Oh, love [*ren'ai*], which revolutionizes man's spirit and body!
> Love, which cultivates a new frontier of taste and imagination!
> Love, which creates a hero and a brave being!
> Love, which unites the family and the nation!
> Love—may a great poet appear and astound those numerous writers who
> have distorted you![15]

As if in response to this demand, in February 1892, Kitamura Tōkoku wrote an essay for *Jogaku zasshi* entitled "Disillusioned Poets and Women" ("Ensei shika to josei"), which had an enormous impact on the younger generation.[16]

> Love [*ren'ai*] is the key to life's secrets. Love comes first, and then human life. If there is no love, what is the significance of life? . . .
> How can love be mere affection? Only love can offer a citadel for a poet who is a vanquished general in the battle of the world of ideas [*sōsekai*] against the actual world [*jissekai*].[17]

Tōkoku argued that "love" (*ren'ai*), for which man must sacrifice himself, is an "unsullied mirror that reflects man's true self."[18] In 1893 Tōkoku—together with his young Christian followers Shimazaki Tōson and Hoshino Tenchi—established a new literary journal called *Bungakukai* (1893–98), which, as noted earlier, began as the literary supplement to the *Jogaku zasshi* but soon became an independent literary journal that eliminated the religious, educational, and social orientation of its parent publication. Tayama Katai, who had been associated with the Kenyūsha group led by Ozaki Kōyō, began contributing lyrical travelogues to *Bungakukai* in 1894 and was undoubtedly influenced by the new journal, which was responsible for introducing such European romantic poets as Byron, Keats, and Wordsworth to Japan and which became the cornerstone of the Japanese Romantic movement.

Futon reveals how the ideology of "love," together with that of "literature," exercised its authority on Meiji intellectuals. For Tokio, *ren'ai* implies a fashionable ideal cherished primarily by young people with Christian educations. He considers his love (*koi*), by contrast, to be more natural and genuine. Tokio's attraction to Yoshiko, however, in fact derives from and is reinforced by literary (and Western) ideals of love. Indeed, for Tokio, who lectures

Yoshiko "on literature, novels, and love" (chap. 5, p. 155), love and literature
are two complementary aspects of the same order, which he considers essential to a "true modern individual." Despite his contempt for Christians (here
represented by Tanaka), Tokio's own *koi* has quietly assimilated and naturalized the ideology of *ren'ai* to the extent that he believes his love for Yoshiko
to be different from that associated with Christianity.

The following passage reveals the narcissistic nature of Tokio's ideals of
love, a narcissism also latent in the ideals espoused by Kitamura Tōkoku and
other writers: "Old-fashioned education simply could not equip a girl to be
the wife of a modern Meiji man. His own view was that women too had to
stand on their own feet and exert their will power" (chap. 5, pp. 154, *62*). In
Tokio's view, women in the new age must be "awakened" and "independent"
so that they can be an appropriate match for a modern Meiji man. When the
"modern," "educated" and "literary" Yoshiko enters his life, Tokio becomes
enraptured with his own self-image, by an appropriate female partner who
turns his vision into reality. But Tokio's high-spirited advocacy of the "free
behavior of an independent modern woman" lasts only as long as he believes
that Yoshiko is his partner. When he is informed that Yoshiko has gone to
greet Tanaka, he becomes furious.

> That twenty-one-year-old boy Tanaka had actually come to Tokyo. Yoshiko
> had gone to meet him. Who knows what they did? What she had just told him
> [Tokio] might be a pack of lies. . . . They had no doubt held hands. Their hearts
> would have pressed against each other. Who knows what they were doing
> upstairs in that travel lodge, out of the sight of others? It was only a fleeting
> moment between purity and impurity. Tokio could not bear such thoughts.
> "This concerns my responsibility as her supervisor!" he cried out angrily to
> himself. "I can't leave things like this! I can't allow such freedom to a capricious-
> minded woman." (chap. 4, pp. 141–42, *52*)

The omniscient narrator's presentation of Tokio's emotions reveals a fundamental discrepancy between the ideals to which Tokio subscribes and the
more immediate drives that work inside him, thereby disclosing the basic
narcissism and blindness residing in his ideals of love.

"Objective Description" and "Subjectivity of Great Nature"

From around the time of *Futon's* publication, Naturalist writers such as
Shimazaki Tōson and Tokuda Shūsei started to write heavily autobiographical works almost entirely in the third person. Tōson's series of autobiographical novels—*Haru* (Spring; 1908), *Sakura no mi no jukusuru toki* (The time when
the fruit of the cherry ripens; 1914–18), and *Shinsei* (New life; 1918–19)—all

of which have a common protagonist (Kishimoto Sutekichi), reveal Tōson's growing consciousness of the potential of a third-person narration to create a literary autobiography with a double perspective. While presenting the inner thoughts of the protagonist, the third-person omniscient narration provides the reader with commentary on the protagonist's behavior, thus giving the reader a more complete vision of the protagonist.[19] Indeed, in practice third-person narration gravitated toward the protagonist's perspective and became one of the formal conventions of the autobiographical novel, and both readers and authors came to identify the third-person objective narration as none other than the author's own self-commentary.[20] It is questionable, however, whether Katai intended, at least at the time of writing and publication, to have *Futon* read as an autobiography in the third person and to have this work ultimately reduced to "his self" or to his "self-consciousness."

Literary history has generally characterized Katai both as the pioneer of the I-novel and as the advocate of "flat description" (*heimen byōsha*), which claims to depict the object "without a grain of subjectivity and without an abstract plot."[21] Thus, Katai is considered to have faithfully recorded the facts of his own personal life with flat description, without critical perspective or distance. Katai, however, made this comment about flat description, which appeared in *Waseda bungaku* (Sept. 1908) in an interview with a Naturalist journalist, in an attempt to defend himself against criticism of his works for being excessively sentimental and subjective.

The association of Katai with "flat description" has obscured his concern with objectively describing the internal world of his characters. In July 1907, two months before the publication of *Futon*, Katai published an essay entitled "On *Shasei*" ("Shasei to iu koto") in which he expressed his view of Masaoka Shiki's (1867–1902) notion of *shasei* (literary sketch, drawing).

> Sheer *shasei* inevitably tends to be an external description. The writer draws on a two-dimensional surface, what he sees in front of him, as if he were painting. As a result, the feelings of the writer (observer) can be expressed to a certain degree, though the internal feelings of the characters in the work cannot be represented. As long as one uses the *shasei* method, one cannot help but feel unnatural when one dares to depict those internal feelings. Those who have faith in *shasei* must think that they can suggest those internal feelings through the character's external attitudes. . . . In my opinion, this seems to derive from the fact that the notion of *shasei* is bound to a particular stylistic technique. Man has both surface [*heimen*] and depth [*rittai*]. . . . When you have mastered the surface, you should attempt to observe matters three-dimensionally.[22]

Katai here was paying tribute to Shiki's *shasei / shaseibun* movement, which had a deep impact on the development of *genbun-itchi*, but more important he was attempting to clarify his own attitude toward description by juxtaposing it with *shasei*, which he improperly reduced to the notion of "external [surface] description."[23] The essay suggests that when Katai wrote *Futon*, he was probably conscious of attempting to be both two-dimensional (surface) and three-dimensional (depth), that is to say, he was trying to depict objectively the subjective "internal feelings" of a protagonist modeled on himself.

Katai developed a coherent view of description (*byōsha*) in a 1901 essay entitled "The Subjectivity of the Author: In Response to a Critique of *Wild Flower*" ("Sakusha no shukan: No no hana no hihyō ni tsuite"), which was written in response to Masamune Hakuchō, a writer and critic who had condemned Katai's novel *No no hana* (Wild flower; 1901) for being "too sentimental, subjective, and contrary to the claim of its preface, which had rejected 'the narrow subjectivity of the novelist.' " Much like the protagonist of *Futon*, Katai was often criticized for being overly sentimental, lyrical, and subjective even after he began writing Naturalistic works under the influence of Zola and Maupassant. This essay is Katai's rebuttal.

> I am dissatisfied with those critics who, when they come across a passage in which the protagonist laments the vagaries of fate, immediately criticize the author for allowing his narrow subjectivity to reveal itself in his work. I am stunned when critics, lacking the power of judgment, go so far as to assert that the author's self can be directly observed in the character whom the author has created to be realistic and believable. . . . In any event, the author tries to represent the characters as objectively as possible while also attempting to reveal the subjectivity of great nature as much as possible. This is where my work differs from the novels of external realism now in fashion among Meiji writers; and this is probably why a certain critic has mistakenly taken my work to be a subjective novel written in contradiction to the claims of the preface.[24]

While severely criticizing the critic for confusing the subjective emotions of the characters with those of the author, Katai emphasized the importance in Naturalism of "the subjectivity of great nature" (*daishizen no shukan*), which he distinguished from the author's "narrow subjectivity" (*sakusha no shōshukan*).[25] In an article entitled "On Subjectivity and Objectivity" ("Shukan kyakkan no ben"; September 1901), Katai further argued that a novelist should transcend his "narrow," "sporadic," "personal" subjectivity, which is full of "personal prejudices," and should attain, through "concrete and objective description," "the subjectivity of great nature," which embraces and transcends various ideals and doctrines and which constitutes the innermost principle of human life.[26] In Katai's words, the "naturalism of Zola, Flaubert, and Goncourt" "has the great subjectivity of nature at its root" in "boldly depicting the vices of society and the weaknesses of the individual, while at the same time representing the images and forms of great nature as objectively as possible."[27] (Katai's statement resonates with Mori Ōgai's emphasis on the *Idee* in art in the famous *Botsu risō ronsō* debate of 1891–92 between Ōgai and Tsubouchi Shōyō concerning the vastness of nature/reality and the importance of ideals in art.) While emphasizing "objective depiction," Katai repeatedly stressed the importance of "the subjectivity of great nature" without which "realism descends to superficial imitation."[28] Katai was here attempting to distinguish himself from the Naturalist novelists of the Waseda school (Hirotsu Ryūrō [1861–1928], Kosugi Tengai [1865–1952], and others), whom Katai criticized for being "obsessed with external description and thus incapable of exploring the depths of human nature."[29]

Although some contemporary readers interpreted *Futon* as an autobiography written in the third person, Katai's own literary concerns at this time were probably focused not so much on self-portraiture as on an "objective portrayal" of a man from a new literary perspective, that of "true Naturalism," which had an overwhelming aura for Katai and his contemporaries. Katai's primary concern appears to have been objective description of the subjective world of the protagonist, an objective description that assumes the transcendental perspective that he called the "subjectivity of great nature."

Sexuality and the Ideology of Nature

The standard literary histories divide Japanese Naturalism into two stages: "early Naturalism" (*zenki shizenshugi*), which emerged around 1900 under the direct but undigested influence of Emile Zola, and "late Naturalism" (*kōki shizenshugi*), a more domesticated form of naturalism represented by such writers as Tōson, Katai, Masamune Hakuchō, and Tokuda Shūsei.[30] Early Naturalism is generally thought to be a superficial adaptation of Zolaism, whereas late Naturalism, whose direction *Futon* is thought to have irreversibly determined, is characterized as a factual description of the author's private life, without the wider social dimension found in European naturalism.

Immediately after the publication of *Futon* in September 1907, Shimamura Hōgetsu, an influential Naturalist critic, wrote:

This work is a bold and outspoken confession of a man of flesh. In this regard this work has clearly and consciously explored what had been initiated earlier— ever since the "novel" first emerged in the Meiji era—by such writers as Futabatei, Fūyō, and Tōson. This work has advanced that aspect of the Naturalist movement that advocates "description without falsification in regard to both beauty and ugliness" and that tends to concentrate on depicting ugliness. Although what is represented is ugly, it is the undeniable voice of nature. Contrasting this natural aspect with that of reason, this work boldly presents to the public a self-conscious, modern character who is difficult for the reader to bear witness to. Herein lies the life of this work as well as its value. Had this work been published in an earlier period, those concerned with morality would have attacked it by now. However, we have yet to hear those voices. Is this due to a change in time or to some other reason? This is not to say that no one, aside from the writers mentioned above, has attempted to deal with this problem. Most of these writers, however, only depicted ugly actions [*shūnaru koto*] and not ugly minds [*shūnaru kokoro*]. By contrast, the author of *Futon* described not ugly actions but ugly minds.[31]

While drawing a contrast between "reason" and "flesh," Hōgetsu praised *Futon* for its depiction of "ugly minds" as opposed to "ugly actions." What did Hōgetsu mean by the "ugly minds" he found so striking in *Futon*? Why was their presence significant?

Kosugi Tengai, a popular novelist considered a forerunner in the adoption of European naturalism, gives us a clue in the preface to his novel *Hayari uta* (Popular songs; 1902).

> Nature is nature. It is not good [*zen*] or evil [*aku*]; neither is it beautiful or ugly. It is simply that a particular people in a particular nation in a particular period selects a particular aspect of nature and calls it good or evil, beautiful or ugly. The novel is nature in the world of ideas. Whether it be good, evil, beautiful, or ugly, there is no reason why the novelist should be restricted in the range of his depiction. The novel should let the reader imagine the phenomena in the novel as if the reader were encountering those phenomena in the natural world.[32]

In a tone reminiscent of Shōyō's statements in his debate with Ōgai, Tengai argued that a novelist should not discriminate among "good, evil, beautiful, and ugly." The early Naturalist writers who were attracted to Zola such as Tengai and the young Nagai Kafū in fact emphasized and tried to depict the evil and the ugly. In the postface to his novel *Jigoku no hana* (A flower in hell; June 1902), the young Kafū revealed his ultimate objectives.

> One aspect of man cannot but be animalistic. . . . In human society as it exists today, the human mind has long been shaped by religion and ethics, both of which are products of particular customs and circumstances. This dark side of man has come to be considered completely evil. What is going to happen to the animality that has been condemned in this fashion? If we want to create a perfect, ideal human life, I believe that we must start by making a special study of this dark side. . . . Therefore, I would like to concentrate on boldly and vividly depicting the various dark desires of man, the physical power, the violence, all of which derive from the environment and from the hereditary elements transmitted from our ancestors.[33]

Kafū is obviously relying on the authority of Zola, whose series of novels *Les Rougon-Macquart* (1869–93) and whose theoretical principles were being introduced to the Japanese literary world at the time.[34] Kafū declared that he would represent the dark animalistic side of man suppressed and condemned by civilization. In *Jigoku no hana* he crudely depicted the gross sexual desires and violence of the wealthy, Meiji upper-middle class. An aspiring Christian writer has a secret relationship with the lascivious wife of a bourgeois man, who made a fortune by marrying the mistress of a wealthy Westerner; a school principal rapes a young female teacher, who works as a private tutor to the wealthy man's son. Each character is explained in terms of his or her heredity and environment, but the simplistic, good-versus-evil characterization is reminiscent more of late Edo and early Meiji *gesaku* popular narratives than of Zola's *Les Rougon-Macquart*. Ultimately Kafū reduces the "animalistic, dark side" of man to the attributes of the evil characters. Nevertheless, *Jigoku no hana* was praised for attacking social hypocrisy and for describing the "hitherto undescribed reality" of man.[35]

As Kafū's early novels suggest, Zola's naturalism, which had a profound impact on the literary world of the early 1900's, provided a new foundation for romantic protest against social tradition. In 1902, the critic Hasegawa Tenkei (1876–1940), attempting to clarify the notion of "nature" in Naturalism (*shizenshugi*), which did not refer simply to Zolaism, summarized contemporary notions.

> Now Naturalism [*shizenshugi*] is much in fashion in the literary world. This notion does not necessarily overlap with the "natural" [*shizenteki*] as a word synonymous in the artistic domain with the "realistic" [*shajitsuteki*] or the empirical [*keikenteki*]. In other words, this Naturalism is the name given to the thought [*shisō*] of a group of people who claim that "man should maintain a natural state." The people who advocate this Naturalism are those who consider all institutions and manners in today's society as false, artificial, hypocritical, and unnatural, and who believe that man should act by following his "natural nature" [*shizensei*] and that man should follow his instincts and original nature [*honsei*].[36]

Tenkei regarded "Nietzsche's instinctivism" (*honnōshugi*) and Rousseau's slogan "return to original nature" as the central principles of Naturalism as conceived by the "intellectual world" (*shisōkai*).[37] Another article on Naturalism written in 1902 by a young critic and student at the University of Tokyo called Fukada Yasukazu reveals that various other Western literary and philosophical trends were also covered by the umbrella of Naturalism.

> "Nature" indicates that which does not use artificiality, that which does not undergo forging and deliberation. Thus, in scholarship, Naturalism rejects spec-

ulation and respects facts. . . . In ethics, Naturalism advocates Tolstoy's original man, affirms sexual drives, regards all restraints as being unworthy of consideration, advocates Nietzsche's instinct, supports the so-called aesthetic life [*biteki seikatsu*]. . . . In the literary world, Naturalism means, first and foremost, "realism."[38]

The notion of Naturalism, which garnered a large following as well as critical opposition in the literary and intellectual world of the 1900's, indiscriminately embraced Nietzsche-ism, Rousseau-ism, Tolstoy-ism, and Zola-ism, all of which were thought to emphasize human instincts, particularly sexual drives, as a means of criticizing established socio-ethical restraints and customs. Fukada's definition of "nature"—" 'nature' refers to that which does not use artificiality"—also suggests that the "nature" (*shizen*) in Naturalism had already assumed the traditional connotation of the word *shizen* (originally pronounced *jinen*), which had been used as an adjective or an adverb (rather than a noun)—meaning "as is" (*ari no mama*), or "by itself," "naturally" (*onozukara*)—before becoming the standard translation for the Western word "nature."[39]

The polysemic implications of "nature" and Naturalism are evident in *Jūemon no saigo* (The end of Jūemon; May 1902), a novella that established Tayama Katai as the rising star of Naturalism. *Jūemon no saigo* depicts the life of Jūemon, a savage rebellious man with a hereditary physical defect—his scrotum is abnormally large—who is ostracized by the surrounding community. The story is told by a first-person narrator who speculates on the causes of Jūemon's desperate criminal life in Zolaistic terms ("Does the reason for his rebellion lie in his inherent nature or in his environment?")[40] and is deeply moved by his life and tragic death.

> I thought to myself, "If man is completely natural, then it's bound to end in tragedy. For then nature must come into conflict with present-day conventions. In this case, doesn't nature itself end up in this world as unnatural? Six thousand years of history and customs—that goes a very long way toward making a second nature. As a result of this history, society sometimes dominates nature or embellishes it. But can nature always remain subjugated by six thousand years of history? Perhaps it could be argued that this isn't a subjugation of nature but an improvement of it. But, then, to what extent could man, with his superficial knowledge and petty mind, possibly be able to improve on nature? There are gods, and there are ideals, but they are all less than nature. There are principles, and there are imaginative visions, but none is greater than nature. And to those who would ask me on what grounds I say this, I believe I would answer: the analysis of the innate individual."[41]

> "The child of nature simply cannot exist in this impure world. Woe to those who are born full of nature into the world, for are they not children of nature

born into the world of man, to die unknown and in defeat? No, no, no. To die in defeat! Such might be the sad fate of the child of nature. And yet, like the death of the warrior on the battlefield, doesn't this defeat possess infinite life? Doesn't it reveal infinite tragedy? Doesn't it call for infinite reflection upon the life of man?"

I thought the matter over deeply for a while.

"Considered from a broader point of view, the whole life of this poor child of nature is a question of living in accordance with his birth and fate. That Jūemon died like an animal, with no one to bury him, doesn't mean that his life was in vain!"[42]

Nature, which is contrasted with society and history (as well as with limited knowledge and mind), is regarded as being of the highest order and having the highest value. In *Jūemon no saigo*, this nature manifests itself through Jūemon, the "child of nature," who is born with an abnormally large scrotum and who ends up leading a criminal life in a rural village. His excessive sexuality, which society regards as ugly and evil, becomes a symbol of the "great nature" suppressed by society.

In contrast to *Jūemon no saigo*, in which the first-person narrator directly sets forth his Naturalistic philosophy (a crude mixture of Zola and Rousseau), *Futon* does not make overtly Naturalistic statements through either the protagonist or the narrator. The words "heredity" and "environment," which appear repeatedly in *Jūemon no saigo*, are absent in *Futon*. Unlike Jūemon, a biologically abnormal criminal, Tokio is a middle-aged, ordinary intellectual. Significantly, however, Tokio also has "dark, sexual desires," which become one of the focal points of the narrative. These, however, are emphasized more discreetly, with the narrative focusing on sexual desires of which Tokio himself is not fully aware.

Persistent desire [*yokubō*] and reproductive power [*seishoku no chikara*] never hesitate to take possession of a woman when she is of suitable age. (chap. 3, pp. 136, 47)

Like a being oppressed by the unbearable forces of nature [*taegatai shizen no chikara*], Tokio once again laid down his bulky frame, this time on a nearby bench. (chap. 4, pp. 147, 56)

The pain in life that a man in his mid-thirties is most prone to suffer from— agony over his work and sexual frustrations—those things pressed his heart with tremendous force. . . .

He thought seriously about Yoshiko's love and about her future life. Reflecting on his own experience, he thought about the boredom, the tedium, the callousness that would come into the young couple's life after they had lived together for a while. He thought about the pitiful situation of a woman after she had given her body to a man. His heart was now filled with the weariness of life,

a weariness of that dark power lurking in the hidden reaches of nature.   (chap.
7, pp. 172, 76–77)

The familiar smell of the woman's hair oil and sweat excited him beyond words.
The velvet edging of the quilt was noticeably dirty, and Tokio pressed his face to
it, immersing himself in the familiar female smell.
    All at once he was stricken with desire [*seiyoku*], with sadness [*hiai*], and
with despair [*zetsubō*]. He spread out her mattress, lay the quilt out on it, and
wept as he buried his face against the cold, stained, velvet edging.
    The room was gloomy, and outside the wind raged.   (chap. 11, pp. 193–
194, 95–96)

In a manner characteristic of Naturalist works written from the early 1900's
under the influence of European naturalism, Katai repeatedly used such terms
as *yokubō* (desire), *seiyoku* (sexual desire), and *seishoku no chikara* (reproductive
power) to describe the character's internal state.
    But instead of simply being a matter of biology, sexual desire in *Futon* is
closely related to the protagonist's fascination and infatuation with Western
literature.

Then suddenly, by some chain of thought or other, he called to mind Hauptmann's *Lonely People*. Before things had turned out as they had, he had thought
about teaching her this drama as part of her curriculum. He had wanted to teach
her about the hero's—Johannes Vockerat's—mind, about his grief. He had read
the work some three years before, before he had even known of her very
existence. He was already a lonely man. He did not go so far as to try to compare
himself to Johannes, but he did feel, with much sympathetic understanding, that
if such a woman as Anna appeared, then it was only natural that things would
end in tragedy. He let out a long, deep sigh, thinking that he couldn't even
become Johannes anymore.
    He did not dare to teach her *Lonely People*, but he had once taught her
Turgenev's short work *Faust*. There in the little study, bright with the light of
the lamp, her heart had been filled with longing by that colorful love story, and
her expressive eyes had sparkled with a still deeper significance. The lamplight
shone on the upper part of her body, on her chic and fashionable hairstyle, her
comb, her ribbons; and when she had drawn her face close to the book, that
indescribable perfumed smell, that fleshy, feminine smell. . . . As he explained to
her the part in which the protagonist reads Goethe's *Faust* to his former lover, his
own voice too had trembled with passion.
    "But it's no good now!" he exclaimed to himself, and pulled at his hair
again.   (chap. 1, pp. 126–27, 37–38)

As the opening paragraphs of *Futon* reveal, Tokio has molded his life to
resemble that of Johannes, an alienated writer who falls in love with a beautiful, intellectually awakened university student named Anna. Tokio, whose
life is steeped in literature, specifically late nineteenth-century Western litera-

ture, teaches Yoshiko about works such as Turgenev's *Faust* (1856) and *On the Eve* (1860), Hermann Sudermann's *Hometown* (1893), and Henrik Ibsen's *Doll's House* (1879). Whenever he feels lonely or depressed, he recalls the fate of the tragic characters in the novels of Hauptmann, Turgenev, and Maupassant. Although Tokio himself believes that he is deeply alienated, the manner in which he superimposes his "agony" on that of his favorite literary heroes makes him appear to be a complacent narcissist enraptured with his own "tragic" and literary image. Reading as fallacious identification—one of the central motifs of the European novel as exemplified by *Don Quixote* and *Madame Bovary*—no doubt had a particular poignancy for Meiji writers and intellectuals, including Katai himself. Katai not only imitated Hauptmann's *Lonely People* in his earlier novel *Jokyōshi* (A female teacher; June 1903), Katai's own life immediately after the publication of *Jokyōshi*—when Okada Michiyo (Yoshiko's model) came to Tokyo to study with him—seemed to be shaped by both *Jokyōshi* and *Lonely People*.

In *Futon* Tokio's attraction to Yoshiko is aroused and reinforced by such literary heroines as Anna Mahr (in *Lonely People*), who brings spiritual energy to a progressive thinker stifled by traditional morality and weary of everyday life. In contrast to *Jokyōshi* or its model *Lonely People*, which turns on the conflict between romantic love and the constraints of traditional society,[43] however, Tokio's spiritual attraction to Yoshiko polarizes his carnal desire. In the following passage Tokio reacts to the realization that Yoshiko has had a physical relationship with Tanaka.

> He was furious to think how he had done his best to help their love, only to have Yoshiko taken from him body and soul by some student. If things had reached that stage—if she had given up her body to Tanaka—then there would have been no need for him to respect her chastity as a virgin. It would be in order for him, too, to make a bold move and satisfy his sexual desire. Such thoughts led him to look upon Yoshiko, whom he had formerly worshipped as a heavenly figure, as a kind of prostitute whose beautiful attitude and expressions, let alone her body, were nothing but contemptible. In such terrible torment, he hardly slept at all that night. A wild assortment of feelings passed through his heart like dark clouds. Placing his hands on that troubled heart, Tokio thought things over. . . . Well, for a start it was a fact that she was now soiled, having given her body to a man. Should he simply send Tanaka back to Kyoto, and then exploit her weakness to make her his own? This prompted all sorts of thoughts. . . . However, a force arose within him to oppose his dark imagination, and a sharp conflict followed.   (chap. 9, pp. 184–85, 87)

This is probably one of the places in which Hōgetsu saw the "description of the ugly mind." Tokio, who persistently questions whether Yoshiko's love for Tanaka is spiritual or carnal, is himself helplessly caught between these two poles. Tokio's sexual desire takes shape under the perception that such desire is ugly and improper and should be concealed and suppressed. Indeed, this almost exaggerated emphasis on base and ugly carnal desire sharply separates *Futon* from earlier Meiji literary works, which, although dramatizing the incompatibility of love and marriage, do not deny the ideal of romantic love itself so much as reinforce the longing for this ideal as something unattainable in Japanese society. By contrast, *Futon*'s disclosure of Tokio's hidden, carnal desire not only dramatizes the fundamental discrepancy between his literary ideals and the reality to which he is blind, it also demystifies and diminishes the ideal of romantic love in the face of "uncontrollable, dark force of nature." In contrast to earlier Naturalistic works such as *Jūemon no saigo* in which sexuality as the embodiment of "natural force" was celebrated as an emancipatory power, the "dark force" concealed inside Tokio reveals the narcissistic fallacy of the Meiji intellectual as a rebel against traditional society.

Why, then, did this "description of the ugly mind" have such a sensational impact? When *Futon* appeared in September 1907, Naturalism continued to possess a fascinating aura for intellectuals and writers. In a critical essay entitled "Naturalism in the Literary Arts" ("Bungei-jō no shizenshugi"; January 1908), Hōgetsu wrote: "Both in creative writing and in critical essays, the word "Naturalism" carries a mysterious aura in today's literary world."[44] Hōgetsu then emphasized the essential relationships among Naturalism, ugliness, and truth.

> Realism aims to represent reality.
> Idealism aims to represent ideals.
> Naturalism claims to represent Truth.
> The word Truth is the life [*seimei*] and the motto of Naturalism. . . .
> In order to depict reality [*genjitsu*] as faithfully as possible, it is necessary to eliminate all artificial embellishments. If naked man, the natural wildness, and ugliness are depicted according to this principle, they will come close to Truth and become poignant.[45]

The close association of Naturalism, "truth," and the "ugliness" of human life was emphasized in a number of essays that appeared between 1906 and 1908.

> Only that art which is based on truth itself [*shinjitsu sono mono*] and which excludes those artistic embellishments—created at the time when illusion dominated—should be the art of the coming years. In times of disillusionment, people seek unaffected art that represents the truth.[46]

> Our future path should directly face and find the significance of the real world, throwing away the relics of religion, ethics, and philosophy inherited from our ancestors. People of the past might also have created certain ideals based on their

experience of reality, but those ideals have become obsolete today, concealing and excluding a vital part of true reality, that is to say, the carnal aspect of the human being.[47]

In the final analysis, the Naturalist school argues that the ideal of art is ultimately the truth and that art should represent the ultimate truth of man's inner life, without embellishment. . . .

The art of Naturalism represents the reality of ordinary, ugly human life [*heibon shūakunaru jinsei*]. At the same time it seeks those immeasurable ideals that lie at the heart of human life.[48]

It was in this kind of literary and discursive environment that *Futon* was enthusiastically received, as the "first Japanese novel of true Naturalism," the first to describe fully the "ugliness" and "dark secret" in contemporary man.

The particular aura of this ugliness, which was specifically associated with "hidden, dark, secret, improper sexual desires," reveal how Meiji intellectuals perceived the ideological centrality of sexuality in late nineteenth-century Western literary and cultural discourse. As Michel Foucault notes in *The History of Sexuality*:

The society that emerged in the nineteenth century—bourgeois, capitalist, or industrial society, call it what you will— . . . put into operation an entire machinery for producing true discourses concerning it. Not only did it speak of sex and compel everyone to do so; it also set out to formulate the uniform truth of sex. As if it suspected sex of harboring a fundamental secret. As if it needed this production of truth. . . . Thus sex gradually became an object of great suspicion; the general and disquieting meaning that pervades our conduct and our existence, in spite of ourselves; the point of weakness where evil portents reach through to us; the fragment of darkness that we each carry within us: a general signification, a universal secret, an omnipresent cause, a fear that never ends. And so, in this "question" of sex . . . two processes emerge, the one always conditioning the other: we demand that sex speak the truth . . . and we demand that it tell us our truth, or rather, the deeply buried truth of the truth about ourselves which we think we possess in our immediate consciousness. . . . From this interplay there has evolved, over several centuries, a knowledge of the subject; the project of a science of the subject has gravitated in ever narrowing circles, around the question of sex.[49]

According to Foucault, the nineteenth century witnessed a sudden proliferation of representations of sexuality as a dark, omnipresent secret, the revelation of which was thought to lead to the truth of human existence. In a manner that supports Foucault's hypothesis about the deployment of sexuality in nineteenth-century European cultural discourse, in works published after *Futon* it was truth or desire for truth that served as a medium for the sudden manifestations of sexual consciousness and for the desire to narrate about sex.

Although the centrality of Western discourse on truth and sex, backed by the authority of science, no doubt provided the value system that informed and supported the omniscient narrator's descriptive statements in *Futon*, contemporary readers who praised *Futon* especially valued the critical "self-consciousness" that they thought separated *Futon* from the "narrow subjectivism" and "sheer objectivism" of earlier Naturalist works. This perception overlaps with the distinction Katai made in the years following 1901 between the "author's narrow subjectivity" (*sakusha no shukan*) and the more transcendental and critical perspective of "the subjectivity of great nature" (*daishizen no shukan*), which Katai advocated. As we have seen, the latent irony prevailing in *Futon* reveals how Tokio's perceptions of reality and of himself are deeply immersed in and shaped by his blind acceptance of Western literary ideals, particularly the notion of romantic love and the impossibility of its realization in Japanese society. And it is the perception of the more immediate, sexual drives (of which Tokio himself is not completely aware) that provides a critical view of Tokio's "narrow subjectivity," which, the text suggests, is conditioned both by the ideological authority of Western literary and cultural practices and by the hidden forces of sexuality.

The Naturalist doctrine that emphasized the association between the "dark secret" of sexuality and truth probably owed its particular persuasive power not only to the evolutionist perspective of European literary movements but also to the relative familiarity of the notion of "ugly, filthy, and base carnal desires." What Shōyō had criticized as "vulgar, obscene desires"— the "animalistic lust" (*jūjō, jūyoku*) that he found in Tamenaga Shunsui's Edo period *ninjōbon* and that he believed must be surpassed by the "pure love between man and woman"—was now reformulated and reconceptualized as the secret key to the truth of man's inner life. In contrast to the Western notion of love, which was thought essential for the "modern individual" yet seemed to remain a mirage in Japan, the notion of dark, ugly sexual reality was probably more readily accepted as a natural, immediate, and universal reality inherent in everybody. Following the sensational reception of *Futon*, many writers began to describe their own sexual life in relationship to a yearning for love, disillusionment in marriage, and domestic, family life. The increased focus on women of the demimonde as the subject of the *shōsetsu* and the reevaluation of Tokugawa "pleasure literature" in subsequent years were no doubt also related to the Naturalist belief in the essential relationship between sexuality and truth.[50]

From Productive to Reproductive Reference

The initial ideological nature of the "ugly facts of human life" was soon dissipated and became invisible as a result of the ideology of description that Naturalist novelists and critics claimed represented the true reality of life. Those ugly facts of life were now regarded as if they existed prior to and independently of Naturalistic description. Literary historians and critics claim that after the appearance of Katai's *Futon* Japanese Naturalist novelists and their successors, the I-novelists, mistook facts for truth and consequently provided little more than a factual description of their immediate, private lives. As *Futon* ironically reveals, however, immediate experiences are highly problematic. What Tokio believes to be the facts of his life are immersed in and shaped by his literary consciousness and perceptions and projected back on reality, thereby dramatizing the power of authoritative narratives to shape life and form reality. Reconceptualizing the notions of representation and referent, Paul Ricoeur makes a useful distinction between the concept of a "productive reference," in which the reference creates and produces new realities, providing new perceptions of the worlds, and the notion of a "reproductive reference," in which the reference reduplicates or re-presents existing realities or worlds.[51] The initial impact of *Futon* doubtlessly derived from the fact that the character Tokio was not merely a caricature but a revealing portrait of the position of "literature" in Japan. *Futon* created a new mythos of reality, a productive reference, that provided contemporary Japanese intellectuals with a new way of perceiving their reality and their lives. Paradoxically, however, Naturalist writers and critics, including Katai himself, spread the belief in the absolute authority of literature, specifically the value of the "facts" described in their novels, as something directly leading to the truth.

In November 1908, Natsume Sōseki, who had been deeply involved in Western literature—particularly the eighteenth-century English novel—questioned the ideology of literature, particularly that promoted by the Naturalists, and criticized Tayama Katai's recent remarks about his dislike of "artificiality" (*sakui*) and "fabricated stories" (*koshirae-mono*).

> Katai says that, although he was struck with admiration by Hermann Suder-mann's *Der Katzensteg* when he translated it into Japanese six years ago, he now regards it as being no more than a fabrication, full of artificiality. . . .
>
> In my view . . . Katai's *Futon* is also a fabrication. His *Sei* [Life] is less fabricated than *Futon*. . . .
>
> I suggest that instead of being bothered by fabrications, Katai should take

pains to fabricate lively characters and natural settings. When the characters cannot but be taken as living characters and the setting cannot but be taken as natural, the author who fabricated them becomes a kind of creator. Such an author should be proud of having fabricated. Needless to say, well fabricated yet bad works (such as Alexandre Dumas's *Black Tulip*) are out of the question. At the same time, even when the works have fewer traces of artifice, if the authors write about facts and actual practices that have no significance whatsoever, then they are equally out of the question. No doubt Katai will also agree with this view.[52]

Sōseki, whose criticism of Katai should not be reduced to an opposition between facts and fiction, regarded all literary works, including that of the so-called Naturalists, to be fabrications and observed that the descriptions of ordinary "ugly facts" that writers such as Katai value are not necessarily valuable unless the reader is blinded by the ideological aura that had come to be associated with those facts. Sōseki criticized Katai and others for coming to believe that the ordinary, ugly reality that their fiction represented was the only objective reality,[53] thereby suggesting that Katai himself unknowingly transformed his productive reference into a reproductive reference.[54]

After the success of *Futon*, Katai published one work after another. These included works closely based on his domestic family life such as *Sei* (Life; 1908), *Tsuma* (Wife; 1908), and *En* (The bond; 1910); an ambitious long work called *Inaka kyōshi* (A country schoolteacher; 1909) portraying the life of an obscure young man in the provinces; and collections of critical essays such as *Inki tsubo* (An inkpot; 1909) and *Katai bunwa* (Katai's literary essays; 1911).

By 1910, however, Naturalism had begun to lose its earlier aura and authority. In an essay written in August 1910 called "The Present Condition of Our Stifled Time" ("Jidai heisoku no genjō"), Ishikawa Takuboku (1886–1912), a poet and critic, noted that a "scientific, fatalistic, static, and self-negating" tendency had emerged after the Russo-Japanese War and was represented by Naturalist slogans such as the "disclosure of reality" (*genjitsu bakuro*), "no solution" (*mukaiketsu*), "flat description" (*heimen byōsha*), and "observing life from a distance" (*kakuitsusen no taido*). Recently, however, the focus had shifted to a more active, self-assertive attitude as revealed in the emphasis on such phrases as "original desire" (*daiichigi yoku*), "the criticism of life" (*jinsei hihyō*), "the authority of subjectivity" (*shukan no ken'i*) and "the romantic element in Naturalism" (*shizenshugi-chū no rōmanteki bunshi*).[55]

In a newspaper article called "Naturalism as an Ideal of Self-Assertion" ("Jiko shuchō to shite no shizenshugi"; August 1910), which Takuboku was reacting against, Uozumi Setsuro (1883–1910) pointed to the unique fusion in Naturalism of a self-assertive spirit and a deterministic, pessimistic world-view, a fusion that occurred in opposition to the authority of the nation and of the family, both of which had prevented the independence and development of the individual. Although Takuboku agreed with Uozumi's remark on the strange coexistence of these two opposing forces, he argued that neither before or during the Naturalist movement had there been an opposition to or confrontation with the authority of the nation. In Takuboku's view, the failure of Meiji intellectuals to recognize the absence of confrontation was a tragedy worse than any unsuccessful confrontation. Takuboku argued that at a time when people had lost direction, ideals, and means of escape, all that remained was a strong desire for self-assertion. Since the Sino-Japanese War, "we the Meiji people" passed through three unsuccessful self-assertive stages: Takayama Chogyū's "individualism," the attraction to religion—which grew out of a reaction to this individualism—and now Naturalism. Having had these experiences, they should devote themselves to exploring the future by "rejecting illusory ideals [*kūsō*] such as Good [*zen*] and Beauty [*bi*]" and by "making Necessity [*hitsuyō*] an ideal."[56]

Takuboku's remarks articulate the commonly shared perceptions in 1910 of the stagnation of Naturalism and of the desire to move forward. As we will see in the next chapter, notions of "individual character" (*kosei*), "personality" (*jinkaku*), and "self" (*jiko*) suddenly proliferated in the early 1910's. Indeed, Naturalist critics such as Katagami Tengen and Sōma Gyofū also started to emphasize such notions as "fully releasing one's individuality" or "achieving the true self."[57]

To return to the beginning: Tayama Katai stated in 1909, two years after publication of *Futon*, that he had had no intention of making a personal confession in *Futon*.

> As for *Futon*, I had no particular motives. It was not a confession. Nor did I deliberately select those ugly facts. All that I did was to present reality as I had found it in life. . . . My only concern as an author was to know to what extent I had succeeded in depicting that reality, to know to what degree I had approached the truth through my writing.[58]

However, in 1917, ten years after the publication of *Futon* and in keeping with contemporary developments, Katai noted, in his literary memoirs *Tōkyō no sanjūnen* (My thirty years in Tokyo), that *Futon* had been a personal confession, a transcription of the facts of his life.

> In those days my body and soul were fascinated by Gerhart Hauptmann's *Einsame Menschen*. I felt as though [Johannes] Vockerat's loneliness were my own. Both with regard to my family life and my career, I felt that I had to destroy the old patterns and somehow open up a new path. Fortunately, through my imper-

fect but extensive reading, I had been exposed to new ideas from abroad, particularly from Europe. I felt that the agony of the fin de siècle also manifested itself fully in the philosophies of Tolstoy, Ibsen, Strindberg, Nietzsche, and other such writers. I, too, wanted to tread that painful path. I decided to fight bravely against society as well as against myself. I decided to try to reveal what I had kept secret, to disclose what might destroy my own spirit. I decided to write about my own Anna Mahr, who had caused me to suffer for two or three years, ever since the spring of the year that brought the Russo-Japanese War.[59]

These remarks reinforced later autobiographical readings, including that of Nakamura Mitsuo. Katai proudly identified *Futon*'s protagonist with himself, stressing the courage of his self-disclosure. This kind of attitude—the idea of renewing life and art through the art of confession—would flourish from the mid-Taishō period. After several years of productivity following the publication of *Futon*, Katai suffered from repeated bouts of depression; and by 1917, when he published *Tōkyō no sanjū-nen*, the literary center had shifted from Naturalism to the Shirakaba group, which emerged in opposition to the pessimistic, dark outlook of the Naturalists. It is probably no accident that Katai's remarks on *Futon* in 1917 reflect contemporary trends as represented by the Shirakaba group, which advocated the development of the individual self through sincere, direct, and immediate self-expression. Ironically, Katai's retrospective remarks in 1917 helped to erase the critical distance that had once made this work, to quote one of his early readers, a "remarkable achievement of true Naturalism."

~✑

CHAPTER 5

Shaping Life, Shaping the Past: Shiga Naoya's Narratives of Recollection

> Ever since Katai discovered the value of real, everyday life, no writer has turned life into art with as much intensity and dignity as Shiga Naoya. No writer has pursued with such devotion the path of the I-novel, where the principles of everyday life become the principles of creative writing.
>
> —Kobayashi Hideo, 1935

Whereas modern literary histories regard Tayama Katai as the founder of the I-novel, Shiga Naoya has been considered the consummate and most successful practitioner in this genre, the writer who brought this tradition to its apex. Shiga's writings invite the kind of reading that assumes a single, continuous personality at work in them. The name of the protagonist (Ōtsu Junkichi, Tokitō Kensaku, or "I") differs from work to work, but most have similar perceptions, problems, and backgrounds. Furthermore, in personal essays addressed directly to the reader, Shiga noted that the background and characteristics of these protagonists were actually those of himself. One consequence has been that many have considered Shiga an author who wrote about nothing other than himself.

The Narrative of Personality

Shiga has been variously described as "a sensitive, moral soul" (Akutagawa Ryūnosuke), "an ultra-egotist" and "a man of action" (Kobayashi Hideo), "a primitive man" (Inoue Yoshio), "a man of moods" (Tanigawa Tetsuzō), "a man of harmony" (Itō Sei, Hirano Ken), "a self-conceited amateur" (Dazai Osamu), "an immature and narrow writer" (Nakamura Mitsuo), a writer of "gentleman's realism," who possessed a "natural, uncritical ego" (Honda Shūgo).[1] As these remarks suggest, critical response to Shiga's literature has often taken the form of comments on the author's personality and moral life. Fusing the content of his literature with the "facts" of his life, critics and scholars have formulated what they believed to be a coherent picture of the living Shiga and have used this biographical narrative to analyze Shiga's personality and to interpret his literary works.

Pursuing the self through art was a common goal of the Shirakaba (White Birch) group to which Shiga belonged. Influenced by such humanitarian philosophers and writers as Tolstoy and Maeterlinck, the Shirakaba group espoused an idealistic humanism rooted in the belief that the pursuit of the self was a goal of the highest value. Comments made in 1911 in their literary journal *Shirakaba* by Mushakōji Saneatsu, the leader and spokesman of the Shirakaba group, suggest "self," "individuality," and "personality" were key terms for the group.

> The value of one's existence is acquired only by giving life to one's own individual personality.
> Those who commit themselves to work that cannot make the best of their own individual personality [*kosei*] are insulting their own selves [*jiko*].
> I despise all those people who do not give full play to their own individual personality.
> Those whom I like are all those who are fully displaying their own individual personality.
> Without an individual personality, an individual has no dignity.[2]

For the Shirakaba group, "work" (*shigoto*) meant artistic activity. According to Mushakōji, the value of this art lay "in the writer's heart and personality."[3] The Shirakaba group was composed primarily of graduates of the prestigious Peers' School, who were scions of upper-class, relatively wealthy families, and its members believed in art for art's sake, or more precisely, they regarded art as the ultimate means of developing and realizing their "true selves."

Victory in the Russo-Japanese War in 1905 made the Japanese feel that they had finally become respected members of the "world." The adherents of the Shirakaba group, whose adolescence was spent in the first decade of the twentieth century, considered their closest contemporaries to be Whitman, Rodin, Maeterlinck, Verhaeren, and Bergson, all of whom they referred to as "we."[4] In 1911, Mushakōji wrote that the members of the Shirakaba group were "the spiritual children of the world."[5] It was no accident that, from the start of his literary career, Mushakōji wrote the dates of all his works according to the Western system rather than the Japanese.[6] The Shirakaba group in fact tended to accept Western discourse as universal. For them, there were no Japanese: there was only Humanity (*ningen*), or Mankind (*jinrui*), which stood side by side with such "universal" notions as Love, Art, Nature, Justice, Beauty, and Life. All these notions were defined in relation to Humanity, which was both a universal abstraction and a concrete manifestation, directly represented by each of their individual selves. In 1912, in his first comprehensive essay on the notion of the Self, Mushakōji wrote:

> What I call the "Self" [*jiko*] includes everything that can be referred to as the Self. For me, the notion of the Self is as clear or as obscure as the notion of Humanity [*ningen*]. The notion of Self is as mysterious as that of Humanity. . . .
>
> For me, there is nothing that possesses more authority than my Self. . . .
>
> I believe that the Self embraces the following desires [*yokubō*]: desire as an individual [*kojin*], desire as a social being [*shakaiteki dōbutsu*], desire as a human being [*ningen*]—to distinguish this desire from that of an individual, I also refer to this desire as "desire as mankind" [*jinrui*] or "blood of mankind" [*jinrui no chi*]—desire as an animal [*dōbutsu*], desire as earth [*chikyū*], desire as the thing-in-itself [*butsujo*]. . . .
>
> When I say that "one should work for the sake of one's Self," I mean that one should harmonize and fulfill these desires as much as possible. . . .
>
> The greatest problem is how to harmonize and unite these desires. I believe that the only way to resolve this problem is to exert oneself for the sake of the Self.[7]

Mushakōji continued to express his optimism in exploring and developing the Self through Work (or Art, for the Shirakaba group), a process believed to lead directly to the exploration of true Humanity. Individual differences existed among the members of the Shirakaba group, but ultimately they shared a belief in the universal value of self-respect and pursuit of the self. In a diary entry dated March 7, 1912, the year he began publishing in the prestigious literary journal *Chūō kōron*, the young Shiga Naoya wrote:

> I was reading Rousseau in the train, that passage in which Rousseau is considered clever but worthless by those whom he encounters. . . . It all applied to myself. I don't know how great Rousseau is. I don't believe that he is that great. I thought that even now I was no worse than Rousseau and that I was more interesting than he in many ways.
>
> It is sufficient if a man [*ningen*]—or at least oneself [*jibun*]—commits one's life to exploring what is in oneself. To mine what is in oneself—that is everything.[8]

As the passage suggests, Shiga's artistic activity was motivated in large part by a deep sense of respect for the self and a strong desire to explore that self in the belief that it had universal value. This basic assumption, together with his manner of writing, further reinforced the practice of reading Shiga's "personality" into his works. In his last years, even Akutagawa Ryūnosuke, who had earlier condemned the confessional mode of Japanese Naturalist literature and had excelled in "fiction-like fiction," expressed a special admiration for Shiga's works: "Shiga Naoya is the most genuine of writers—more genuine

than the rest of us. . . . Shiga's literature is, above all, the work of a writer who
leads a respectable and dignified life."[9]

Shiga was admired as the "god of literature" (*bungaku no kamisama*) and
the "god of the novel" (*shōsetsu no kamisama*), but in the years following
World War II Shiga was attacked for stunting the growth of modern Japanese
fiction. Dazai Osamu, for example, expressed disgust at the "conceited nature" of Shiga's literature,[10] and in an influential study entitled *Shiga Naoya ron*
(1954), Nakamura Mitsuo criticized Shiga's novels for preventing the reader
from discussing more than the "author's personality." In Nakamura's view,
since no critical distance existed between the protagonist and the author,
Shiga's novels were comprehensible and meaningful only to those who had a
biographical knowledge of the author. Shiga's contemporary readers could
accept "a character as abstract as Kensaku," the protagonist of *An'ya kōro* (A
dark night's passing; 1921–37), because they could superimpose the concrete
image of the living author on the abstract protagonist.[11]

Shiga and Genbun-itchi

The interpretive tradition that assumed that Shiga's works were a direct
transcription of his personal experience was closely related to his position in
the development of *genbun-itchi*. Since the latter half of the 1920's, Shiga has
been regarded as the writer who perfected the "true, modern, colloquial"
genbun-itchi written language, a language with "directness" and "precision."
In *Ōtsu Junkichi* (1912), one of Shiga's early works, the protagonist Junkichi
notes: "Having had almost no opportunity to write in the traditional episto-
lary style [*sōrō-bun no tegami*], I found it terribly difficult to write to my aunts
and uncles" (*Zenshū*, 2: 283). "Writing" here means the *genbun-itchi* style. For
the generation that grew up after the first decade of the twentieth century,
genbun-itchi was already the standard written language.

According to Yamamoto Masahide, who has studied the historical development of the modern written language extensively, the primary-school
textbooks edited and published by the government in 1903–4 adopted, to a
significant degree, the colloquial *genbun-itchi* style, thus promoting a standardized national written and spoken language. This style was also used in school
compositions and essays (*sakubun*). The number of newspaper articles written
in the colloquial style also vastly increased after the mid-1900's, and in 1922
the editorial columns of the major newspapers, which had long preserved the
tradition of writing in the traditional expository style, shifted to the *genbun-
itchi* style, meaning that entire newspapers were now written in this style.[12] By
1923, the modern colloquial style had penetrated not only the literary world
but society at large. As Yamamoto points out, the writings of the Shirakaba

group, especially the works by Mushakōji and Shiga, were instrumental in further refining and elaborating the *genbun-itchi* style. According to Uno Kōji, Mushakōji "perfected the *genbun-itchi* style in the strict sense of the word," developing a style that was "spontaneous" and "totally free from traditional writing conventions."[13] Satō Haruo (1892–1964) and other younger contemporaries of Mushakōji such as Akutagawa Ryūnosuke made similar statements. In his last literary work, *Bungeitekina amarini bungeitekina* (Literary, all too literary; 1927), Akutagawa wrote:

> Satō Haruo has argued that since we are supposed to be writing in the colloquial style, we should write in the same manner that we speak. . . . "Writing in the same way that one speaks" has become the primary objective of modern prose writers. Recent examples of this trend are the works of Mushakōji Saneatsu, Uno Kōji, and Satō Haruo. Shiga Naoya's prose is no exception. . . . It is not that I have no desire to "write in the same manner that I speak." I do, however, hope to "speak in the same manner that I write." . . . What I am concerned with is not "speech" but "writing."[14]

From the mid-1920's, writers took issue with the concept and institution of *genbun-itchi*. Under the influence of European futurism, Dadaism, and expressionism, Yokomitsu Riichi, the leader of the Shinkankaku-ha, the Neo-Perceptionist school, emphasized the uniqueness of writing and claimed in 1929 that the novelist should "write as he writes" (*kaku yō ni kaku*), a remark intended as an ironic echo of Satō Haruo's earlier statement. In the same year, Tanizaki Jun'ichirō argued that a novelist should fully utilize the "spoken language," which he believed retained the character of the "original Japanese language," possessed a subtle honorific system, and embodied the character of particular locales and social groups. For Tanizaki, all of these had been destroyed by the *genbun-itchi* style, which he regarded as westernized, artificial, and neutral.[15] By the late 1920's, the *genbun-itchi* style was considered the dominant norm that regulated all writing. And it was Shiga Naoya who was seen as the great writer who had perfected this mode through his direct and precise colloquial style. Shiga has also been criticized for his "naive belief" in the "directness" and "transparency" of the colloquial written language.[16] What is important here is that the widespread view of the immediacy of Shiga's written language assumes that his writing and his voice are identical and both originated in the "living man Shiga." This belief has in turn led to a highly thematic reading of Shiga's texts, particularly of his personality and life.

Genre Distinctions

From August 1907 when Shiga wrote an unpublished story entitled "Ryokugashi" until around 1910 (the year the *Shirakaba* journal was estab-

lished), Shiga used the word *shōsetsu* in the title of a number of works such as
"Shōsetsu: Abashiri made" (Fiction: On the way to Abashiri; 1908), "Shōsetsu: Hayao no imōto" (Fiction: Hayao's younger sister; 1908), and "Shōsetsu: Wakai ginkōin" (Fiction: A young bank officer; 1909). The original
manuscript (written in 1908) of what was published in 1918 as "Aru asa" (A
certain morning),[17] a work that Shiga later considered his real "maiden" work
(*shojosaku*) and that he believed gave him the "knack for writing *shōsetsu*"
("Sōsaku yodan," 1928; *Zenshū*, 8: 3), was originally entitled "Hi-shōsetsu:
Sobo" (Nonfiction: Grandmother) and was a sketch of what actually happened one morning to young Shiga and his grandmother. The genre distinction made by the young Shiga seems close to the modern Western distinction
between "fiction" and "nonfiction."

Shiga, however, ceased using such headings from around 1910. In subsequent years, exactly when is unclear, Shiga's notion of *shōsetsu* underwent a
significant transformation. For the older Shiga, some of his *shōsetsu* were
extensively "imaginary," and others were almost entirely based on "facts." A
shōsetsu does not have to be factual, but being almost entirely factual is not
incongruous with being a *shōsetsu*. Factuality and fictionality are no longer
relevant generic criterion. Instead, for Shiga "creative writing" (*sōsaku*) signifies *shōsetsu*. The differences among *shōsetsu*, *zuihitsu* (essay), and *nikki* (diary) derive not from the form or the subject matter but from the writer's
attitude toward what he is writing, by the intensity of the creating spirit.[18] In
response to an essay that praised Shiga as "one of the most skillful novelists,"
Shiga wrote in an essay called "Rizumu" (Rhythm; 1931):

> Although people talk about the content and form of art, the effect of the work
> of art on us is not that gentle. I believe that it is rhythm. . . . If the rhythm is
> weak, then even when the work is skillfully constructed or is superb in content,
> that work is not genuine and is thus worthless. In the case of the *shōsetsu*, the
> impression left after reading the work is obvious. The strength or weakness of
> the artist's spiritual rhythm that moves the artist while he is creating—this is all
> that matters. (*Zenshū*, 7: 8)

For Shiga "rhythm of mind" or "spiritual rhythm" is a quality common not
only to good *shōsetsu* but to the activities of all great men. The *shōsetsu* is,
above all, a medium into which the author pours his spiritual energy. The
artistic experience implies spiritual communion between the creator and the
recipient through the art form, which is, for Shiga, the *shōsetsu*. To present a
work as a *shōsetsu* is a sign of the writer's sincerity and zeal in writing. This
definition of the *shōsetsu* focuses on the mental attitude of the author, but
given that Shiga's artistic ideal was the spiritual communion achieved through
the work of art, it is clear that the notion of spiritual rhythm or spiritual

resonance also implies an ideal reading mode in which the reader enters into a communion with the author's spirit. This particular view of the *shōsetsu* contributed to and became part of the larger I-novel discourse.

Shiga's "Sōsaku yodan" (Digression on my works; 1928), his first substantial commentary on his own works (which appeared as the notion of the I-novel was becoming popular), has also provided critics and scholars a foundation for interpreting him in the I-novel reading mode.[19] In this introduction to a collection of his works, Shiga pointed out that many of them were based on, and some replicated entirely, the facts of his personal life.

> I am trying to write down some of my memories with regard to the works that I have included in this volume. . . .
>
> "Aru asa" (A certain morning). In the afternoon of the thirteenth of January, the day of the third anniversary of my grandfather's death, when I was twenty-seven, I wrote down what had happened that morning. This work might be considered my maiden work. I had tried to write a *shōsetsu*, but I had never been able to put it together. Although the content of "A Certain Morning" was simple, I felt as if I had acquired the knack of writing for the first time. . . .
>
> "Jūichigatsu mikka gogo no koto" (On the afternoon of the third of November) is a diary [*nikki*] that dealt with things as they were. Although I should have written down the facts immediately, I did not actually write until several days later. The result was an unsatisfactory piece for me, since I could not express the excitement that I had felt during the actual incident.
>
> "Kinosaki nite" (At Kinosaki) is also a *shōsetsu* based completely on facts. The death of a rat, that of a bee, and that of a water lizard were real incidents that I witnessed over the period of several days. I believed that I could honestly and naturally express the feelings that I felt during those occurrences. . . .
>
> With regard to the subject material, *Ōtsu Junkichi*, *Aru otoko sono ane no shi* (A certain man, the death of his sister), and *Wakai* (Reconciliation) are like three branches of one tree. *Ōtsu Junkichi* and *Wakai* are facts [*jijitsu*], and *Aru otoko sono ane no shi* is an amalgamation of facts and fiction.   (*Zenshū*, 8: 3–14)

"Sōsaku yodan" and its sequel "Zoku sōsaku yodan" (1938) suggest that many of Shiga's texts were largely, if not entirely, drawn from the facts of his life. In comments on *An'ya kōro*, Shiga revealed that some readers, including literary critics, had taken the protagonist Kensaku for Shiga himself, although for Shiga, Kensaku was an amalgamation of Shiga and his fictional imagination. However, Shiga's distinction between fact (*jijitsu*) and fiction (*tsukurigoto*, *fikushon*) ultimately reinforced the referential, autobiographical readings of his works, both those labeled as "facts" and those that were not. The so-called fictional elements were incorporated into a larger biographical reading.

Anyone who reads the "autobiographical trilogy"—*Ōtsu Junkichi* (1912), *Wakai* (1917), and *Aru otoko sono ane no shi* (1920), which were presented together for the first time in 1928 in the one-volume *Shiga Naoya shū*—

alongside other more or less autobiographical works is led to reconstruct the "story" of Shiga's life and its development in a chronological and more or less causal, developmental order. These other works include "Nigotta atama" (Muddy mind; 1911), "Haha no shi to atarashii haha" (The death of my mother and a new mother; 1912), "Sobo no tame ni" (For my grandmother; 1912), "Ko o nusumu hanashi" (The kidnapping; 1914), "Haha no shi to tabi no kioku" (The death of my mother and the memory of socks; 1917), "Kinosaki nite" (At Kinosaki; 1917), "Nijūdai ichimen" (An aspect of my twenties; 1923), "Puratonikku rabu" (Platonic love; 1926), "Kako" (My past; 1926), "Yamagata" (Yamagata; 1927), "Kumori-bi" (Cloudy days; 1927), and An'ya kōro (1921–37), particularly the first half.

Throughout Shiga's oeuvre, recurrent characters—family members and close literary friends—appear and reappear like figures in various episodes of a larger myth: the father with whom the Shiga hero, to use William Sibley's apt term,[20] has a long antagonistic relationship; the mother, who died when the Shiga hero was still young; the grandmother, who raised the hero from his childhood and with whom he had an intimate and ambivalent relationship; the grandfather, whom the hero respected greatly; the uncle; the younger (half-)brother and sisters; and the close literary friends (of the Shirakaba group), who share with the Shiga hero certain artistic ideals and ambitions. Recurrent and conspicuous motifs also constitute the fabric of Shiga's oeuvre: the hero's daily moods as an uncontrollable and undeniable reality; the strong awareness of irrepressible sexual forces; adultery and sin; the problematic relationship between actions and motives; complex familial relationships, particularly an antagonistic relationship with the father; and a peculiar attention to small creatures combined with a sense of intimacy with nature and an awareness of an all-encompassing natural forces. When read as an oeuvre, Shiga's works invite referential and thematic readings that seek to reconstruct Shiga's life as a continuous entity with regard to which each text takes on full meaning.

The Space of Recollection: Ōtsu Junkichi

Shiga's texts, however, also make the reader aware that any experience ultimately is knowable only through narration. Shiga's self-commentary on his works reveals two deep, interlocking concerns: a tenacious belief in the absolute nature or truth of the past; and a strong awareness of the act of recollecting and writing, which ultimately gives shape to the events of the past and transforms those events into "historical facts."[21] Many of Shiga's narratives take the form of a first-person recollection in which past events (including dreams) are recalled with such immediacy as to resist retroactive reorganization, and yet the "true" significance of those past events is tenaciously sought through the act of recollecting and narrating.

In the extremely short piece "The Death of My Mother and the Memory of Socks" (written in 1912 but published in 1917), the first-person narrator recalls a minor childhood incident related to his mother, who died when he was thirteen. One evening about a year before his mother's death, the "I" had ignored his mother when she brought *tabi* socks for him. Busy with preparations for dinner, the mother placed the socks on his head and started to leave, causing "I" to suddenly fly into a rage and leaving his mother perplexed and sad. The narrator "I" recalls that long after this event (his mother had already passed away) his father told him that she had often wept over the waywardness of her son, who had been spoiled by an indulgent grandmother.

> But I didn't remember that I gave her that much trouble. The incident of the *tabi*, however, remained in my mind. Imagining my mother's feelings at that time, I realized how sad she probably had been. The Aoyama Cemetery was not that far out of the way for me on the way back from school, and so I visited my mother's grave once in a while. And I often recalled the *tabi* incident. Every time I recalled it, I apologized in my heart to my mother as she lay in her grave. (*Zenshū*, 1: 357)

Both the childhood memory of the past event and the recognition of its significance are recalled in the present act of recollection. The later recognition turns the amorphous memory of the past into a symbolic reality that emerges as something lost only to be reinstated as a trace of the "real" past. Here the vivid presence of this trace sustains and strengthens the "I" 's tie with the dead mother. A similar dialectical tension between what is believed to have occurred in the empirical past and the act of reinstating it through recollection sustains many of Shiga's texts. While inducing an autobiographical and thematic reading that seeks to reconstruct a coherent story of Shiga's life, the text also dramatizes and problematizes such causal narrativization.

Shiga himself expressed his ambivalence about framing his past works according to the author's original intentions. At the beginning of "Zoku sōsaku yodan" (1938), the second substantial essay on his own work, Shiga expressed the hope that his works would "exist independently of the author."

> In the preface to the "one-yen edition" of my selected works (*ichi-en-bon zen-shū*), I expressed the hope that I would like, if possible, to write the kind of work that exists independently of the author. To tediously record my memories of

past works would go against this hope. In this sense, I feel rather reluctant to make any comments, but since I have been asked by the publisher to provide some help to my readers, I have agreed to write something. (*Zenshū*, 8: 15)

The following is from Shiga's "preface" to his one-volume *Shiga Naoya zen-shū*, published in 1931 by Kaizōsha: "I do not know how many of these works can stand on their own, independent of the author. If any exist, I want them to exist on their own. That feeling reflects both my self-conceit and my indifference" (*Zenshū*, 8: 128).[22]

Shiga Naoya started to write between 1905 and 1910, long before the notion of the I-novel came to the fore in the mid-1920's. The I-novel critical discourse that emerged after the mid-1920's tended to emphasize the "imme-diacy" of Shiga's writing and regarded Shiga's texts as faithful accounts of his personal life. This discourse regarded the retroactively reconstructed person-ality and life story of Shiga not only as the key to reading his works but as embodying a significant aspect of the Japanese literary tradition, either posi-tively or negatively. As I shall argue, however, Shiga and his works not only contributed to the formation of I-novel discourse but placed that discourse in a relative and critical perspective. Many of Shiga's early texts such as *Ōtsu Junkichi* (1912) were in fact sustained by a tension between two opposing forces: a concern for some strong ordering force, which shaped "life," "art," and the "self"; and a tenacious suspicion of and resistance to these ordering forces.

Ōtsu Junkichi is a first-person self-portrait realized in the space and time of recollection. The widespread assumption about the immediacy and direct-ness of Shiga's writing has, however, led to the ignoring of the significance of this temporal distancing between past and present. In his influential *Shiga Naoya ron*, Nakamura Mitsuo considered *Ōtsu Junkichi* to be "Shiga's first realization of his literary self," a prototypical work that determined the basic method of Shiga's later personal works. According to Nakamura, *Ōtsu Junki-chi* is an uncritical self-glorification of the author's moral life, a single-voiced, subjective self-account devoid of any critical or ironical distance between the protagonist and the author, who remains completely unaware of the ludicrous and deficient aspects of his own perspective.[23] As we shall see, however, the "I" 's (Junkichi's) awareness of selfhood emerges through the act of recollec-tion, in the tension between the narrating "I" and the narrated "I."

When Shiga Naoya made his literary debut with *Ōtsu Junkichi* (1912), his first extensively autobiographical work, he had already published such short stories as "Abashiri made" (On the way to Abashiri; published 1910), "Ka-misori" (The razor; 1910), "Nigotta atama" (1911) and "Sobo no tame ni"

(1912) in the literary journal *Shirakaba*. *Ōtsu Junkichi*, however, was the first work by Shiga (or, for that matter, by any member of the Shirakaba group) to be printed by a major publisher. It appeared in the autumn 1912 issue of *Chūō kōron*, one of the most prestigious literary journals of the time. Shiga later remarked that the work was based entirely on fact.[24] The entries for 1907 in Shiga's diary and his recently published personal notes of the same year reveal that the events treated in *Ōtsu Junkichi*, particularly Junkichi's "love relationship" with his maidservant Chiyo, actually occurred in 1907, five years before the composition and publication of *Ōtsu Junkichi*.[25] In many ways *Ōtsu Junkichi* epitomizes Shiga's initial literary concerns before they were framed by later I-novel discourse.

> "I will probably never, in my entire life, experience love." There was a time when, filled with such thoughts, I felt desolate. I had no confidence in my work, and I could hardly boast that I did not care about love.
>
> In those days I was a lukewarm Christian. Being far removed from various temptations, I almost made Paul's phrase "Avoid fornication" my motto. For me, following this motto in the broad sense meant being determined not to fall in love with a woman unless I was sure that I would marry her. The result was a life in which I had less and less contact with women.
>
> I became a Christian in the summer of my seventeenth year, and from the time I reached twenty my desire for women intensified. I became somewhat obstinate. I was disgusted by my own obstinacy and periodically felt the impulse to become a freer individual. Despite these circumstances, it took a long time and various events before I forsook my Christian faith.   (pt. I, chap. 1; *Zenshū*, 2: 241)

Ōtsu Junkichi is divided into part I, consisting of seven short chapters, and part II, of thirteen equally short chapters. The first two chapters reveal young Junkichi's relationship to Christianity, his personal attraction to his Christian mentor U-sensei, and his growing awareness of the sinfulness of sexual desire, an awareness that emerged after his encounter with Christianity. The rest of part I focuses on a particular autumn in the past. Part II describes several months from the end of the following spring to the end of the summer. Both parts deal with young Junkichi's attraction to young women: his interest in Okinu, his friend's sister, a "noble" girl of mixed parentage (British and Japanese), is dealt with in part I; and his relationship with Chiyo, a housemaid, in part II. The narrator ("I") recalls all these episodes, which presumably were the direct and indirect causes for the irreversible changes that divide his past from the present time of recollection.

Junkichi's recollections are marked by the daily "moods" (*kibun*) that he experienced in "those days." These recollected moods, which are ephemeral yet unforgettable, are, for Junkichi, the most tangible tie to the past and spur him to embark on a retrospective self-examination. Junkichi's recollecting can in fact be seen as an attempt to objectify and explain these nebulous and uncanny moods. During the dance party at Okinu's residence, Junkichi's displeasure, discomfort, and irritation increase, and he becomes "poisoned by his own unpleasant mood," turning into a "congelation of unpleasantness" (pt. I, chap. 4, p. 258). It is at this moment that Okinu, after a period of mutual awkwardness, approaches Junkichi and begins to talk to him "in a childish fashion" (p. 260). While chatting, Junkichi is somehow relieved, as if a stiff knot had been undone. The relationship between his moods and his feelings of "love" emerges again in part II, which begins with a description of Junkichi in a bad mood in early summer. Junkichi becomes aware of his "love" for Chiyo when he realizes that his bad moods (*fukigen*) disappear when talking to her (pt. II, chap. 6, p. 285); she momentarily frees him from his painful and awkward self-consciousness.

The narrating "I" describes and analyzes the young Junkichi's sense of unnaturalness and discomfort at Okinu's dance party from the narrator's present perspective.

> Considering my character and taste, I should have been delighted by this sort of thing [the dance party]. But I believed in an ascetic ideal and was guided by a secondary character and taste that were the products of my faith in that ascetic ideal. Furthermore, since this secondary character and taste existed on a more conscious level than my original character and taste, I could not help being more loyal to my secondary character and taste. I gazed quite contemptuously at the people dancing with flushed faces. Now, however, looking back, I am ashamed by my own weak mind, consumed as it was by an ideal. On the other hand, if the same thing were to occur to me now, I doubt if I, who have already become who I am, could be faithful to my original character and taste.   (pt. I, chap. 4, pp. 257–58)

In contrast to the young Junkichi, who was frequently assaulted by uncontrollable bad moods, the present narrator considers this condition to have resulted in part from a disjunction and discordance between his "secondary character and taste" and his "original character and taste." At the same time, the narrator "I," who has already forsaken his Christian beliefs and ascetic ideals and is now conscious of his "original character and taste," is not so naïve as to believe that he can easily regain that original nature. He is well aware that the present "I" is a product of his past experiences and that his "original character and taste" have been retroactively "discovered" as something already lost or altered, and thus as only a trace or memory. The recollection of Junkichi's love relationship with Chiyo is filled with a strong awareness of irreversible change, of layers of selves—the "original," the "secondary," and the present selves—rather than, as in standard I-novel readings, as a unity of narrated and narrating selves.

Christianity and Romantic Love

The awareness of these layers of selves as well as the young Junkichi's relationship with Chiyo are directly related to his struggle with Christian "ideals." Chiyo, who initially frees the young Junkichi from his discomfort, soon intensifies his obsession with the Christian prohibition of "fornication" (*kan'in*). "Soon after I became acquainted with Christianity, I began to abhor my own body" (pt. I, chap. 1, p. 242). The young Junkichi, who "had confidence only in sports and reading novels," "entrusted his religious and philosophical matters to U-sensei," who becomes a spiritual father figure. For the young Junkichi, the "sin of fornication," which eventually becomes for him the essence of Christianity, is the aspect that affects his view of life most deeply, paradoxically arousing in him an awareness of his own strong "physical desires" as well as of his temptation to "sin."

> On one occasion, U-sensei told us, "Christianity is the first religion to emphasize the sinfulness of fornication. Fornication is a sin as great as murder." I felt a terribly unpleasant reverberation. As my body and soul searched for someone to love, I was held back by my "social circumstance" [*kyōgū*] and "ideals" [*shisō*]; the resulting discordance caused me unbearable pain. (pt. I, chap. 2, p. 244)

The young Junkichi begins to realize that his growing feeling of discord results not so much from the conflict between the body and the soul as from the tension between his aspiration for love (which both his body and soul seek) and his social circumstances and ascetic ideals. Before meeting U-sensei, he wanted to amass a fortune through foreign trade, but after meeting this teacher, he desired to become first an evangelist, then a philosopher, and finally a writer of "pure literature" (*junbungaku*). Chiyo enters Junkichi's life at the point at which he begins to feel alienated by U-sensei's ideas, thus intensifying the tension that Junkichi feels between his aspiration for mutual love and the shackles of "social circumstance and ideals," which he sees as suppressing his more genuine impulse to love and be loved.

The citations from Junkichi's diary in chapter 6 of part II ironically reveal the process by which he grows more attached to Chiyo. When Junkichi becomes aware of his affection for Chiyo, he simultaneously realizes that he is reluctant to marry her (since he feels that she is not the kind of woman who can understand him and his work). Only four days after writing that one reason he is reluctant to marry Chiyo is that she is not beautiful, he writes:

"Now Chiyo has become the only woman who is beautiful and dear to me" (pt. II, chap. 6, p. 286). No sooner does the young Junkichi write (in the diary) that Chiyo has freed him of a fixed notion of a beautiful woman than he becomes aware of another source of dissatisfaction, the social gap that lies between them. This, he believes, prevents the mutual understanding, reciprocal love, and respect for his work that constitute his ideal of marriage. Five days later, however, he writes in his diary that he "has become sympathetic toward those of the servant class" (chap. 6, p. 286). In the following section, the young Junkichi regards his hesitation over Chiyo as the unfortunate result of his "prejudice" and "vanity," "or, rather, it was as if I were forced to think that way." The young Junkichi, attempting to overcome his "vanity" and "hesitation," so that he may "truly love" Chiyo, who has freed him from his "obstinate obligation to ideals," is unaware that he is meanwhile being carried away by an obligation to egalitarian humanism and an obsession with romantic love.

The ironical first-person recollection in *Ōtsu Junkichi* reveals that the young Junkichi is also unknowingly carried away by the force of literary narratives. While at a resort, the young Junkichi reads Futabatei Shimei's Japanese translation of Turgenev's *Sportsman's Sketches* (*Katakoi*; 1896) and is struck by one particular passage that seems to foreshadow his own fate: "Since I was young, I thought that my future had no limit and that I would have plenty of an even better kind of experience [of love]. . . . However, I have never had such an experience." Superimposing the Russian story of lost love on his relationship with Chiyo, the young Junkichi decides to take this relationship seriously. Tolstoy's *Resurrection*, which was translated into Japanese in 1905 and enthusiastically received by the young intellectuals of the time, is also implicitly behind the drama of Junkichi's attachment to Chiyo. As the sons of wealthy bourgeois or aristocratic families, the members of the Shirakaba group seemed to have been particularly attracted to and influenced by this story of a Russian noble's affair with a housemaid and his subsequent repentance and atonement.[26]

The most powerful of these literary narratives, which the young Junkichi both unconsciously and willingly yields himself to, is the Western romantic opposition between the genuine impulse of love or nature and "social and ideological constraints," the very story that informed "Sekiko and Shinzō," Junkichi's first completed *shōsetsu*, which he wrote in reaction to U-sensei's teachings about fornication. Chiyo, who initially frees Junkichi from his discomfort and his obstinate preoccupation with U-sensei's teachings, soon becomes associated with love and nature, a linkage intensified by an affectionate puppy that Junkichi regards as a symbolic tie between himself and Chiyo.

As soon as Junkichi labels his attraction to Chiyo "love," however, he also becomes aware of the gap between his ideals of love and marriage and his actual feelings toward Chiyo. This gap threatens Junkichi; the critical difference proposed in "Sekiko and Shinzō" is not the opposition between the soul and the body or between love and marriage but that between a male-female relationship based on love and one "without love." The young Junkichi views a "loveless" physical relationship (whether married or unmarried) as nothing other than "sinful fornication."

At this point, the young Junkichi resorts to the opposition between love/nature *and* socio-ideological constraints as a means of explaining his hesitation toward Chiyo; that is, he feels that the socio-ideological constraints within him (his "prejudice" and "vanity") prevent him from truly loving Chiyo. For the young Junkichi, the attempt to overcome prejudice and vanity and to turn his relationship into "true love" parallels his romantic resistance to social and ideological constraints. In trying to flee from the commandment against fornication, the young Junkichi unconsciously tries to act out the conceptual drama developed in his novel, unconsciously hoping that he will fall into true love.[27] The first-person recollection in *Ōtsu Junkichi*, in short, ironically casts the young Junkichi as an actor, as someone who unknowingly turns to the romantic notion of heroic rebellion.

Through the interaction between the vivid memory of the past and the retrospective movement that seeks some causal, explanatory perspective for those remembered events, the young Junkichi's past is relived and acquires new significance. Although the narrating "I" looks back on the development of Junkichi's "impetuous love" for Chiyo with a sense of distance, once his recollection touches on the young Junkichi's rage at his father's intrusion into the relationship (his father orders her sent home), the narrator suddenly loses his poise. The narrator's emphasis on the "difference" between the "I"'s present situation and his father's view of the young Junkichi as a "foolhardy warrior carried away by foolish passion" invites the reader to reconsider and question the motives of Junkichi's present act of recollection, which started as a detached, self-assessment of his growing sense of identity and selfhood.

> Indeed, for those people I might have appeared to be no more than an eccentric child. They probably could not help considering our opinions to be what forever remain worthless fancies without ever becoming valuable in actual life. We never could refrain from exaggerating our own importance. And I myself was aware of the imbalance between my passionate ambition toward work [*shigoto*] and my actual self-confidence. In other words, at that time [*sono toki no genzai ni oite*], I had not yet achieved work that could give me a sense of self-confidence. And that fact turned our high opinion into no more than a shriek-

ing tone. . . . Just as I was regarded as a foolhardy warrior carried away by a
foolish passion, for the people outside our circle we must have seemed no more
than foolhardy warriors carried away by some strange passion. But we could not
remain in that state forever. And I think that the fact that they did not even try to
imagine the future possibilities of those ever advancing youths was one of the
reasons that they have had an unfortunate relationship with us. But I also think
that this has been almost inevitable.   (pt. II, chap. 12, pp. 314–15)

The narrator ironically describes the grandiose yet unproved ambitions of the
young Junkichi and his friends, stressing the difference between the young
Junkichi "at that time" and the Junkichi at the "present time." The narrator
implicitly suggests that he can now critically observe, from a higher, more
transcendental perspective, both the limitations of the young Junkichi and
those of his father and family. But the very act of distancing, in which the
narrator "I" suddenly starts using the plural pronoun "we" (watakushidomo) to
describe the young Junkichi's confrontation with his father, as if to support
the young Junkichi's otherwise vulnerable position, undermines the declared
distance and instead reveals the "I"'s strong need, even now, to assert his
"achievement" and "self-confidence."

Instead of being a distanced, objective self-portrayal, as suggested in the
beginning, the recollection of the "past" becomes an effort to assert Junkichi's
identity and independence from the father by deliberately making a distinction between the past and the present. This impression is reinforced in the
next and last section (pt. II, chap. 13), which ends by recalling the young
Junkichi's rage at his father's refusal to talk to him directly about Chiyo. In the
midst of his fury, the young Junkichi throws a cigar box on the tatami floor.

> I had rarely experienced such violent and sudden anger. But I was clearly aware
> *at that time* [sono toki no genzai ni oite] that I was not forced to act in such a
> desperate fashion. I knew that if there had been another person nearby, my
> vanity would not have allowed me to act that way. Yet my feelings of anger made
> me feel like doing it. "I do not have to make an effort to suppress this"—that
> thought came to my mind *at that time*.   (pt. II, chap. 13, p. 317; my italics)

Unsatisfied with the cigar box, the young Junkichi then throws a nine-pound
iron dumbbell to the floor. In his excitement, he is suddenly filled with an
unsuppressible impulse to laugh, imagining the comical figure of the stu-
pefied houseboy sleeping downstairs. Nakamura Mitsuo, in discussing this
passage, criticizes both Junkichi and Shiga for "not being aware of Junkichi's
own comicality" and for his "blind self-glorification."[28] The recollecting
narrator, however, is ironical, clearly making the young Junkichi (who believes he is not getting carried away) appear comical. The narrating "I" places
the young Junkichi in a critical perspective, revealing that he did in fact lose

his romantic struggle against his father (who represents "social and ideological forces") and that the young Junkichi's "romantic struggle" was in fact "play-acting." But the narrating "I" also implies that he, the self-declared mature Junkichi, ultimately won that struggle over the two fathers, his Christian mentor, U-Sensei, and his biological father. For the narrating "I," recollecting becomes a process by which he attempts to overcome his past by demonstrating that his present self is more mature, by placing his past in an ironic perspective, and by showing a deeper and more comprehensive understanding of his past self.

At the same time *Ōtsu Junkichi* reveals that the narrating "I" never completely masters the past. Instead, the conflict and tension (particularly with the father) implicitly continues into the present, becoming the motive for the recollection and retroactive analysis. *Ōtsu Junkichi* both demystifies and reinforces the story of romantic rebellion against Christianity and the father. But the fact that the significance of the act of recollecting is not made clear inside *Ōtsu Junkichi* forces the reader to seek some cause, motive, or the larger framework of his recollection and eventually entices the reader into an I-novel reading mode.[29] Later, in the novella *Aru otoko sono ane no shi* (A certain man, the death of his sister), which was serialized in the newspaper *Ōsaka mainichi shinbun* from January to March 1920, Shiga retroactively situated *Ōtsu Junkichi* in an autobiographical context. At the time he wrote *Ōtsu Junkichi*, however, Shiga did not further frame the recollecting/narrating "I," probably because of his skepticism about, and resistance to succumbing to, an authoritative, transcendental perspective that imposes a causal order on a story of life—a profound resistance that informs *Ōtsu Junkichi*.

Resisting Master Narratives: "Muddy Mind," "Claudius's Diary," "Han's Crime"

Shiga's early writings, including *Ōtsu Junkichi* (1912), and a number of short stories written at this time—"Nigotta Atama" (Muddy mind; April 1911), "Kurōdiasu no nikki" (Claudius's diary; September 1912), "Han no hanzai" (Han's crime; October 1913)—pursue the problem of the power of order-inducing master narratives: specifically, the stories of romantic love and the sin of fornication and, most important, the "progress of the self" (the quest for a "truer life"), which includes the first two narratives. The following passage is from Shiga's diary, in an entry for January 10, 1911 (Shiga used English words for the words italicized below).

> All in all, I understand the *Details* of things but am quite weak when it comes to understanding the *Whole*. As a shōsetsu writer, I believe that it would be appro-

priate for me to write the *Details* of *Life*, but the idea that I am not grasping the *Whole* is somewhat disturbing. On the other hand, I also believe that one can never comprehend the *Whole*. It seems to me that *Details* are truthful and that the *Whole* contains fallacies. I am also afraid that comprehending the *Whole* or facilely applying a specific notion to the *Whole* at this stage in my life might result in thwarting the development of my self. In any event, at present, I hope to have the ability to see the *Details* of *Life* precisely.   (*Zenshū*, 10: 463)

Here Shiga revealed his resistance to making facile generalizations about the "whole" as well as his desire to understand it. The passage also suggests the young Shiga's belief in the progress of the Self, a grand narrative of the whole that he did not seem to be fully aware of here but that he questioned in various works throughout his career, such as "Han's Crime," *Wakai*, and *An'ya kōro*.

"Muddy Mind," which was written before *Ōtsu Junkichi*, represents a more abstract or conceptual version of the main conflicts and tensions in *Ōtsu Junkichi*. The protagonist Tsuda, like Ōtsu Junkichi, becomes a Christian in his youth, and then suffers more and more from his growing awareness of sexual desire. Tsuda similarly attempts to break the spell of the Christian condemnation of fornication by having recourse to the notion of romantic love, which he believes will justify a physical relationship. Gradually, however, he becomes aware of the discrepancy between his physical relationship with an older woman (Onatsu) and his romantic ideal of love, and he kills the older woman, who, he believes, is preventing him (by implicating him in the sin of fornication) from having a "truer life" (a theme to be developed in "Han's Crime"). Tsuda, who ends up in an insane asylum, cannot escape from the weight of two ideological conceptions—Christian guilt over fornication, and romantic love as the prerequisite for an emancipated "true life"—except through madness.

"Claudius's Diary," which was written from February to August 1912, during the time Shiga was working on *Ōtsu Junkichi*, shows how a dominant narrative shapes one's life and one's interpretation of that life. Claudius's diary records the psychological process by which Claudius, who is presented as innocent in the death of his brother (Hamlet's father), becomes spellbound by Hamlet's belief that Claudius killed his brother out of an adulterous desire for Hamlet's mother, a belief that Claudius calls "nothing but the product of Hamlet's imagination, the demonic result of cheap literature" (*Zenshū*, 2: 13). Claudius gradually internalizes Hamlet's beliefs and eventually admits that he was overjoyed at his brother's death. In the end he realizes that there is no firm line between his "imagination" and his "action." "Spontaneity and naturalness [*shizen*]" momentarily free him from his feeling of being trapped by "cheap" yet powerful "literature," but his conscious effort to be "spontaneous and carefree" makes him lose this sense of freedom. "Claudius's Diary," which is not fully developed as a narrative, depicts only the psychological process by which Claudius falls under the spell of the "story" of the "sin of adulterous desire" (and fratricide) and does not fully explore the issues that it raises—such as the relationship between imagination and action, the connection between motives and interpretations, and the interrelated questions of spontaneity, moral effort, and freedom—all of which are taken up more fully in "Han's Crime."

"Han's Crime" (1913) dramatizes two interrelated master narratives: the ideal of romantic love (or rather, the failure to achieve the ideal of romantic love as a result of carnal sin) and the pursuit of a "truer life" (*hontō no seikatsu*), a truer existence or truer self. The short story revolves around interpretation of the killing by a skilled Chinese knife thrower (Han) of his wife while performing his act. Taking the form of a court trial, "Han's Crime" consists of Han's first-person testimony in which he reflects on his past life (as did both Tsuda and Claudius). The main question is whether the act was intentional murder or merely an accident.

Han notes that although he loved his wife from the day of their marriage until the death of their prematurely born child, he firmly believed that the child was not his own but the result of his wife's premarital relationship with her cousin. Han suspects that his wife killed the baby even though she claimed it was an accident. Afterward, Han lost all his affection for his wife, which in turn resulted in the loss of her affection for him. He came to hate and resent his wife, whom he thought was preventing him from achieving a "better, truer sort of existence," but he could do nothing because he wanted to act in a "morally proper way." The night before the incident, Han, unable to sleep, considered killing his wife instead of cowardly hoping for her death. On the day of the incident, Han was totally exhausted because of the agitation of the night before. He did not think about anything until the moment he threw the knife, at which point he suddenly realized the risk of choosing this particular performance for that day. His own self-consciousness made Han suddenly feel that he could not rely on his intuitive skill, and he consciously attempted to avoid hitting his wife with the knives. His loss of intuitive balance, the normal concentration of mind and body, caused his knife to hit his wife. Immediately afterward Han thought that he had murdered his wife, but then he began to question that position.

> The previous night I had thought about killing her, but might it not be that very fact which now caused me to think of my act as deliberate? Gradually I came to the point that I myself did not know what had actually happened! Suddenly I became excited. I became excited to the extent that I could not stand still. I became unbearably happy. I felt like shouting for joy at the top of my lungs.[30]

Han's joyful excitement derives not from an interpretation of this incident as an unintentional accident but from his realization of the fallacy of causal interpretation that sees a situation as an effect and finds a cause for that effect. Han realizes that his initial belief in the nature of this incident as murder was nothing other than an interpretation of the past, a construction of a spatio-temporal sequence that *a priori* assumes a continuity between a subject and its deeds.

"Han's Crime," in short, radically questions the belief in a fixed identity of a subject as the origin of its actions. Han's realization is concerned not so much with some physical, bodily forces beyond the control of the mind (a theme underlying Naturalist literature) as with the irreducibility of his bodily action to his reflective thinking or to the fixed subject normally considered to be the origin of his thought and action. Han's realization frees him from his unquestioned presupposition about his life as a causal continuity, a life hitherto filled with regret over an irreparably damaged "origin" (failure in romantic love because his wife had "sinned" prior to their marriage) and with the frustration of not yet having achieved a "truer existence" or "self." Han's aspiration for a "better, truer sort of existence" and his conscious effort to be morally correct had only made him sense an unbridgeable gulf between the insufficient present and the forever deferred state of a truer existence. Han's joy comes from the realization of the uniqueness of the present, a present that does not attempt to dominate the past by retroactively constructing a continuous historical identity, a present not dominated by the fixed ideal of a true self.

"Han's Crime" ends with Han's happy realization of the undecidability of the agent of the killing and his unreserved joy at his wife's death, which exterminates the origin of his agony. This sudden removal of the object of intense hatred carries no moral burden. In this regard, it represents a wish fulfillment for the Shiga protagonist in "Muddy Mind" and subsequent works. The irony is that this lucky extinction of the obstacle, while radically questioning the belief in the fixed identity of the subject, yields to and reinforces the story of an unbound celebration of the self and leads to the belief in the supremacy of the self, an ideal espoused by Mushakōji and the Shirakaba group, including Shiga himself. As we have seen, in Ōtsu Junkichi, the "I" attempts to put his coming-of-age in perspective by revealing that the young Junkichi was unknowingly formed and bound by a strong master narrative, specifically, the story of romantic love and the sin of fornication. In the process, the narrating "I" unwittingly reveals a strong desire to claim a certain identity, particularly one as an "independent" shōsetsu writer. "Han's Crime," by contrast, not only dramatizes Han's preoccupation with a continuous identity but also problematizes the narrative and temporal shaping of life, a concern that becomes Shiga's dominant focus in Wakai.

Temporal Modalities in Wakai

Shiga's preoccupation with shaping life through the act of narrating and his resistance to a pre-established and plotted story would become most fully developed in *Wakai* (Reconciliation; 1917), an overtly autobiographical first-person narrative in which the narrator/writer (Junkichi) recounts the near past through two interwoven narrative threads: the "I's" interaction with his family, particularly the process by which the "I" becomes reconciled with his father, and the "I's" struggle to write an autobiographical work entitled *A Dreamer* (*Musōka*) in which he tries to deal with his antagonistic relationship with his father. Not only are the two narrative threads closely interwoven, but they influence and frame each other. When the "I" becomes reconciled with his father, he loses the incentive to write *A Dreamer* and instead decides to write about their "reconciliation."

The basic temporal framework of the recounted story unfolds from the end of July to the middle of September, which the narrator refers to (in chap. 11) as the "present time" (*ima*) of narrating and writing. The climax of the narrative is, as the title suggests, the reconciliation between the son and the father, which we are told (in chap. 13) takes place on August 30. The following passage from chapter 13 reveals that the process of reconciliation is being recalled and retrospectively reassessed by the "I," who has already experienced this reconciliation.

> The tone in which I talked to my father was totally different from the gentle and calm tone that I had promised my mother that I would use. But now I feel that it was the most natural and spontaneous tone for that moment and that, for our relationship, there could have been nothing more appropriate. (*Zenshū*, vol. 2, chap. 13, p. 403)

The narrative unfolding of *Wakai*, however, cannot be reduced to a single, fixed, retrospective perspective as this passage may suggest. In fact, one of the main experiences in reading *Wakai* is a peculiar sense of time in which different modes of temporality unfold in and through the act of narrating, a temporal experience inextricably related to the structure of *Wakai* as well as to the life of the "I."

An interesting shift in narrative perspective and in the temporal sequence occurs in chapter 3 when the narrator begins recollecting a more distant past in connection to the difficulty that he had, around August 19, in writing *A Dreamer*. In contrast to the beginning of *Wakai*, in which the events of the near past are recounted in loosely chronological order, without a particular unifying perspective or theme, the narrative sequence that unfolds from the middle of this chapter emerges specifically out of the narrator's effort to explain and reassess the complexity of his relationship with his father, which both motivates and thwarts the writing of his present project.

The "I" has difficulty writing because he is attempting—unsuccessfully—to find an appropriate causal perspective on his conflict with his father. The narrator mentions a "certain attitude" toward his father that he took eleven years earlier and that led to his father's negative attitude toward him, but he does not explain this "certain attitude," as if to imply that the origin of their long-standing conflict can never be determined. Instead, the narrator recalls a more recent episode, the so-called Kyoto incident, in which the "I" 's refusal to meet his father led to further antagonism. This, the narrator claims, is a more "direct" cause of his father's "present" hostility. This recollection, which begins as a retroactive, causal explanation of his father's "*present* hostility," generates an extended narrative, stretching from chapters 3 to 10, in which the narrator/writer retraces his life subsequent to this episode. A curious shift in temporal sequence and narrative perspective occurs: the account, which begins by retrospectively explaining the father's hostility, continues to the end of *Wakai* without returning to the present time mentioned in chapter 3 and gradually transforms itself into an account of a reconciliation between the father and the son.

The following chart outlines three consecutive temporal sequences, giving the "story time" and the textual indications of time. The narrative sequence from the beginning of chapter 1 to the middle of chapter 3, which I refer to as Sequence I, recalls the near past, from "this July 31" to around August 19 (prior to reconciliation with the father). Out of this account emerges a recollection of a more distant past, the events that began "two years prior to the present," which are described from the middle of chapter 3 through chapter 10 (Sequence II). The narrative from the beginning of chapter 11 to the end of *Wakai* (chap. 16), or Sequence III, unfolds as a direct extension of Sequence II, and yet it turns out to be narrated by a narrator who has already experienced a reconciliation with his father. Although Sequence II begins as a sub-episode or flashback within Sequence I, it does not remain subordinate to Sequence I. Instead, as Sequence II and III unfold, the primary story (Sequence I) level and the subordinate story level (Sequence II) become twisted together.

Sequence II

Chapter 3: Spring of two years ago.
Incident in Kyoto. Beginning of October.
Settles in Abiko. Confrontation with
father.
Chapter 4. June (of a year ago). Wife

comes to Tokyo. First baby born. End of
July, baby taken to Tokyo.
Chapter 5. Night of July 30. Baby, back in
Abiko, struggles with illness.
Chapter 6. July 31, dawn. Death of the
baby.
Chapter 7. Anger over the father's refusal
to bury the baby in the family graveyard.
Chapter 8. August 20. The couple visits
the baby's grave and go on a trip. In
November sister gives birth to baby. "I" 's
resentment toward grandmother
disappears.
Chapter 9. "Soon after" above. Wife
becomes pregnant. Best friend (M) moves
to Abiko. In February desire to write
returns.
Chapter 10. Expected day of delivery
approaches. July 22, delivery of baby. July
23, birth of baby.

Sequence I

Chapter 1. July 31. Visits deceased baby's
grave.
Chapter 2. Works on a novel. August 13,
changes subject. August 15, finishes novel.
August 16, comes to Tokyo. Sees the
father after two-year lapse. Stays in bed for
two days.
Chapter 3. August 19, works on *A
Dreamer*. "The unpleasantness that my
father expresses toward me *at present* does
not derive from what happened eleven
years ago. *It was two years ago in the spring.*"

Sequence III

Chapter 11. "And *it was about four weeks
ago*." August 23, "I" goes to Tokyo. Visits
the family in Azabu.
Chapter 12. "Next day" (August 24),
attempts to write a letter to father. "Next
day" (August 25), works again on *A
Dreamer*.
Chapter 13. August 30 (anniversary of
mother's death), comes to Tokyo.
Reconciliation.

Chapter 14. Reconciliation continued.
Chapter 15. "Next day" (August 31),
Father and sisters visit the "I" 's house in
Abiko.
Chapter 16. Decides to give up *A Dreamer*.
"Next morning" (September 2), visits
Azabu. Goes to restaurant with the entire
family. Decides to write about
reconciliation. "Half a month has past."
Receives a letter from uncle.

Sequence II is shaped by the need to explain retroactively and teleologically the causal connection of past events to the father's "present" hostility toward the "I." As the narrative proceeds, however, Sequence II becomes part of Sequence III, forming a Möbius strip in which a recollection of past events turns into a narrative of events that occurred after the initial point of the recollection. It is as if a fragmentary, episodic, diary-like record of the "I" 's recent experience (Sequence I) turns into an autobiographical, memoir-like narrative that grasps the passage of time from the present results, without revealing exactly where or how this transformation from a diary-type record to a memoiresque narrative occurs.[31] This peculiar narrative unfolding causes the reader to experience two different modes of temporality, neither of which dominates the other: a loosely chronological, open-ended mode in which various events unfold without having a specific, predetermined focus or goal, and a retrospective, teleological, structured mode that organizes history according to its effects and consequences.

The peculiar temporal unfolding of *Wakai*, which refuses to reduce the process of the "I" 's reconciliation to a strictly coherent causal order, is inextricably related to the relationship between the "I" 's life and the act of writing fiction, which mutually frame and shape each other. As the diary-like record of his daily life (in Sequence I) reveals, writing fiction, which he refers to as "work" (*shigoto*), occupies a central part of the "I" 's life as a *shōsetsu* writer. On the other hand, the "I" 's chief artistic project is to write about his personal relationship with his father, to give "objective" meaning and coherence to the "facts" of his life. In chapter 3, the "I" reflects on the difficulty of this project.

> When I write about actual events, I have often been tempted to enumerate one event after another haphazardly. I recall various events and feel as if I should record all of them. Indeed, they all have a causal relationship to each other. But I could not write down every detail. When I try to write down the events, I find the connections between the events unsatisfactory and unpleasant. I had to

make an effort to select from among the occurrences, all of which I wanted to write down.

Now that I was attempting to write about my troubles with my father, I encountered this same problem on a greater scale. There were too many incidents related to the conflict.

Furthermore, as I have already mentioned, my desire not to vent my personal spite toward my father through my writing prevented me from making progress on my writing. But the fact is that part of my self held a personal grudge against him. But that was not my entire self. There coexisted another part that wholeheartedly sympathized with my father.   (chap. 3, p. 334)

In *A Dreamer*, the "I" tries to retrace the "actual events" (*jijitsu*) in order to view his "experience accurately and to make a fair judgment" (chap. 2, p. 328). The "I" becomes keenly aware, however, that he cannot find the "true significance" of the past by haphazardly linking various events and that he must shape the past in order to understand it correctly. The "I" suspects the difficulty derives from the contradiction inherent in his persistent desire to write a narrative with no preconceived aim or intention. The "I" wants to write about his past antagonistic relationship with his father in order to master it, by "viewing it objectively," but the more he proceeds with the writing, the more he becomes haunted by a recurrent sense of not wanting to impose a totalizing, teleological perspective on the past—a circular process that generates the desire to write *A Dreamer*.

Sequence II unfolds out of a recognition of this dilemma, out of the narrator's attempt to explore retrospectively his "present" antagonistic relationship with his father. The episode concerning the birth and death of the first baby in Sequence II (chaps. 4–7) occupies a central position as the event primarily responsible for damaging the already antagonistic relationship between the father and the son. Following the recollection of the baby's death struggle, the narrator proceeds to recount the "I"'s intense anger toward the father, a hatred engendered by the father's attitude toward the death of the baby. This recollection, which generates yet another recollection of an earlier experience, curiously reenacts the "I"'s recurrent and contradictory desire to narrate the story of his intense relationship with his father.

That morning I received a telegram from my uncle in Akasaka telling me to send the coffin to Akasaka. It implied that my father had refused to have the coffin brought to his house in Azabu. I was completely disgusted. If no one had attempted to use the baby to change my relationship with my father, the baby would not have died. Of course, I deeply regretted the fact that I had allowed the baby to be taken to Tokyo. Now I wanted to do everything for the dead baby. . . . As I watched the baby, from the night before last through the next morning, resist with all her might the unnatural death that gradually took her away, I was disgusted by the shift of my father's anger from me to the baby—an unpleasantness that I could not bear to recall later. I thought that everything derived from my clouded relationship with my family at Azabu. I was irritated. But I could not sacrifice my relationship with my grandmother in order to straighten out the relationship.

The "I" attributes his difficulties with writing to this tension.

I cannot count how many times in the past five or six years I have tried to write a long novel dealing with my discord with my father. But the attempt has always failed. I did not have enough perseverance. I was also trying to avoid using my pen to carry out a personal grudge. But most of all, the thought of the actual tragedy that the publication would cause, particularly the dark shadow that would be cast on my relationship with my grandmother, depressed me. Three years ago, when I was living in Matsue, I conceived of the following plot for a long novel, out of a desire to avoid such a tragedy. A gloomy-looking young man, who is serializing a work in a local Matsue newspaper, visits me. I read the installments that he sends me. It describes his troubled relationship with his father. Somewhat later, the newspaper column suddenly stops appearing. The young man, extremely upset, visits me and explains that, although he published the work under a pseudonym, his father has noticed and managed to stop the serialization by bribing the publisher. A number of unpleasant events subsequently occur between the young man and his father. I record all of this as a bystander. . . . I wanted to describe various unpleasant events that could have occurred between me and my father under such circumstances.

The "I" hoped that the act of writing would be apotropaic or a kind of auto-therapy. Indeed, as he proceeded to plan the scene of writing, unanticipated developments occurred to him.

By explicitly writing those events down, I hoped to prevent them from actually taking place. I believed that we could avoid acting out what had happened in my fiction. The climax of the plot was to be an unpleasant tragedy at my grandmother's deathbed: the excited young man tries to enter the house despite his father's efforts, thus triggering a violent conflict, more violent than a mere fistfight. I planned to create either a scene in which the father kills the young man or a scene in which the young man kills his father. All of a sudden, however, I suddenly imagined the father and the son, at the height of the confrontation, embracing each other and bursting into tears. I had never dreamed of such a scene. My eyes dimmed with tears.

I did not decide, however, to write the catastrophe in this reconciliatory manner. I decided that the climax should not be determined in advance and that I should not know what happened until I actually proceeded with the writing. But I imagined how pleasant it would be if the writing actually resulted in this unexpected ending. I tried writing part of the long novel, but I could not continue. After this attempt at writing, my relationship with my father worsened again because of my marriage. Nevertheless, I continued to feel that the scene that I imagined so spontaneously and so naturally was not far from what could happen one day between my father and me.   (chap. 7, pp. 366–68)

The recollection of the confrontation with his father almost immediately becomes interlocked with his difficulty in writing, a difficulty that frames this very recollection (in Sequence II). The retrospective narrative here unfolds in a curious way, gradually sliding away from the original focus. While the narrator explains that his murky relationship with his family derives from his concern for his grandmother, he recalls an earlier writing experience in which he planned to describe a violent and catastrophic confrontation between a fictional father and son in order to prevent it from happening in his real life. In this recollected episode, however, the "I" imagines, much to his surprise, a scene in which the two embrace each other. The "I"'s desire to narrate the story of his tempestuous relationship with the father reveals itself to be a desire to be cured or freed of that very desire. One suspects that the "I" may have refused to predetermine the end of his narrative because he intuitively sensed that that would imply the self-destruction of the narrative itself—of his "work" and his identity. After this point (in Sequence II), the narrative focus shifts and begins to trace the gradual diminution of the "I"'s intense anger toward his father in inverse proportion to the growth of his harmonious state of mind (*chōwatekina kibun*), a process that leads to the final reconciliation narrated in Sequence III. The ambiguous temporal perspective in Sequence II is no doubt related to the involuntary reenactment of an earlier experience that suspends the linear temporal process and generates an oscillation between retrospection and anticipation. The narrative from Sequence II to Sequence III unfolds as if the "I"'s contradictory desire to narrate the story of his relationship with his father is reaching an end that is not predetermined, that could be both the destruction and fulfillment of these contradictory desires, both the destruction of *The Dreamer* and the fulfillment of *Wakai*.

Two different temporal modalities appear in *Wakai*: an open-ended, generative temporality in which various events unfold without a predetermined focus or goal, and a recollected, retrospective temporality, which structures the past. During the course of the narrative, however, another temporal mode emerges, a kind of extra-temporal mode. In Sequence II, there are two long, dramatic scenes that are presented with such a sense of immediacy that they almost seem to stand independent of the larger narrative: the death struggle of the first baby (chaps. 5 and 6) and the birth of the second baby (chap. 10).

At the request of the grandmother, the "I" reluctantly allowed the new-born baby to visit his father's house in Tokyo. After a rough train ride home, the baby suddenly fell ill and, despite a valiant struggle and the help of many, died the next morning. The "I" recounts this incident as an occurrence that irreparably damaged the already antagonistic relationship between himself and his father. As his recollection of the incident proceeds, however, the death struggle of the first baby is recalled with such a sense of immediacy that the reader feels as if he or she is directly witnessing the unfolding events. Chapter 5, three times the length of the other chapters, consists mainly of bare dialogue with little narrative description. As the infant fights for her life, the "I" becomes absorbed in the effort to help her. This intense "within-timeness," in which the demarcation between the recollecting present and the recalled past, the act of recollection and the recalled experience, becomes blurred, overshadows the larger, chronological sequence as well as the retrospective, causal framework established by the narrator, both of which seem to disappear temporarily. The same can be said of the scene in chapter 10 that depicts the birth of the second baby.

Many readers have felt that both scenes attain a special extra-temporal "presentness" in which both the narrator and the reader relive a past event in the present moment, transcending the usual distinctions between the past and present, action and reflection, cause and result. Referring to the baby's death in *Wakai*, Kobayashi Hideo emphasizes Shiga's penetrating intuitive vision, one that "sees and remembers without any conscious effort to observe or remember."[32] In Kobayashi's words, Shiga's essential temporality is always the "present." Referring to the baby's death scene in *Wakai*, Sudō Matsuo suggests that the more intensely and purely the past is experienced, the more precisely and compellingly it is selected, shaped, and depicted in the present writing. Attempting to explain the impression of directness and immediacy in Shiga's texts, Sudō points out that in climactic scenes an action is realized in a "constant present by immediately leaving behind the preceding action through the use of short sentences that all end with *ta,* the past or perfect verb ending."[33] Sudō argues that the essence of Shiga's writing is highly lyrical, especially in the way the scenes of the death and birth of the babies can be appreciated independently from the rest of the narrative. For Sudō, *Wakai* represents the embodiment of the Japanese literary tradition in that the focal points of the text are lyrical passages (such as the death of the baby) in the first-person, "present" mode that climax in the expression of intense emotion coupled with physical action in the fashion of "ancient lyrics" or like the Japanese classical *utamonogatari,* or poem-tale, in which climactic moments of lyrical poetry are loosely framed by a prose narrative that otherwise has little significant order.[34]

This sense of "presentness" or extra-temporality also plays a critical role in the "reconciliation," which occurs on the anniversary of the mother's death (in chap. 13). In both his dreams and his visits to the graveyard, the "I" apparently has an extraordinary temporal and spatial experience in which the ordinary distinctions between the present and the past, life and death, disappear. When he decides to see his father on the twenty-third anniversary of his mother's death (in chap. 13), the "I" seems to be intuitively attuned to the special quality of this day.[35] Indeed, the reconciliation in *Wakai* is a reconciliation between father and son as well as a reconciliation within the "I" between two opposing temporal and interpretive perspectives. In an passage in chapter 3 (Sequence II), the narrator recounts a confrontation with his father that occurred about two years ago, half a year after the Kyoto incident. Although the "I" shows sympathy toward the father over the Kyoto incident and claims that his feelings have changed, he still insists that he was correct in acting as he did.[36] For the "I," the meaning and value of the past cannot change with the passage of time if he is to maintain his identity, which he insists is a consequence of the past, of temporal continuity. The father, on the other hand, expects the "I" to repent for his past misdeeds: no reconciliation can take place until his son has retroactively denied or altered the significance of his past actions. In the course of recounting the past, however, the "I" recognizes and reconfirms a change in his feelings toward his father. On the day prior to the reconciliation, the "I" again reflects on his present feelings toward the father.

> I started to work again on *A Dreamer*, which I planned to submit for the October issue of the journal.
>
> At the present moment, I did not hate my father. . . . But I was not certain whether I could maintain this feeling toward my father if he acted in a hostile manner. . . .
>
> It would be best if I could withdraw effortlessly and in a composed manner from my father's presence without being affected by any negative attitude that my father might take toward me. But I thought that having decided to act in such a fashion was to think in a rash manner, overlooking a deep gulf.　(chap. 12, pp. 396–97)

Although the "I" is still concerned about the continuity between his past and his present, he becomes aware that he does not desire to continue his present relationship with his father. He is at the same time wary of predetermining the future (in the same manner as in his earlier writing experience). He wants to break away from a linear, causal mode of temporality, which he has hitherto unknowingly relied on, but at the same time he senses that he cannot break away from this form of continuity simply by anticipating or narrating the future according to his present desires. Such a prefiguration would be no more than another version of the same causal fallacy and would teleologically delineate an unknown, contingent future as a causal extension of the present.

On the anniversary of the mother's death, on the day of the reconciliation, however, the "I" acts "spontaneously," without premediation.

> "I think that it is meaningless to continue my present relationship with you."
> "Yes, I agree."
> "I could not control myself before. I believe that I caused you considerable trouble. I also think that I acted wrongly in regard to certain matters."
> "Yes," nodded my father. In my excitement, I spoke as if I were angry. It was far from the calm, tranquil tone that I had promised my mother to use. However, I now realize that it was the most spontaneous and natural tone and that there could have been nothing more appropriate for our relationship. . . .
> "I understand. Is what you say true only as long as your grandmother is alive? Or will it be for good?" my father asked.
> "Until now I was only thinking of the present. I simply wanted you to let me visit this house while grandmother is alive. But if this could be forever, I couldn't ask for more." I was about to cry, but I held back.
> "I understand," my father said, shutting his mouth tightly. His eyes were filled with tears.   (chap. 13, pp. 403–4)

Initially the "I" hopes to improve his relationship with his father primarily because he wants to see his aging grandmother without being constrained by his father, but in this privileged and spontaneous moment of the present, the desire for reconciliation frees itself from the constraints of a premeditated, original motive and transcends the obsessive preoccupation with the incompatibility between the two opposing interpretive attitudes toward the past: a progressive temporality in which cause appears to lead to result, and a retroactive, teleological mode in which the past is given meaning in light of the present. In the scene of reconciliation, the "I," while not denying the validity of his past, calmly accepts his father's perspective when the father reports to his mother that "Junkichi has just told me that he truly repents the past and wishes to establish a lasting father-son relationship" (chap. 13, p. 405). The "I" not only frees himself from his preoccupation with his identity (based on continuity with the past), he projects his present intention (to remain reconciled with the father) into the future, neither of which he could do earlier.

At the reconciliation, the "I" is freed, not unlike Han in "Han's Crime," from his preoccupation with causal continuity. What the "I" experiences in the reconciliation, however, is not just a sublimation of, or emancipation from, causal temporality in an extratemporal, privileged present moment, as in "Han's Crime," but the recognition of the inevitability and necessity of a narrative and temporal shaping of life, a shaping inevitably more or less intentional and teleological. This realization was to have profound implications for Shiga's subsequent writings. In this respect, it is significant that the narrator "I" suddenly uses a heavily metaphorical expression (very rare in *Wakai* or in Shiga's texts in general) to describe the "fatigue" he experienced after the reconciliation.

> "It was not an unpleasant fatigue. It was a fatigue accompanied by a sense of tranquillity, as if I were fainting away in the tranquillity, like a small lake deep in the mountains enveloped in a heavy mist. It was a fatigue like that experienced by a traveler who has finally come back home after a long, long unpleasant journey." (chap. 14, p. 408).

The process leading to the reconciliation is now metaphorically refigured as the experience of "homecoming," as a return to the family as well as to nature.

Autobiographical Shaping and An'ya kōro

From the late 1910's Shiga became intensely conscious of giving his past works an autobiographical frame. *Aru otoko sono ane no shi* (A certain man, the death of his elder sister), which was serialized in a newspaper from January to March 1920 and which would later form part of Shiga's "autobiographical trilogy" (with *Ōtsu Junkichi* and *Wakai*), appears to be a third-person autobiography that attempts to give a comprehensive and balanced portrayal of Shiga's antagonistic relationship with the father by adopting an external, "objective" perspective of a fictive witness, thereby enhancing the process of self-distancing and self-commentary. The narrator of *Aru otoko* talks about "a certain man," Yoshiyuki, his "elder brother by a different mother," and about the antagonistic relationship between this brother and his father. The family background, the personality of Yoshiyuki and the father, and the circumstances of their antagonistic relationship resemble those of the characters in *Ōtsu Junkichi*, but they are portrayed from an "external" perspective, through the eyes of the sympathetic younger brother, the "I." Yoshiyuki mentions, in a letter addressed to his elder sister, the *shōsetsu* he wrote at the request of a publisher, for which he received, for the first time, a significant amount of compensation—the "market value" of which he had dreamed and through which he secretly hoped to gain his father's recognition of his "work" (*shi-*

goto). In the midst of the citation of this letter, the narrator "I" intrudes, making sympathetic comments that attempt to give a more objective and neutral perspective to both father and son.

> Concerning this incident, however, my elder brother was rather inattentive to the contradictory nature of his position. The *shōsetsu* with which he hoped to please his father by earning financial compensation was directly based on the trouble that was caused earlier when my brother insisted that he marry our maid Chiyo. In this *shōsetsu*, the father was given a role that was far from pleasing. He was characterized as an incorrigible, stubborn materialist. I was afraid of what would happen if my father should read this work. My brother, on the contrary, assumed that our father would not read it. I wonder, however, how he would have reacted if our father had wanted to read the *shōsetsu*, becoming interested in the work as my brother had secretly hoped. In any event, I have to say that my brother, who wanted to please his father with the money that he received for this *shōsetsu*, was after all very carefree and self-centered.   (*Zenshū*, 2: 501.)

Aru otoko, which explicitly invites an identification between Yoshiyuki and Ōtsu Junkichi, and between these two figures and Shiga himself, suggests the autobiographical nature of *Ōtsu Junkichi* as well as Shiga's assumptions around 1920 about the reader's practice of identifying the protagonist with the author.

In the 1920's, Shiga published some earlier sketches (written in early 1910's) that dealt with adolescent friendships and personal relationships among the ambitious yet still unestablished writers of the Shirakaba group. The publication of these works, which make little sense without an interest in Shiga's biographical context, testifies to the formation of the I-novel reading mode in the contemporary world of journalism. From 1925 to 1926, Shiga also wrote a series of short narratives later labeled the "Yamashina series": "Saji" (Trifles of life; September 1925), "Yamashina no kioku" (Memory of Yamashina; January 1926), "Chijō" (Foolish passion; April 1926), and "Banshū" (Late autumn; September 1926). These works, which overtly encourage an identification of the protagonist with the author (and which, as Shiga notes in the preface to the hardcover edition, are based on personal experiences), deal with the *shōsetsu* writer's liaison with a young geisha, his description of this experience, and the repercussions caused by publication of this *shōsetsu*. This series both presupposes and thematizes an I-novel reading and writing practice that regards the text as a faithful record of the author's personal life, in which "art" and "life" form and transform each other, a self-perpetuating process that provides the writer with more to write about. In 1926 Shiga also published a short narrative called "Kako" (My past), a straightforward personal essay narrated by the "author" himself who (as a result of recent interaction with a distant relative) recalled and retraced from a more detached perspective his relationship with the housemaid Chiyo, the episodes presented in *Ōtsu Junkichi*, and the subsequent demise of the relationship.

However, the most significant creative activity for Shiga from the late 1910's, while he was becoming conscious of and participating in the formation of the I-novel reading and writing mode, was the publication of *An'ya kōro* (A dark night's passing), Shiga's only long, extended narrative fiction (published in installments from January 1921 to 1928, with the last section completed in 1937 after a nine-year lapse; parts of the first half appeared earlier in a slightly different and independent form in April 1919 and January 1920). Tokitō Kensaku, the aspiring young writer who is the protagonist of *An'ya kōro*, is the son of his mother and his putative grandfather—a fact known to everyone but himself. During the course of the narrative, he discovers this secret and attempts to come to terms with it. Eventually he finds a woman whom he loves and marries, but while he is away, she ends up having a physical relationship with his cousin. In a fashion reminiscent of the protagonist of "Han's Crime," Kensaku tries to overcome the fact of the adultery, which he regards as a kind of karmic fate and which he attempts to deal with by himself. He retreats to Mount Daisen, where, one day, while climbing the mountain, he faints from fatigue. The novel ends when the wife comes to the rescue of her unconscious husband.

In his first substantial commentary on his own writings, "Sōsaku yodan" (1928), which was appended to a collection of his works that included the first half (parts I and II) of *An'ya Kōro*, Shiga stated that although some readers and critics equated the protagonist Tokitō Kensaku with himself, "it is impossible to explain to what extent Kensaku is the author himself and to what extent he is not" (*Zenshū*, 8: 14). In 1938, when Shiga finally completed the last section of *An'ya kōro*, he remarked that whereas Tokitō Kensaku was by and large modeled on himself, *An'ya kōro* differed significantly from its aborted, unpublished predecessor, a long autobiographical narrative called *Tokitō Kensaku*, which Shiga at this point retroactively called "a so-called I-novel" ("Zoku sōsaku yodan," *Zenshū*, 8: 16).[37]

Shiga's remarks in "Zoku sōsaku yodan" about the transformation of the aborted *Tokitō Kensaku* into *An'ya kōro* are revealing.

> The subject of *Tokitō Kensaku*, the predecessor of *An'ya kōro*, was the long-standing antagonistic relationship with my father. Perhaps the difficulty of transcending my own personal grudge prevented me from completing it. Some years later, however, I had a very pleasant reconciliation with my father, which I described in my *shōsetsu Wakai*. Once I had accomplished the reconciliation, my feelings about the *shōsetsu Tokitō Kensaku* started to change. Particularly after writing *Aru otoko sono ane no shi*, in which I dealt with my past relationship with my father from a relatively fair and critical standpoint, from the perspective of

the brother of the protagonist, I started to lose the motivation to continue *Tokitō Kensaku*. Although I still wanted to write a long narrative, I gradually lost interest in the subject.

Memories of a childhood incident provided the spark that would later transform *Tokitō Kensaku* into *An'ya kōro*.

At my mother's deathbed (she died at thirty-three, when I was thirteen), my grandfather wept, saying "It was a pity that she passed away without experiencing anything truly enjoyable." My father did not cry at that time. This scene deeply impressed me, causing antipathy toward my father, but when I imagined that I might have been my grandfather's child, this old memory suddenly returned to me with a completely different significance. . . . I woke up the next morning to find this idea to be utterly silly, but years later, when I was in Abiko thinking about the unfinished work that had lost its initial significance, this old notion suddenly came back to me, inspiring me to write about the various ways in which a protagonist suffers from not knowing what others know about his origins. This inspiration transformed *Tokitō Kensaku* into *An'ya kōro*. . . .

But I could not easily write *An'ya kōro* either. There were times when I thought of writing a number of short pieces to collect into one extended work. It was with such an idea in mind that I separately published what later became the Prologue to *An'ya kōro* under the title "Kensaku no tsuioku" [Kensaku's reminiscences; January 1920] and the last section of the first half of *An'ya kōro* under the title "Aware na otoko" [A miserable man; April 1919].

The descriptions in the first half of *An'ya kōro* were for most part from what I had written for the earlier *Tokitō Kensaku*. It was hard to throw away completely what I had once written with such great effort, so I tried to revive the earlier piece as much as possible. I wrote the second half, the part that had not existed in *Tokitō Kensaku*, solely for *An'ya kōro*. There is consequently a difference in style between the first half and the second half. It was an inconsistency I could not avoid. . . .

The main theme of *An'ya kōro* revolves around a woman whose past error not only caused her to suffer but caused others to suffer even more. . . . The protagonist is doomed to suffer from his mother's past mistake, and no sooner has he freed himself from this suffering than he is doomed to experience a similar error by his own wife. . . .

My main concern in *An'ya kōro* was not the external development of the events but rather the development of the protagonist's inner feelings as he experiences these events. (*Zenshū*, 8: 17–21)

According to Shiga, what transformed *Tokitō Kensaku* into *An'ya kōro* was an imaginative construction of the origin of his long-standing antagonistic relationship with his father, a relationship that was the subject of *Tokitō Kensaku*. The construct in question is a fictional scenario about one's true origin, what Freud called the "family romance."[38] In the words of Peter Brooks:

Freud, in his well-known essay "Family Romances," develops the typical scenario based on the child's discovery that *pater semper incertus est*: the phantasy of being an adopted child whose biological parents are more exalted creatures than his actual parents, which is then superseded when the child accepts the actual mother but creates a phantasized, illegitimate father, and bastardizes siblings in favor of his own sole legitimacy. It may be significant, as Roland Barthes notes, that the child appears to "discover" the Oedipus complex and the capacity for constructing coherent narrative at about the same stage in life. The most fully developed narratives of the child become a man all seem to turn on the uncertainty of fatherhood, to use this uncertainty to unfold the romance of authority vested elsewhere, and to test the individual's claim to personal legitimacy within a struggle of different principles of authority.[39]

In Shiga's account, this reconstruction of his life and his relationship with the father came to his mind as a plausible and convincing explanation of his personal experience, which, he realized, acquired a new significance within this imaginative scenario. Although Shiga rejected this scenario as a "silly fancy" at the time he was writing *Tokitō Kensaku*, he resurrected it as the main motif of *An'ya kōro* when his antagonistic relationship with his father ended.

As we have seen, Shiga struggled between the desire to write about life "as it is," without imposing on it an interpretive, explanatory, or causal narrative, and the desire to understand the significance of life, by implicitly seeking an underlying structure or order. What I have called the "recognition" in *Wakai*, the realization that writing about life inevitably means giving it shape and order, seems to have played a significant role in Shiga's acceptance of a fictional scenario as a driving force in *An'ya kōro*. Indeed, *An'ya kōro* assumes all the narrative motifs that had hitherto emerged in Shiga's texts—an uncontrollable mood or feeling (*kibun*) as the most immediate reality, an antagonistic relationship with the father, the young man's concern for self-progress and development, the young man's artistic ambition to contribute to the well-being of humanity, a longing for the dead mother, an incestuous attraction to her surrogate, uncertainty over one's origins, a preoccupation with physical desire, romantic love as a way to a truer life, the sin of fornication, and the problem of adultery. If in *An'ya kōro* Shiga used what Freud called the "family romance" to explain the "origins" of the hero's uncertainty about his existence and identity, then the hero's quest finally takes, as we shall see, the form of the story of a return to nature. (It is unclear whether Shiga got the idea of "family romance" through reading nineteenth-century Western novels, or whether his conception attests to a certain universality of this motif in bourgeois social structure, or whether it resulted from a combination of the two.) The metaphor that emerges toward the end of *Wakai* in which the protagonist compares his experience to a homecoming after a long journey, to a return to an all-embracing nature, becomes the narrative that embraces all the other narratives in *An'ya kōro*.

Generation of the Narrative, Narrative of Generation: The Return to Nature

The narrative of *Wakai* does not end with the climactic reconciliation; rather, it continues to describe the "I" 's writing. Having achieved a reconciliation, the "I" loses the incentive to continue writing about his past antipathy toward his father and instead decides to write about the reconciliation, which occupies his mind at this time.

> I had lost the incentive to keep writing *A Dreamer* as I had originally planned, as a novel dealing with my discord with my father. I had to look for some other material. I had some material in hand, but my heart would not embrace the material immediately, and sometimes it would not embrace it at all, even after a time. If I force myself to write under those circumstances, the work will be a lifeless fabrication, a failure. I wondered if I could finish something satisfactory by the September 15 or 16 deadline.
>
> Even as I thought about these problems, I began to ruminate on what had just happened between my father and myself. I wanted to see him in the near future.   (chap. 16, p. 413)
>
> When we parted, I saw that my father's eyes sparkled with affection. I had no more doubt about our reconciliation. We parted at Ginza.
>
> I felt uneasy about the fact that there were fewer and fewer days left to the deadline. *I finally decided to write about the reconciliation that occupied my mind.*
>
> About half a month has passed since then. I received a letter from my uncle, who had just returned to Kamakura from Kyoto. It was a reply to the letter of thanks that I had sent him at the beginning of the month.   (chap. 16, p. 418; my italics)

Wakai's referential modality encourages not only an identification between the "I" (Junkichi) and the author Shiga but also an identification between the act of writing (about the reconciliation) and the act of writing *Wakai* itself, an identification reinforced by the date of *Wakai*'s first appearance in the literary magazine *Kokuchō* in October 1917.[40] The date of completion ("September 18, 1917") is clearly indicated in the October issue of *Kokuchō*. The initial readers were no doubt under the impression that the months mentioned in *Wakai* ("this past July," "August," "September") were those of 1917. Shiga's subsequent comments on the process of writing *Wakai* also reinforce this identification.[41] If one adopts this autobiographical reading mode, identifying the narrator with the author and the act of writing about the reconciliation (*wakai*) mentioned *in* the narrative with the act of writing of *Wakai*, the italicized sentence in the above passage becomes the text's self-referential remark about its own generation. The act of writing *Wakai* from the beginning to this point is now situated inside the story, which catches up with the narration itself. As Gérard Genette notes, one common practice of autobiographical narrating (in which a narrator retrospectively talks about his/her distant past to the present) is for the narrative to "bring the hero to the point where the narrator awaits him, in order that these two hypostases might meet and finally merge."[42] The text of *Wakai*, however, does not end at the point at which the now unified hero/narrator has become the author/creator of the narrative of his own life. The last short paragraph, which introduces a letter that the "I" received "about half a month later" returns the reader to the story level, which overtakes the act of writing mentioned in the previous sentence.

The text of *Wakai* ends by reinforcing and substantiating the "I" 's narrative and the metaphorical shaping of his life, not as a subjective soliloquy or artificially imposed order, but as a fait accompli, as part of a natural process. The last paragraph of *Wakai* consists entirely of a citation from a letter from the uncle that emphasizes the "natural course" (*jisetsu in'nen*) of the recent reconciliation and that includes a passage from a classical Chinese poem.

> I firmly believe that the recent reconciliation took place according to the natural course of the events in time. Your father also told me that he felt assured of the firmness of this reconciliation. Your letter indicated your conviction of the permanence of this reconciliation, and I had also felt that way on the spot. I am filled with the excitement expressed in the old poem:
>
> > From east, west, south, and north,
> > Having come back home
> > Deep into the night,
> > Together we view the snow on the thousand cliffs.
> > (chap. 16, p. 419)

The motif of "homecoming" is reinforced here through multiple voices, which absorb the narrator "I" 's earlier metaphorical reshaping of his experience as a "homecoming," as part of a collective memory of a natural and spontaneous flow of time that brings about a collective communion within and with nature.

Takemori Ten'yū sees *Wakai* as a text sustained by strong kinship affections: the protagonist awakens to these affections as a result of his new experience as a father, following the death of a baby and the birth of another.[43] Yamada Yūsaku stresses the symbolic significance of the scene in which the father's entire household celebrates the reconciliation by silently and ceremonially exchanging a cup of sake, "all filled with a common, warm joy that none of us could articulate with words" (chap. 14, pp. 406–7). Yamada interprets this as a "ritual that celebrates the family stability regained through Junkichi's belated acceptance of his father as the new 'patriarch' of the kinship community, replacing his late grandfather."[44] Sekiya Ichirō argues that the ritualistic ceremony is the kinship community's celebration of Junkichi's belated "coming-of-age": the death of the first baby becomes the symbolic death of Junkichi's old self and the birth of the second baby the birth of Junkichi's new self, which has awakened to an all-encompassing natural power larger than itself.[45] In this reading of *Wakai* as a story of kinship communality, the return to kinship communality implicitly becomes a return to nature. Takemori argues that the "long journey of Shiga's antagonistic relationship with his father, which actually led Shiga to wander to such distant places as Onomichi, Matsue, Kamakura, Akagi, and Abiko, and which, in the end, immersed him in the emotions of kinship blood ties that can be called his home," can best be summarized in the phrase *jisetsu in'nen* (natural process), an all-nurturing natural process.[46]

The main thesis of Sudō Matsuo's study of Shiga is that Shiga's relationship with "nature" (*shizen*) is transformed from an antagonistic one into a harmonious union. Sudō, who attempts to trace this transformation from Shiga's earlier years to his later years, points out that his relationship with nature is best represented in two almost symmetrical passages in *An'ya kōro*: the famous passage (set at Mount Daisen) toward the end of the narrative (pt. IV, chap. 19) in which Kensaku experiences an ecstatic unity with cosmic nature, and an earlier passage (set on a ship from Tokyo to Onomichi) (pt. II, chap. 1) in which Kensaku attempts to "stand firm as if representing all mankind" against nature.

> He felt his exhaustion turn into a strange state of rapture. He could feel his mind and his body both gradually merging into this great nature that surrounded him. It was not nature that was visible to the eyes; rather, it was like a limitless body of air that wrapped itself around him, this tiny creature no longer than a poppy seed. To be gently drawn into it, and there be restored, was a pleasure beyond the power of words to describe. The sensation was a little like that of the moment when, tired and without a single worry, one was about to fall into a deep sleep. Indeed, a part of him already was in a state hardly distinguishable from sleep. He had experienced this feeling of being absorbed by nature before; but this was the first time that it was accompanied by such rapture. In previous instances, the feeling perhaps had been more that of being sucked in by nature than that of merging into it; and although there had been some pleasure attached to it, he had at the same time always tried instinctively to resist it, and on finding such resistance difficult, he had felt a distinct uneasiness. But this time, he had not the slightest will to resist; and contentedly, without a trace of the old uneasiness, he accepted nature's embrace. . . . He felt as if he had just taken a step on the road to eternity. Death held no threat for him. If this means dying, he

thought, I can die without regret. But to him, this journey to eternity did not seem the same as death.   (pt. IV, chap. 19, *Zenshū*, 5: 578–79)[47]

Arguing that the narrative development of *An'ya kōro*, particularly from part II to part III, does not prepare the basis for Kensaku's change in attitude toward nature, Sudō presents two explanations, both of which represent what I call the "I-novel discourse" surrounding Shiga. First, Sudō argues that the disjunction between the halves of *An'ya kōro* derives from the fact that the protagonist or the plot is not shaped according to the principles of narrative fiction but rather by the circumstances of composition. Over the long period of writing, the author's view toward nature underwent a significant transformation. Sudō's second point is that this transformation embodies an archetypal characteristic of Japanese literature: namely, an emphasis on harmony and unity with nature through physical and emotional ties of *aware*, of affection and sympathy.[48]

Sudō and other scholars, including recent Western critics, regard Shiga's texts as the culmination of a long Japanese lyrical tradition of communality, which gave priority to "presentness" and emotional communion, and which lacks an ordered structure and fictional imagination. *Wakai* and Shiga's oeuvre, regarded as the quintessence of the I-novel, have, in short, generated a broader narrative about literary continuity and cultural identity. It can be argued, however, that the so-called cultural tradition and the perceived continuity between classical texts and the I-novel were in significant part created and constructed teleologically through the attempt to define and frame Shiga's works in a larger, cultural context. These critics may in fact have been induced to narrate the story of the communal, nature orientation of the Japanese "tradition" by Shiga's powerful metaphor of homecoming and of a return to nature. Although the cause and result remain uncertain, Shiga's texts have undoubtedly contributed not only to the formation of I-novel discourse but to the refiguration and consolidation of cultural identity, while at the same time exploring and problematizing the narrative shaping of that identity. The cultural origin of Shiga's fiction does not precede his fiction so much as the fiction calls for and creates its own origins.

PART III

Traces of the Self

CHAPTER 6

~⋇

Crossing Boundaries: Truth and Fiction in Nagai Kafū's 'Strange Tale from East of the River'

Bokutō kidan (A strange tale from east of the river) is a first-person narrative about an aging novelist whose personal experience appears to reflect that of the author, Nagai Kafū (1879–1959). The work, published by Kafū in 1937 when he was fifty-eight years old, was enthusiastically received by his contemporaries.[1] Some readers considered it to be a "lyrical novel" (*jojō shōsetsu*), others saw it as a "social novel" (*shakai shōsetsu*), and still others understood it to be an I-novel.[2] Kafū first established his name as an advocate of Zola, writing such works as *Yashin* (Ambition; 1902), *Jigoku no hana* (Flowers in hell; 1902) and *Yume no onna* (A woman of a dream; 1903), all of which were inspired by the French writer.[3] At the end of 1903 he went to America, where he stayed for almost four years. During his years abroad, the last of which was spent in France, his literary interest shifted from Zola to Maupassant and such French romantic poets as Lamartine and Musset.[4] Upon returning to Japan from America (via France), he successively published *Amerika monogatari* (Tales of America; 1908), *Furansu monogatari* (Tales of France; 1909), *Kanraku* (Pleasure; 1909), *Kichōsha no nikki* (Diary of a returnee; 1909; later titled *Shin-kichōsha nikki* [Diary of a recent returnee]), *Sumidagawa* (The Sumida River; 1909), and *Reishō* (Sneers; 1909). He also began publishing translations of such French symbolist poets as Baudelaire, Verlaine, and Régnier, which appeared together in a poetry collection called *Sango-shū* (Coral anthology; 1913). Kafū's return from France and America in 1908 coincided with the peak of Japanese Naturalism, and he soon became— or so it was thought—a leader of the Tanbi-ha, the School of Aestheticism, which was strongly anti-Naturalist.[5] One consequence of this affiliation was that Kafū generally has not been considered an I-novelist.

By the late 1920's the I-novel was commonly understood by the reading public to be a thinly veiled fiction in which the author faithfully recounts the details of his personal life and through which he reveals his true self even more directly than he would in an autobiography. In the mid-1930's, when *Bokutō kidan* appeared, the I-novel was the subject of serious literary and intellectual debate and stood in a dominant position, both for its advocates and for its critics. It was, for example, in 1935 that Yokomitsu Riichi (in "Junsui shōsetsu ron") and Kobayashi Hideo (in "Watakushi shōsetsu ron") severely criticized the narrow perspective and "naïve realism" of the Japanese I-novel. The introduction of Marxism and the importation of autobiographical novels by Gide, Proust, and Joyce in the late 1920's and in the first half of the 1930's triggered this debate. Many Marxist "proletarian writers," who abandoned communism following their party leaders' repudiation of Marxism in 1933, began writing confessional novels in which they described their own act of renunciation. In 1937 Japan launched its war on China, an act that eventually resulted in World War II and led to the silence and suppression of many writers.

A Kafū revival occurred after World War II. Some critics praised Kafū for his "aloof individualism" and for being one of the few writers who had not followed the militarism and ultra-nationalism of the 1930's and early 1940's. Others, however, particularly younger critics, scoffed at Kafū's postwar popularity and argued that his individualism was little more than self-defensive cynicism, lacking a real social consciousness, and that his lyrical lamentations were no more than a literary pose and style.[6] Kafū's satirical commentary on the superficial westernization and rapid modernization of contemporary Japan and his lyrical lamentation and sense of nostalgia for a lost past, particularly for the dying culture of Edo, are recurrent features of his writings, as they are of *Bokutō kidan*.

It was thus no accident that, in the 1950's, when the I-novel again became a central literary concern, literary critics, many of whom were concerned with the problem of the self in the Japanese novel and society, judged and assessed Kafū's works in terms of his lyricism and aloof self-isolation. Although no critic ever called Nagai Kafū an I-novelist, many of them ultimately read *Bokutō kidan* and other of his works as I-novels. As I shall argue, *Bokutō kidan*, considered by many to be Kafū's most representative work, not only plays upon the I-novel phenomenon by dramatizing and defamiliarizing I-novel reading and writing practices—which tacitly reduces the text to the author's true self—but also underscores and reinforces the I-novel as a literary and cultural institution even while it undercuts and undermines that institution.

Defamiliarizing the I-Novel

The first-person narrative of *Bokutō kidan*, which begins in a casual essay style, makes the reader wonder who is narrating the text and what kind of text it is.

> I almost never go to see a moving picture. If vague memories are to be trusted, it was toward the end of the last century that I saw, at a Kanda theater, a moving picture of a San Francisco street scene. I suppose it must have been about then, too, that an expression "moving picture" was invented. Over forty years have passed since then, and today this expression has been discarded. The expression one has learned first comes most easily, however, and I shall here continue to use the old, discarded one.
>
> A young literary acquaintance, telling me one day shortly after the earthquake that I had fallen behind the times, dragged me off to a moving picture in Tameike. It was a moving picture much admired at the time, and it turned out to be an adaptation of a Maupassant story. I might better have read the original.
>
> Yet young and old delight in moving pictures and make them the subject of daily conversation, and even a person like me sometimes feels inclined to wonder what the conversation might be about. I always make it a special point, therefore, to look at billboards when I pass moving picture houses. One can tell from the billboards, without seeing the pictures themselves, what the general plots are, and what delights people so.
>
> Asakusa is the part of town where one can see the most moving picture billboards at a single viewing. One can see all the several varieties and compare their virtues and defects. When I am in the vicinity of Asakusa or Shitaya, I always remember to go to the park and have a walk around the lake. It was on a late spring evening when the wind was getting warmer.   (chap. 1, pp. 95–96, 278)[7]

The first-person narrator, the "I" (*watakushi*), who has peculiar habits and tastes, speaks of his periodic visits to Asakusa Park in downtown Tokyo and then describes an incident that occurred one late-spring evening. On the way back from an old-fashioned, secondhand bookseller near the Yoshiwara Licensed Quarter, the "I" is apprehended by a suspicious policeman, who takes him to a police box and interrogates him.

> "Where are you coming from at this hour of the night?"
>   "I've been over there."
>   "Over where?"
>   "By the canal."
>   "What do you mean, the canal?"
>   "The canal that is known as the San'ya Canal at the foot of Matsuchi Hill."

"What's your name?"

"Ōe Tadasu." The policeman took out his notebook. "You write Tadasu the way it is in the *Analects*. 'Having unified and rectified the world.' Remember? 'Rectified'—that's the character."

He glowered, ordering me silent. . . .

"Where do you live?"

"Number 6 Otansumachi 1-chōme, Azabu."

"What do you do?"

"Nothing at all."

"Unemployed? How old are you?"

"I was born in the Year of the Hare, Lesser Earth Sign."

"I asked how old you are."

"Hare, Lesser Earth. 1879." I thought I would say no more, but silence seemed risky.

"Fifty-seven years old."

"Pretty young for your age, aren't you?" I giggled.

"What did you say your name was?"

"Ōe Tadasu."

"How many in your family?"

"Three." As a matter of fact I am a bachelor, but I knew from experience that if I told the truth I would come under yet stronger suspicion.

"Your wife and who else?" The policeman took the charitable view.

"The wife and the old woman."

"How old's your wife?"

I had to think for a minute, but then I remembered a woman with whom I had kept company some four or five years before. "Thirty. Born July 14, Year of the Horse, Great Fire Sign."

I thought if asked her name I would give the name of a woman in a story I was then writing, but the policeman said nothing more. He felt the pockets of my coat and overcoat. (chap. 1, pp. 101–3, *282–83*)

The episode ends with a remark that playfully raises the question of the "I"'s identity: "It occurred to me afterward that if I had not had the family register and the certified seal, I would indeed have spent the night in a cage" (pp. 106, *284*). The same essay or journal-like style continues in chapter 2, which begins: "I have drawn up plans for a novel called *Shissō* (Whereabouts unknown), in which I have some confidence. If I can finish writing it, this new novel will not be among my worst efforts" (pp. 106, *284*).[8]

The "I" gives an outline of the planned novel, in which an elderly schoolteacher Taneda, after leaving a noisy home on the day of his retirement, chances to meet a young woman named Sumiko, his family's onetime maid, now working in a bar. The description of the planned novel ends with:

I do not know what I should do with my story hereafter.
. . . .
   I am thinking about the path to his [Taneda's] downfall, and his feelings at
various stages along the way; his discomfiture when he is handed over to his wife
and children, and so on. On my way back from having bought an old singlet in a
San'ya alley, I was apprehended by a policeman and admonished at a police box.
There can be no better material than this for describing the feelings of poor
Taneda.
   The things that most interest me when I write a novel are the choice and
description of background. I have from time to time fallen into the error of
emphasizing background at the expense of characterization.   (chap. 2, pp. 109,
286)

   Until the middle of the second chapter, *Bokutō kidan* resembles a daily
journal in which the "I" reflects on recent events and in which he records his
thoughts as they come to mind. In the middle of that chapter, however, the
"I" sets out on a walk to find material for his fiction writing and, as a result of
a sudden shower, becomes acquainted with an unlicensed prostitute Oyuki
and visits her house (chap. 3). At this point, in the middle of chapter 3, the
first-person narrator "I" suddenly becomes the "author of this book" and
begins to address the reader accordingly.

Those who have read the stories of Tamenaga Shunsui will remember how from
time to time Shunsui breaks the narrative to apologize for himself or his characters. . . .
   After the manner of Shunsui, I should like to make a remark or two here.
The reader may feel that the woman was just a little too familiar when she met
me there by the road. I merely record the facts of our meeting, however, and add
no coloring, no shaping or contriving. Inasmuch as the affair had its beginning
in a sudden thunder shower, moreover, certain readers may be smiling at me for
having used a well-worn device. I do not want to give the incident another
setting for fear of being suspected of creating fiction. Put in motion by an
evening shower, it seemed to me interesting for the very reason that it was so
much in the old tradition. Indeed I began this book because I wanted to tell of it.
   . . . The fact that the woman who took me in from the rain belonged to the
old-style minority made me think the tired old device appropriate. I cannot
bring myself to do injury to what happened.   (chap. 3, pp. 119–20, *292*)

These playful comments by the "author" of *Bokutō kidan* suddenly call the
narrative levels of the text into question. The "I" now states that he began
"this book" because he wanted to recount his encounter with Oyuki. When
the first-person narrator talks about his walk near Yoshiwara (chap. 1) or of
his plan for a new novel (chap. 2), he could not have known of this encounter
with Oyuki, and yet we are now told that this is why the "I" began writing

"this book." The novelist "I," who calls himself Ōe Tadasu and who has been revealing his personal life and his plans for his novel *Shissō*, suddenly becomes the writer of *Bokutō kidan*.

Knowing that Nagai Kafū wrote *Bokutō kidan*, the reader is led to identify this "author/I" with Kafū, an association reinforced by a postscript entitled "Sakugo zeigen" (literally, "a redundant postscript"), in which Kafū addresses the reader as the author of the *shōsetsu Bokutō kidan*. The continuity between the writer in *Bokutō kidan* (Ōe Tadasu, which in fact might or might not be the "I"'s real name), who is working on a manuscript called *Shissō*, and the author of *Bokutō kidan* (Nagai Kafū) is hinted at from the beginning of the narrative.

> "In the early years of this century I once wrote a story about a prostitute of the Suzaki quarter." (chap. 2, pp. 110, *286*)

> "In the days when my old friend, the good Kōjiro Sōyō, was still alive, I would go to the Ginza every night." (chap. 5, pp. 130, *297*)

> "These haiku of mine came back to me one evening when I found a mosquito net hanging in Oyuki's backroom. Perhaps half of them were composed on visits to my late friend Inoue Aa, who was then living in a Fukagawa tenement with a woman not approved of by his family. It would have been in about 1910 or 1911, I suppose." (chap. 6, pp. 139, *304*)

> "The inquisitive reader who has wanted to know more about the person I am will have found his wishes only too well satisfied by a reading of certain inadequate works from my middle years: among them the dialogue 'Early Afternoon,' the fugitive essay 'House for a Mistress' and the story 'Unfinished Dream.'" (chap. 7, pp. 150, *310*)

In 1903 Kafū published a novel entitled *Yume no onna* about the life of a prostitute in the Suzaki licensed quarter. Kōjiro Sōyō and Inoue Aa are actual names of Kafū's deceased friends. "Early Afternoon" ("Hirusugi"; 1912), "House for a Mistress" ("Shōtaku"; 1912), and "Unfinished Dream" ("Mihatenu yume"; 1910) are titles of early works. The year of birth that the "I" gives to the policeman is that of Kafū and the address, "Number 6 Otansumachi 1-chōme, Azabu," is a slight modification of Kafū's address at the time: Number 6 Ichibeimachi 1-chōme, Azabu.[9] The reader who recognizes these references will no doubt associate the writer in *Bokutō kidan* with Kafū, but the same reader will also be aware that Kafū never wrote a novel entitled *Shissō*, which the "I" claims to have successfully finished (chap. 9). Even for those who do not recognize these references, the postscript "Sakugo zeigen" will induce an identification between Kafū, the author of *Bokutō kidan*, and the writer in *Bokutō kidan*.

This narrative posture of playfully and provocatively inviting the reader to assume that the work is depicting the author's actual lived experience and of using a protagonist who, while different in name, possesses recognizable characteristics of the author has indeed induced past readers to discuss this text in relationship to I-novel writing and reading practices. In 1937 Satō Haruo wrote that "although *Bokutō kidan* is not a so-called I-novel, Kafū's righteous indignation [*gifun*] and humanistic love [*ningen-ai*] are directly expressed through the voice of Ōe Tadasu, who represents Kafū."[10] Criticizing Satō Haruo for seriously considering *Bokutō kidan* an I-novel, Hirano Ken wrote in 1954 that Nagai Kafū utilized the I-novel setting to give a sense of reality to his romantic and anachronistic dream of love.[11] Hirano Ken was in turn criticized by Etō Jun in 1959 for "falling prey to Kafū's use of I-novel conventions," confusing the protagonist for the author, and consequently "naïvely believing in Kafū's dream of having an anachronistic love affair."[12] According to Etō, Kafū skillfully manipulated the I-novel formula to make the reader believe that Ōe Tadasu was Kafū himself. By doing so, Kafū created the deceptive impression that he himself had actually been involved in the kind of human conflict that constituted the "essence of the novel," an essence that Kafū's literary works fundamentally lack.[13] Although these critics oppose equating the "I" in the text with Kafū himself, many of them ultimately attempt to find or pin down Kafū's "real" or "true self" in the work, thus reading *Bokutō kidan* as an I-novel. It is precisely this temptation that *Bokutō kidan* both elicits and exploits.

Throughout *Bokutō kidan* the "I" calls the reader's attention to the problem of his "true identity." Out of "sympathy toward the people in the world who are labeled 'dark and unrighteous'" (pp. 150, *310*) and out of a professional interest in experiencing the lives of other social classes, the "I" wanders in disguise, changing his clothes, adopting the language of his interlocutor, and concealing his true identity. As an anonymous stroller, the "I" wanders freely around Tokyo, but he always attempts to avoid the police box, which is the only place where his name (written on a legal document) can be disclosed.[14] If the "I" 's proper name were revealed, he would no longer be able to freely traverse the territorial and social borders that provide material for his writing. Disclosure would be a fatal blow to his writing and identity as a writer. This fact becomes even more significant when we realize that this "writing" is concerned not only with *Shissō* but with *Bokutō kidan* itself.

Oyuki is the Muse who has accidentally called back into a dulled heart nostalgic shadows of the past. If she had not been drawn to me, or if I had not thought she was, I would without doubt have torn up the manuscript that had long been waiting on my desk. Oyuki is the strange force to make a forgotten old author finish a manuscript, in all probability his last work.   (chap. 9, pp. 170, *321–22*)

The "I" repeatedly notes that although he is thankful to Oyuki for being his muse, he cannot reveal his true identity to her. Because of the ambiguous use of the personal pronoun "I," we do not know if the "manuscript" refers to *Shissō* or *Bokutō kidan* itself. The first instance in the passage above seems to refer to *Shissō*, but the second can also refer to *Bokutō kidan*, an impression reinforced in the next chapter (the last chapter), when the narrator refers to *Bokutō kidan* as "this manuscript" (p. 180). The "I" 's relationship with Oyuki becomes not only the core of *Shissō* but also that of *Bokutō kidan*. A disclosure of the "I" 's true identity would thus implicitly cause the disintegration of *Bokutō kidan* itself.

Most critics tie the identity of the "I" either to Ōe Tadasu as the "protagonist" or to Nagai Kafū as the "author." This division corresponds to the classification of this work by critics as either an "essay-like fiction" or a "fiction-like essay," a classification based on the binary opposition between "fiction" and "truth." The identity of the "I," however, floats between the two proper names Nagai Kafū and Ōe Tadasu (a name that may be a fiction in a fiction) and ceaselessly crosses territorial boundaries, both topologically and narratologically, a movement that dramatizes and problematizes the gap and tension between the enunciating subject and the enunciated subject, as well as the hierarchical dichotomy between fiction and truth.

Art Versus Life, Fiction Versus Truth

On one level, *Bokutō kidan* seems to dramatize the interrelationship between art and life by maintaining a binary opposition between fiction and facts. The "I," working on his novel *Shissō*, tries to nourish his fiction by going to the east side of the Sumida River. Up through chapter 5, the "I" is concerned primarily with the novel *Shissō*, the story of Taneda and Sumiko. As the narrative progresses, however, this fiction is swallowed up by the story of Oyuki and the "I." In chapter 6, the "I," bewildered by Oyuki's expression of affection, tries to remind himself that he is visiting her as a novelist gathering experiential material. After citing a passage from *Shissō* (chap. 8), as if to emphasize his position as a writer of fiction, the "I" 's concern for *Shissō* fades away. By the last two chapters (9 and 10), the "I" is concerned only with the story of Oyuki and himself. The journal-like record, in which the writer of *Shissō* jots down his day-do-day experience and thoughts in relation to his fiction writing, gradually takes on the shape of a story of an affair between Oyuki and the "I." The narrative ends with the following passage.

> I must now lay down my brush, my strange tale from east of the river finished. To give it an ending in the old fictional style, I should perhaps add a chapter describing how, quite by accident, six months or a year later, I met Oyuki in a wholly unexpected place. She had changed her profession. . . .
>
> In the end, neither Oyuki nor I knew the other's name or home. We became friends in a house by a canal east of the river, amid the roar of mosquitoes. We were such that once we parted, there would be neither chance nor means to bring us together again. One might say that we played frivolously at love. Still, there was a particular warmth in knowing from the outset that we would part and not meet again. If I try to describe it, I will only exaggerate, and if on the other hand I toss it off lightly, I will know the distress of having been unworthy of the occasion. The power with which just such feelings are described at the end of Pierre Loti's *Madame Chrysanthemum* is enough to bring tears to one's eyes. If I were to attempt that particular shading of fiction for my strange tale, I would bring ridicule upon myself as an imitator of Loti who has not imitated well enough. . . .
>
> There remain a few blank lines on the back of my page of the manuscript. So let my brush go where it will, to console the night with a few lines of poetry or prose, I scarcely know which.   (pp. 178–80, *326–28*)

The entire narrative is presented here as the "tale" of Oyuki and the "I." Even as the narrator emphasizes the nonfictional authenticity of *Bokutō kidan*, he superimposes Pierre Loti's *Madame Chrysanthemum* on the text, thereby associating the "nonfictional" story of Oyuki and the "I" with lyrical, exotic fiction. Here the authentic record of the writer's life is crystallized into a work of art. Interestingly, it is *Bokutō kidan*, the record of the "I"'s wanderings, rather than his work of fiction *Shissō*, that successfully realizes the "I"'s ideal of the novel. In chapter 2 the "I" notes that when he writes a novel, he is most interested in the depiction of places—amply presented in *Bokutō kidan* but not in the lengthy excerpts from *Shissō*.

In "Sakugo zeigen," the author notes that *Bokutō kidan* emerged from his visits to Tamanoi, mentions his friendship with the late Kōjiro Sōyō, and suggests that many of "I"'s habits and tastes were based on his (Kafū's) own.[15] He does not, however, mention any relationship similar to that between Oyuki and the "I." In the postscript, *Bokutō kidan*, which has hitherto stood on the side of "real life" as opposed to the "fictional" world of *Shissō*, is referred to as a *shōsetsu* and takes on the aura of fiction, in contrast to the postscript, which claims to stand on the side of real life. "Sakugo zeigen" thus not only reintroduces the binary oppositions established in *Bokutō kidan* be-

tween life and art and between facts and fiction, but it once again transforms
life into art.

> The rain and wind that came a few days earlier cleared away the cloudy Novem-
> ber weather; the balmy weather of autumn (which Su Tung-p'o spoke of as
> "The best scene of the year—describe it!") is now with us. One could still hear
> the singing of insects like thin threads in the air, but now that, too, has com-
> pletely ceased. The sounds that ring in my ears are all different from those I
> heard until yesterday. I realize that autumn has completely passed away. The
> dreams I had on late summer nights as I slept restlessly in the lingering summer
> heat, the scenes I gazed upon during cool moonlight nights—I feel as if that all
> happened a long time ago. . . . The scenes I view every year do not change. Nor
> do the feelings I have each year when I see the same scenes. Just like the blossoms
> and the leaves that fall, my close friends have gone one after another. I know that
> I will follow them before long. I will go today under the cloudless sky, and sweep
> their graves. The fallen leaves have probably buried their gravestones as they
> have my garden.   (*Kafū zenshū*, 9: 206)[16]

The high-toned style of "Sakugo zeigen," full of Chinese loanwords and
rhetorical flourishes, initially contrasts with that of *Bokutō kidan*, which is
written in a far more colloquial style, but in the end the postscript returns to
the style and journal-like form of *Bokutō kidan*. Just as *Bokutō kidan* ends with
a comment on the deepening autumn, "Sakugo zeigen" finishes with a description of the coming winter. The boundary between the two, between
fiction and real life, once more becomes blurred, making us aware that
"Sakugo zeigen," supposedly standing on the side of the author's real life, is in
fact a highly stylized literary text, or art.

The endless transformation of life into art is further amplified by *Danchōtei nichijō*, Kafū's literary diary, which he kept from September 1917 until the
day before his death in April 1959. Although it was not until 1951 that much
of the diary was made public, it is clear that from the beginning Kafū kept a
diary not just as a private record but as a work to be read.[17] The diary for 1936
reveals that Kafū repeatedly visited the east side of Sumida River from March
through December. In an entry for September 7, Kafū described a non-
chalant prostitute whose house he "accidentally found to be a most conve-
nient resting place" during his trips to Tamanoi, which he began in March or
April for the purpose of investigating the quarter.[18] Kafū noted what he
learned about the past and the possible future of this woman and described his
favorable impressions of her and her home. He even drew a sketch of the
interior of the house. In the entry for September 21, Kafū noted that he had
started to write a novel, which he called *Bokutō kidan* on October 10 and
which he completed on October 25. The diary, which reveals that Kafū
visited Tamanoi not only while writing *Bokutō kidan* but even after he fin-

ished the manuscript, suggests both the parallels and the contrasts between "reality" (the diary) and "fiction" (*Bokutō kidan*).

Both detractors and admirers of the Kafū diary, which was maintained for over forty years without a lapse of a single day, however, regard it not only as a factual record but as a self-conscious dramatization of his life.[19] Nakamura Shin'ichirō (1918–), a contemporary novelist and critic, effectively summarizes the feelings of many readers.

> The Kafū diary was reworked later by Kafū, and most of it was edited and reworked for dramatic effect. As we turn one page after another, the deliberateness of the style gradually makes us feel as if we are reading not a record of facts but a long novel. It would not be an exaggeration to say that Nagai Kafū the author created, after many years of effort, Kafū a man of letters, a fictional, imaginary character. Probably no diary can conceal the face of the writer as skillfully and as successfully as Kafū's diary can. It is, more than anything, his refined and elegant literary style that makes this possible. For me, however, the charm of the Kafū diary extends beyond these characteristics. Recently I have become interested in penetrating the mask of the diary to find Kafū's true diary, to discover Kafū's true face. . . . Underneath the fiction—that of a man of letters relaxing and enjoying his daily life—is the desolate emptiness of Kafū's real life.[20]

If the "record of real life" appears to transform itself into a work of art with a fictional and imaginative protagonist, this same process of transformation invites the shadow or trace of yet another presence: the so-called "real" Kafū, the enunciating subject who can never be completely identified with the enunciated subject. The moment we think that we have caught the "real" Kafū, he eludes us, leaving behind a highly stylized literary figure.

No matter how closely life resembles art, or fiction imitates reality, or vice versa, there is a strong tendency, as dramatized by *Bokutō kidan* and its reception, for people to assume a firm distinction between the two, giving priority to one over the other, or regarding one as the origin of the other. When, in chapter 3 of *Bokutō kidan*, the "I" suddenly reveals his motive for writing "this text," he notes that his description of his first encounter with Oyuki may appear too fiction-like to be true, thereby giving the reader the suspicion that it is only a fabrication when in fact it did occur.[21] According to the narrator, he was interested precisely in the fact that part of his real life was indistinguishable from the worn-out conventions and clichés of traditional prose fiction. The fiction-like quality of lived experience has, he claims, motivated him to write. Interestingly, the "factual record" of the "I" 's first encounter with Oyuki is directly followed by passages from *Shissō* describing the protagonist Taneda's reunion with the young girl Sumiko. (Chapter 4 consists entirely of passages from *Shissō*.) Both have similar dialogues, characters, and relationships. It is stylistically and thematically impossible to distinguish the two descriptions, the one supposedly a faithful transcription of fiction-like real events and the other supposedly realistic fiction. The juxtaposition playfully undermines the self-prescribed genre distinctions and suggests that it is impossible to differentiate narrative fiction from a record of real life without a framing meta-narrative that provides a norm for such differentiation.

On one level, the narrator "I" seems to suggest this kind of normative differentiation by giving priority to truth/facts as the origin of fiction. In the following passage, the "I" reveals how he decided to develop his fictional narrative.

> I have not yet finished my novel *Shissō*, which I began in early summer. It had been three months since the first encounter, said Oyuki tonight, reminding me that it has been even longer since I began writing it. I left Taneda Jumpei and the girl Sumiko, with whom he shared lodgings, out walking on Shirahige Bridge, refugees from the heat of their rented room. . . .
>
> My first plans for the novel had the girl Sumiko, in her early twenties, falling easily into the deepest of relationships with Taneda, then already fifty; but as I proceeded with the writing, I came to feel there was something unnatural about the relationship. That fact, and the blistering heat, have made me stop writing.
>
> But now, as I lean against the railing and listen to the music and singing from the park downstream, and think of Oyuki in the upstairs window, and her tone and manner as she spoke of these three months—I know that there is nothing at all unnatural about the relationship between Taneda and Sumiko. There is no need whatsoever to dismiss it as a forced contrivance, a fabrication of an inept novelist. Indeed I have come to feel that the results would be unfortunate if I were to change my original plans.   (chap. 8, pp. 159–60, *316*)

The fictional relationship between Taneda and Sumiko that the "I" originally planned becomes an implausible fabrication in the "I"'s eyes. It is not that readers would necessarily find the fabricated fiction implausible. On the contrary, the "I" is aware that people often give more credence to a fabricated story than to the truth. As the "I" notes after being interrogated by a policeman (chap. 1), "I knew from experience that if I told the truth I would come under yet stronger suspicion" (pp. 103, *282*). The "I" almost discards his original plan for *Shissō* not because it is a fabricated story but because he is afraid that it may not be well enough fabricated to be plausible. The "I," in short, is concerned with the principle of *vraisemblance*, or verisimilitude, which the original plan seemed to lack. His experience that night, however, has changed his perception. Encouraged by what has just happened to himself and Oyuki, the "I" finally decides to carry out his original plan for *Shissō*. Although the end result is the same (the "I" decides to develop his fiction as originally planned), the "I" finally makes the decision based not on the principle of verisimilitude but on that of experiential truth, of what actually happened to himself and Oyuki. The "I" thus completes *Shissō* by redefining it as the imitation of truth (facts), giving hierarchical priority to the "imitated" as the origin—the very principle used to characterize the so-called Japanese I-novel.

In *Bokutō kidan*, however, this truth (as the origin of the fiction) is already permeated with fiction. When Oyuki reveals her affection for the "I" and mentions marriage, the "I," though pleased, is bewildered since he knows that Oyuki's true affection toward him is based on a fictional identity she has unknowingly fabricated. (Oyuki has come to believe that the "I" is involved in illegal publishing, the same sort of obscure profession as her own.) The "I," however, will not reveal his true identity because he does not want to hurt her by making her realize that he is not the kind of person she thinks. He is also convinced that she is more likely to misunderstand the truth, which is less plausible than fiction. The text here suggests that people tend to believe a fabrication more than actual fact, not because they do not value truth but because they tend to view and interpret reality by unconsciously creating desirable fictions, which, although often far from being true, seem to be truer than truth. Significantly, it is, of all characters, the "I" himself, who indulges most in fabricating such fictions.

When the "I" crosses the Sumida River by train to visit the Labyrinth, he reads *Twenty-four Views of the Sumida* (a literary account in *kanbun* of scenic places and historical sites) by his favorite poet Yoda Gakkai (1833–1909), an Edo/Meiji scholar of Chinese literature, in order to superimpose the literary past upon the actual locale. This same process of poeticizing reality applies as well to his relationship with Oyuki. When the "I" first encounters Oyuki, he is fascinated by her old-fashioned hairstyle and clothes, which evoke the nostalgic image of Meiji-era prostitutes.

> The figure of Oyuki, her hair always in one of the old styles, and the foulness of the canal, and the humming of the mosquitoes—all of these stir me deeply and call up visions of a past now dead some thirty or forty years. I want, if it should ever be possible, to express my thanks to the agent of these ephemeral yet marvelous visions. More than the actor in the Namboku play, more than the Shinnai singer—someone called Tsuruga—who tells of Ranchō and his tragic love, Oyuki was the skillful yet inarticulate artist with the power to summon the past.   (chap. 6, pp. 137, *303*)

For the "I," Oyuki is above all an unknowingly skillful agent or catalyst for phantasmic evocations and nostalgic visions of a lost past. The "I" suspects that Oyuki's own personal history as she has presented it to him is not entirely true. Yet, he does not care to ask her the truth. He prefers and takes pleasure in his imaginative and self-contained vision of Oyuki, who, as the real origin of his fiction, is already fiction itself. Although the "I" gives priority to truth as the origin of fiction, this truth is no more and no less than fiction.

On another level, however, the "I"'s placing of priority on truth over fiction is playfully undermined from the start. The "I"'s statements in the third and eighth chapters about his decision to continue writing about an implausible reality, of things as they actually happened, without being concerned about the principle of verisimilitude, are framed by his reference to Tamenaga Shunsui's (a late Edo-period *gesaku* fiction writer) technique of authorial intrusion into a fictional narrative in which the "author" defends the truthfulness of what is being described in the text (chap. 3, p. 119). The "I"'s statement about the truthfulness of what he describes, in other words, is presented as an imitation of an anachronistic narrative convention. Whether fiction frames reality or reality frames fiction, the hierarchical priority of truth over fiction is so playfully subverted that we do not know which is the imitation and which the imitated or which is the origin of the other.

Bokutō kidan, however, does not dissolve the hierarchical opposition between reality and fiction. Instead, it stresses this distinction even as it undercuts it. What actually excites the "I" is not the projected fictional image itself but the double vision, the juxtaposition of the fiction and the real. In reading Yoda Gakkai's *Twenty-Four Views of Sumida* while he crosses the Sumida River, the "I" enjoys not so much the vision of the evoked past itself as the interaction between the literary vision and the present raw reality. The "I," in fact, selected this area for the setting of *Shissō* because he "wanted to describe the transformation that took place to this historical site" (of villas belonging to Edo and early Meiji literati) "after the Great Kantō Earthquake," to describe the "change into a shabby new town that bears no traces of the past" (pp. 109–10). It is the gap between the literary vision of the lost past and the present site of squalid alleys that defamiliarizes and enlivens both. A similar process of double vision underlies the "I"'s visit to the Labyrinth as well as his relationship to Oyuki. The "I" is drawn to Oyuki not so much out of a blind infatuation with his fictional image of Oyuki as an embodiment of a lost past as out of an attraction to her as a powerful agent who summons ephemeral visions of the lost past in the midst of contemporary reality. The "I" appreciates both the revitalized anachronistic fiction and the defamiliarized, unpoetic, shabby real—a point that has fascinated Kafū admirers—because he confidently believes in his ability to juxtapose the two while firmly distinguishing between them. Even as he travels in disguise, adopting the same language as his interlocutor to appreciate the "essence" of the place and the people, the "I" always carries his identification papers with him. And when he comes home late at night, he takes a bath, changes his clothes, and writes about what happened to him during the day while in disguise. The multilayered "I" in *Bokutō kidan* satirically criticizes the rapid changes in contemporary Japanese social manners—especially the drastic transformations in the spoken and written languages—which resulted from the aggressive process of modernization. This critical perspective is sustained by the juxtaposition of nostalgic memories of a lost past (prior to the Great Kantō Earthquake, which erased the last traces of old Edo) with contemporary reality, which is deplored as a degradation or loss, or by the juxtaposition of "true" Western literature and culture "untampered by the Japanese" with contemporary reality, which is regarded as a cheap and imperfect imitation of "true" Western culture. As the postscript "Sakugo zeigen" notes, "When the essence of something, whatever it may be, is spoiled, I am filled with sorrow. I prefer to appreciate foreign literature as foreign literature. Even when it comes to such things as food or drink, I don't like anything that has been tampered with by the Japanese" (p. 193). Instead of fully involving himself in the degraded conditions of contemporary Japanese life, the "I" seems to entertain himself from a privileged position that gives him the knowledge of the truth and a critical distance toward reality.

This aloof distance has also frustrated and irritated many postwar readers. Etō Jun, for example, says that the "protagonist visits Oyuki not to see her but to escape from her."[22] According to Etō, this is yet another example of Kafū's egotistical refusal to become involved with reality and real human relationships. Etō's criticism, however, assumes that the "I" can, as a privileged authority, always distinguish and choose between truth (reality) and fiction. Indeed, in contrast to Oyuki and the policemen, who unknowingly create fictions about the "I"'s identity, the "I" is aware that his image of Oyuki is, like Oyuki's image of himself, fabricated. Thus, when Oyuki mentions marriage, the "I" is taken aback because he believes that these two realms—the fictional and the real—belong to different orders.

> From my youth I have been making my way into the streets of the heavily painted, and even now I have not awakened to the evils of the practice. Under the pressure of circumstances, I have more than once followed the wishes of a woman and brought her into my house and set her at broom and dustpan. Always the experiment has been a failure. When such a woman leaves behind her old surroundings and no longer thinks herself lowly, she soon becomes unmanageable, either the slovenly wife or the fiery wife. Oyuki has, as time passes, come to think of leaving her old surroundings, with my help. She is by way of becoming the slovenly wife or the fiery wife. To make her neither the one nor the other in her later years, to make her an ordinary, happy housewife,

must be the work not of me, whose experience is rich only in failure, but of
someone who still has months and years before him. If I were to say as much to
Oyuki, it is not likely that she would understand. She knows but one side of my
double nature. It would be very easy to reveal the side she has not guessed, to
show her where it is inadequate. Still, I hesitate, less for my own sake than
because I fear the terrible disappointment Oyuki must have in seeing her mistake.   (chap. 9, pp. 169, *321*)

Although the "I" states that he does not want to disappoint Oyuki by
destroying her fictional image of himself, his remarks ironically reveal his fear
that Oyuki will transgress the boundary between fiction and reality. Trans-
gression will lead not only to her disillusionment but, more crucially, to the
extinction of his own fictional image of Oyuki as muse, as his artistic inspiration, and as the origin of his "manuscript." Even more ironical and to the
point, however, is the fact that, despite the "I" 's confidence in his ability to
distinguish fiction from reality, the passage reveals that the "I" himself is now
beginning to confuse the two. Although Oyuki expresses love for the "fictional I," the "I" takes Oyuki's proposal as addressed to his "real self." The
moment that the "I" thinks that Oyuki is drawn to his "real self"—which is
the moment that gives the "I" the power to "complete the manuscript"—is
the same moment that the "I" almost takes fiction for truth and begins to
withdraw into his own territory. Throughout *Bokutō kidan*, the "I" crosses
narratological and socio-geographical boundaries, constantly suggesting and
displacing his true identity. In a passage cited earlier, the "I," after finding a
"moving picture" that was much admired after the Great Kantō Earthquake
as an adaptation of a Maupassant story, thinks that it would be "better to read
the original." But the "I" cannot resist periodically visiting Asakusa to see the
movie billboards, the emblems of a mass culture of "cheap imitation." The
"I" 's ceaseless traversal of geo-narratological borders generates a space that
calls for the "original"—the memory of what is already and always absent—
and the "imitation," both of which are given life through the constant interplay of truth and fiction. The "I" 's self-confinement in his "true identity,"
whatever it may be, thus implies the end of this particular textual movement
and the close of the narrative. Kafū's writings provocatively evoke traces of
the self without ever revealing the ultimate "true self" that those texts tan-
talizingly suggest. In this manner, Kafū's elusive writings, at once the product
and ironical critique of the preoccupation with the autonomy of the true self
as the emblem of modernity, paradoxically intensify the myth of the "true
self" even as they play with and undercut that myth. And of all of Kafū's
works, it is *Bokutō kidan* that epitomizes this literary phenomenon most
visibly.

CHAPTER 7

Allegories of Modernity: Parodic Confession in Tanizaki Jun'ichirō's 'Fool's Love'

This is a long novel [*chōhen*], but it is a kind of "I-novel" [*watakushi shōsetsu*]; and so far the plot is quite simple. The "I," the son of a rich farming family outside Utsunomiya, is a graduate of the Higher Technical School in Tokyo, and he is now working for a company as an engineer. His name is Kawai Jōji. His wife, Naomi, a former cafe waitress, was taken in by Jōji when she was fifteen years old. Jōji has cherished her; and she has been raised in luxury and "fashionable style" [*haikara*]. At this stage of the story, Jōji is thirty-two years old and Naomi is nineteen. (*Zenshū*, 23: 83)[1]

Tanizaki Jun'ichirō (1886–1965) made these comments on *Chijin no ai* (A fool's love; translated into English as *Naomi*)[2] in November 1924, when he began re-serializing the novel after a four-month hiatus.[3] Nomura Shōgo, Noguchi Takehiko, and other modern critics have interpreted Tanizaki's comments to be a "declaration of the I-novel."[4] We should remember, however, that it was not until 1924–25 that the term *watakushi shōsetsu* came to refer to "I-novel" as a recognized literary category.[5] Here Tanizaki seems to use the term simply to mean a first-person novel narrated by an "I," but the larger literary context no doubt made the term provocative.[6] Was Tanizaki poking fun at the so-called autobiographical *watakushi shōsetsu*, which was just becoming a dominant literary notion? Or was he suggesting an autobiographical reading, as some critics argue, despite the apparent difference between the protagonist and the author? Or was Tanizaki simply indifferent to the literary climate surrounding the *watakushi shōsetsu*?

I'm going to try to relate the facts of our relationship as man and wife just as they happened, as honestly and frankly as I can. It's probably a relationship without precedent. My account of it will provide me with a precious record of something I never want to forget. At the same time, I'm sure my readers also will find it instructive. (chap. 1, *Zenshū*, 10: 3, 3)[7]

The opening passage of *Chijin no ai* directly echoes Jean-Jacques Rousseau's *Confessions*, generally thought to be the first modern autobiographical work to attempt to "reveal faithfully the self in its true nature"[8] and a work that had a profound impact on the autobiographical novels of the Japanese Naturalists.[9] The first-person narrator of *Chijin no ai*, however, tells the story of his life without making the position of the real author an issue. In the literary milieu of the late Taishō period, where the novel was often assumed to be a record of the author's true self, this provocative imitation of *Les Confessions* no doubt sounded like a parody of autobiographical confessions. *Chijin no ai*, however, is neither a parody in the narrow sense nor simply an anti-I-novel.

Literary history has portrayed Tanizaki as an opponent of Japanese Naturalism and the autobiographical I-novel, a position reinforced by the famous literary debate in 1927 (February to June) between Tanizaki and Akutagawa Ryūnosuke over the "plot of the novel" (*shōsetsu no suji*). The following passage from *Jōzetsu-roku* (Record of verbosity), Tanizaki's serialized essay that sparked the debate, has often been cited as evidence of Tanizaki's position as an "anti-*watakushi shōsetsu*" writer.

> Recently I have contracted a bad habit. I find myself interested only in fabrication, whether it be my own writings or those of others. I have not the least interest in writing or reading those novels that use bare facts or even works that are realistic. I think this is one reason why I am reluctant to read contemporary works that appear in the monthly magazines. When I glance at the first five or six lines and realize that the author is depicting his private life, I immediately lose interest. (*Zenshū*, 20: 72)

In the debate, Tanizaki stressed the importance of an "interesting plot" and "architectural structure," praising Stendhal's *Charterhouse of Parma* as a model of a "richly orchestrated" novel (*Zenshū*, 20: 76). Akutagawa, by contrast, questioned the value of an "interesting plot" and emphasized the "depth of poetic spirit" as the essence of the "genuine novel" (*junsuina shōsetsu*), giving Jules Renard and Shiga Naoya as examples of authors of "genuine novels" "created by perceptive eyes and sensitive hearts."[10] Akutagawa's enthusiastic praise of Shiga Naoya's novels, which he thought reflected the author's "sensitive morality" and "pure life," suggests an affinity between Akutagawa's "poetic spirit" and Kume Masao's *shinkyō* (state of mind).[11] The debate over the "plot of the novel" can be seen as part of the larger literary controversy, which emerged around 1924–25, over the *honkaku shōsetsu* (authentic novel) and the *watakushi shōsetsu* and then later over the *tsūzoku shōsetsu* (popular novel) and the *junsui shōsetsu* (pure novel).

The impact of the I-novel on the literary scene is apparent in the fact that even Akutagawa, who was well known for his carefully constructed short stories, advocated "depth of poetic spirit" and expressed high respect for Shiga Naoya's "pure" attitude toward life. By emphasizing "plot" and "structure" and by openly showing contempt for overtly autobiographical works, Tanizaki likewise confirmed—or so it has been thought—his position as an "anti-*watakushi shōsetsu*" novelist. It is significant, however, that in *Jōzetsuroku* Tanizaki ardently praised the "autobiographical" works of George Moore: *The Confessions of a Young Man* (1888) and *Memoirs of My Dead Life* (1905, revised 1921), which Tanizaki read in English around 1921 or 1922. Tanizaki was also attracted to two recent historical novels by Moore (*Héloïse and Abélard* and *Ulick and Soracha*): "Although the plots of these two recently published historical novels are simple, and the structure and design [*kekkō haichi*] are not particularly interesting, they are lyrical and full of poetic spirit like his autobiographies" (*Zenshū*, 20: 83).

Tanizaki was overjoyed to find Moore's recent historical novels as interesting as his autobiographical works, especially after being disappointed by the "plain realism" of Moore's "non-autobiographical" novels, *A Mummer's Wife* (1885) and *Esther Waters* (1894), which reminded him of Tokuda Shūsei. In discussing the charm of Moore's two historical novels, Tanizaki paid particular attention to their lyrical elements and formal qualities, observing that the fusion of dialogue and descriptive prose (without quotation marks or indentations) and the continuous dialogue without narrational intrusions (such as "he said") created a fresh narrative style reminiscent of traditional Chinese and Japanese *monogatari* (prose fiction). Tanizaki would explore this specific stylistic interest in the fusion of dialogue and descriptive prose in subsequent years. Although *Jōzetsuroku* has often been cited as evidence of Tanizaki's position as an opponent of the autobiographical I-novel, the work reveals that Tanizaki did not necessarily focus on the question of whether a work was "autobiographical" or even on the question of whether it had "an interesting and well-constructed plot." In fact, from 1910 through the early 1920's, when the autobiographical confession became an increasingly conspicuous literary trend, Tanizaki himself wrote a number of heavily autobiographical works. Almost all of these were presented in the third person, a narrative convention established by the autobiographical novels of the Japanese Naturalists. Throughout his literary career, however, Tanizaki was fond of the form of the first-person confession. These two major interests came together for the first time in *Chijin no ai*.

The Autobiographical Novel and Dramatized Confessions

In the preface to *Itansha no kanashimi* (Sorrow of a heretic; 1917), Tanizaki stated that in this "confession" he recorded as faithfully as possible his adolescence and early family life as he perceived it (*Zenshū*, 23: 23).[12] *Shindō* (A prodigy; 1916) and *Oni no men* (Demon mask; 1916) are also autobiographical works about the author's coming-of-age. Heavily autobiographical elements also appear in works written from the end of the Meiji period through the early Taishō period: "Akuma" (A devil; 1912), "Atsumono" (Broth; 1912), "Zoku Akuma" (A devil, part II; 1913), "Suterareru made" (Until abandoned; 1914), and "Jōtarō" (Jōtarō; 1914), all of which focus on the so-called masochistic sexual perversity of the protagonist.[13] These works relied heavily on the mystifying allure of abnormal sexuality, a theme popular among Japanese intellectuals of the time.[14] Tanizaki, in fact, was one of the foremost promoters of this literary and intellectual trend, which directly derived from the fin de siècle European decadent movement.

In May 1916, Tanizaki published an essay in the journal *Chūō kōron* entitled "Chichi to narite" (Having become a father) in which he looked back on the relationship between his art and his life.

> On March 14, I became a father for the first time. Those who know me personally are extremely surprised by that fact. I myself feel as if I have encountered an unexpected fact. Although most men are naturally prepared to become a father after they marry, I was not prepared at all. . . .
>
> Why did I hate children so much? Because I was an absolute egotist. Since I ultimately cared for and loved only myself, I wished to live solely for my own pleasure.
>
> I was also afraid that a child might spoil my art. It seemed that if my egotism perished, so too would my art. . . .
>
> I gave art first priority; life came second. Initially, I attempted to unite my life and art as much as possible, or rather, I tried to subordinate my life to my art. When I wrote "Shisei" [Tattoo; 1910], "Suterareru made," and "Jōtarō," that seemed to be possible. I was also secretly leading an abnormal sexual life. Later on, when I recognized an unbridgeable gap between my life and art, I attempted to use my life for my art. I wanted to devote the greater part of my life to perfecting my art. I also wanted my marriage to contribute to a more profound art. Even today, I give priority to art over life. Recently, however, these two—art and life—have become temporarily separated. When my heart ponders art, I long for diabolic beauty, and when I look at life, I feel threatened by its humanity. . . .
>
> Although I planned to express my feelings about having become a father, I have ended up writing a confession about my feelings prior to becoming a father. I have very little experience being a father. Even today, one month after

the baby's birth, I do not find the child endearing. I presume that I will never find her endearing. Of the two evils, I find my wife slightly more endearing than my child.   (*Zenshū*, 22: 24–31)

This "confessional" essay (written and published in 1916) reflects the literary and journalistic milieu of the time. It reveals that Tanizaki was highly conscious of his own literary image or persona as a "diabolist," as an "egotistic" novelist who lived solely for the sake of art. In fact, this essay, which emphasizes Tanizaki's egotistic concern for art, appears to be yet another attempt to reinforce that self-created public image. Tanizaki suggests that in his early years he did not separate his art from his life and that he had tried to shape his life according to the ideals and demands of his art. In the latter part of this confession, however, Tanizaki also mentions a growing awareness of a gap between his art and his life, a conflict and tension enacted by the essay itself, which, despite Tanizaki's declaration of diabolic indifference toward his wife and new-born baby, humorously reveals his concern for them.

This conflict between art and life, a central concern of the autobiographical novels of the Japanese Naturalists, would constitute one of the major thematic concerns of Tanizaki's novels and plays in the following years, from the middle to the late Taishō period, particularly, "Aru otoko no hanjitsu" (A half-day of a novelist; 1917), *Itansha no kanashimi* (1917), and "Norowareta gikyoku" (A cursed play; 1919). In the meantime, what is widely known as the Odawara Incident (Odawara jiken) occurred in 1920 and 1921. Satō Haruo (1892–1964), a poet and novelist and Tanizaki's close literary friend, became involved with Tanizaki's wife, Chiyo, who had learned of Tanizaki's illicit relationship with her younger sister Seiko (later one of the models for Naomi in *Chijin no ai*). Tanizaki proposed that he and Chiyo get divorced and that she marry Satō, but at the last moment Tanizaki backed down, to the dismay of Chiyo and Satō, who, in his fury, broke off his hitherto close relationship with Tanizaki.

Immediately after the "incident," Satō Haruo expressed his longing for Chiyo in "Sanma no uta" (A song of mackerel) and in a number of poems included in *Junjō shishū* (Lyrical poems; July 1921), his first poetry collection. Tanizaki, in turn, dealt with the triangular relationship in such works as "A to B no hanashi" (A story of A and B; August 1921) and "Aisureba koso" (Because of love; December 1921). In plays such as "Eien no gūzō" (An eternal idol; March 1922) and "Kanojo no otto" (Her husband; April 1922), he depicted an artist (a sculptor and a novelist, respectively), his abused wife, her younger sister (who seduces the artist), and the artist's friend, who longs for the artist's wife. From January 1923 to December 1924 Tanizaki serialized (in *Fujin kōron*) a roman à clef entitled *Kami to hito to no aida* (Between man and god), which deals with a psychological struggle between two novelists: Soeda, the leader of the "Diabolist school," and Hozumi, modeled on Satō. *Kami to hito to no aida*, which refers to a number of Tanizaki's recent works as well as to those of Satō Haruo, focuses on the artistic pressures that shaped the triangular relationship involving these two novelists. During the same period (from January to April 1923), Tanizaki serialized (in *Tōkyō Asahi shinbun*) yet another roman à clef, *Nikukai* (A lump of flesh), a story of the protagonist's desire to create a movie using his favorite lover as the main actress. *Nikukai* was a thinly disguised depiction of Tanizaki's recent personal life, particularly his enthusiasm for creating a film using Seiko, his sister-in-law and lover.[15] Indeed, three works written during this period, *Nikukai*, *Kami to hito to no aida*, and *Chijin no ai* (March 1924–July 1925), are closely related.[16]

Satō Haruo also serialized (from June 1925 to October 1926) a long roman à clef called *Kono mittsu no mono* (These three things), in which he attempted to record the triangular relationship as faithfully as possible from his own point of view. Satō abandoned this work, however, following his reconciliation with Tanizaki in October 1926. The reconciliation then became the material of Satō's next novel, *Kozo no yuki ima izuko* (Where are the snows of yesteryear; 1927). Although Tanizaki's *Tade kuu mushi* (Some prefer nettles; 1928–29) apparently contains many fictional elements, the relationship between the protagonist Kaname, and his wife Misako (and her lover Aso), reflects this triangular relationship. In the summer of 1930, after Satō divorced his wife, Tanizaki, his wife Chiyo, and Satō Haruo mutually agreed that Tanizaki and Chiyo would divorce and Chiyo and Satō would marry. In August 1930, Satō Haruo published a memoir of this affair called "Bokura no kekkon" (Our marriage), and from November to December of 1931 Tanizaki published a long essay called "Satō Haruo ni ataete kako hansei o kataru sho" (For Satō Haruo: an account of my past life) in which he described the entire history of their relationship. In this long essay Tanizaki stated that the two novelists saw themselves, even in the midst of their struggle, as model characters for as yet unwritten literary works, works that constantly occupied their minds and influenced how they acted and thought (*Zenshū*, 20: 328–32).

Despite the close bond between Tanizaki's private life and his writings in this period, Tanizaki has never been considered an I-novelist. In this regard, Nakamura Mitsuo has quite astutely observed that both Tanizaki and the so-called I-novelists transformed their personal lives into literary personae. Nakamura also argues that Tanizaki was able to espouse and carry out the childish role of a "diabolist" and "heretic" because of the literary climate of the 1910's, which stressed the emancipation of the individual self, an ideal advocated chiefly by the Japanese Naturalists.[17] Although labeled an anti-

Naturalist or anti-I-novelist, Tanizaki shared many of the basic assumptions and objectives of the Japanese Naturalist writers: the belief in the high value of literature (particularly that of the novel), the emphasis on man's sexual desire as a key to the revelation of truth, the stress on unity of life and art, and the need for autobiographical self-portrayal. In this regard, Tanizaki and the Shirakaba group are much closer to each other than generally perceived. When the autobiographical confession and writers' accounts of their own personal life became a major literary trend from the late 1910's to early 1920's, Tanizaki was much more a part of this literary milieu than he himself was aware. Despite his public opposition to the I-novel, Tanizaki continued to write autobiographical novels, which not only drew on but shaped his personal life.

All the heavily autobiographical works written by Tanizaki from the 1910's to early 1920's—"Jōtarō," *Shindō, Itansha no kanashimi,* and *Kami to hito to no aida*—are basically presented in the third person, a convention of autobiographical novels written by the Japanese Naturalists. During this period, when the autobiographical confession was becoming a discernible literary trend, Tanizaki wrote not only heavily autobiographical works in the third person but a series of novels in the first person, which took the form of a dramatized confession but were not overtly autobiographical. Most of these dramatized confessions, which appeared from around 1918, were labeled *hanzai shōsetsu,* or "crime stories."

Tanizaki was fond of first-person narratives from the beginning of his literary career and wrote a large number of first-person fiction, beginning with "Shōnen" (Early youth; 1911), one of his first works, and extending all the way to *Fūten rōjin nikki* (The diary of a mad old man; 1961–62), written a few years before his death in 1965. In some works, the narrator records his own experience.[18] In others, he introduces himself as the "novelist Tanizaki" and narrates a story heard from another person who narrates in the first person.[19] The narrator sometimes claims to have found the story in "historical documents," which he occasionally cites.[20] If we look at the broad scope of Tanizaki's career, an obvious change can be detected between the first-person narratives written before the mid-1910's and those written after. At this time Tanizaki began seriously experimenting with the first-person dramatic monologue, paying particular attention to the performative aspect of narrating.

Prior to this period, the first-person narration seemed to play little more than a mechanical role in introducing the "story." For example, "Shōnen," which was published in *Subaru* in June 1911 and which Nagai Kafū enthusiastically praised, is told by a first-person narrator ("watakushi") who looks back over some twenty years to his childhood. After the introductory paragraph, the entire narrative is devoted to a description of a "childhood experience," which unfolds as if it were being lived for the first time. This sense of directness, however, is occasionally interrupted by the use of peculiar expressions (e.g., use of English words such as "ecstasy" and highly stylized similes) that inevitably suggests an adult consciousness. Although certain expressions evoke the distance between the "I" as the subject of enunciation and the "I" as the subject of the enunciated story, this distance or relationship never becomes problematized. The first-person recollection functions as a rhetorical space for the unfolding of an exotic sensual experience, without raising the question of the enunciating situation.

From the mid-1910's onward, however, first-person narration became an integral and necessary part of the narrative. In the confessional crime stories—"Zenka-mono" (An ex-convict; 1918), "Hakuchū kigo" (A bluster in daytime; 1918), "Yanagi-yu no jiken" (An incident at the Yanagi bathhouse; 1918), "Norowareta gikyoku" (A cursed play; 1919), and "Watakushi" (The I; 1921)—the truth of the first-person confession is placed in question by an unreliable, "abnormal," and eccentric narrator. There is a thematic parallel between these works and the third-person autobiographical narratives written during the same period: many of the narrators are masochists (such as the "I" in "Zenka mono" and Sonomura in "Hakuchū kigo") who talk about their life and loneliness as "evil men."

All these dramatized confessions draw attention to the performative aspect of narration—the motive and the effect of the confession, the ironic gap between the statement and the manner in which it is made, and the intertwined psychology of the confessor and listener. In "Watakushi," for example, a first-person narrator reminisces casually about his life "in the dormitory of the First College [Ichikō, or Daiichi Kōtō-gakkō]."

> It was years ago, at the school where I was preparing for Tokyo Imperial University.
>
>   My dormitory roommates and I used to spend a lot of time at what we called candlelight study (there was very little studying to it), and one night, long after lights-out, the four of us were doing just that, huddled around a candle talking on and on.
>
>   I recall that we were having one of our confused, heated arguments about love—a problem of great concern to us in those days. Then, by a natural course of development, the conversation turned to the subject of crime: we found ourselves talking about such things as swindling, theft, and murder. . . .

"I hear there's been a rash of stealing in the dormitory lately." This time it was Hirata who spoke. "Isn't that so?" he asked, turning to Nakamura, our other roommate.

"Yes, and they say it's one of the students."

"How do they know?" I asked.

"Well, I haven't heard all the details—"

Nakamura dropped his voice to a confidential whisper. "But it's happened so often it must be an inside job." (*Zenshū*, 7: 363)[21]

The opening sentence sounds as if it refers to the personal experience of the author, who lived, as is well known, in the dormitory of the First College before entering Tokyo Imperial University. Before long, the narrator "I" describes his uneasiness as he gradually came to be suspected of the thefts.

It sounds foolish to worry about such a thing, but during that brief silence all sorts of thoughts raced through my mind. "In this kind of situation what difference is there, really, between an innocent man and an actual criminal?" By then I felt that I was experiencing a criminal's anxiety and isolation. Until a moment ago I had been one of their friends, one of the elite of our famous school. But now, if only in my own mind, I was an outcast. It was absurd, but I suffered from my inability to confide in them. (*Zenshū*, 7: 368)[22]

The reader assumes that the narrator is attempting to convey the psychological reality of being suspected of a crime until the revelation, toward the very end, that the "I" is in fact the thief. The story of the "I"'s dormitory theft at an elite school was probably directly inspired by Edgar Allan Poe's "William Wilson," whose title character cheats his Oxford classmates at gambling without being suspected.

As Itō Sei notes, Tanizaki continued to pursue the problem of criminal psychology in subsequent works: "A to B no hanashi" (August 1921), "Aru chōsho no issetsu" (A paragraph from a police report; November 1921), and "Aru tsumi no dōki" (A motive for a certain crime; January 1922).[23] In these stories of crime and criminal psychology, written from around 1918, the influence of Edgar Allan Poe's works—"William Wilson," "The Imp of the Perverse," "The Black Cat," and "The Tell-Tale Heart"—is evident, particularly in the Doppelgänger motif and in the monologue in which the "criminal" or "madman" confesses his crime and philosophy of evil.[24] Although Tanizaki's crime stories do not have the religious and ethical tone of Poe's stories, it is significant that in a period when the autobiographical personal confession was becoming a salient literary phenomenon, Tanizaki became aware of the performative aspects of personal confession through his close encounter with Poe's works.[25]

Chijin no ai *and Western Decadence*

Chijin no ai, written during the heyday of autobiographical confessions, integrates for the first time two of Tanizaki's major but hitherto separate concerns: autobiographical portrayal, particularly of a "masochist," and the dramatized first-person confession emphasizing the performative aspects of narration (previously limited to Tanizaki's crime stories). In *Chijin no ai,* Tanizaki combines these two concerns with two major interrelated topoi— the masochistic adoration of the femme fatale and the exoticism of the West —preoccupations since the beginning of his literary career. In contrast to Tanizaki's earlier works, which did not seriously question the absolute authority of the West or the allure of masochism and abnormal sexuality, the dramatized first-person confessional form of *Chijin no ai* places both the attraction to the West and the obsession with masochism and abnormal sexuality in an ironic and critical perspective, one that also explores in allegorical form the sociohistorical and geopolitical conditions of modern Japan as well as the basic assumptions of the modern Japanese novel.

> I'm going to try to relate the facts of our relationship as man and wife just as they happened, as honestly and frankly as I can. It's probably a relationship without precedent. My account of it will provide me with a precious record of something I never want to forget. At the same time, I'm sure my readers will also find it instructive. As Japan grows increasingly cosmopolitan, Japanese and foreigners will eagerly mingle with each other; all sorts of new doctrines and philosophies will be introduced; and both men and women will adopt up-to-date Western fashions. No doubt, the times being what they are, the sort of marital relationship that we've had, unheard of until now, will begin to appear everywhere.
>
> In retrospect, I can see that we were a strange couple from the start. It was about seven years ago that I first met the woman who is now my wife, though I don't remember the exact date. At the time, she was a hostess at a place called the Cafe Diamond, near the Kaminari Gate of the Asakusa Kannon Temple. She was only in her fifteenth year and had just started working when I met her. She was a beginner—an apprentice, a budding hostess, so to speak, and not yet a full-fledged employee.
>
> Why I, a man of twenty-eight, had my eye on a child like that, I don't understand, but at first I was probably attracted by her name. Everyone called her "Nao-chan." When I asked about it one day, I learned that her real name was Naomi, written with three Chinese characters. The name excited my curiosity. A splendid name, I thought; written in Roman letters, it could be a Western name. I began to pay special attention to her. Strangely enough, once I knew that she had such a sophisticated name, she began to take on an intelligent, Western look. I started to think what a shame it would be to let her go on as a hostess in a place like that.   (chap. 1, *Zenshū,* 10: 3–4, 3–4)

Kawai Jōji, the first-person narrator and protagonist of *Chijin no ai,* begins his story in a tone that recalls the opening passage of Rousseau's *Confessions.* The first-person narrator of *Chijin no ai,* however, proceeds to tell the story of his life without making the position of the real author an issue. Unlike many of the protagonists who appear in the works after "Jōtarō" (September 1914), who declare themselves to be masochists, perverse eccentrics, or "artists of vice," Kawai Jōji describes himself as "having been an exemplary office worker: frugal, earnest, conventional to a fault, even colorless, doing the work every day without the slightest complaint or discontent" (chap. 1, p. 5). Jōji goes on to recall how his life, particularly his sexual life, was shaped by what we could call a single, magical signifier: that of the West. Jōji is initially attracted to Naomi not by her character or even by her appearance but by her name, which sounds Western to him. (Jōji visualizes her name in Roman letters, as NAOMI.) The magical signifier calls for a corresponding "substance"; once Jōji is attracted to her Western name, he notices that she indeed looks like a Westerner, in particular, the movie actress Mary Pickford. They later move into a "cheaply built Western-style house—what is now called a 'modern culture dwelling' [*bunka jūtaku*]" (chap. 2, p. 20). Jōji allows Naomi to take English, music, and dance lessons in the hope that she will acquire refined and respectable "Western manners" as well as the "physical and spiritual beauty of Western women," both of which Jōji considers to be indispensable attributes of a "modern and fashionable" (*haikara*) woman. Jōji's dream, however, materializes in an unexpected way: Naomi gradually grows into a coarse beauty completely beyond Jōji's control, an "animal-like harlot" who freely carries on liaisons with various men. Knowing Naomi's "baseness," Jōji cannot help being infatuated with her powerful, erotic charm. Eventually, following Naomi's wish to "live in a Western house on a street where Westerners live, a house with a beautiful bedroom and dining room, a cook, a houseboy. . . ." (chap. 27, pp. 298, 232), they move to a Western house in Yokohama, where Jōji is now called "George" by Naomi and her Western boyfriends.

The central motifs of *Chijin no ai*—the self-destruction/salvation of a powerless man through his masochistic worship of an unrestrained, imperious, beautiful woman; the transformation of the woman from a weak and lowly creature into a cruel and powerful femme fatale whose harlot-like character becomes the source of her charm; and the establishment of exotic space for the fulfillment of hidden desire—are recurrent motifs of fin de siècle European Decadence, which profoundly influenced Tanizaki from the beginning of his career. As is well known, Tanizaki read not only the works of Poe, Baudelaire, Oscar Wilde, and Anatole France but also such works as

Krafft-Ebing's *Psychopathia sexualis* in his college and university days.[26] Looking back at his formative years, the largely autobiographical protagonist of "Jōtarō" defines himself as a "masochist."

> To speak frankly, Jōtarō is an inborn, intense *Masochisten* [*sic*]. In other words, he is the kind of person who not only enjoys being despised by the opposite sex but who derives the greatest pleasure in feeling intense physical pain and in being treated cruelly.   (*Zenshū*, 2: 402)

> When, as a freshman in the Department of Letters, he encountered the work of Krafft-Ebing, he experienced such astonishment, joy, and excitement! . . . He discovered that many brilliant men, Rousseau, Baudelaire, and others, had possessed the same *masochistic* desire. He also learned that upon careful scrutiny, the works of Dante, Shakespeare, and Goethe also revealed the same conspicuous tendency. He came to realize that this personal tendency did not prevent him from becoming a man of letters and that he had no other alternative but to establish himself as an artist of *Masochisten*. In fact, he chose his present profession not because he had any particular ideology or philosophy but because, as a *Masochisten*, he could do nothing else. His "literature," therefore, is no more than a record of the morbid pleasure he derived from this perversity.   (Ibid., pp. 405–6)

In claiming to be a masochist, the protagonist is implicitly consecrating himself and giving himself the privilege of joining the fraternity of the great European literary artists. His self-awareness and definition of himself as a "masochistic artist" serve, despite his statement to the contrary, as an "ideology or philosophy" that shapes his sensibility and life according to a particular, empowering ideal.

The education of erotic sensibility through particular works of art and the realization of artistic ideals in one's personal life were characteristics not simply of Tanizaki's literary personae but of European romantic and Decadent literature as well, as suggested by Oscar Wilde's famous axiom "Nature imitates art" (*The Decay of Lying*). In *The Romantic Agony*, the classic study of the literary transmission of erotic sensibility in romantic and decadent literature, Mario Praz traced the genealogy of the Decadent motifs—the preoccupation with the perversities of pleasure and pain (especially masochism), the figure of the femme fatale, the bond between eroticism and exoticism, and other interrelated themes—from Gautier to Baudelaire and Flaubert to Swinburne and Walter Pater, and then to Oscar Wilde, D'Annunzio, and others. Scatology and foot fetishism—recurrent motifs throughout Tanizaki's works—were also part of this web of Decadent motifs, which clearly stimulated and influenced Tanizaki (although he may also have had some "inborn" propensities in this direction). Had Tanizaki pursued these Decadent motifs without exploring the position of the West as a specific space of exoticism in his literature, a pursuit that culminates in *Chijin no ai*, these motifs would have remained simply a set of Decadent literary and cultural clichés.

The exoticist transports himself via his imagination from his immediate circumstances to a "distant" place and time where he can freely realize his erotic desires. Mario Praz comments on this close tie between exoticism and eroticism (aroused by the Fatal Woman) in European Decadence.

> It was Merimée who localized in Spain the type of the Fatal Woman which towards the end of the century came to be placed more generally in Russia: the exotic and the erotic ideals go hand in hand, and this fact also contributes another proof of a more or less obvious truth—that is, that a love of the exotic is usually an imaginative projection of a sexual desire. This is very clear in such cases as those of Gautier and Flaubert, whose dreams carry them to an atmosphere of barbaric and Oriental antiquity, where all the most unbridled desires can be indulged and the cruelest fantasies can take concrete form.[27]

The writers (including Tanizaki) of the so-called Tanbi-ha, or Aesthetic school, which opposed the then dominant Japanese Naturalist movement, did not overlook the central position of exoticism in European Decadence. The poet Kinoshita Mokutarō (1885–1945), a promoter of the Pan no kai (1908–12), the literary society where the Tanbi-ha first came together, retrospectively described that society's orientation.

> At the core of our ideas was the principle of "l'art pour l'art," which had been elaborated by Gautier and Flaubert. Exoticism was attached to this principle at its origin. . . . For us, European literature itself was the object of exoticism. But we also discovered an exotic longing for the "culture of Nanban, the early European visitors to Japan," which made the exotic tone mellow and complex. We also loved *ukiyoe*, and the music and drama of the Edo period, not out of traditional, classical, or nationalistic interest, but because of our interest in exoticism. It was through our encounter with Goncourt, Monet, and Degas that we came to appreciate *ukiyoe*.[28]

In a number of early works written around 1910–15, Tanizaki located the exotic space in the world of Edo, which functions as a site of erotic fantasy—a fact no doubt related to the contemporary "rediscovery" of Edo culture as a result of the encounter (by the Tanbi-ha and others) with Western decadent exoticism. From early in his literary career, however, the idealized West also functions as the space or site of such erotic exoticism. In "Shōnen," for example, the femme fatale appears in two exotic settings. On the day of the Inari festival, the "I" is invited to the wealthy Shin'ichi's estate, which reminds the "I" of "a faraway mysterious world" and which is divided into two parts: a traditional Japanese-style house and a Western-style house. The Japanese-style house reminds the "I" of the "inner palace of the Chiyoda

[Edo] Castle painted by [the Edo *ukiyoe* artist] Chikanobu" (*Zenshū*, 1: 148).
The "I" here experiences "hitherto unknown pleasure" when he is bound,
beaten, and licked by the pale, effeminate, and androgynous Shin'ichi, who
becomes a cruel tyrant. When the "I" helps Shin'ichi beat and bind (half in
play) Mitsuko, Shin'ichi's half-sister (by his father's concubine), he is reminded of an illustration from a late Edo *kusa-zōshi* in which a beauty is
abused by a young *hatamoto* (high-ranking samurai) and his retainers.

Significantly, however, it is in the Western-style house, full of exotic
ornaments, that the most dramatic power reversal takes place and that the true
femme fatale emerges. On the evening of the shrine festival, Mitsuko appears
in front of the "I" like an "angel-like," "pure-white" "Western girl," who
"began to treat the three of us [Shin'ichi, the "I," and another classmate] as if
we were her slaves. After taking a bath, she made us cut her nails, clean her
nose, and drink her urine" (p. 184). The "ecstatic joy" that the "I" experiences inside the Western-style house is similar to that experienced in the
Japanese-style house, but the masochistic pleasure experienced in the Western-style house is far more intense, sensual, and dramatic. The "I" and his
playmates are ordered by this "cruel queen" to become candle holders. As the
burning candle wax flows over his face, the "I" sees an unearthly dim light,
smells the fragrance of Mitsuko's dense perfume, and hears the "mysterious
sounds of a piano" (pp. 183–84). In this mixed state of agony and sensual
ecstasy, the "I" is "burnt" by Mitsuko's "flames" and transported to "another
world."

As "Shōnen" clearly reveals, of the two exotic spaces, the West was the
more dazzling and powerful. The world of Edo, "rediscovered" through the
encounter with the Western Decadence, was not yet remote enough to be
truly exotic for Tanizaki, a native Tokyoite. The imagined West was not only
the origin (via Western Decadent literature) of erotic ideals and ideology for
Tanizaki; it became, as it most fully does in *Chijin no ai*, the very space in
which those erotic ideals were to be realized. During the Taishō period, in
the years prior to *Chijin no ai*, the worship of the West and its women was a
prominent motif in Tanizaki's writings, particularly in "Jōtarō," "Dokutan"
(A German spy; 1915), "Ningyo no nageki" (Grief of a mermaid; 1917),
"Honmoku yawa" (Evening talk at Honmoku; 1922), "Ave Maria" (1923),
and *Nikukai*. In "Jōtarō," for example, the protagonist Jōtarō has the following
thoughts:

> How I would like to go to the West! It is my misfortune that I was born in a
> country where I cannot view such sublime female bodies. What of art? What of
> literature? How can I create great art when I live in Japan, where I have only a
> tiny physique, where there are only vague colors, and where there is so little
> stimulation. (*Zenshū*, 2: 458)

In these works by Tanizaki, masochistic sensual pleasure is derived from an intense worship of the West as the origin of eroticism. The sense of inferiority toward that same West paradoxically intensified the masochistic pleasure, whose value Tanizaki never questioned.

The importation and influence of Western Decadent literature released the sensual eroticism that had been confined (from the late Edo period through the late Meiji period) to the domain of the popular illustrated books called *kusa-zōshi*, which were not considered proper or serious literature. As Noguchi Takehiko points out, the Tanbi-ha movement not only restored (hitherto suppressed) sensual eroticism to serious literature, it gave this eroticism high status.[29] The basis for this change was established by Japanese Naturalism, against which Tanizaki and the Tanbi-ha were reacting. Japanese Naturalism posited sexual desire as a hidden or suppressed force, whose disclosure in the novel could lead directly to the revelation of the truth of human nature. This focus on sexual desire as the origin of the truth of human nature was disseminated by the Naturalist movement and formed the basic premise of the modern Japanese novel.[30] Tanizaki's absolute belief in the value of literature and his unflinching exploration of eroticism were thus rooted in the literary and ideological soil first cultivated by Japanese Naturalism. For Tanizaki, the West, as the origin of erotic pleasure, was the origin not only of beauty but also of truth and power.

Modern Girl and New Woman

In contrast to many of Tanizaki's earlier protagonists, who are presented as "abnormal masochists," Kawai Jōji's background and life-style, including his attraction to "modern, fashionable" (*haikara*) trends, reflect contemporary urban life in Tokyo in the 1920's. Jōji is in fact presented as an exemplary middle-class urban "salary man" (a graduate of the Higher Technical School and an engineer) who spends his free time going to Western films and lounging in cafes (where he first meets Naomi, who reminds him of Mary Pickford). Critical of traditional arranged marriages and the constraints of conventional "family life," Jōji has a "fairly advanced and modern" (*haikara*) view of marriage and moves with Naomi into a "cheaply built Western-style house—what is now called a 'modern culture dwelling' "—in the suburbs of Tokyo.

Chijin no ai began serialization in March 1924, half a year after the Great Kantō Earthquake (September 1, 1923), which destroyed most of downtown Tokyo.[31] The massive industrialization during World War I greatly expanded the urban, educated middle class, including female professionals such as teachers, nurses, typists, and office workers. After the earthquake, the entire urban infrastructure, particularly the transportation system and housing (including the suburban *bunka jūtaku*), was radically modernized and Americanized, geared to the newly expanded middle class. From the early 1920's, a chronic economic recession (which followed the postwar depression) left this expanded middle class with little opportunity for advancement. The liberal political movement called Taishō Democracy, which sought universal suffrage, peaked in 1919 and subsequently led some toward socialism and communism. The Maintenance of Public Order Act (Chian-iji-hō), which was promulgated in 1925, immediately before the expansion of the (still limited) suffrage, almost completely deprived the middle class of any significant political power. The leisure time of this class was directed toward consumption of new cultural goods. The modern department stores, movie theaters, restaurants, cafes, and dance halls, which sprang up during the rapid rebuilding in the wake of the earthquake, were filled with fashionable youths called *mobo* (modern boys) and *moga* (modern girls).[32] Younger readers were apparently attracted to Naomi as a dynamic representative of the liberated modern girl, the woman who violates all the traditional rules and social conventions.[33]

Jōji's relationship with Naomi not only reflects the new sociocultural reality and the collective fantasy of the Japanese in the early 1920's but also parodies both contemporary sociopolitical conditions as well as the collective cultural fantasies, placing them in an amusing, ironical light. The following dialogue occurs between Jōji and Naomi.

> " . . . I'll buy anything that'll make you beautiful. I'll give you my whole salary."
> "That's all right, you don't need to. My English and music lessons are more important."
> "Oh, yes, yes. I'm going to buy you a piano soon. You'll be such a lady, you won't even be ashamed to mix with Westerners."
> I often used phrases like "mix with Westerners" and "like a Westerner." Clearly she was also pleased.   (chap. 5, pp. 42, *36*)

> Even while I was indulging her this way, I hadn't abandoned my original desire, which was to give her a good education and bring her up as a fine, respectable woman. I didn't have a clear idea of what "respectable" and "fine" meant, but I must have been thinking of something vague and simplistic like "a modern, sophisticated woman whom I wouldn't be ashamed to present in any company." Was "making Naomi a fine woman" compatible with "cherishing her like a doll"? It seems ridiculous now, but I was so befuddled by my love for her that I couldn't see such an obvious inconsistency.   (chap. 6, pp. 48, *40*)

Jōji's "original desire" to give Naomi "a good education and bring her up as a fine, respectable woman" is equated with the desire to cultivate (westernize)

Naomi both physically and spiritually so that she can become a "modern, sophisticated" companion, the "full equal of a Western woman," an idea that also pleases Naomi. This situation strongly evokes the earlier figure of the "new woman," or rather, the modern Japanese man's aspirations for a modern "new woman."

The figure of the modern "new woman" (which must be distinguished from the "modern girl" or *moga*), the enlightened and Western-educated woman who seeks spiritual freedom and independence, emerged in the 1890's together with the powerful literary ideal of *ren'ai*, the romantic "love between enlightened, modern individuals," the ideal advocated by Kitamura Tōkoku and his followers, which spread rapidly among young Japanese intellectuals. The ideal of the emancipated, individual modern woman soon produced a group of young educated women such as Hiratsuka Raichō (1886–1971), who led a feminist movement first based on the journal *Seitō* (Blue stockings, 1911–16) and then later centered on the progressive commercial magazine *Fujin kōron* (1916–). Hiratsuka and her fellow *Seitō* feminists proudly called themselves by the hitherto pejorative term "new woman," challenged such social conventions as the patriarchal marriage system, and sought the full development of the individual talent in the manner of the Shirakaba humanists. From the late 1910's, Hiratsuka expanded the hitherto elitist feminist movement to include a newly expanded population of educated middle-class housewives, seeking equal opportunity for men and women, and in 1924, they established an organization that sought female suffrage.[34] By the 1920's, under the influence of the humanistic individualism of the Shirakaba school and the feminist movement led by the Seitō group, the figure of the educated and enlightened "new woman" had lost much of its initial negative connotations. The gradual integration of the enlightened new woman into modern Japanese literature is discernible in Futabatei's *Ukigumo* (1887–89), Katai's *Futon* (1907), Sōseki's *Sanshirō* (1908), and Arishima Takeo's *Aru onna* (A certain woman; 1919).

Naomi, whom Jōji attempts to transform into a "modern," "respectable" woman, becomes a degraded version of the ideal of the modern "new woman." *Chijin no ai* parodies, if not satirizes, the contemporary sociocultural phenomenon of the modern girl and modern boy, whose "freedom" and "emancipation" are depicted as nothing more than the cheap products of the new consumer society. When Jōji offers to "buy anything that will make her beautiful," Naomi replies that "English and music lessons are more important" for her than material goods. Despite their distinction between spirituality and materiality, "spirituality," represented by the cultural capital of "English and music lessons," is hardly distinguishable from the fashionable clothes that decorate Naomi's body. Naomi is completely indifferent and unrelated to the struggle and consciousness of the modern "new woman"—as explored, for example, in the heroine Yōko in Arishima Takeo's *Aru onna*—a point underscored by the following ironic passage.

> Taking care not to awaken her, I sat by her pillow, held my breath, and stealthily gazed at her sleeping form. . . . Rough sleeper that she was, Naomi had shed her coverlet and was gripping it between her thighs. . . . A book lay open at her nose. It was the novel *Descendants of Cain* by Arishima Takeo, "the greatest writer today," in Naomi's judgment. My eyes moved back and forth between the pure white Western paper in the book and the whiteness of her breast.   (chap. 13, pp. 154–55, *120*)

Before long, Jōji realizes that Naomi is completely lacking in the intellectual and spiritual virtues that would make her comparable to a "sublime Western lady." Naomi's physical beauty, however, develops far beyond Jōji's initial expectations and comes to resemble that of a Western woman. Naomi starts to have a carefree "friendship" with fashionable male college students— known at this time as *mobo*—with whom she frequents dance halls. Through a veil of rumors and lies, Jōji discovers that Naomi has developed "free" relationships not only with these college students but with many other "boy friends" as well. By emphasizing the materiality and superficiality of modern girls and modern boys, *Chijin no ai* recalls, by contrast, the "spirituality" and "depth" of the earlier sociocultural figures of the new woman and the modern man, who sought her as his spiritual companion. The modern girl is parodied here as a degraded version of the new woman: the modern girl's materialistic and superficial culture becomes a mass-produced reproduction of the new woman's spiritual cultivation. The modernism represented by the modern girl turns out to be a phony imitation of the authentic Western modernity aspired to by the new woman.

Jōji's half-unconscious equation of his desire to educate Naomi as a "fine, respectable woman" with the "vague and simplistic idea of making her a modern, sophisticated woman" whom he "wouldn't be ashamed to present in any company," as well as with his desire to "cherish her like a doll," ironically evoke modern man's attachment to the new woman—for example, Takenaka Tokio's attachment to the female student Yoshiko, to whom Tokio teaches Western literature and the ways of the modern, independent woman. Rejoicing that he has finally found a spiritual companion indispensable for the true self-realization of a modern man, Tokio is overjoyed with his own self-image as a fully realized modern individual. Jōji's explanation of his ideal woman thus satirically exposes the narcissistic and self-complacent attitude latent in the original ideal of the new woman and in *ren'ai*, the "romantic and spiritual love" aspired to by the modern man, who hopes to be a truly modern individual. The unexpected outcome of Naomi's education, from a "tame and simple-looking" girl (whom Jōji dreams of possessing like a "precious diamond") into an uncontrollable, animal-like "whore," allegorically explodes modern man's narcissistic longing for a new woman.

Allegorical Vision

Following the paradigm of the Fatal Woman in Western Decadent literature, Naomi's transformation from a pale, little girl into a fierce animal-like woman is only to be expected. In Western Decadent literature, the irresistible sexual charm of the exotic Fatal Woman, often equated with savage "nature," transports the man beyond the confines of modern civilization to a realm where he experiences total self-realization, the fulfillment of all unconscious desire. While following the narrative grammar of the Decadent femme fatale, however, Naomi simultaneously acquires a specific geopolitical significance, which does not correspond symmetrically to that of the exotic, Oriental femme fatale in European Decadent literature. Naomi's physical charm, which is tied to that of a "true Western woman," enslaves Jōji through its association with an imagined West. The materiality of Naomi's erotic charm, in which Jōji sees no spiritual or intellectual quality, is in fact highly charged with ideological values, whose foundation is the blind belief in the authority of the West.

Chijin no ai here radicalizes and parodies the Japanese Naturalist absolutist emphasis on the "natural," the "physical sexual forces" of man. The Japanese Naturalists emphasized and demystified contemporary man's narcissistic attachment to conceptual and ideological ideals (such as the influential Western literary ideal of love), a narcissism blind to uncontrollable physical and sexual forces (called "nature"). As we saw earlier, this emphasis on natural, physical, and sexual forces, which had provided the Naturalists with a critical perspective, subsequently became an absolute principle: the Naturalists became oblivious of the ideological origins of this critical perspective and came to regard these forces as absolute facts.

Jōji's first-person confession in *Chijin no ai* is a parody and satire of the basic premises of modern Japanese literature as well as the sociohistorical and geopolitical conditions of modern Japan, but this is not a detached parody so much as a tragicomical self-parody that exposes the absurd but intense nature of the narrator's unconscious and blind infatuation with the West. In the following passage, Jōji unpretentiously discloses what this "West" means for him.

When Madame Shlemskaya presented her white hand, my heart skipped a beat and I hesitated, uncertain whether it was all right to take it.

Naomi's hands were elegant, too—graceful and sleek, with long, slender fingers. But the countess's white hand was both sturdy and lovely. . . . What set her apart from Naomi most of all was the extraordinary whiteness of her skin. Her pale lavender veins, faintly visible beneath the white surface like speckles on marble, were weirdly beautiful. I'd often complimented Naomi on her hands as I toyed with them. "What exquisite hands you have. As white as a Westerner's." But now, to my regret, I could see that there was a difference. Naomi's hands weren't a vivid white—indeed, seen after the countess's hand, her skin looked murky. . . . The first time she [Madame Shlemskaya] said, "Walk with me!," placed her arm around my back, and showed me the one-step, how desperately I tried to keep my dark face from grazing her skin! I'd have been satisfied just to gaze at her smooth, immaculate skin from a distance. It had seemed irreverent even to shake her hand. Now, drawn to her breast with only her soft, thin blouse between us, I felt as though I were doing something absolutely forbidden. . . .

What's more, her body had a certain sweet fragrance. "Her armpits stink," I heard the students in the mandolin club say later. I'm told that Westerners do have strong body odor, and no doubt it was true of the countess. She probably used perfume to hide it. But to me, the faint, sweet-sour combination of perfume and perspiration was not at all displeasing—to the contrary, I found it deeply alluring. It made me think of lands across the sea I'd never seen, of exquisite, exotic flower gardens.

"This is the fragrance exuded by the countess's white body!" I told myself, enraptured, as I inhaled the aroma greedily.   (chap. 9, pp. 83–85, 68–69)

Juxtaposed to that of a "true Western lady," a Russian dance teacher, Naomi's glossy "Western" beauty is here degraded to an imperfect imitation of a "true Westerner," whose "pure white skin" dazzles Jōji. What is beneath this "white skin"—the "substance" of the "true Westerner"—is unattainable or even irrelevant for Jōji, since it is the strong radiance of the pure white surface that enraptures and blinds him. The absolute hierarchy constructed here between the true Westerner and the fake, however, is almost immediately demystified by Jōji's multi-voiced narration. The exquisite object of Jōji's blind adoration, who evokes "unseen lands across the sea . . . exquisite, exotic flower gardens," is bluntly described by Naomi's friends with such expressions as "Her armpits stink!" Whereas the true Westerner remains an absolute ideal in Jōji's eyes, she is placed in an ironical light and reduced from a transcendental absolute to an element in Jōji's world of fantasy.

The hierarchical polarity between the true Westerner and the fake imitation has invited criticism of the position of Western modernity in this work. In 1951–52 Nakamura Mitsuo remarked: "This novel is a historical monument that embodies the modern manners of Taishō society. These modern

manners, however, have become comically outdated and have lost their
flavor—an effect that derives both from the protagonist's myopic understanding of the adored West and from the author's wholehearted and uncritical
support of the protagonist's perspective."[35] Jōji's and the other characters'
attempts at assimilating Western manners are indeed superficial, myopic, and
comical. Jōji's "West" can be reduced, in the final analysis, to the "white skin"
of a Western woman. It is literally no more than skin deep. It is also true, as
Nakamura suggests, that Tanizaki was incurably infected by Western manners
at this time. In 1921 Tanizaki moved to a Western-style house in Yokohama,
a district inhabited by many foreigners. He sported Western-style clothes,
wore shoes even inside his house, started to take English lessons, and learned
dancing from a Russian lady.[36] Indeed many of the episodes described in
Chijin no ai appear to be based on Tanizaki's personal experience.

But it is precisely this comically or, rather, tragicomically blind adoration
of the West, which derived both from Tanizaki's personal fantasy and from
the collective unconscious of contemporary Japanese, that *Chijin no ai* ironically dramatizes. At the Ginza dance hall, for example, Naomi and her
friends ridicule a Japanese girl named Kikuko (literally, "chrysanthemum
girl"), who wears a pink dress and puts on heavy Western-style makeup.

" . . . And look at the way she's dressed. I don't mind if somebody tries to look
like a Westerner, but she doesn't look like one at all. Pathetic. She's a monkey." . . .

"A monkey? That's good. She's a monkey, all right."

"You're a fine one to talk. Didn't you bring her? Really, Ma-chan, she
looks just awful and you ought to tell her so. She'll never look Western with that
face. It has 'Japan,' 'Pure Japan' written all over it."

"In other words, a pitiful effort."

"That's right, a monkey's pitiful effort. Some people look Western even
when they wear Japanese clothes, you know."

"Like you, right?"

Naomi gave her impudent nasal laugh. "That's right, I look more like a
Eurasian than she does."

. . . Kumagai squeezed into our group with the Pink Dress in tow. . . . Like a
Western doll with the head of a Kyoto doll, her clothes and her features just
didn't go together. It wouldn't have been so bad if she'd accepted the situation,
but she'd been at pains to harmonize them with all sorts of devices, only to spoil
her good looks. . . .

"Ma-chan, do you like monkeys?" Naomi asked abruptly.

"Monkeys?" Kumagai fought back a guffaw. "That's a strange question,
isn't it?"

"I have two monkeys at home, and I thought I'd give one of them to you, if
you like. Well? You do like monkeys, don't you?"

"Think of that. Do you really have monkeys?" Kikuko asked gravely.

Encouraged by her success, Naomi forged ahead, her eyes shining. "Yes, I do. Are you fond of monkeys, Miss Kikuko?"

"Oh, I like all kinds of animals—dogs, cats, and . . ."

"And monkeys?"

"Yes, monkeys, too." (chap. 10, pp. 105–21, 84–94)

Naomi's blunt criticism of the "monkey's pitiful effort" makes its point, but the ironical effect of the passage derives from Naomi's unwitting revelation of her own coarseness and superficial understanding of things Western. Kikuko is indeed unaware of her comic appearance or the others' ridicule. But the same is true of Naomi. Those who laugh at other people's superficial and comical imitation of Western manners immediately become the object of their own biting criticism. In the same scene, Jōji himself is unknowingly ridiculed by Naomi and her boyfriends, with whom Naomi has been on intimate terms—a fact known to everyone except Jōji. Although Nakamura Mitsuo's irritation with Japan's blind attempt to modernize and westernize is understandable, his harsh attack on *Chijin no ai* from the point of view of someone with a more profound knowledge of "true" Western modernity than the objects of his criticism makes him part of the chain of ridiculers and the ridiculed that *Chijin no ai* so effectively dramatizes.

Jōji's unsuccessful education of Naomi paradoxically succeeds in transforming her into a true Fatal Woman. Naomi eventually degenerates into an uncontrollable, fierce animal-like harlot, whom Jōji ejects from his house. When she returns, apparently having nowhere else to go, Jōji literally takes her for a Western woman.

"Who's there?"

"It's me." The door flew open with a bang, and a large, black shape like a bear burst into the room from the darkness outside. Whipping off a black garment and tossing it aside, an unfamiliar young Western woman stood there in a pale blue French crepe dress. The exposed arms and shoulders were as white as a fox. Around her fleshy nape, she wore a crystal necklace that glowed like a rainbow; and beneath a black velvet hat pulled low over her eyes, the tips of her nose and chin were visible, terrifying, miraculously white. The raw vermilion of her lips stood out in contrast.

"Good evening," said the Western woman. When she took off her hat, the first glimmer of recognition flashed across my mind. As I studied the face, I finally realized that it was Naomi. I know it sounds strange, but that's how much Naomi's appearance had changed. It was her face that deceived me most. Through some magic, her face was utterly changed, from the color of her skin and the expression of her eyes to the profile and features themselves. Even after she'd removed her hat, I might still have thought that this woman was some unknown Westerner if I hadn't heard her voice. Then there was the terrifying whiteness of her skin. Every bit of rich flesh protruding from the dress was as white as the flesh of an apple.   (chap. 25, pp. 263–64, *207–8*)

I was only conscious of Naomi's form lingering as a rapturous feeling of plea-sure, like a memory of beautiful music—the high, pure song of a soprano, reverberating from some sacred realm outside this world. It was no longer a question of lust or love—what my heart felt was a boundless ecstasy that had nothing to do with these. I considered again and again. The Naomi of tonight was a precious object of yearning and adoration, utterly incompatible with Naomi the filthy harlot, the whorish Naomi, given crude nicknames by so many men. Before this new Naomi, a man like me could only kneel and offer worship. If her white fingertips had touched me even slightly, I'd have shud-dered, not rejoiced.   (chap. 25, pp. 267–68, *210*)

Jōji tells us that he later learned that Naomi had put on "new" Western-style makeup. The intensity of Jōji's personal fantasy, however, does not fade away even when the object of his fantasy is recognized for what it is. In this climactic scene, the lowly becomes the sublime, the "harlot" an angel, and the fake a "true Westerner." The ultimate object of Jōji's attachment, the "terrifying whiteness" of Naomi's skin, which fills him with "boundless ecstasy," is presented not as that of a true Westerner but as a *symbol* of the true Westerner, a symbol that simultaneously marks the absence and negation of what it symbolizes. Jōji's attachment to Naomi and the West is exposed as a fetishistic project(ion) in the sense that it (mis)takes for present and real what is absent and unreal.

Freud argues that fetishism is rooted in the (male) infant's perception of the mother's lack of a penis as a menace to himself, as a sign of castration. The infant attempts to deny this absence by seeking out its presence in surrogate objects. The fetishist tragically continues to maintain the presence of this object by investing in its absence—that is, in some object that recalls, without ever being, the ineluctably absent maternal penis.[37] Foot fetishism, as is well known, is a recurrent motif in Tanizaki's works from "Shisei" (The tattoo; 1910), his debut piece, to the late masterpiece *Fūten rōjin nikki* (The diary of a mad old man; 1961–62). What is important here is not the foot fetishism per se, which belongs to the larger nexus of Western Decadent motifs, but the fundamentally fetishistic nature of the exoticism explored in Tanizaki's texts. *Chijin no ai* dramatically exposes not only the fetishistic structure of Jōji's desire but also that of Tanizaki's exoticist project in its entirety. Here, for the first time, Tanizaki engages in self-deconstruction and self-demystification.

In contrast to Tanizaki's earlier works, which tend to assume the absolute authority of the West as well as that of masochism, *Chijin no ai* turns on an ironic narration, a dramatic irony in which the reader stands at a critical distance from the protagonist's perspective and yet is never at a safe distance from the object of its biting irony. This ironic narration demystifies the absolute value of the protagonist's fetishistic attachments (Naomi and the West) without subverting the intensity of his personal and collective fantasy. In the process, the symbolic function and position of the West are revealed in a manner that undercuts its absolute authority as a transcendental source of power and truth while stressing the tragic fetishistic obsession of seeking the West in surrogate Japanese objects (the West as conceived in Japan allegorically becomes the ineluctably absent mother's penis). While following the literary paradigm of the adoration of the exotic Fatal Woman in Western Decadence, *Chijin no ai* offers an allegorical vision of contemporary Japanese society that cannot define (or stop defining) itself except in relationship to the imagined West.

Tanizaki's Speaking Subject and Creation of Tradition

From *Chijin no ai* on, Tanizaki's interest in the performative aspects of narration deepened, and his encounter with the dialect and speech of Kansai women (after his move to Kansai in 1923, following the Great Kantō Earthquake) apparently provided the Tokyo-born author with the opportunity to defamiliarize the modern spoken and written languages and to reflect further on the impact and effect of speech acts. Soon after his move, Tanizaki began to write about the speech and voice of the Osaka woman, which he praised for being warm, rich, resonant, and suggestive. In a July 1929 essay entitled "Talking About Kansai Women" ("Kansai no onna o kataru"), Tanizaki noted that the language used by men of the Osaka area was a form of *hyōjungo* (standard Japanese), but it was not the genuine Tokyo dialect, on which it was supposedly based, but a type of neutral, artificial language developed in the process of modernization by adapting Western syntax and expressions. By contrast, the speech of Osaka women, Tanizaki believed, still retained its local and historical roots (*Zenshū*, 22: 242).[1]

Tanizaki experimented with the Kansai dialect in his novel *Manji* (Swastika; 1928–30), which has both a narrator, an Osaka woman named Sonoko, and an addressee, a novelist Sonoko calls *sensei*. The presence of this novelist, who claims to be a genuine Tokyoite and reminds the reader of Tanizaki, highlights Sonoko's Osaka dialect, an exotic "tongue" that draws as much attention to itself as to her long confession. Although *Manji* is narrated almost entirely in the first person, Sonoko's speech envelops other voices, specifically rumors and stories she has heard from others. The text initially places these other voices in quotation marks, but they are gradually integrated into Sonoko's speech and often become indistinguishable from her own narration.

As the narrative unfolds, the various rumors gradually prove to be true and have an irreversible impact on Sonoko's life. Sonoko and her beautiful friend Mitsuko pretend to be lesbians (in order to deceive others), but in the process Sonoko falls in love with Mitsuko. Sonoko then creates more stories and rumors to conceal and continue this forbidden relationship. In the beginning, the difference between fact and fiction, reality and imagination, seems self-evident, but the stories gradually transform Sonoko's entire life, which becomes the product of her own stories.

Reflections on the Japanese Language

While serializing *Manji*, Tanizaki reflected on modern Japanese written languages in an essay entitled "On the Defects of the Modern Colloquial Written Style" ("Gendai kōgobun no ketten ni tsuite"), published in November 1929. Here Tanizaki sharply criticized the *genbun-itchi* style, which had become "standard Japanese," urging readers to reconsider and recover the "uniqueness" of the "original Japanese language."

> The so-called *genbun-itchi* style, the *kōgo* (colloquial written) style that has evolved into its present state since the middle of the Meiji period, has almost been perfected. But for someone like me, who makes a living writing and who deals with this style all the time on a practical level, the various defects of this style are obvious. I cannot help but be keenly aware that this style still requires vast improvement. . . . It seems to me that today's "colloquial written" style strangles the beauty and strength of our national language. (*Zenshū*, 20: 183)

Tanizaki astutely pointed to the historical and ideological origins of the *genbun-itchi* style, which had, by this time, come to appear both neutral and natural. Tanizaki examined *no de aru*, the standard sentence ending of the *genbun-itchi* style, and argued that it had not existed in the Tokyo dialect, on which standard Japanese was generally thought to be based. It was an artificial concoction, deriving from a *kanbun* (Japanese reading conventions for classical Chinese) ending, created by people from Shikoku and Kyūshū, who, after acquiring political power in the Meiji regime, used it to conceal their rural origins and to lend authority to their speech (*Zenshū*, 20: 185–86). Tanizaki stressed that the so-called neutral *genbun-itchi* style, which made simplicity and lucidity its main objectives and attempted to transcend locality and history, was in fact an artificial product of a newly established regime interested in the centralization of the nation-state.

Tanizaki argued that the formation of the *genbun-itchi* style was closely linked to the adoption of Western syntax and expressions. Those who had contributed most to this westernization and artificiality of style were novelists in the Japanese Naturalist movement, which had decisively influenced almost all subsequent writers (including Tanizaki himself), most of whom continued to move in the direction of the westernization of the written language. Tanizaki noted that in his younger days, he had always been "concerned with whether or not his sentences could easily be translated into English" (p. 204). Recognizing that the *genbun-itchi* style was firmly established and imposed severe constraints on the writer, Tanizaki urged Japanese novelists to explore the possibilities of the spoken language, which, in contrast to the artificial, westernized *genbun-itchi* style, still retained the "unique characteristics of the original Japanese language."

Tanizaki's stress on the "unique characteristics of the original Japanese language" not only prefigures his so-called conversion to Japanese tradition in the subsequent prewar years, but also reflects a larger reaction by writers of the time against the *genbun-itchi* style, which began to be widely perceived from the end of the Taishō period as a "unitary" norm and an established institution. By the early 1920's, the *genbun-itchi* written style had become institutionalized both in the literary world and in society at large, and by 1923 almost all major newspapers were written in it. In an essay cited earlier ("Bungeitekina amarini bungeitekina"), Akutagawa Ryūnosuke wrote:

> Satō Haruo has argued that since we are supposed to be writing in the colloquial style, we should write in the same manner that we speak. . . . "Writing in the same way that we speak" has become the primary objective of modern prose writers. Recent examples of this trend are the works of Mushakōji Saneatsu, Uno Kōji, and Satō Haruo. Shiga Naoya's prose is no exception. But, putting aside for now the question of how Westerners speak, it is undeniable that our "way of speaking" is less musical than that of our neighbors the Chinese. It is not that I have no desire to "write in the same manner that I speak." I do, however, hope to "speak in the same manner that I write." . . . What I am concerned with is not "speech" but "writing."[2]

In *Shin bunshō dokuhon* (New essays on written styles; 1950), Kawabata Yasunari looked back on his youth, when he, together with Yokomitsu Riichi, shared Akutagawa's concern for the "written language," which they believed could not be reduced to a simple transcription of the spoken language. Under the influence of European futurism, Dadaism, and expressionism, which flourished after World War I, Yokomitsu Riichi, the leader of the Neo-Perceptionist school, concerned himself with the renovation of the written language. He made the following remarks in 1929.

> "Writing in the same manner that one speaks" was a literary principle of the Naturalists, who usurped the power and the position of the Ken'yūsha group. This descriptive style has become the mainstream and now includes such recent

writers as Sasaki Mosaku, Murō Saisei, and Takii Kōsaku. Those writers (such as myself), who gathered around the journal *Bungei jidai* [October 1924–May 1927], by contrast, followed the principle of "writing as one writes," as opposed to "writing as one speaks."

People condemned this movement, deriding it as "the style in the last days of capitalism" or "literature of the Great Earthquake." The style of "writing as one speaks" has flooded every corner. How much further can we let it go? We must shift our effort to "writing as one writes." . . .

As long as literature is destined to use letters [*moji*], it should be "written as one writes" rather than "written as one speaks." How else can we explore the real value of letters?[3]

Despite the obvious differences between Yokomitsu's phrase "writing as one writes," which deliberately inverts Satō Haruo's famous "write as one speaks," and Tanizaki's stress on the "spoken language," both men shared a similar awareness that the literary possibilities of the *genbun-itchi* written language had been exhausted and that it had become an unhealthy norm stifling all kinds of writing.

Tanizaki stressed the notion of the spoken language, but his argument has little to do with the belief in the immediacy and directness of the voice or in the idea that speech more directly reflects one's thoughts than the written language—a notion advocated by Mushakōji Saneatsu and the ideology that underlay and promoted the *genbun-itchi* movement. Instead he was concerned with the nature of the speaking subject. The following summarizes Tanizaki's argument about the "unique merits of the Japanese language."

English sentences formally require a grammatical subject even when the subject is self-evident. In Japanese, by contrast, it was normal for sentences to forgo a grammatical subject, at least in poetry and the novel. That was true from the Heian through the Tokugawa period, before it became fashionable to imitate the West. [Tanizaki here cites the opening passage of "Shiramine," from Ueda Akinari's *Ugetsu monogatari* (1776).] This entire passage, which is one extended sentence, has not a single word to indicate the subject. The identity of the protagonist who made the long journey is left to the reader's imagination. The name Saigyō and his Buddhist name En'i do not appear until three or four pages later. And yet, if the reader has a knowledge of classical Japanese literature, he or she can guess the identity of the protagonist. Here lies the secret to this sentence's refined suggestiveness. The absence of an overt subject also allows the reader to feel as if he or she were going on the journey, viewing the scenes and places of historic interest. The reader thus closely identifies with Saigyō's circumstances. This is one of the major merits of the Japanese sentence, whether or not the author is conscious of it. (*Zenshū*, 20: 195).

I have heard that Latin sentences often do not have an explicit subject [*shukaku*], that they differentiate person by verbal conjugation. When honorifics are used in Japanese, the subject should also be left out. In fact, that is why honorifics exist. I have never seen a Japanese grammar book with a section on gender. When I was a student, we were taught that the Japanese language had no gender distinction except for literal translations of European pronouns such as "elle" (*kanojo*) or "elles" (*kanojora*). But in the past gender distinctions existed in pronouns such as *ware*, *mimoto*, and *onmae*, even if they were not used with regularity. Even today, although individual Japanese words do not have the gender distinctions found in European languages, in actual practice we can easily differentiate between male and female speech. . . . I believe that the fact that we can identify gender in conversation is a unique characteristic possessed only by the Japanese language. (*Zenshū*, 20: 197–99)

Tanizaki emphasized the indefiniteness of the grammatical subject as a merit of the Japanese language. This allows the reader to identify closely with the narrated characters and to experience an "eternal beauty" that transcends a specific personal or historical context. At the same time, the specificity of the speaking subject, created through the use of honorifics and various pronouns, can give the Japanese novelist a marked advantage over a Western novelist, who must indicate the speaker each time (as in "he said," "she answered").

These two seemingly incongruous, contradictory "characteristics of the Japanese language"—the indefiniteness and the specificity of the speaking subject—constitute the central argument of Tanizaki's *Bunshō dokuhon* (Essays on written styles; November 1934), which elaborates ideas first presented in 1929 in "On the Defects of the Modern Colloquial Written Style."

I want to emphasize this first and foremost: a grammatically perfect sentence is not necessarily a good sentence. Don't be constricted by the grammar. Indeed, the Japanese language does not have as complicated a grammar as those found in Western languages. . . . It is not that our language is devoid of the rules of tense but that no one follows them strictly. Indeed, if you are concerned with such rules, you cannot write. *Shita* [to have done] means the past, *suru* [to do] the present, and *shiyō* [will do] the future, but they are extremely flexible and their meanings change depending on the context. Even in describing one continuous action, we use *shita*, *suru*, and *shiyō* simultaneously, or in reverse order. In short, it is almost as if there were no rules. And yet we experience no inconvenience and are able to distinguish easily the present from the past, depending on the situation. (*Zenshū*, 21: 131–32)

The word "grammar" in the expression "Don't be constricted by the grammar" does not refer to a system of linguistic rules underlying the structure of the Japanese language but to what Tanizaki called "school grammar," which he believed was "uncritically adopted from Western grammar" (*Zenshū*, 20: 194) and which made clear distinctions in both tense and person. Tanizaki argued that even though the Japanese language lacks strict rules for tense, one can easily understand the temporal state from the context.

What, then, is the merit of vagueness and ambiguity in tense and in grammatical subject? Tanizaki made a revealing assertion toward the end of *Bunshō dokuhon* that "the unique merits of the Japanese language can also be observed in the Chinese language" (*Zenshū*, 21: 239) and gave the example of a Li Po poem.

> The eternal life of this poem, its ability to move the hearts of readers of all periods, cannot be attributed to any single cause, but two elements contribute greatly: the fact that the grammatical subject is left out and that there is no definite indication of tense. If it were a Western poem, . . . the poem would be reduced to what a particular person viewed or felt on a particular night. Such a poem would never possess the appeal of Li Po's poem.   (*Zenshū*, 21: 239–40)

Tanizaki praised the indefiniteness of "tense" (time) and of "grammatical subject" (person) for imparting "eternal life" to the literary work and for enabling it to transcend the historical and personal context of the particular subject. He then cited the opening passage of Ueda Akinari's "Shiramine," which "allows the reader to feel as if the reader were wandering around the country with Saigyō" (*Zenshū*, 21: 240). Paradoxically, Tanizaki's aspiration of transcending the confines of an individual subject presupposes a strong consciousness of the individual subject, which Tanizaki (earlier in this essay) regarded as a negative characteristic of Western languages. For the indefiniteness of tense and subject to become a merit, one must have, as Tanizaki obviously did, a strong awareness of the individualized subject as well as of what Tanizaki regarded as Western grammar.

Tanizaki did not regard these two apparently contradictory characteristics of "original Japanese"—the indefiniteness and specificity of the speaking subject—as points of conflict but as "merits" that complement each other. His particular interest in honorifics and the specificity of the speaking subject reveals his awareness that enunciation takes place not in an abstract space but in a particular speaker-listener relationship, even when the listener is only implied. As noted earlier, Tanizaki criticized the standardized *genbun-itchi* language for pretending to be neutral and for attempting to erase the historical, social, personal, or interpersonal context of the speaker/writer. In fact, the deliberate use in *Bunshō dokuhon* of the *de arimasu* sentence ending, a lecture style that shows respect for the listener, implies that Tanizaki is speaking in a specific context and to a specific audience: to contemporary educated general readers and not just to novelists and literary critics.

Constructing Japanese Tradition

The dialectical relationship between these two seemingly contradictory aspects of "original Japanese" indeed lies at the heart of the narrative fiction that Tanizaki wrote between the publication of "On the Defects of the Modern Colloquial Written Style" and *Bunshō dokuhon*. *Manji, Yoshino kuzu* (Arrowroot in Yoshino; 1931), *Mōmoku monogatari* (A blind man's tale; 1931), *Ashikari* (Reed cutter; 1932), and *Shunkin shō* (A portrait of Shunkin; 1933) are all layered narratives that explore and depend heavily on both the indefiniteness and the specificity of the speaking subject. *Manji* is the only work narrated in the Osaka dialect, but the others have distinctive spoken voices or, more precisely, layers of both distinctive and indistinguishable voices. These voices are generated by a new experimental written style that not only reflects the speaking voice but employs devices found exclusively in written languages, specifically, the visual effects derived from manipulating the use of *kanji*, the *kana* syllabary, punctuation, and sentence divisions (or absence thereof).

Tanizaki's rediscovery and exploration of the "unique merits" of "original Japanese" were closely related to the transformation of the object of his exoticist quest from a radiant modern Western woman to the dim, suggestive, "traditional Japanese" woman. This geo-cultural conversion to Japanese tradition, which developed through the symbolic reconceptualization of Kansai (represented by Kansai women) into an exotic place that simultaneously evoked his lost home (downtown Tokyo before the earthquake and modernization), is foreshadowed and probed in the highly autobiographical novel *Tade kuu mushi* (Some prefer nettles; 1929) and then later dramatized in the new experimental written languages that Tanizaki claimed resuscitated the "unique merits" of the original Japanese language.

In *Yoshino kuzu* the narrator/writer "I" relates a story told by his friend Tsumura concerning Tsumura's yearning for his dead mother, a story interwoven with legends and classical tales about the historical site of Yoshino, a noted "poetic place" (*utamakura*). Tsumura's longing is reinforced and shaped by layers of legends, songs, and classical plays (*kabuki*, puppet theater, Noh drama) familiar since childhood. In his search for his mother's original birthplace, Tsumura discovers the image of his lost mother in a young girl who is a distant relative of his mother and who becomes Tsumura's wife. The narrator, who relates Tsumura's personal story, remembers a distant past when he too was taken to Yoshino by his young mother. In the process, Tsumura's story of yearning for a lost mother merges with the narrator's own.

This erotic yearning for an eternal female figure who merges with one's lost mother is most fully explored in the first-person narrational layers of *Ashikari*. In a casual essay-like style, the narrator ("I") describes an evening visit to Minase, the site of the former palace of the thirteenth-century Emperor Gotoba, an accomplished poet who spent his last years in exile. As the

"I" recalls the ancient glory of Gotoba's palace and the legendary courtesans who once lived on the nearby waters, a man suddenly appears in the reeds like a shadow of the "I" and relates to him a story of his father's yearning for a sublime lady named Oyū-san, a story that the man claims was narrated to him by his now-deceased father.

The man's father, Serihashi, became enamored of the beautiful Oyū-san, but since she, as a widow of a wealthy merchant, was obliged to stay with her husband's family and raise the family heir, Serihashi married Oyū-san's younger sister Oshizu (at Oyū-san's request) in the hope of seeing Oyū-san often. Aware of Oyū-san's warm feelings toward Serihashi, Oshizu proposes to Serihashi on the eve of their wedding that their marriage be a mere formality and that he make Oyū-san happy. The three of them spend time together, with both Serihashi and Oshizu serving Oyū-san as if she were their mistress. In the meantime, Oyū-san's son dies from illness, Oyū-san leaves the family, and (at the suggestion of Serihashi, who does not have the wealth necessary to support Oyū-san in proper style) remarries a rich merchant, who promises to treat her like a princess. After Oyū-san leaves, Serihashi and Oshizu consummate their conjugal relationship for the first time. According to the man in the reeds, he is the son of Serihashi and Oshizu. Every year on the night of the harvest moon, the man visits the nearby villa where Oyū-san plays the koto and her maidservants dance under the full moon. Finding the man's statement odd, the narrator ("I") asks if Oyū-san is not by now an elderly woman, close to eighty years of age. The man does not reply and vanishes, as if melting into the moonlight.

Ashikari's long sentences interweave the speech of the narrator ("I") and the man in the reeds without using quotation or other punctuation marks. As the man relates the story of his father's longing for Oyū-san, his voice occasionally blends with that of the father. Consequently, the father's desire merges with the son's yearning for his "mother." Just as Oyū-san is the ideal woman for Serihashi, while Oshizu functions as his formal wife, Oyū-san is the idealized mother for the son even if his physical mother might be Oshizu. The man's long monologue clouds the subtle gap between the father's and the son's longing. In a stimulating critical essay, the modern novelist Hata Kōhei argues that it is a mistake to see the man in the reeds as Oshizu's son, that he is in fact Oyū-san's son. Hata argues that unless the man in the reeds is the son of Serihashi and Oyū-san, both Serihashi's desire to transmit his yearning for Oyū-san to his son and the son's motive for telling the story would be unnatural.[4] Hata, who seems to assume that the man has to be either Oshizu's son or Oyū-san's son, is preoccupied with the question of authentic origin and true identity, which the text of *Ashikari* invites but ultimately evades.

Before long, Oshizu entered my father's house as a bride. Yes, Oshizu should therefore be my mother and Oyū-san my aunt. But the situation is not that simple. (*Zenshū*, 13: 472)

I understand. But, then, if the relationship between Oyū-san and your father was as you have described, whose son are you really? (*Zenshū*, 13: 486–87)

While raising the question of the man's identity, the text of *Ashikari* leaves the answer ambiguous. It is no accident that the man in the reeds appears and vanishes in a manner reminiscent of a two-part Noh dream play (*fukushiki mugen nō*) in which the spirit of a dead person appears before a wandering priest and relates a story of regret or attachment. Given the Noh framework, it is impossible to tell whether the man is the son of Serihashi or the spirit of the dead Serihashi, or the product of the narrator's imagination. The indeterminacy of the speaking subject does not, however, completely dissolve the subtle differences among the three first-person narrators: the "I," the man who claims to be Serihashi's son, and Serihashi. Indeed, it is through this layered narration that Oyū-san becomes a luminous and hazy figure, who is simultaneously a graceful lady, a cruel child, a warm mother, an erotic woman, and a distant goddess. This all-encompassing figure, who represents both lost origins and the unattainable, is fully appreciated only when one recognizes the subtle differentiation among the male speakers.

Significantly, Tanizaki's statements in *Bunshō dokuhon* on the voice of the speaker/writer reveal a peculiar ambiguity about the subject of the narrational voice. According to Tanizaki, the "merits" of the "conversational style" (*kaiwa-tai*), which he considers to be the "true colloquial written style" (*shin no kōgo-tai*), are flexibility in expression, variety in sentence endings, the ability to make the reader feel the enunciator's voice and emotions, and the power to make the reader perceive the writer's gender (*Zenshū*, 21: 193). Pointing out that the conversational style is now used only "in letters exchanged between female students," Tanizaki urges all writers, particularly novelists, to be aware of its merits. The enunciator and writer are self-evident in the case of a personal letter. But what about a fictional narrative, in which a single writer/author creates various voices? In discussing the merits of honorifics in subsequent sections of *Bunshō dokuhon*, Tanizaki revealed that he had in mind the writers and authors of the fictional text in mentioning the "voice of a speaker" or the "voice of a writer."

I suggest that women write in a style appropriate for women when it comes to practical writing and essays, or even academic articles and creative writing, not to mention personal letters and diaries. Although *The Tale of Genji* is a type of realistic novel, the author uses honorifics even in the descriptive prose [*ji no bun*] to describe the upper ranks. The author does not necessarily remain objectively detached, but this does not reduce the aesthetic quality of the work. On the contrary, it creates a graceful atmosphere, like that of a lady. And we should not forget that *The Tale of Genji* is written in the "same style as spoken at the time." (*Zenshū*, 21: 237)

Although Tanizaki's discussion seems to be limited to the question of the writer's gender, the passage raises the larger question of the writer's subjectivity in his or her written language (*écriture*). Criticizing the standard *genbunitchi* style for concealing its ideological origins and for pretending to be neutral, Tanizaki urged writers to articulate themselves within the historical, social, and personal context that conditions both the world and social views of the subject.

Tanizaki's discussion of Murasaki Shikibu's voice reveals that he did not clearly distinguish the narrator and the author of the text, the rhetorical and the referential functions of language, or fiction and reality. Although seeming to reconsider and reconceptualize the specific sociohistorical contexts that condition and constitute the "speaking subject," Tanizaki's statements in *Bunshō dokuhon* ultimately reinforce the I-novel reading mode that reduces the text to the author's personal voice and identity.

But while Tanizaki's critical statement about the subjectivity of the writer appears to invite or encourage the I-novel reading mode, in practice Tanizaki continued to explore the problem of the enunciating act, an act that could not be reduced to the author's personal voice. In later works such as *Kagi* (The key; 1956), *Yume no ukihashi* (The floating bridge of dreams; 1959), and *Fūten rōjin nikki* (The diary of a mad old man; 1961–62), Tanizaki dramatized the act of writing (as opposed to speaking). At the same time, however, Tanizaki continued to be concerned with the story of his own life and with the identity of his self. In the same period that he wrote *Ashikari*, Tanizaki published a long autobiographical essay on his youth, *Seishun monogatari* (A tale of my adolescence; September 1932–March 1933); and then from 1955 to 1956, he serialized a longer autobiographical essay on his childhood entitled *Yōshō jidai* (My childhood days) in which he wrote extensively about his hometown of Nihonbashi (in downtown Tokyo), destroyed by the Great Kantō Earthquake and by World War II, and about the memory of his now-deceased mother. In his later years Tanizaki attempted to "record" the story of his real life, particularly its origins. Tanizaki's remark in *My Childhood Days* about the "extraordinarily fine and pure white skin of my mother's thigh" (*Zenshū*, 17: 52) has been interpreted by many scholars as the origin of Tanizaki's lifelong theme of longing for an eternal woman. As we have seen, however, Tanizaki's works, like those of many so-called I-novelists such as

Tayama Katai and Shiga Naoya, subvert the commonly held hierarchical divisions between reality and fiction and between origin and result, as well as the myth of the authorial self that precedes and controls the work of art.

Japanese novelists since the mid-Meiji period have been concerned with the critical distinctions of author, narrator, and character in narrative fiction. Yet, ultimately, they have not adhered to the Western hierarchical grading of narrative levels, or *niveaux narratifs* (to use Genette's term), in which the narrative level is graded between two poles, that of reality and that of fiction, according to its closeness or remoteness to the real world. Modern Western narratology as developed by Wayne Booth and French structuralists such as Tzvetan Todorov and Gérard Genette emerged in reaction to the persistent myth of the individual subject (author) as the source and origin of meaning. However, the analytical model that they developed—such as the distinctions among narrative levels or among the levels of person—remains deeply rooted in the psychology and metaphysics of the individual "subject," or self, and of discourse that is thought to be controlled by that self.

Modern Western narratology provides a useful tool for clarifying the textual characteristics of, particularly the multiple voices working in, modern Japanese narrative works hitherto analyzed and interpreted according to an I-novel reading mode that reduced textual differences to the single identity of the author's self. But to use the analytical models of Western narratology blindly or exclusively is also to fall into a similar trap of restricting the text to the ideology of the "subject" as the origin of meaning, which many modern Japanese novels sought out as the prototype of Western modernity as well as demystified and subverted as an unattainable mirage. Once we begin to question the distinction between the reality presented by Tanizaki's autobiographical essays and the fiction developed by his novels, both of which are in fact narrative texts, we can never know if this origin (the memory of the mother's pure white thigh) determined Tanizaki's literary activity or whether his literary activity needed, called for, and created this origin.

The two exoticist quests that we have examined in Tanizaki—the search for the unattainable, true West in a surrogate Japan and the rediscovery or recreation of one's lost origins and identity—seem to epitomize, in a metaphorical way, two complementary forces that have sustained what I have called "I-novel discourse": the untiring search for a "true modern self" and the increasing concern for the origin and identity of the "Japanese self." We have examined the historical formation of this discourse by closely rereading selected texts not in order to show that earlier readings were misreadings but in order to trace the creation of this I-novel discourse and to reveal how this discourse narrated stories of the search for the self in which the writer's self and the collective Japanese self became the twin protagonists. I have also shown how this I-novel discourse generated, in the words of Paul Ricoeur, various "productive references"—that is, how it created new realities and perceptions of the world—which, under the influence of I-novel discourse itself, came to be taken as "reproductive references," which in turn assumed the pre-existence of the described or represented realities.

Since the 1980's, various literary texts as well as historiographical narratives have been re-examined with a postmodern skepticism toward the notion of the subject as an autonomous, controlling consciousness, and with the shared recognition that the subject is culturally and historically constructed within specific discursive positions, including differences such as race, gender, and class. Critics and scholars have also begun to reread and re-evaluate modern Japanese literary texts, including the so-called I-novels, in this light. In re-evaluating those texts labeled I-novels, some scholars have rejected traditional (Western) humanist views of subjectivity, including the view that such subjectivity was underdeveloped or lacking in Japanese literature, and have attempted to pay more attention to the historical and cultural discourses shaping both the production and reception of those texts. This re-evaluation is both welcome and necessary, but the critical appeal to cultural "tradition"— the "indigenous" linguistic, aesthetic, epistemological, and social tradition— as the final frame of reference for evaluating and reading these modern texts is as problematic as the appeal to the humanist assumption about the subject, since these so-called traditions or literary and cultural origins are themselves often the product of modern I-novel discourse. Tanizaki's construction and reinvention of the "original Japanese language" as well as the retroactive construction of the historical origins and continuity of the I-novel tradition are emblematic of this process. The uncritical appeal to cultural tradition unknowingly reproduces and reinforces what I have described as I-novel discourse. To borrow the words of Ricoeur once more, "Culture creates itself by telling stories of its own pasts,"[5] which, in this instance, are generated through a complex relationship to an imagined modern Western self.

Reference Matter

Notes

Unless otherwise noted, all translations are mine. All Japanese names are given in Japanese order, with surname first. For complete author names, titles, and publication data for the works cited here in short form, see the Bibliography, pp. 221–34.

Introduction

EPIGRAPHS: Kume, "Watakushi shōsetsu," p. 111; Takeuchi, p. 69.

1. *Watakushi*, a first-person pronoun used mainly on formal and public occasions, by both men and women, can also signify that which concerns individual matters (as opposed to public matters), personal and often partial feelings, as well as private or secret matters. The Sino-Japanese reading *shi* is not used as a first-person pronoun but as a modifier, to signify the other three meanings of *watakushi*. See *Nihon kokugo daijiten*, ed. Nihon daijiten kankōkai (Shōgakukan, 1976), s.v. When the term "I-novel" first emerged in the 1920's, the compound was read mainly as *watakushi shōsetsu*, but *shi-shōsetsu* became a more common reading (presumably because of its brevity) as the term acquired wide public recognition. Kobayashi Hideo's famous "Essay on the I-novel," written in 1935, is referred to both as "Watakushi shōsetsu ron" and as "Shi-shōsetsu ron" (*Kobayashi Hideo zenshū*, 3: 119–45), but after World War II most people came to favor the reading *shi-shōsetsu*. The two readings are still interchangeable, however, and there are no established semantic distinctions between the two.

2. Keene, *Dawn to the West*, p. 221.

3. Tamiya, p. 60.

4. The Heian poetic diaries by court women—*Kagerō nikki* (Gossamer years), *Diary of Murasaki Shikibu*, *Sarashina Diary*, etc.—started to be read as a faithful record of the author's personal experience after the rise of the Japanese Naturalist movement. Hitherto these women writers had been recognized primarily as *waka* poets whose fame derived from their position in the imperial *waka* anthologies. The status of their works as "literature" was particularly elevated after 1923 when modern literary histo-

rians began to call these poetic diaries *jishō bungaku* (literature of self-reflection) and *nikki bungaku* (diary literature). See Hisamatsu.

5. Fowler, p. 12.

6. Maruyama, pp. 251–55; Fowler, pp. 11–12.

7. I examine I-novel criticism by Kobayashi Hideo and Nakamura Mitsuo at length in Chapter 3.

8. For the most provocative rereading of the I-novels, see Hasumi, *"Shi-shōsetsu" o yomu*, which reads, for example, Shiga Naoya's *An'ya kōro* solely in terms of the semiotic dynamics of numbers (the interplay of one and two).

9. Lejeune, *Le pacte autobiographique*, pp. 13–46. The first chapter of this book, "Le pacte autobiographique," is translated into English as "The Autobiographical Contract" in Todorov, *French Literary Theory Today*, pp. 192–222. Lejeune uses this criterion to define autobiography and other genres of *littérature intime* (diary, self-portrait, personal essay). Lejeune's full definition of the genre of autobiography is "a retrospective prose narrative produced by a real person concerning his own existence, focusing on his individual life, in particular on the development of his personality" ("The Autobiographical Contract," p. 193).

10. Lejeune, "The Autobiographical Contract," pp. 210–11.

11. For a revealing study of Kasai Zenzō's works, see Fowler, pp. 248–89.

12. Hijiya-Kirschnereit, *Shi-shōsetsu*, pp. 455–62.

13. Ibid., p. 256; Masaoka, pp. 361–69.

14. Genette, "Frontières du récit"; "Discours du récit," in his *Figure\ III*, trans. as *Narrative Discourse*.

15. Benveniste, *Problèmes de linguistique générale*; trans. as *Problems in General Linguistics*.

16. Michel Foucault, *L'archéologie du savoir*; trans. as *The Archaeology of Knowledge*.

Chapter 1

1. Terada, "Shinkyō shōsetsu, watakushi shōsetsu" (1950), in his *Bungaku*, pp. 145–46. See also Terada, "Shi-shōsetsu oyobi shi-shōsetsu ron" (1954; in ibid., pp. 106–7).

2. Kume, "Watakushi shōsetsu," p. 109.

3. When Terada further develped his argument in his 1954 article, he discussed "various forms of the writer's *watakushi*" in the modern Japanese *shōsetsu* and revealed his deep interest in the problem of *watakushi*, which Terada also called *jiga* (self, ego) and which he characterized as being "incredibly flexible, protean, divisible, and yet constant and traceable" ("Shi-shōsetsu oyobi shi-shōsetsu ron," p. 113).

4. DeWoskin, p. 45.

5. See Nakamura Yukihiko, "Kogidō no shōsetsukatachi," in his *Kinsei sakka kenkyū*, pp. 131–51.

6. See Nakamura Yukihiko, "Yomihon no dokusha," in his *Kinsei shōsetsu shi no kenkyū*, pp. 314–33.

7. Writers and readers of the *shōsetsu* from the mid-eighteenth century, including Ueda Akinari and Takizawa Bakin, were heavily influenced by Ming-Ch'ing critics

such as Chin Sheng-t'an and Mao Tsung-kang (see Nakamura Yukihiko, *Kinsei bungei shichō kō*, pp. 252–82, 283–305, 330–75).

8. Kyokutei (Takizawa) Bakin, "Author's Preface to the Third Sequel," in his *Chinsetsu yumiharizuki: ge*, p. 129.

9. Shikitei Sanba, "Author's Preface to Part II," in his *Ukiyo buro*, p. 111.

10. Fowler, for example, asserts that in Japan "the notion of what is 'real' or 'authentic' is traditionally limited to personal observation and experience, with the result that fiction, insofar as it deviates from what 'actually happens,' connotes a 'fabrication' inapplicable to reality rather than a plausible, equally valid version of it" (p. 7).

11. Despite the firm conceptual distinction between *seishi* and *haishi*, the actual production of both forms of narratives was interrelated. The "official histories" that Bakin drew on included not only Chinese official histories but various Japanese war chronicles (such as *Genpei seisui ki* and *Taiheiki*), which, though filled with apparently fictional elements, were thought to record the canonical truth of Confucian teachings in the same way that the Chinese official histories did. See Nakamura Yukihiko, "Takizawa Bakin no shōsetsu kan," in his *Kinsei bungei shichō kō*, pp. 330–75. See also Plaks, p. 312.

12. From an article entitled "A Means of Disseminating the Seed of Freedom in Our Country Lies in Reforming Our *Haishi* and Drama," *Nihon rikken seitō shinbun* (June 9 and June 29, 1883); reprinted in *Kindai bungaku hyōron taikei*, 1: 15–19.

13. Yanagida, *Seiji shōsetsu kenkyū: jō*, pp.10–60, 97–233.

14. Yano, p. 4.

15. Ibid., pp. 3–4.

16. Ryūkei cited (at the end of his "Author's Preface") books on ancient Greek history written in English between the 1820's and the 1870's. The authors include George Grote, John Gillies, Connop Thirlwall, and George Cox (Yano, pp. 5–6).

17. Tōkai, pp. 3–110.

18. Tsubouchi Shōyō, *Shōsetsu shinzui*, p. 48.

19. Ibid., p. 96.

20. See the classification of contemporary fiction writers in Kyokutei (Takizawa) Bakin, *Kinsei mono no hon*.

21. Shōyō expanded the category of the *shōsetsu* by using the term in three different capacities: (1) to refer to late Edo *yomihon* (the traditional notion of the *shōsetsu*) by occasionally writing the word *yomihon* in small *kana* letters alongside the Chinese graphs for *shōsetsu* and *haishi*—a stylistic practice characteristic of *yomihon*, in which words that originated in China and were written in Chinese characters were accompanied by more familiar colloquial Japanese readings in small *kana* letters; (2) to refer to the Western novel by occasionally placing the *kana* transcription *noberu* (novel) alongside the Chinese characters for *shōsetsu*; and (3) to refer to all previous Japanese prose fiction. In *Shōsetsu shinzui*, these different usages of *shōsetsu* eventually give way to the word *shōsetsu* as a general term.

22. Tsubouchi, *Shōsetsu shinzui*, pp. 69–73. The importance of the depiction of "human feelings" (*ninjō*) in the novel had earlier been stated in Oda Jun'ichirō's short postface to *Karyū shunwa* (The spring tale of flowers and willows, 1878), a free

Japanese adaptation in *yomihon* style of Bulwer-Lytton's *Ernest Maltravers* (1837) and its sequel *Alice* (1838); see Oda Jun'ichirō, p. 109. Oda also emphasized that the "human feelings" depicted in Lytton's *shōsetsu* are "deep and touching" because "his books are basically grounded on historical facts" (ibid.).

23. Terry Eagleton (pp. 223–25) argues that the literary-critical discourse of the Victorian period (represented by Matthew Arnold) also constructed the notion of "English literature," which provided an ideological function, a unifying social "cement," in an age when religion had ceased to provide the affective values and basic mythologies by which a socially turbulent class-society could be welded together. The following passage from Arnold's "The Study of Poetry" (1880) reveals his basic stance. "More and more mankind will discover that we have to turn to poetry to interpret life for us, to console us, to sustain us. Without poetry, our science will appear incomplete; and most of what now passes with us for religion and philosophy will be replaced by poetry" (*The Norton Anthology of English Literature*, 3d ed. [New York: Norton, 1974], 2: 1425).

24. Tsubouchi, *Shōsetsu shinzui*, pp. 48, 75. This same phrase appears both in the first chapter "General Introduction" ("Sōron") and in the third chapter "The Principles of the Novel" ("Shōsetsu no shugan"). Shōyō revealed in the latter that he adapted this phrase from John Morley's essay on George Eliot. Although this particular essay has not been identified, Shōyō later wrote in a letter that he had started to read such English magazines as *The Fortnightly Review* (1865–), *The Nineteenth Century* (1877–), and *The Contemporary Review* (1866–), which included articles by such writers as Herbert Spencer, Charles Allen, T. H. Huxley, Thomas Carlyle, Matthew Arnold, and John Ruskin. John Morley was the editor of *The Fortnightly Review*. Articles on George Eliot appeared in these magazines following her death in 1880. For the sources of *Shōsetsu shinzui*, see Seki Ryōichi, "*Shōsetsu shinzui* kō," and "*Shōsetsu shinzui* to senkō bunken," in his *Shōyō, Ōgai*; Kawazoe Kunimoto, "Bungaku kakushin ki to Eikoku no hyōron zasshi"; and Ojima Kenji, "*Shōsetsu shinzui* to Bain no shūji-sho." In *Shōsetsu shinzui*, Shōyō also cited the eighteenth-century *kokugaku* scholar Motoori Norinaga's discussion of *mono no aware* (pathos of things)— in which Norinaga praises *The Tale of Genji* for "revealing various aspects of human feelings" (Tsubouchi, *Shōsetsu shinzui*, pp. 76–78)—to support his notion of the mimetic depiction of *ninjō*. For a convincing argument that Shōyō's advocacy of the "mimetic depiction of *ninjō* as criticism of life" was stimulated more directly by Alexander Bain's and Morley's (Arnold's) discussions, which reminded him of their affinity to Norinaga's discussion of *mono no aware*, see Seki, *Shōyō, Ōgai*, pp. 194–97.

25. Tsubouchi, *Shōsetsu shinzui*, pp. 69–73.

26. Shōyō defined *ninjō* as *jōyoku*, to which he added the *kana* reading *passhon* (passion). *Jōyoku* was used at the time as the standard translation for "passion," a term in the newly introduced field of psychology that denoted "durative, intense emotion such as love, affection, hatred, jealousy, and ambition" (see Ochi Haruo, "*Shōsetsu shinzui* no botai").

27. Shōyō also explained *ninjō* as *hyaku-hachi bonnō* (108 earthly desires), the various desires that must be overcome in order to achieve Buddhist salvation. The word *hyaku-hachi bonnō* reactivates the morally negative connotation of *jōyoku*, which was originally a Buddhist word meaning "carnal desires" before it became a translation for

a neutral term of psychology. The morally negative connotation of the word *jōyoku* is further evoked in Shōyō's *retsujō* (vulgar, obscene desires) and in his contrasting of *jōyoku* and *retsujō* with *dōriryoku* (reason, morality) (see Tsubouchi, *Shōsetsu shinzui*, p. 69).

28. Tsubouchi, *Shōsetsu shinzui*, p. 88.

29. Shōyō's own *shōsetsu, Tōsei shosei katagi* (Manners and lives of contemporary students; serialized from June 1885 to Jan. 1886) deals with the internal conflicts of elite students between their affections toward women and their ambition, and between their "idealism" and their more realistic, practical concerns.

30. Tsubouchi, *Shōsetsu shinzui*, pp. 70, 47–48, 84.

31. Tsubouchi, "Tamenaga Shunsui no hihyō" (Feb.–Mar., 1886), p. 420.

32. Ibid., p. 421. In *Shōsetsu shinzui*, Shōyō frequently used English words (such as "novel," "artistic," "didactic") together with their Japanese translations. The word "realism" or "realist," however, does not appear in *Shōsetsu shinzui*. For *mosha* or *mogi* (imitative description or imitation) Shōyō adds the *kana* transcription *ātistikku* (artistic). In this instance he classifies novels into two types: "artistic" and "didactic," into *mosha* (imitative/mimetic) *shōsetsu* and *kanchō* (encouraging virtue and punishing evil / didactic) *shōsetsu* (Tsubouchi, *Shōsetsu shinzui*, p. 79).

33. Tsubouchi, "Ryūtei Tanehiko no hyōban," pp. 425, 427. In this article, the key word of which is *shinri*, Shōyō praised the Edo *gesaku* (popular fiction) writer Ryūtei Tanehiko, who was still popular at the time, "for his superb ability to adapt classical works such as the *Tale of Genji* and for his smooth and elegant written style." Shōyō, however, criticized Tanehiko for being no more than a talented "adapter" (*hon'anka*) which, he emphasized, is very different from being a "novelist" (*shōsetsuka*), whose objective is to "reveal the truth by depicting new ideas [*shinki no myōsō*] never presented before" (ibid., p. 425).

34. Ibid., pp. 426, 428.

35. Having been stimulated and encouraged by Shōyō's *Shōsetsu shinzui* (serialized from Sept. 1885 to Apr. 1886) and his *shōsetsu, Tōsei shosei katagi* (serialized from June 1885 to Jan. 1886), Futabatei visited Shōyō and eagerly exchanged literary ideas, starting in January 1886. At Shōyō's encouragement, Futabatei decided to write the monumental *shōsetsu Ukigumo* (Drifting clouds; 1887–89).

36. See Kitaoka, pp. 162–79.

37. Futabatei Shimei, "Shōsetsu sōron," in his *Futabatei Shimei shū*, p. 407.

38. Futabatei Shimei, "Bijutsu no hongi" ("The Essence of Art"—translation of Belinsky's *The Idea of Art*, 1841); unpublished during Futabatei's lifetime. Published in 1928 in *Meiji bunka zenshū* and now included in *Futabatei Shimei zenshū*, 5: 136–55. It is assumed that Futabatei started to translate it before 1886. Futabatei, "Katokofu-shi bijutsu zokkai" (Introduction to Katkov's Aesthetics; May–June 1886, a translation of Katkov's "Practical Significance of Art" from the *Anthology of Russian Literature*), *Futabatei Shimei zenshū*, 5: 12–21.

39. Futabatei, "Bijutsu no hongi," in *Futabatei Shimei zenshū*, 5: 136.

40. On several occasions, Futabatei translated Belinsky's Hegelian notion "the divine, absolute idea" simply as *shinri*, deliberately omitting the word "divine" or "God" (see Kitaoka, p. 166).

41. *Futabatei Shimei zenshū*, 5: 16–17.

42. *Shinri* was used as a synonym for such Buddhist terms as *shinjitsu*—"ultimate principle" (Sk. *uttama-artha*), "true [Buddhist] teachings" (*tattva*), "the way things exist" (*tathatva*)—and *shinnyo* (universal principle, the way things exist [*tathatā, tathātā, tathātva*] and the way laws are established [*dharmatā*]) (see *Kokugo dai jiten* [Shōgaku-kan]; and Nakamura Hajime, *Bukkyōgo dai jiten* [Tōkyō shoseki, 1981]).

43. Futabatei Shimei, "Ochiba no hakiyose: futakagome," in *Futabatei Shimei zen-shū,* 6: 49–51, 63–65, 67. In one passage, written in 1889, Futabatei expressed his ad-miration for an early Ch'ing Neo-Confucianist Wei Shu-tzu (1624–80), who argued: "The marvel of writing resides in acquiring *ri* [Chinese *li,* "principle, unchanging es-sence"] and in cultivating *shiki* [*shi,* "knowledge"], . . . which makes *ri* the true *ri* [*shin no ri; zhen li*]" (ibid., pp. 58–59). Futabatei, who had studied the Chinese classics (like other intellectuals of his generation) before he studied Russian, probably translated Belinsky's (Hegelian) notion of "Idea" as *shinri* (true *ri*) under influence of the Neo-Confucian, metaphysical notion of *ri.* For Futabatei's educational background in Chi-nese classics, see Yanagida Izumi, "Gi Shuku-shi to Futabatei Shimei."

44. Futabatei, "Ochiba no hakiyose: futakagome" and "Ochiba no hakiyose: mikagome," in *Futabatei Shimei zenshū,* 6: 49–141, esp. pp. 63–65.

45. Ibid., p. 63.

46. In November 1886, for example, a politician Ozaki Yukio (1859–1954) wrote a "Preface to the Second Volume of *Setchū-bai* (Plum blossoms in the snow; 1886), a *seiji shōsetsu* by Suehiro Tetchō, and praised *Setchū-bai* as a "realization of the respect-able and useful *shōsetsu,*" the basis of which, Ozaki said, "is the realistic depiction of *ninjō* without becoming absurd" ("*Setchū-bai* jo" in Suehiro Tetchō, *Setchū-bai, Meiji seiji shōsetsu shū II,* Meiji bungaku zenshū 6, pp. 135–36). In 1887, the editorial column of *Jogaku zasshi* (Journal for female students), a Christian humanist and feminist journal founded in 1885, claimed that reading *shōsetsu* could be beneficial for women as long as they knew how to read and judge *shōsetsu.* The editorial confidently asserted that "the most advanced *shōsetsu* depict the realities of life and human feeling [*jissai no sejō ninjō*]" ("Shōsetsu ron," *Jogaku zasshi,* Oct. and Nov. 1887, reprinted in *Kindai bungaku hyōron taikei,* 1: 49–50).

47. Ōgai, a high-ranking government medical officer, returned from Germany in 1888, after five years of studying medicine, philosophy, and literature. Ōgai's rationale for starting *Shigarami zōshi* is explained in his "*Shigarami zōshi* no honryō o ronzu" (Mori, 11: 131–33).

48. Saganoya Omuro (or Hokubō Sanshi—both pen names for Yazaki Shinshirō), pp. 83–85.

49. Mori Ōgai, "Gendai shoka no shōsetsu ron o yomu," *Shigarami zōshi,* no. 2 (Nov. 1889): 4–21; the revised edition entitled "Ima no shoka no shōsetsu ron o yomite," was published in 1896 in *Tsukikusa,* a collection of Ōgai's critical essays; see Mori, 11: 161–81. Ōgai's discussion of the novel deals with problems of style, subject matter, realism vs. idealism, the relationship between beauty and moral virtues, genre theory, and the problem of journalism. See Kobori Keiichirō, "Kaisetsu" in Mori, 11; see also Kobori's *Wakaki hi no Mori Ōgai,* pp. 377–433.

50. Tsubouchi, "Shakespeare kyakuhon hyōchū" (Oct. 1891), p. 190.

51. Mori Ōgai, "Emile Zola ga botsu risō" (Jan. 1892), in Mori, 12: 98–101. Ōgai

had been superimposing Zola on Shōyō's advocacy of the realistic depiction since "Gendai shoka no shōsetsu ron o yomu" (Nov. 1889).

52. Ōgai, "Shōyō-shi no sho hyōgo" (Sept. 1891); "Waseda bungaku no botsu risō" (Dec. 1891); "Waseda bungaku no bokkyaku risō" (Mar. 1892); "Shōyō-shi to Uyū-sensei to" (Mar. 1892); in Mori, 12: 6–21, 21–29, 31–39, and 39–65, respectively.

53. In the following statements by Tayama Katai, which reflect the literary and intellectual environment around 1900, we can hear the resonance of Shōyō and Ōgai. Praising the contemporary Belgian writer Maurice Maeterlinck and two German writers, Gerhart Hauptmann and Hermann Sudermann for "depicting the innermost and subtlest mysteries of human feelings [*ninjō no himitsu*] while depicting the defects and weakness of human nature," Katai compared them with Maupassant, who "remains at the stage of vividly drawing human beings on paper by depicting them in a strictly objective way without presenting ideals [*risō o bosshitaru*]." Katai praised Maeterlinck and others for "presenting ideals [*hyōjun*] and valuing subjectivity [*shukan*]" and for "having marvelous plans and colors [*kyakushoku to shikisai*]" (Tayama Katai, "Seika yokō" [June 1901], cited in Hisamatsu et al., *Kindai I*, pp. 229–30).

54. Anonymous, "Bungaku gokusui" (Dec. 1889); Hototogisu (pen name for Kitamura Tōkoku), "Tōsei bungaku no ushio moyō" (Jan. 1890); anonymous, "Bungaku sekai no kinkyō" (Feb. 1890); Tokutomi Sohō, "*Fujō monogatari* jo" (Apr. 1890); all reprinted in *Kindai bungaku hyōron taikei*, 1: 89, 90–92, 98–99, 102, respectively. Shōyō's works subsequent to *Shōsetsu shinzui* and *Tōsei shosei katagi* and the works of Shōyō's followers such as Yamada Bimyō's *Kochō* (1889), Ozaki Kōyō's *Ninin bikuni irozange* (1889), and Futabatei's *Ukigumo* (1887–89) as well as Mori Ōgai's *Maihime* (1890) were initially received as a kind of new *ninjō shōsetsu*. For a concise summary of the reception of *Ukigumo*, see Hata Yūzō, "*Ukigumo* no hyōka," in Miyoshi Yukio and Takemori Ten'yū, 2: 3–10.

55. Tokutomi Sohō, "*Fujō monogatari* jo," in *Kindai bungaku hyōron taikei*, 1: 102.

56. First and third quotations—Uchida Fuchian (Roan), "*Fujō monogatari* o yomu" (May 1890), in *Kindai bungaku hyōron taikei*, 1: 109–10, 108 and 111; second quotation—Ishibashi Ningetsu, "Hōchi ibun" (Apr. 1890), in *Kindai bungaku hyōron taikei*, 1: 105.

57. Those who criticized *Fujō monogatari* and emphasized the importance of the realistic depiction of *ninjō* also expressed their dissatisfaction with the contemporary *ninjō shōsetsu* (primarily works by Ken'yūsha writers), although they claimed that these *ninjō shōsetsu* were far more advanced than the "childish story of *Fujō monogatari*."

58. From around the late 1880's to the early 1890's, the notion of *bungaku* became interchangeable with "literature" in the modern Western sense of the word. Nishi Amane, an early Meiji scholar of Western Studies, adopted the word *bungaku* in the early 1870's as a translation for "literature" in his *Hyakugaku renkan* (lecture notes from 1870 but published posthumously in 1945), but it was not until after the early 1890's that this usage of *bungaku* prevailed. In *Shōsetsu shinzui*, which emphasized the central position of the novel in modern Western literary art, Tsubouchi Shōyō did not even use the word once. Before the early 1890's, the term *bungaku*, which originated in

Confucius' *Analects*, meant "learning," "studies," or "scholars" ("official Confucian scholars" in particular). The first group of modern Japanese *bungaku shi* ("history of *bungaku*"), which appeared in 1890, continued to use the word *bungaku* in this traditional fashion; see Hasegawa Izumi, pp. 138–42.

59. The revival of Saikaku was initiated by the dissemination of the phrase "Saikaku, the Realist of Japan." Uchida Roan's article, "Nihon shōsetsu no san taika" (Three greatest writers of Japanese novels; Nov. 1889, in *Kindai bungaku hyōron taikei*, 1: 428–29), which clearly echoes Shōyō's discourse on the *shōsetsu*, praises Saikaku as "the best Japanese *shōsetsu* writer, whose works are not inferior to the contemporary Realist work . . . in depicting the actual realities of the society." Next to Saikaku, Roan gives the names of Santō Kyōden and Shikitei Sanba, both of whom Roan defines as "not pure *shōsetsuka* but the best Japanese satirists [*fūkaika*], who excelled in penetrating the depths of *ninjō*." Roan had barely read Saikaku when he praised him as the "best Japanese *shōsetsuka*." In an earlier article that appeared in October and November 1888, Roan discussed Edo period writers, but made no mention of Saikaku. The original (woodblock) printings of Saikaku's works had become extremely rare by the Meiji period, and they were hardly read until the late 1880's. The first of Saikaku's works to be reprinted were a part of *Kōshoku ichidai onna* and a part of *Kōshoku gonin onna*, which appeared in a literary journal *Bunko* in July and December 1889, respectively (see *Zadankai Meiji bungaku shi* [Iwanami shoten, 1961], pp. 89–90). Influenced by Fukuzawa Yukichi, Awashima Kangetsu, who collected Saikaku's rare books from around 1880 and triggered the Saikaku revival in late 1880's, was eager to live permanently in the United States. According to his memoirs, he became interested in the Japanese classics when he began to ponder how to explain Japan to Americans (see Ochi Haruo, *Kindai bungaku no tanjō*, p. 89). The first modern Japanese literary history, *Nihon bungaku shi* (History of Japanese literature, 1890), written by the first graduates of the Kokubungaku (National Literature) department at the University of Tokyo (Mikami Sanji and Takatsu Kuwasaburō) and the three earliest modern anthologies of classical Japanese literature (published in 1890), all presented Saikaku as the most important "novelist" (*shōsetsuka*) in the Tokugawa period. Significantly, at the same time, Saikaku's contemporary, Chikamatsu Mon'zaemon, the noted *bunraku* playwright, was elevated to the position of "Japan's Shakespeare."

60. Futabatei Shimei, "Ochiba no hakiyose: futakagome," in *Futabatei Shimei zenshū*, 6: 73.

61. The modern historian Inoue Kiyoshi (pp. 382–86) points out that this petition and the party platform were monumental in that they advocated the political rights of the people for the first time and in that they propagated the modern notion of the "patriotism for the nation" (*aikoku*), which was distinctly different from the more dispersed loyalties to a local feudal lord.

62. The abolition of the feudal system (in 1871), the abolition of the traditional four-class system (in 1870–71), and the adoption of the national conscription system (announced in 1872–73) caused many former samurai to become unemployed and impoverished (see Irokawa, *Kindai kokka no shuppatsu*, pp. 57–84, 109–40, 255–68). The fact that the promotors of the Meiji Restoration were low-ranking samurai from the western provinces awakened other low-ranking samurai to their own potential.

63. The restrictions on the publication of newspapers (in 1875) were repeatedly

strengthened, particularly from 1883. The restrictions on public gatherings (established in 1880) were also increased in 1882, dealing the various political organizations a severe blow (see Irokawa, *Kindai kokka no shuppatsu*, pp. 134–35, 194–96).

64. See the "Yukoku" of "Zenkoku bohei no mikotonori"; cited in Inoue Kiyoshi, pp. 217–18.

65. See Maeda Ai, "Meiji risshin-shusse-shugi no keifu," in his *Kindai dokusha no seiritsu*, pp. 90–97.

66. Ibid., pp. 97–98. On the administrative and curricular change in the compulsory elementary school system, see Gluck, pp. 19, 108. Fukuzawa's own views of independence also changed in the early 1880's, shifting from an emphasis on individual independence to a focus on national unity, which he considered a necessity in the face of accelerated Western imperialism in the 1880's. On the transformation in Fukuzawa's social stance, see Walker, pp. 22–24.

67. Itō Hirobumi, the political leader who promoted the centralization of the bureaucracy and became the first prime minister under a cabinet system that he himself established, went to Prussia from 1882 to 1883 to study the constitution, the parliamentary system, government institutions, and local administration. (see Irokawa, *Kindai kokka no shuppatsu*, pp. 432–36). On the relationship between early nineteenth-century European popular national movements and self-conscious governmental efforts to create national unity, see Anderson, pp. 83–111.

68. By 1885, the major political parties formed at the height of the Freedom and People's Rights movement—such as Jiyūtō (Freedom Party, founded in 1881), Rikken-seitō (Constitutional Party, founded in 1882), and Rikken-teiseitō (Constitutional Imperial Party, founded in 1882)—were forced to dissolve (in 1884, 1883, and 1883, respectively).

69. Toda Kindō (1850–90), whose short allegorical work *Minken engi jōkai haran* (Storms in the sea of passions: a story of people's rights; 1880) is thought to be the first *seiji shōsetsu*, was a son of a feudal lord and went to the United States in 1871, where he became a Christian. After returning to Japan, he devoted himself to the spread of Christianity and then to the People's Rights movement. Sakurada Momoe (1859–83), whose adaptation of the beginning part of Dumas *père's Mémoires d'un médecin* (from an English translation)—entitled *Futsukoku kakumei kigen: nishi no umi chishio no saarashi* (Small storms on the tide of blood in the western sea: the origin of the French Revolution; 1882)—studied the Chinese classics, German, and English. He joined the Freedom and People's Rights movement in its early years. Miyazaki Muryū (1855–89), a son of a samurai in Tosa province, the birthplace of the Freedom and People's Rights movement, studied Chinese poetry in his youth, and joined the People's Rights movement as a journalist. His *Furansu kakumei no ki: jiyū no kachidoki* (The triumph of freedom: a record of the French Revolution; 1882–83), a free adaptation of Dumas's *Taking the Bastille*, was serialized and widely read. Yano Fumio (pen name—Yano Ryūkei, 1850–1931), whose *Keikoku bidan* (Commendable anecdotes on creating a nation: young politicians of Thebes; 1883–84) was one of the most influential and enthusiastically received *seiji shōsetsu*, was the son of an important feudal clan official. He received an orthodox Confucian education and then entered Fukuzawa Yukichi's progressive Keiō-gijuku, where he mastered English and Western learning. Yano devoted himself to the People's Rights movement both as a

journalist and as a politician. When Ōkuma Shigenobu, with whom Yano had long collaborated, became foreign minister in 1896, Yano was appointed ambassador to China. Shiba Shirō (pen name—Tōkai Sanshi, 1842–1922), whose *Kajin no kigū* (Chance meetings with beautiful women; 1885–97) was received enthusiastically in the late 1880's, was the son of a samurai from Aizu, which was loyal to the Tokugawa shogunate. He studied the Chinese classics and then French and English, and was eventually sent to the United States, where he studied economics at the University of Pennsylvania. After a limited constitution and the national Diet were established, Shiba became a representative to the Diet in the second election (1892). Suehiro Shigeyasu (pen name—Suehiro Tetchō, 1849–96), whose *Setchū-bai* (Plum blossoms in the snow; 1886) was another well received *seiji shōsetsu*, was a son of a samurai (his father excelled in Chinese poetry) and received a solid Confucian education. After serving in the Ministry of Finance and becoming disillusioned, Suehiro became a journalist for a political newspaper and devoted himself to the Freedom and People's Rights movement both as an activist and as a journalist. He too eventually became a representative to the Diet in 1890 and 1894–96 (see Yanagida, *Seiji shōsetsu kenkyū*).

70. In 1884, at the height of the Freedom and People's Rights movement, Shōyō translated and published Shakespeare's *Julius Caesar* as *Jiyū no tachi: nagori no kireaji* (The sword of freedom: a final thrust of the point).

71. "Futabatei Shimei no isshō" (1925), in Uchida, p. 118.

72. Futabatei Shimei, "Rokoku bungaku no Nihon bungaku ni oyoboshitaru eikyō" (written ca. 1907–8), in *Futabatei Shimei zenshū*, 5: 283, 284.

73. Futabatei, "Yo ga hansei no zange," in *Futabatei Shimei zenshū*, 5: 265–67.

74. Kitamura, *Kitamura Tōkoku shū*, p. 289.

75. Ibid., p. 290.

76. Ibid.

77. In his literary memoirs, *Kindai no shōsetsu* (Modern novels; 1923), Tayama Katai revealed the deep impact that Futabatei's "Aibiki" (1888) and "Meguriai" (1888–89)—both partial translations of Turgenev's *A Sportsman's Sketches*—had on himself and on contemporaries such as Tōson and Doppo: "One can write those kinds of sentences if one makes an effort. To be so detailed and precise! I was deeply impressed" (cited in Yamamoto Masahide, *Kindai buntai hassei*, p. 6).

78. Futabatei Shimei, "Ochiba no hakiyose: futakagome," in *Futabatei Shimei zenshū*, 6: 73.

79. The second half of *Shōsetsu shinzui* is devoted to discussing technical problems such as written styles, plot, structure, characters, description, and narration. Shōyō divided the possible written styles into three categories: (1) *gabuntai* (elegant, classical style), found in *Genji monogatari*; (2) *zokubuntai* (vernacular, colloquial style), found in the dialogue in Shunsui's *ninjōbon*; and (3) *gazoku-setchūtai* (blending elegant and colloquial styles), which Shoyō further divides into (A) the *yomihon* style (represented by Bakin) with greater use of *gabuntai* than *zokubuntai* and with the heavy use of Chinese characters and *kanbun* syntax; and (B) the *kusa-zōshi* style (represented by Shunsui) with less use of Chinese words and greater use of colloquial language. Shōyō argued that future Japanese novelists should explore the *kusa-zōshi* style (using a blend

of *gabuntai* and *zokubuntai* for the descriptive part and *zokubuntai* for the dialogue) in order to create a new narrative style suited for the realistic depiction of *ninjō* in contemporary society.

80. Futabatei was convinced that the "future written language of Japan should be united with the spoken language." In August 1888, Futabatei expressed his view of *genbun-itchi* as follows: "Language is the reflection of man's ideas and thoughts. . . . Both the spoken discourse and written language are manifestations of the same ideas and thoughts, one in the form of voice, the other in the visual form. . . . Why should the same thought or the same word become different when it is written and when it is spoken? . . . I would like to assert that the future written language of Japan should be united with the spoken language" ("Kuchiha-shū: hitokagome," in *Futabatei Shimei zenshū*, 6: 11–13).

81. As Shōyō himself states (*Shōsetsu shinzui*, p. 108), his argument about blending the colloquial language and the established literary languages is a variation of Bakin's view of written styles. In fact, Shōyō's specific discussions of stylistic, rhetorical, and composition problems (plot, structure, characterization, etc.) are all heavily based on Bakin's principles of the *shōsetsu* (*yomihon*), which themselves drew on the composition theories developed for Ming-Ch'ing vernacular *hsiao-shuo*.

82. Futabatei Shimei, "Yo ga genbun-itchi no yurai" (1906), in *Futabatei Shimei zenshū*, 5:170–72.

Chapter 2

1. Based on an extremely limited franchise, the Diet opened in 1890. A little over 1 percent of the entire population (males over 25 who had paid a significant amount of tax) were given a right to vote for members of the House of Representatives (Irokawa, *Kindai kokka no shuppatsu*, pp. 485–86). Also in 1890 the Rescript on Education was promulgated to create a collective sense of the nation through a moral education that emphasized filiality and loyalty. Carol Gluck (pp. 120–27) persuasively argues that although the actual content of moral education ranged from the ethical instruction (*shūshin*) developed by Confucian moralists to the *settliche Bildung* advocated by the educational vanguard, which drew on Johann Friedrich Herbart's theories of character training, the drive for national unity through moral education in the late 1880's created the sociocultural basis for favorable reception of the Rescript on Education.

2. For the interiorization of the political ideal of individualism, see also Walker.

3. See Sumiya, *Kindai Nihon no keisei to kirisutokyō*, pp. 78–84.

4. Kitamura, *Kitamura Tōkoku shū*, p. 300.

5. Ibid., pp. 291–92.

6. Sumiya, *Kindai Nihon no keisei to kirisutokyō*, p. 9.

7. The number of Christian churches increased from 44 in 1878 to 168 in 1885, and the number of Christians from 1,617 in 1878 to 11,000 in 1885. Most of the increase occurred outside the major cities (see Irokawa, *Kindai kokka no shuppatsu*, p. 467).

8. The number of churches increased from 168 in 1885 to 300 in 1890, and the number of Christians from 11,000 in 1885 to 34,000 in 1890. The government policy

of rapid westernization during the so-called Rokumeikan period, which began in the early to mid-1880s, also increased the access of people from various social classes to Christianity (Sumiya, *Kindai Nihon no keisei to kirisutokyō*, pp. 80–84).

9. Yamaji, p. 288. Christian missionaries began arriving in Japan in 1859, after the conclusion of the commercial treaties, and taught English and the Bible to young students in various areas of Japan. The first Japanese church (Nihon Kirisuto kōkai) was secretly established in 1872 in Yokohama. The modern historian Sumiya Mikio (*Kindai Nihon no keisei*, pp. 17–18) notes that at the end of the Tokugawa period the supporters and retainers of the shogunate favored opening the country to foreign intercourse. This contrasts with attitudes in the western provinces, which advocated *sonnō-jōi* (revere the emperor and expel the barbarians). After the Meiji Restoration, talented sons of former supporters of the shogunate came to centers for Western education such as Yokohama, Tokyo, and Kōbe. Hoping to enhance their opportunities, they studied English and Western culture and came to believe that they should serve and save the nation through Christianity, which they considered to be the essence of advanced Western civilization.

10. Karatani, "Shi-shōsetsu no keifugaku," p. 117.

11. Tōkoku's January 1888 letter to Ishizaka Mina reveals that his metaphors of "battles" draw on a passage in Patrick Henry's "Liberty Speech" (1775): "Besides, Sir, we shall not fight our battles alone. There is a just God who presides over the destinies of nations" (*Kitamura Tōkoku shū*, p. 300). Tōkoku's shift from politics to Christianity might have been conceived not as a disjunction but as a continuity within the same Western discourse of winning "freedom."

12. Kitamura Tōkoku, "Nihon bungaku shi kotsu" (Outline of the history of Japanese literature; Apr.–May 1893); also known as "Meiji bungaku kanken" (My view of Meiji literature); in *Kitamura Tōkoku shū*, p. 127.

13. Ibid., pp. 131, 125; "Naibu seimei ron" (On the inner life; May 1893), in *Kitamura Tōkoku shū*, p. 146.

14. Tōkoku's younger contemporaries such as Shimazaki Tōson and Iwano Hōmei entered mission schools in order to receive a Western-style education, which seemed to prepare them for social success. Tōson entered Meiji Gakuin, a Calvinist school in Tokyo in 1887; Hōmei started at Taisei Gakkan in Osaka in 1887 and then transferred to Meiji Gakuin in 1888. They subsequently became Christians.

15. Disraeli's novel *Contarini Fleming*, translated into Japanese and serialized in a Tokyo newspaper in 1887, takes the form of an autobiography written by the title character. Tōkoku's account (Aug. 1887) of his family and childhood days closely resembles Contarini's description of his childhood days in which a sensitive and imaginative youth in rebellion against an authoritarian stepmother is inspired by the heroes of drama and history books and dreams of worldly success before finally attempting to write a novel (see notes by Oketani Hideaki in Kitamura, *Jinsei*, pp. 341–42). In a letter to his father written toward the end of Aug. 1887, Tōkoku wrote: "If you want to know about my personality, please read the biography of the poet Contarini, which is now being serialized in *Tōkyō nichi-nichi shinbun*" (*Kitamura Tōkoku shū*, pp. 292–93).

16. Uemura's *Shinri ippan* (On truth; 1884), which emphasized the "spiritual freedom" at the height of the Freedom and People's Rights movement, was widely read

by young intellectuals, including Futabatei Shimei. Uemura began to participate in the translation of Old Testament in 1884. In 1890, he established a Christian journal, *Nihon hyōron*, in which he dealt with political and social issues and introduced Western literature, particularly such romantic poets as Byron, Browning, Tennyson, and Wordsworth. Uemura attracted and converted to Christianity such future writers as Kunikida Doppo (who converted in 1891) and Masamune Hakuchō (1897). For Uemura's literary essays, see *Uemura Masahisa chosaku shū*, vol. 3. Uchimura Kanzō, whose strong personality had a great impact on young students, introduced Western writers through his lectures. Masamune Hakuchō, a later Naturalist writer, became deeply attracted to European literature after he heard Uchimura's lectures on Carlyle and Dante in the late 1890's. See Masamune Hakuchō, "Uchimura Kanzō" (1950), pp. 295–361. In the 1900's Uchimura also attracted, among other young students, Shiga Naoya and Mushakōji Saneatsu (1885–1976), future writers of the Shirakaba group.

17. Kitamura Tōkoku, "Jinsei ni aiwataru to wa nan no ii zo?" (What does it mean to commit to life?; Feb. 1893); "Naibu seimei ron" (Essay on the inner life; May 1893), in *Kitamura Tōkoku shū*, pp. 114, 145.

18. Kitamura Tōkoku, "Naibu seimei ron," in *Kitamura Tōkoku shū*, pp. 145–46.

19. Kitamura Tōkoku, "Nihon bungaku shi kotsu," and "Naibu seimei ron," in *Kitamura Tōkoku shū*, pp. 125–26, 145.

20. Togawa, "Katsudō ron" (On life as activity; Feb. 1894), p. 272.

21. Togawa, "Henchō ron" (Time for change; Jan. 1894), p. 269.

22. Togawa, "Katsudō ron," p. 273.

23. Takayama Chogyū, "Nihon-shugi o sansu" (Praising Japanism; June 1897) in Takayama et al., p. 25.

24. Takayama Chogyū, "Walt Whitman o ronzu" (Discussing Walt Whitman; June 1898) in Takayama et al., pp. 35–36.

25. Ibid., p. 38.

26. Takayama Chogyū, "Bunmei hihyōka to shite no bungakusha" (The man of letters as critic of civilization; Jan. 1901), in Takayama et al., p. 63.

27. Takayama Chogyū, "Biteki seikatsu o ronzu" (Discussing the aesthetic life; Aug. 1901), in Takayama et al., p. 84.

28. Ibid., pp. 80–83.

29. Although the growth of Christianity slowed after the early 1890's due to the growth of state control and nationalism, there was a resurgence of Christianity from 1901, primarily among urban, middle-class intellectuals and students whose numbers increased with the spread of industrialization, particularly after the Sino-Japanese War. Takakura Tokutarō (1885–1934), a Protestant pastor and the successor to Uemura Masahisa, left this description of his adolescence. "My mind had long been preoccupied with the question of the self. When I graduated from high school in Kanazawa, I expressed my thoughts at the time in the boarding school commemorative book. I remember writing, 'That which we must love most is the self [*jiko*]. What is the thing called the self [*jiga*]? How can we have an emancipated, fulfilling self?' In those days I thought with great enthusiasm that I would readily sacrifice anything to solve the question of the self. . . . I was baptized in December 1906. My motive for baptism was the hope that the question of the self would be solved, at least in part, by

Christianity" (Takakura Tokutarō, *Onchō no ōkoku* (1921), cited in Sumiya, *Nihon no shakai shisō*, p. 42). Of particular interest here is the fact that in this period young intellectuals such as Takakura were attracted to Christianity out of a deep desire to "pursue and understand the self."

30. Yosano Tekkan, "Shinshisha seiki" (Principles of the New Poetic Society), in *Myōjō*, no. 6 (Sept. 1900); reprinted in Yosano and Yosano, pp. 386–87. Tekkan and Yosako Akiko (1878–1942), a Myōjō poet who became Tekkan's wife, proudly celebrated their aspiration for love in their poems. Akiko's new expressions of sensuality had considerable impact on her younger contemporaries as exemplary expressions of a new attitude toward life. The modern *tanka* poet Sasaki Yukitsuna (1938–) astutely notes that a formal characteristic of the *waka* poetry as a first-person lyric form promoted the living poet's identification with the first-person subject of the *waka*. Sasaki suggests that the act of writing *waka* thereby shaped the perception and life of the Myōjō poet (see Sasaki Yukitsuna, pp. 59–82).

31. Takayama Chogyū, "Bunmei hihyōka to shite no bungakusha," in Takayama et al., p. 68.

32. Futabatei Shimei, "Watakushi wa kaigi-ha da" (I am a skeptic), in *Futabatei Shimei zenshū*, 5: 233.

33. Shimazaki, *Tōson zenshū*, 6: 10

34. Ibid., p. 11.

35. Hattori Nankaku, "Gakokō ni kotau" (Answering to Lord Gako, around 1754), in Hattori, p. 227. Written, of course, in *kanbun* or classical Chinese.

36. Shimazaki, "Preface to *Tōson shishū*" (1904), in *Tōson shishū*, p. 565.

37. Kanda Kōhei, "Bunshō o yomu," *Tōkyō gakushikaiin zasshi* 7, no. 1 (Feb. 1885), cited by Yamamoto Masahide, *Kindai buntai hassei*, p. 333.

38. See Yamamoto Masahide, *Kindai buntai hassei*.

39. Cited in ibid., p. 285.

40. Ibid., p. 286.

41. Ibid., pp. 665–71.

42. Yamamoto Masahide, *Genbun-itchi no rekishi ronkō*, pp. 173–89, 451–68, 469–502, 503–33.

43. Yamamoto Masahide, *Kindai buntai hassei*, pp. 47–49; idem, *Genbun-itchi no rekishi ronkō: zokuhen*, pp. 431–47. From the 1900's, grammar books on the colloquial language began to be published and contributed to the normalization of the newly standardized colloquial written language. In 1904, the national textbooks for elementary school *kokugo* (national language) were edited and published by the government, including a number of texts written in the colloquial, *kōgo* written style; a revised edition in 1910 further increased the number of *kōgo* texts (see Doi, pp. 223–26). For the decisive role of the notion of "private-property" language and of the formation of vernacular as a national language-of-state (materialized through print-capitalism) in the nineteenth-century European conception of nation-ness, see Anderson.

44. This movement eventually led, from the 1890's, to three linguistic systems, which were constructed in close relationship to one another: (1) the standardized colloquial written language (*kōgo*), which was thought to be a transcription of Tokyo *yamanote* spoken language (used by the educated middle class, as opposed to the more specifically local *shitamachi* "downtown" dialect), but which was in fact a mixture of

written practices, including *kanbun* and Western syntax; (2) the standardized national spoken language, which was constructed and disseminated through the *genbun-itchi* written language; and (3) the Tokyo *yamanote* spoken language, which was thought to be the "origin" of the standardized *genbun-itchi* written and spoken languages, but was in fact affected and transformed by the *genbun-itchi* languages. The "imitating" constructed and transformed the "imitated," in a circular process. See also Doi, pp. 222–36.

45. Yamamoto Masahide, *Kindai buntai hassei*, p. 51. According to Yamamoto, the secondary-school textbooks edited by Tsubouchi Shōyō in 1908 (revised in 1909), which adopted more readings in the colloquial style than any other school textbooks, and which influenced subsequent school textbooks, included "Inukoro" by Futabatei, *Wagahai wa neko de aru* by Natsume Sōseki, "Musashino" by Doppo, "Nogi shōgun" by Mori Ōgai, and works by Masaoka Shiki, Takahama Kyoshi, and Tayama Katai (Yamamoto, *Genbun-itchi no rekishi ronkō: zokuhen*, pp. 187–93).

46. Yamamoto Masahide, "Shaseibun to genbun-itchi," in his *Genbun-itchi no rekishi ronkō: zokuhen*, pp. 466–87.

47. Masaoka Shiki, "Joji-bun" (Jan. 1900), in Masaoka, p. 369. Until 1893, Shiki was opposed to the "unification of spoken and written languages." See also Yamamoto Masahide, *Genbun-itchi no rekishi ronkō: zokuhen*, pp. 466–68.

48. Takahama Kyoshi, "Genbun-itchi" (May 1900). See Yamamoto Masahide, *Genbun-itchi no rekishi ronkō: zokuhen*, pp. 469–70. Stimulated by Sōseki's *Wagahai wa neko de aru* (I am a cat; 1905), many of these writers began to write *shōsetsu* after the mid-1900's.

49. Kunikida Doppo, "Shizen o utsusu bunshō" (Written language for describing nature), in *Kunikida Doppo shū*, p. 299.

50. Karatani Kōjin, *Nihon kindai bungaku no kigen*, pp. 7–113.

Chapter 3

1. The novelist and critic Kume Masao proudly stated in 1934 that in 1920 he had been the first to use the term "I-novel." In 1926, the novelist Chikamatsu Shūkō wrote in his memoir that the journalist Nakamura Murao had coined the term. Neither claim has been confirmed (see Katsuyama, p. 175).

2. Nakamura Murao, p. 93.

3. Ibid.

4. Ibid.

5. Chikamatsu Shūkō, "Shōsetsu no honkei to bōkei," in *Jiji shinpō* (Feb. 1916), cited by Katsuyama, p. 255.

6. Nakamura Seiko, "Kokuhaku bungaku no ryūkō," *Waseda bungaku* (Aug. 1918); Maeda Akira, "Gyōshi to kanshō no seikatsu," *Bunshō sekai* (Aug. 1918); Ikuta Shungetsu, "Jiden to jidenteki sakuhin," *Jiji shinpō* (1920), cited in Katsuyama, pp. 255–56. In an annual survey of the literary world in 1920 ("Taishō kunen-do no bungei-kai"), Akutagawa noted a recent increase in "autobiographical novels" (*jiden shōsetsu*) that drew material directly from the writer's private life within a small, closed literary circle (*bundan*). Akutagawa criticized the kind of roman à clef that used real-life models (other writers in the literary circle) to slander specific individuals. Akuta-

gawa's remarks reveal that from the late 1910's to the early 1920's autobiographical narratives, which assumed and induced referential readings, had become a noticeable trend. Akutagawa's review also reveals that I-novel critical discourse had yet to be formed, that the autobiographical element did not yet constitute the primary criterion in discussing novels. In fact, when Akutagawa reviewed novels written in 1919 in "Literary World of 1919" ("Taishō hachinen-do no bungei-kai"), he categorized the writers by school: namely, "the writers of Naturalism, who espoused Truth [*shin*]," "the writers of Aestheticism, who espoused Beauty [*bi*]," "the writers of Humanism, or the Shirakaba school, who espoused Virtue [*zen*]," and "the more recent writers," namely, "new Waseda school—in the vein of Naturalism," "the new Tokyo University school [*shin Akamon-ha*]," "the new Keiō University school [*shin Mita-ha*]." This classification seems to reflect the standard literary perception of writers in the mid-Taishō period. Eguchi Kan's "General Trends of the Literary World and the Position of Each Writer" ("Bundan no taisei to kaku sakka no ichi"; 1918), for example, also uses the same classifications as those employed by Akutagawa (see *Kindai bungaku hyōron taikei*, 5: 63–81).

7. Kume, "Watakushi shōsetsu," p. 109.

8. Uno, " 'Watakushi shōsetsu' shiken," p. 115.

9. Ibid., p. 116.

10. Ibid., pp. 117–18.

11. For example, Tokuda Shūsei (1871–1943) wrote in 1926: "As for *shinkyō geijutsu* [state-of-mind art], I find the model for *shinkyō geijutsu* in the works of Bashō and Saigyō in which they express their personal feelings about their solitary lives" ("Shinkyō kara kyakkan e" in *Shinchō*, June 1926; cited by Katsuyama, p. 182). This view of the I-novel as part of the "long Japanese tradition of ascetic self-cultivation [*shugyō*] and search for the Way [*gudō*]" was more fully developed by Yamamoto Kenkichi in his *Watakushi-shōsetsu sakka ron* (1943), which discusses Kasai Zenzō, Makino Shin'ichi, Kamura Isota, Uno Kōji, Okamoto Kanoko, Hōjō Tamio, Takii Kōsaku, Shiga Naoya, and Kajii Motojirō.

12. Kume, "Watakushi shōsetsu," p. 111.

13. Ibid., 113.

14. Kawasaki et al., 2: 134–38.

15. See Abe Jirō, "Jinsei hihyō no genri," pp. 145–56. Abe's *Santarō no nikki* (Santarō's diary; 1914–15), which celebrates introspection as a way to "the knowledge of the universal," became one of the most popular and widely read books among college students from the Taishō period until World War II.

16. Akutagawa, "Ano koro no jibun no koto," in *Akutagawa Ryūnosuke zenshū*, 1: 380–81.

17. Mushakōji, "Jibun no fude de suru shigoto," pp. 25–26.

18. In 1911, Mushakōji wrote that the members of the Shirakaba group were "the spiritual children of the world" (*Shirakaba*, Sept. 1911, p. 162). In *Santarō's Diary*, Abe Jirō also called himself an "universal man" (*sekaijin*) who "could absorb and synthesize everything by [his] dialectical mind" (Kawasaki et al., 2: 135).

19. Mushakōji, *Shirakaba*, May 1918, p. 39.

20. Abe Jirō, "Jinsei hihyō no genri," pp. 145–56.

21. Arishima, pp. 211–15.

22. Represented in such articles as Hirotsu Kazuo, "Burujowa bungaku ron: Arishima Takeo-shi no kyūkutsuna kangaekata" (Jan. 1922); Arishima Takeo, "Hirotsu-shi ni kotau" (Jan. 1922); Sakai Toshihiko, "Arishima Takeo-shi no zetsubō no sengen" (Feb. 1922); Eguchi Kan, "Kaikyū to bungaku to no kankei o ronzu" (May 1922); Mushakōji et al., "Bungei to kaikyū ishiki" (Mar. 1922); Kikuchi Kan, "Bungei sakuhin no naiyō-teki kachi" (July 1922); Satomi Ton, "Kikuchi Kan-shi no 'Bungei sakuhin no naiyō-teki kachi' o bakusu" (Aug. 1922); Kikuchi Kan, "Sairon: Bungei sakuhin no naiyō-teki kachi" (Sept. 1922), reprinted in *Kindai bungaku hyōron taikei*, 5: 216–19, 220–24, 225–31, 231–45, 251–64, 269–73, 273–81, 281–91, respectively; Hirotsu Kazuo, "Sanbun geijutsu no ichi" (Sept. 1924), reprinted in *Kindai bungaku hyōron taikei*, 6: 33–37.

23. *Minshū geijutsu* (literature for the populace) was discussed from the mid-Taishō period. In 1916, the critic and scholar of English and Japanese literature Honma Hisao (1886–1981), influenced by Romain Rolland's *Le théâtre du peuple* and Ellen Key's advocacy of "recreative culture" for the working classes, emphasized the importance of developing a "healthy popular art, which could be easily understood by middle- and low-class working people and which would elevate their spirit" ("Minshū geijutsu no igi oyobi kachi," Aug. 1916; see Senuma, pp. 19–29; see also Maeda Ai, "Shōwa shotō no dokusha ishiki: geijutsu taishūka ron no shūhen," in his *Kindai dokusha no seiritsu*, pp. 229–50). After the Russian Revolution, the emphasis rapidly shifted from the notion of populace to that of class. The Proletarian literary movement came to the fore with the establishment of the journal *Tanemaku hito* (1921), which took on a Marxist stance. *Tanemaku hito* ceased publication after the Great Kantō Earthquake of September 1923, but reappeared in June 1924 as *Bungei sensen*, becoming an influential anticapitalist journal and the center of the Proletarian literary movement.

24. Kume, "Watakushi shōsetsu," p. 113.

25. Ibid., p. 109.

26. Ibid., p. 110.

27. Ibid., p. 113.

28. Akutagawa Ryūnosuke, " 'Watakushi' shōsetsu ron shōken" (My view of the discussions of the 'I-novel' "; June 1925), in *Akutagawa Ryūnosuke zenshū*, 5: 61–64. Kume's defense of the "artistic novel" can in fact be interpreted as his self-justification for a series of autobiographical novels or romans à clef, beginning with *Hotarugusa* (1918), modeled on his own experience of unrequited love for his mentor Natsume Sōseki's daughter, who married one of Kume's fellow writers. These romans à clef made him journalistically popular but were regarded by fellow writers such as Akutagawa as "sophisticated popular novels" (*tsūzoku shōsetsu*) as opposed to "artistic novels." However, when Akutagawa, in the annual literary review of 1920 ("Taishō kunen-do no bungei-kai"), called Kume's recent series of works new "popular novels" that "attested to the recent infiltration of literature into larger society," the question of whether the novel was autobiographical was not considered pertinent to the distinction between the "popular novel" and the "artistic novel." Significantly, Akutagawa himself became deeply concerned with the problem of the self in his last years.

29. It was also during the late Taishō period that the *zuihitsu*, the personal essay or *pensée*, was institutionalized as an established journalistic literary genre comparable in

status to the novel, poetry, and drama. *Bungei shunjū*, whose first issues appeared in January 1923, regularly published a section entitled "Zuihitsu." In November 1923, a literary magazine called *Zuihitsu*, which carried only this genre, appeared; and one of the major publishers, Kaizōsha, published *Zuihitsu sōsho*, a series of *zuihitsu*. It is from this time that writers specializing in the *zuihitsu* appeared (see Shioda; and Takada).

30. Satō, "Ich Roman no koto" (May 1926), pp. 121–22.

31. Ibid., p. 123. Radio broadcasting started in March 1924 in Japan and rapidly became popular throughout the country. It played a decisive role in spreading standardized *genbun-itchi* Japanese (*hyōjungo*) as a spoken language (see Doi, pp. 233–34).

32. Yokomitsu, "Junsui shōsetsu ron," pp. 144–45.

33. Ibid., pp. 150–51.

34. Kobayashi Hideo, "Watakushi shōsetsu ron," in *Kobayashi Hideo zenshū*, 3: 121–22.

35. Ibid., pp. 133–39. In "Watakushi shōsetsu ron," Kobayashi talked mainly about Gide's *Faux-monnayeurs*. Kobayashi had earlier translated Gide's *Paludes* (1928) and written an introductory essay called "André Gide" (1933) in which he discussed not only Gide's autobiography *Si le grain ne meurt . . .* but also *Les cahiers d'André Walter, Les nourritures terrestres, Paludes, Le Prométhée mal enchiné*, all in terms of Gide's expressions of his self (though Kobayashi did not use the term "I-novel" here). Kobayashi also translated Jacques Rivière's essay, "André Gide" in 1933 (see Kobayashi Hideo, *Kobayashi Hideo zen hon'yaku*).

36. Fujita Shōzō discusses Fukumoto's theoretical emphasis on the "self-reflective" and "self-determining" subject's "active decision" (in opposition to the intellectuals' hitherto sentimental sympathy for an "unobjectified," uncritical identification with the proletariat), a stance that was later turned around and used by the government (in its effort to suppress the movement) to cause the same intellectuals to actively renounce communism (*tenkō*). These former communists renounced the "abstract foreign theory" of Marxism as part of their "active decision" to reunite with the "people" (*taishū*) of Japan. Fujita points to Fukumoto's "decisive break" from the idealistic humanism of Taishō Democracy, that is to say, Fukumoto's emphasis on rigorous theoretical principles (as opposed to the humanistic Personalism of Taishō Democracy), while also pointing out Fukumoto's continuity with Taishō intellectuals, especially his belief in the absolute authority of the ideological principles that he introduced from contemporary Europe (see Fujita, pp. 33–65). Karatani Kōjin astutely points out the structural parallelism between Fukumoto Kazuo and Kobayashi Hideo in their decisive separation from and continuity with Taishō Humanism ("Kindai Nihon no hihyō: Shōwa zenki I," pp. 46–53).

37. This also is the central theme of Kobayashi Hideo's "Literature That Has Lost Its Homeland" ("Kokyō o ushinatta bungaku"; May 1933).

38. Of the many major special issues on the I-novel that appeared in literary journals after World War II, see especially *Bungaku* 21 (Dec. 1953): 38–76; and *Kokubungaku kaishaku to kyōzai no kenkyū* 11, no. 3 (Mar. 1966): 8–92.

39. Itō, *Shōsetsu no hōhō*, p. 21; hereinafter cited in the text.

40. Itō further developed his reflections on the I-novel in a larger cultural context in a series of articles from 1949 to 1953, which were published together in book form

in 1955 as *Shōsetsu no ninshiki*. Available in *Itō Sei zenshū*, vol. 13 (Kawade shobō, 1956), pp. 151–288.

41. Hirano Ken, "Watakushi shōsetsu no niritsu haihan," pp. 25–26.

42. Hirano, *Geijutsu to jisseikatsu*, p. 329.

43. Nakamura Mitsuo, "Watakushi shōsetsu ni tsuite" (Sept. 1935), in *Nakamura Mitsuo zenshū*, 7: 121–22, 133.

44. Nakamura Mitsuo, "Tenkō sakka ron" (Apr. 1935), and "Puroretaria bungaku undō" (Apr. 1935), in *Nakamura Mitsuo zenshū*, 7: 42–43 and 71–72, respectively.

45. Nakamura Mitsuo, "Tenkō sakka ron," in *Nakamura Mitsuo zenshū*, 7: 38–39, 46.

46. Nakamura Mitsuo, *Fūzoku shōsetsu ron*, p. 106.

47. Ibid., pp. 24–25.

Chapter 4

1. Nakamura Mitsuo, *Fūzoku shōsetsu ron*, pp. 51–52.

2. Shimamura, "*Futon* gappyō" (Oct. 1907), p. 204.

3. For example, in 1907, Matsubara Shibun (1884–1945), a critic, enthusiastically praised *Futon* for vividly depicting the character of a self-conscious, 36-year-old intellectual of his time (see Matsubara, p. 197).

4. Nagayo (née Okada) Michiyo, Katai's literary disciple and the model for Yoshiko, published "*Futon, En*, oyobi watakushi" in the journal *Shinchō* (Sept. 1915) and revealed how much she and her husband, Nagayo (the model for Tanaka), had been troubled by the prejudice that people had toward them as a result of Katai's misrepresentations (see Nagayo, pp. 264–66).

5. Katagami Tengen, "Tayama Katai-shi no shizenshugi" (Apr. 1908), p. 205. Katagami's essay for the joint review in the October 1907 issue of *Waseda bungaku* was published under the name of Katagami Tengen, his pen name, whereas "Tayama Katai-shi no shizenshugi" was published under Katagami Noburu, his real name, which he used in his later years.

6. Ibid., p. 214.

7. Sōma Gyofū, "*Futon* gappyō" (Oct. 1907), p. 201.

8. Okumura Tsuneya, a Japanese linguist, has studied the increase, from the mid-Meiji period on, in the use of pronouns in Japanese sentences. Futabatei's *Ukikusa* (1897), a translation of Turgenev's *Roudin*, uses *kare* ("he," or "him") only four times, while Yonekawa Masao's translation of the same novel in 1952 uses *kare* 302 times, *kanojo* ("she," "her") 154 times, and *karera* ("they," or "them") twice. Okumura points out that the increase is due primarily to the addition of the grammatical subject (Okumura Tsuneya, "Daimeishi kare, kanojo, karera no kōsatsu," *Kokugo kokubun* 23, no. 11 [1954]; cited in Yanabu, *Hon'yakugo seiritsu jijō*, pp. 200–201). Yanabu argues that in Meiji novels *kare* and *kanojo* were not equivalent to the third-person pronoun "he" and "she" and that, since the two words did not exist in the "living Japanese" of the time, *kare* in Tayama Katai's "Ippeisotsu" (One soldier) and in *Futon* was closer in linguistic effect to a proper name than to a third-person pronoun (ibid., pp. 205–12).

9. In surveying various linguistic theories concerning the "subject" in Japanese,

Okutsu Keiichirō ("Shugo to wa nani ka?") points out that the presence of the grammatical subject on the phenomenal level should not be confused with the presence (or absence) of the grammatical subject on the implied level. According to Okutsu, even when there is no grammatical subject on the phenomenal level, one can often clearly identify the subject from the context. There are also cases in which the subject cannot be identified (*mushugo bun*).

10. *Jibun* is not the exact equivalent of the first-person "I" since it can work as a reflexive pronoun when used with the second or third person. However, when used independently, *jibun* functions as a first-person pronoun (see *Kōjien*, 2d ed., s.v.; and *Kokugo jiten*, s.v.).

11. "Introduction à l'analyse structurale des récits," p. 20; English trans., *Image, Music, Text*, p. 112.

12. Tayama Katai, *Futon*, in *Tayama Katai shū*, p. 146. All citations of *Futon* are from this edition. This and all subsequent English translations of *Futon* are adapted, with extensive corrections and changes, from *The Quilt and Other Stories by Tayama Katai*, trans. Kenneth G. Henshall. Hereinafter cited in the text: the first page number given indicates the page number in the Japanese text, and the second number (in italics) the page number in Henshall's translation.

13. Noriko Mizuta Lippit makes similar observation in her *Reality and Fiction in Modern Japanese Literature*, pp. 22–38.

14. On the history of Japanese translations of the word "love," see Yanabu, *Hon'yakugo seiritsu jijō*, pp. 94–97.

15. Cited in ibid., p. 98.

16. For example, Kinoshita Naoe, a famous socialist activist and writer, later wrote that, upon reading this essay by Tōkoku, he felt as if he "had been hit by a cannonball." In his autobiographical novel *Sakura no mi no jukusuru toki* (1914–18), Shimazaki Tōson wrote of the protagonist that "in reading these sentences, a deep and piercing convulsion passed through his body as if he had been touched by electricity" (cited in Kitamura, *Jinsei*, by Oketani Hideaki, p. 82).

17. Kitamura Tōkoku, "Ensei shika to josei," in *Kitamura Tōkoku shū*, pp. 64–65.

18. Ibid., p. 66.

19. For an insightful analysis of Tōson's *Shinsei*, see Walker.

20. The fact that Futabatei Shimei's *Heibon* (1907) and the main body of Mori Ōgai's *Vita sexualis* (1909) are narrated in the first person is further evidence of this trend. Both Futabatei and Ōgai, who openly criticized the Japanese Naturalists' absolutist claim of "objectivity," appear to have deliberately used a dramatized first-person narration in order to counteract the rapidly prevailing autobiographical reading mode (of third-person autobiographical narratives) developed by the Naturalists.

21. Tayama, "*Sei* ni okeru kokoromi" (Sept. 1908), p. 448.

22. Tayama, "Shasei to iu koto" (July 1907); cited in Wada, pp. 113–14.

23. In his essay "Joji-bun" (Jan.–Mar. 1900), Shiki wrote that in order to convey one's feelings in response to a scene or event, one "should not use embellished words or exaggerate; instead one should depict [*shasei-suru*] things [*jijitsu*] just as they are and just as one sees them." Shiki, who treated the terms *shasei* and *shajitsu* as synonyms, adds that although *shasei* or *shajitsu* depict things as they really are, the process means that one "should select the interesting aspects and should discard the unin-

teresting ones." Shiki's concept of *shasei* was further developed by *haiku* poets such as Takahama Kyoshi and Kawahigashi Hekigodō and by *tanka* poets such as Itō Sachio, Shimaki Akahiko, and Saitō Mokichi (see Yamamoto Masahide, "Shaseibun no hassei ni tsuite," and "Shaseibun to genbun-itchi," in his *Genbun-itchi no rekishi ronkō: zoku-hen*, pp. 452–87; see also Kamei).

24. Tayama, "Sakusha no shukan" (Aug. 1901), pp. 148–49.

25. Ibid., pp. 147–48.

26. Tayama, "Shukan kyakkan no ben" (Sept. 1901), p. 151.

27. Tayama, "Sakusha no shukan," pp. 149–50; idem, "Shukan kyakkan no ben," pp. 152–53.

28. Tayama, "Shukan kyakkan no ben," p. 152.

29. Tayama, "Sakusha no shukan," p. 148.

30. See, e.g., Hisamatsu et al., pp. 103–17. Shimamura Hōgetsu's comprehensive essay on Naturalism entitled "Bungei-jō no shizenshugi" (Naturalism in the literary arts; Jan. 1908) was the first to present this classification, which has been adopted by subsequent literary histories.

31. Shimamura, "*Futon* gappyō," p. 204.

32. Kosugi, p. 418.

33. "Postface" to Nagai Kafū's *Jigoku no hana* (1902), in Nagai, p. 171.

34. Kafū became fascinated with Zola through the English translations that he read intensively in 1901. In Sept. 1903, he published a translation/adaptation of *Nana*, which he based on an English translation. For his writings on Zola, see Nagai, 18: 1–268.

35. On the contemporary response to *Jigoku no hana*, see "Kafū sakuhin dōjidai-hyō shūsei," in Nihon bungaku kenkyū shiryō kankō kai, *Nagai Kafū*, pp. 218–28.

36. Hasegawa Tenkei, "Shizenshugi to wa nan zo ya" (Sept. 1902), p. 278.

37. Ibid. See also Hasegawa Tenkei, "Shizenshugi ni tsuite" (Aug. 1902), pp. 274–77.

38. Fukada, p. 270.

39. For the historical transformation of the word *shizen* (*jinen*), see Yanabu, *Hon'yakugo seiritsu jijō*, pp. 127–48.

40. Tayama Katai, *Jūemon no saigo*, in *Tayama Katai shū*, p. 88.

41. Ibid., p. 114. The English translation is adapted from Henshall, trans., *The Quilt and Other Stories by Tayama Katai*, p. 142.

42. Tayama, *Jūemon no saigo*, in *Tayama Katai shū*, p. 118; *The Quilt and Other Stories*, p. 145.

43. This conflict between love and marriage had been a primary concern of Kitamura Tōkoku and others who advocated the essential importance of romantic love for the "modern individual." Tōkoku, who married Ishizaka Mina after experiencing intense "spiritual love," emphasized the impossibility of maintaining romantic love in the context of marriage and argued, in such works as "Ensei shika to josei," that this was the difference between ideal and reality.

44. Shimamura, "Bungei-jō no shizenshugi," p. 100.

45. Ibid., pp. 114, 116.

46. Hasegawa Tenkei, "Genmetsu jidai no geijutsu" (Oct. 1906), p. 47.

47. Hasegawa Tenkei, "Ronriteki yūgi o haisu" (Oct. 1907), pp. 80–81.

48. Katagami Tengen, "Heibon shūakunaru jijitsu no kachi" (Apr. 1907), pp. 50, 52.

49. Foucault, *History of Sexuality*, pp. 69–70.

50. Although the "rediscovery" of the prose fiction of the Genroku writer Ihara Saikaku occurred at the end of the 1880's (see Chapter 1), it was in relationship to the growing concern for the essential relationship between sexuality and "truth" that Saikaku's works, especially what are called the *kōshoku-mono* (amorous tales), rose in status as Japan's foremost "classics."

51. Ricoeur, "The Function of Fiction in Shaping Reality" (1979), in *A Ricoeur Reader*, p. 121.

52. Natsume Sōseki, "Tayama Katai-kun ni kotau" (Nov. 1908), in Natsume, 11: 184–85.

53. See also Sōseki's "Kyakkan byōsha to inshō byōsha" (Feb. 1910), and "Bungei to hiroikku" (July 1910), in Natsume, 11: 231–33 and 240–42, respectively.

54. Not only did Sōseki criticize the Naturalist writers for their increasingly absolutist claims about the validity of their "objective descriptions of true reality," but he also considered the Naturalist notions of love and nature much too limited. Sōseki himself pursued the concern for love (not sexuality) and the notion of nature (*shizen, ten*) as an ethical principle that transcends limited human self-consciousness, particularly in the period from *Sore kara* (And then; 1909) through his last work *Meian* (Light and darkness; 1916).

55. Ishikawa, p. 336.

56. Ibid., pp. 337–41.

57. Katagami Tengen, "Kokuhaku to hihyō to sōzō to" (Dec. 1912); idem, "Genjitsu o aisuru kokoro" (Jan. 1913); Sōma Gyofū, "Geijutsu no seikatsu-ka" (Sept. 1912); all cited in Yoshida, *Shizenshugi no kenkyū: gekan*, pp. 409–10.

58. Tayama Katai, "Shōsetsu sahō" (1909), in *Tayama Katai shū*, p. 432.

59. Tayama Katai, "Watakushi no Anna Māru," in his *Tōkyō no sanjūnen*, pp. 206–7.

Chapter 5

EPIGRAPH: Kobayashi Hideo, "Watakushi shōsetsu ron" (1935), in *Kobayashi Hideo zenshū*, 3: 126.

1. Akutagawa, *Bungeitekina amarini bungeitekina* (1927), pp. 14–15; Kobayashi Hideo, "Shiga Naoya" (1929), in *Kobayashi Hideo zenshū*, 4: 16, 21; Inoue Yoshio, "Shiga Naoya to Akutagawa Ryūnosuke" (1932), p. 139; Tanigawa, "Watakushi no mita Shiga-san" (1936), pp. 11–12; Itō, *Shōsetsu no hōhō* (1948), p. 86; Hirano, *Geijutsu to jisseikatsu* (1958), p. 26; Dazai, "Nyozegamon" (1948), pp. 298–300; Nakamura Mitsuo, *Shiga Naoya ron* (1954), pp. 151–52, 228; Honda, *Shirakaba-ha no bungaku* (1960), pp. 105–6, 113.

2. Mushakōji, "Rokugō zakkan," *Shirakaba* (Dec. 1911), in *Mushakōji Saneatsu zenshū*, 23:78.

3. Mushakōji Saneatsu, "Tegami kara," cited in Miyoshi Yukio, *Kindai Nihon bungaku shi*, p. 68.

4. Mushakōji, " 'Jiko no tame' oyobi sonota ni tsuite" (Feb. 1912), p. 59. In 1905

Mushakōji was twenty years old, Shiga twenty-two, Arishima Takeo twenty-seven, Arishima Ikuma twenty-three, Satomi Ton seventeen, and Yanagi Muneyoshi sixteen.

5. Mushakōji, *Shirakaba*, Sept. 1911, p. 162.

6. Honda, *Shirakaba-ha no bungaku*, p. 15.

7. Mushakōji, "'Jiko no tame' oyobi sonota ni tsuite," pp. 57–60.

8. Shiga Naoya, *Shiga Naoya zenshū*, 10: 556. All citations of Shiga Naoya's works are from the sixteen-volume *Shiga Naoya zenshū*, hereafter cited as *Zenshū*. All translations are mine unless otherwise noted.

9. Akutagawa, *Bungeitekina amarini bungeitekina*, pp. 14–15.

10. Dazai, "Nyozegamon," pp. 297–98.

11. Nakamura Mitsuo, *Shiga Naoya ron*, p. 126. In Nakamura's words, "Even for readers who are not familiar with Shiga's literary principles or with his personal life, it is only natural to consider Kensaku to be the author himself and to assume that the experiences described are those of the author himself."

12. Yamamoto Masahide, *Kindai buntai hassei*, pp. 48–52.

13. Ibid., p. 53.

14. Akutagawa, *Bungeitekina amarini bungeitekina*, pp. 18–19.

15. Tanizaki Jun'ichirō, "Gendai kōgobun no ketten ni tsuite" (1929), in *Tanizaki Jun'ichirō zenshū*, 20: 183–218. This essay was later developed into the book *Bunshō dokuhon*, which was published in 1934. These two essays by Tanizaki will be discussed in the Epilogue of this study.

16. Shinoda, pp. 52–53.

17. For the history of the publication of "Aru asa," see Kōno Toshirō's "Kōki" ("Editorial Afterward"), in Shiga, *Shiga Naoya zenshū*, 1: 596–98.

18. See "Sōsaku yodan" (1928), "Zoku sōsaku yodan" (1938), "Zoku zoku sōsaku yodan" (1955), all in Shiga, *Zenshū*, vol. 8.

19. The essay first appeared in *Shiga Naoya shū* (vol. 25 of the series *Gendai Nihon bungaku zenshū*, published in 1928 by Kaizōsha), a one-volume collection of thirty-eight of Shiga's existing works arranged in chronological order.

20. Sibley, *The Shiga Hero*.

21. See comments such as the following in "Sōsaku yodan."

I could not express the excitement that I had felt during the actual incident. (on "Jūichigatsu mikka gogo no koto")

I believe that I could honestly and naturally express the feelings that I had felt during those occurrences. (on "Kinosaki nite")

While the I that appeared in the *shōsetsu* was sentimental, the way of writing it did not become sentimental. (on "Haha no shi to atarashii haha")

I faithfully wrote down the facts, but there is one place in the text where I naturally wrote what was not a fact. Since it came to my mind so clearly, I deliberately wrote it down that way. (on "Kugenuma iki")

22. This preface echoes an earlier statement made by Shiga in 1928: "When I gaze upon the Goddess of Mercy at the Pavilion of the Hōryū Temple, I do not think of the sculptor. The statue exists completely independent of its creator. This is extraordi-

nary. If I could ever create such a literary work, I would not place my name on it"
(*Zenshū*, 8: 126).

23. Nakamura Mitsuo, *Shiga Naoya ron*, pp. 81–85.

24. Shiga Naoya, "Sōsaku yodan" (1928), in *Zenshū*, 8: 14.

25. Diaries for 1907, in *Zenshū*, vol. 10; "Techō 7" ("Personal Notebook 7,"
1907), "Techō 8," and "Techō 9," in *Zenshū*, 15 (1984): 127–200.

26. See Kōno Toshirō, "Tolstoy to Shirakaba-ha"; and Kubo.

27. The recollecting "I" implies a parallel here between the young Junkichi's
"playacting" and that of his grandmother, who (after telling Junkichi of his father's
opposition to the potential marriage and subsequently being cursed by Junkichi) loses
her temper and dashes into a storehouse filled with swords. "I thought that the
grandmother was simply playacting [*shibaige*]. But I also thought that she was so
overwrought as to actually go through with it. And it came to my mind that since she
was not clearly aware that she was playacting, there was a good possibility that she
would be easily carried away to the point that she would really do it" (pt. II, chap. 9,
p. 297).

28. Nakamura Mitsuo, *Shiga Naoya ron*, p.84.

29. One of the few critics to pay attention to the temporal distance between the
narrated time and the narrating moment in *Ōtsu Junkichi* is Sugiyama Yasuhiko.
Citing the passage that describes Junkichi's uneasiness at the dance party (pt. I, chap.
5), Sugiyama points to a "split" between the recollected "I" and the "I writing this
novel" and argues that Shiga should have directly expressed young Junkichi's thoughts
and actions instead of using such explanatory phrases as "I was clearly aware of that at
that time" ("Shiga Naoya," pp. 48–49). According to Sugiyama, the "acting self"
(*kōdō toshite no jiko*) and the "observing, reflective self" (*naisei-suru jiko*) should exist in
the same temporal and spatial framework. Sugiyama complains that the "present self"
(*ima no watakushi*) abruptly intrudes into the story of the "past self." In Sugiyama's
view, the "now" of the "present self" makes sense only in the so-called I-novel, which
is characterized by the use of such temporal markers as "now" and the "present I,"
representing the I-novelist. Although sensitive to temporal differences, Sugiyama
ultimately equates the narrating instance with the act of writing of *Ōtsu Junkichi* itself.
As Emile Benveniste (*Problèmes*, pp. 258–66) has suggested, however, the "now" and
"here" as well as the "I" and "you" indicate the "instance of discourse" without any
immediate extra-textual referents. As we have seen, the I-novel cannot be defined by
person, tense, or grammatical form. Instead, it is determined by how a reader supplies
a contextual referent to such textual signifiers as "now" and "here." When the reader,
including Sugiyama, identifies the "present I" of *Ōtsu Junkichi* with the living person
Shiga Naoya, the text becomes an I-novel. In contrast to Nakamura Mitsuo, who
does not recognize any distance between the narrator/author and the protagonist,
Sugiyama regards the distance between the two as a "split," as a negative factor.
Sugiyama sees the "establishment of the self in Shiga's literature" in the "simultaneous
tension" between the "acting self" and the "reflective self," a tension found in such
works as "Kinosaki nite" and *Wakai* ("Shiga Naoya," p. 49).

30. This translation is adapted from "Han's Crime," trans. Ivan Morris in Keene,
Modern Japanese Literature, p. 270.

31. This ambiguity is embodied in the ambiguous nature of the "now" or "present

time" (*ima*) mentioned toward the beginning of chapter 3, the starting point for Sequence II: "The unpleasantness that my father reveals toward me now did not derive from what happened eleven years ago ("Chichi ga ima akarasama ni jibun ni tsuite itteiru fukai wa sore dewa nakatta"; chap. 3, p. 335). The problem is that the original Japanese sentence, in which the non-past verbal form does not automatically mean the present tense, can also be translated into English as "The unpleasantness that my father *revealed toward me now* did not derive from what happened eleven years ago." The possibility or preference for the latter translation emerges only when one rereads the text, or maybe only when one is forced to translate the entirety of *Wakai* into the tense system of English or other Western languages that require a consistent narrational and temporal perspective. Interestingly, other instances of *ima* in *Wakai* can be more clearly classified as either the "present time" of the narrated events or as the present time of narrating/writing. In either event, the narrating instances of Sequences I and II are left ambiguous and cannot be determined grammatically.

32. Kobayashi Hideo, "Shiga Naoya" (1929) in Kobayashi, 4: 24. Kobayashi saw in Shiga's works a "classical," "primordial" "unity of action, sensibility, and reflection." Kobayashi mentioned that "the readers of *Wakai* are moved to tears because they are moved by the author's powerful nature" and that "great art has always seized the cry of nature" (Kobayashi, 4: 26). Kobayashi contrasted Shiga's intuitive creative process—in which action, sensibility, and reflection are unified—with Edgar Allan Poe's critical self-consciousness about the creative process, but he emphasized that both were firmly rooted in their "own nature" (*shishitsu*). Kobayashi's discussion of Shiga is best understood in relationship to his "Samazamanaru ishō" (Various novel designs"; Sept. 1929), in which he characterized the great novel as a "clear sign of human passion" that "seizes the reader with waves of lively and vital ideas and passions" (1: 23)—the product of an active creative process in which a great artist tries to express his singular vision as directly and faithfully as possible through "realism in the true sense of the word," "according to one's own compelling nature," which, Kobayashi emphasized, is not a matter of philosophical principle but one of existential fate or destiny.

33. Sudō, pp. 33–34.

34. Ibid., pp. 166–67.

35. The special temporal and spatial dimension of this day is foreshadowed in an episode in which the grandmother foresees in a dream that the "I" 's uncle will go to Kyoto. The "I" 's uncle, who actually plans to leave for Kyoto, is surprised to hear of the dream. On the "mystical dimension" in Shiga's literary world, see Saeki Shōichi, "Shiga Naoya no shinpiteki jigen."

36. In the following passage from chap. 3 (Sequence II), the narrator recounts the confrontation that occurred with his father half a year after the Kyoto incident.

"It is perfectly all right for you to visit this house. It would be my pleasure. I would like, however, to settle a matter that must be resolved. What do you think?"

"I sympathize with you for what happened in Kyoto. My feelings toward you have greatly altered since then. But I do not believe that I was wrong in behaving that way toward you at that time."

"All right. If that is the way you feel, I want you to stop visiting this house."

"I understand." I bowed and withdrew from his presence, my heart filled with anger.   (chap. 3, p. 338)

37. According to "Zoku sōsaku yodan," Shiga started to write *Tokitō Kensaku* in the autumn of 1912 (after he had published *Ōtsu Junkichi*) and tried to make progress until the summer of 1914, when he gave up, realizing the insurmountable difficulties. Out of remorse at not being able to respond to the recognition given him by Natsume Sōseki, who had offered Shiga an opportunity to serialize a long novel in *Asahi shinbun*, Shiga noted that he could not publish any work for several years, not until 1917, when he published *Wakai*.

38. Sigmund Freud, "Family Romances" (1908) in *Standard Edition*, 9: 237–41. For the "family romance" as an underlying structure of the modern European novel, see Robert.

39. Brooks, p. 64.

40. The works described in *Wakai* as the works written by the "I" earlier that year (chap. 9, pp. 376–77) are easily identified as Shiga's "Kōjinbutsu no fūfu" (A good-natured couple; Aug. 1917) and "Aru oyako" (Certain parents and child; Aug. 1917), which is referred to in *Wakai* by the same title. *Shirakaba*, the literary journal in *Wakai*, is the name of the famous journal Shiga wrote for. The reader does not have to be a private detective to discover that all the proper names that appear in *Wakai* (except for Junkichi) are the real names or initials of Shiga's close literary friends and family members. Shiga himself later stated that *Wakai* was "all facts." The original publication in *Kokuchō* (Oct. 1917) did not include what is now chapter 10 (concerning the birth of the second child). It was added and inserted when *Wakai* was published in book form in January 1918, as part of a book entitled *Yoru no hikari*. In 1936, *Ōtsu Junkichi, Wakai,* and *Aru otoko sono ane no shi* were published as a trilogy. These three works are included in vol. 6 (subtitled "Chūhen-shū") of the seventeen-volume *Shiga Naoya zenshū* (Iwanami shoten, 1955–56). The present sixteen-volume *Shiga Naoya zenshū* (Iwanami shoten, vols. 1–14 and the one-volume Annex [*Bekkan*] published in 1973–74; and vol. 15 in 1984) arranges these three works together at the end of vol. 2. On the history of the publication of *Wakai*, see Kōno Toshirō's "Editor's Notes" for *Shiga Naoya zenshū*, 2: 660–63.

41. "I wrote *Wakai* according to the facts. I started to write *Wakai* while I was experiencing those events, and I finished writing the work in fifteen days. Nothing was concocted, and I had no trouble in that regard. I was terribly excited from start to finish." "Afterword" in the Iwanami bunko edition of *Wakai, Aru otoko sono ane to shi* (1927), *Zenshū*, 8: 123.

42. Genette, *Narrative Discourse*, p. 226.

43. Takemori, "Shiga Naoya ni okeru chichi to ko," pp. 77–78.

44. Yamada, p. 85.

45. Sekiya, p. 169.

46. Takemori, "Shiga Naoya ni okeru chichi to ko," p. 78. Referring to Junkichi's visit to the graveyard at the beginning of *Wakai*, Takemori remarks that "the image of the dead that is recalled in the communion of strong kinship affections, that image of the dead lives in the midst of quietude and eternity, which are attributes of nature itself, the nature that must have embraced Shiga" (p. 70).

47. Shiga, *Dark Night's Passing*, pp. 400–401; trans. Edwin McClellan.

48. Sudō, esp. pp. 229, 232–33, 252–54.

Chapter 6

1. *Bokutō kidan* was written from September to October 1936 and serialized in the *Asahi shinbun* evening edition from April to June 1937. Kafū printed limited copies of a private edition in April 1937, prior to the newspaper serialization. In August 1937, *Bokutō kidan* was published, together with the postscript "Sakugo zeigen," by Iwanami shoten. On the history of variants, see "Kōki," in Nagai, 9: 430–36.

2. See Satō Haruo, "*Bokutō kidan* o yomu," p. 148; and Hirai, p. 131.

3. As mentioned in Chapter 4 of this study, Kafū also published an abridged translation (from the English) of Zola's *Nana* in 1903.

4. See "Saiyū nisshi shō," the diary which Kafū kept during his stay in America and France and which he published in 1917, for the literary works Kafū read during that interval (in Nagai, 19: 5–54).

5. The emergence of the anti-Naturalist Tanbi-ha movement was marked by the establishment of three literary journals: *Subaru*, established in 1909 by Mori Ōgai and Ueda Bin; *Mita bungaku*, established in 1910 by Kafū; and *Shinshichō*, established in 1910 by students at the University of Tokyo, including Tanizaki. For the relationship between Kafū and the Tanbi-ha, see Miyagi, *Tanbi-ha kenkyū ronkō*, esp. pp. 196–228.

6. Terada, "Henki-sei kanbō," pp. 112–17; Etō, 2: 9–36; Katō Shūichi, "Mono to ningen to shakai," pp. 91–129.

7. All citations from *Bokutō kidan* are from *Kafū zenshū* edition published by Iwanami shoten. The English translation of *Bokutō kidan* is adapted from "A Strange Tale from East of the River," trans. Edward G. Seidensticker and included in his *Kafū the Scribbler*. The first page number cited (in roman type) is from the *Kafū zenshū*, and the second one (in italics) is from Seidensticker's translation.

8. Adapted from the Seidensticker's translation with changes made in the tense. The English requires this section to be placed in the past tense for the sake of narrative consistency. In the original, however, this section is rendered in the present tense, relating the narrator's thoughts as they occur at the time of narration.

9. For basic biographical data on Kafū, see "Nenpu" by Takemori Ten'yū in Nagai, vol. 29.

10. Satō Haruo, "*Bokutō kidan* o yomu," pp. 146–49.

11. Hirano, "Nagai Kafū," esp. pp. 192–95.

12. Etō, p. 28.

13. Ibid., pp. 29–30.

14. I would like to acknowledge Mitsuhiro Yoshimoto, a student in my graduate seminar on Kafū at UCLA in 1986, who made this observation and sharpened my thoughts on this text.

15. "Sakugo zeigen" was written in November 1936 and published in the January issue of *Chūō kōron* (1937) under the title of "Bansatei no yūbe" (Evenings at Bansatei Cafe). The title was changed to the present "Sakugo zeigen" when it was included as the postscript to the private edition of *Bokutō kidan*, which appeared shortly before

the newspaper serialization. All later editions of *Bokutō kidan* include "Sakugo zeigen" as a postscript. See "Kōki," in Nagai, vol. 9.

16. My translation. "Sakugo zeigen" is not included in the Seidensticker's translation of *Bokutō kidan*.

17. From April to October 1917, Kafū published the diary he had kept during his stay in America and France (1903–8). See "Saiyū nisshi shō," in Nagai, vol. 19.

18. Nagai, 22: 88–90. Seidensticker has translated most of the relevant parts from the Kafū diary of 1936; see *Kafū the Scribbler*, pp. 146–48.

19. See, e.g., Ōoka; Endō Shūsaku; and Naruse, esp. pp. 162–64.

20. Nakamura Shin'ichirō, p. 10.

21. Hirano Ken and Etō Jun believe that Kafū tries to enhance the reality of his unrealistic fiction by appearing in the narrative as a living witness. Yoshida Seiichi, on the other hand, claims that "although the author emphasizes the truth of what is described, this statement cannot be taken at face value. The encounter must be a fiction" (*Nagai Kafū*, p. 152). In contrast to those critics who question the validity of the "author's comment" about the "truth" of the encounter, Isoda Kōichi points out that this comment itself contributes effectively toward achieving an anachronistic fiction by transcending the realm of verisimilitude and by paradoxically escaping the banal and the anachronistic (pp. 236–37).

22. Etō, p. 27.

Chapter 7

1. All citations of Tanizaki's works are from the 28-volume *Tanizaki Jun'ichirō zenshū* (Chūōkōronsha, 1966–70), hereafter referred to as *Zenshū*. All translations are mine unless otherwise noted.

2. Tanizaki, *Naomi*, trans. Anthony Chambers.

3. *Chijin no ai* was serialized in a newspaper, the *Ōsaka Asahi shinbun*, from March 1924, half a year after the Great Kantō Earthquake (Sept. 1, 1923). The work was received enthusiastically, particularly among younger readers, but more conservative readers and government censors, disturbed by the overt sexuality, criticized it, causing the prestigious newspaper to discontinue the serialization, much to the dismay of the author, who resumed publication four months later in the monthly magazine *Josei* (Nov. 1924–July 1925).

4. Nomura, *Denki Tanizaki Jun'ichirō*, p. 298; Noguchi Takehiko, *Tanizaki Juni'chirō ron*, pp. 125–26; Donald Keene, *Dawn to the West*, p. 754.

5. Nakamura Murao's "Honkaku shōsetsu to shinkyō shōsetsu to" was published in January 1924, Kume Masao's "Watakushi shōsetsu to shinkyō shōsetsu" in January–February 1925, and Uno Kōji's " 'Watakushi shōsetsu' shiken" in October 1925. See Chapter 3 of this study.

6. In *Bunshō dokuhon*, a long essay on Japanese language and style (published in 1934), Tanizaki also uses *watakushi shōsetsu* to mean a first-person novel (*Zenshū*, 21: 240).

7. The English translation is from *Naomi*. The first number (in roman type) indicates the page in the *Zenshū* edition; the second (in italics) the page number in Chambers's translation.

8. Rousseau, p. 43: "Je forme une entreprise qui n'eut jamais d'exemple et dont l'exécution n'aura point d'imitateur. Je veux montrer à mes semblables un homme dans toute la vérité de la nature; et cet homme ce sera moi. Moi seul. Je sens mon coeur et je connais les hommes. Je ne suis fait comme aucun de ceux que j'ai vus; j'ose croire n'être fait comme aucun de ceux qui existent. Si je ne vaux pas mieux, au moins je suis autre. Si la nature a bien ou mal fait de briser le moule dans lequel elle m'a jeté, c'est ce dont on ne peut juger qu'après m'avoir lu." The first Japanese translation of Rousseau's *Confessions* (by Ishikawa Gian) appeared in 1912. Ikuta Chōkō and Ōsugi Sakae published another translation in 1925.

9. In 1909, in an essay titled "Rusō no *Zange*-chū ni miidashitaru jiko" ("The self discovered in Rousseau's *Confessions*"), Shimazaki Tōson wrote that the *Confessions*, which Tōson first read in an English translation in 1894, at the age of 22, had had a profound impact on him: "In those days I was suffering from various difficulties, and I was depressed when I encountered Rousseau. As I became involved in the book, I felt as if it brought out a self which I had not been hitherto aware of. . . . I felt that through this book I began to understand, even though vaguely, modern man's way of thinking and how to view nature directly" (*Tōson zenshū*, 6: 9–11). Tōson noted that he was guided by Rousseau instead of by Goethe and Heine, who were popular at the time, and that he later returned to Rousseau after he had read Flaubert, Maupassant, Turgenev, and Tolstoy. In Tanizaki's writings, Rousseau is mentioned primarily as a "masochist"; see, e.g., "Jōtarō," *Zenshū*, 2: 406; and "Shunkinshō" (1933), *Zenshū*, 13: 537.

10. Akutagawa, *Bungeitekina amarini bungeitekina*, pp. 8, 14–15.

11. Kume, "Watakushi shōsetsu."

12. Tanizaki's friend Satō Haruo noted that Tanizaki asked him if *Itansha no kanashimi* was inferior to Shiga Naoya's *Wakai*, which was also published in 1917 and which was enthusiastically received ("Jun'ichirō hito oyobi geijutsu" [1927], in *Satō Haruo bungei ronshū*, p. 106).

13. For biographical information, see Nomura, *Denki Tanizaki Jun'ichirō*; and Hashimoto Yoshiichirō.

14. Noguchi Takehiko (*Tanizaki Jun'ichirō ron*, pp. 52–54) notes that a monthly journal *Hentai shinri* (Abnormal psychology) was established in 1915 by an organization called Nihon Seishin-igaku kai (Japanese Society of Psychiatry). The contributors to the journal were not only medical doctors and psychologists but influential critics and intellectuals in various fields, including such socialist critics/scholars as Abe Isoo and Yoshino Sakuzō and such writers as Hasegawa Nyozekan and Ikuta Chōkō. According to Noguchi, this journal published articles on psychopathology, criminal psychology, forensic medicine, psychic phenomena, sex education, suicide, and sexual crimes. The journal published an introduction to Freud's psychoanalysis in 1916, and translations of Freud and Jung began appearing in the 1920's. In 1920, the journal had a special issue on "abnormal sexuality," explaining such terms as "sadism," "masochism," "exhibitionism," and "pygmalionism," in terms of Krafft-Ebing's *Psychopathia sexualis* (originally published in German in 1903). This journal also promoted the view that many artistic geniuses such as Baudelaire, Poe, Wilde, Dostoyevsky, Strindberg, and Ibsen were "mad" in some way.

15. Tanizaki became interested in films from the mid-1910's. From 1920 to 1921

he became seriously involved with a film company called Taishō Katsuei. He wrote several film scenarios—such as "Tsuki no sasayaki" (Whisper of the moon; 1921) and "Jasei no in" (Temptation of a serpent; 1922)—with Seiko in mind as the leading actress (Nomura, *Denki Tanizaki Jun'ichirō*, pp. 235–41).

16. For an illuminating analysis of the relationship among these works, see Saeki, *Monogatari geijutsu ron*, pp. 134–87.

17. Nakamura Mitsuo, "Tanizaki Jun'ichirō ron," in *Nakamura Mitsuo zenshū*, 4: 230–31.

18. "Shōnen" (1911), "Himitsu" (1911), "Akubi" (1912), "Kyōfu" (1913), "Zōnen" (1914), "Shitsū" (1916), "Majutsushi" (1917), "Zenkamono" (1918), "Haha o kouru ki" (1919), "Seiko no tsuki" (1919), "Aru hyōhakusha no omokage" (1919), "Watakushi" (1921), "Fukōna haha no hanashi" (1921), *Chijin no ai* (1924–25), *Mōmoku monogatari* (1931), "Kinokuni no kitsune urushi-kaki ni tsuku monogatari" (1931), *Kagi* (1956), *Yume no ukihashi* (1959), *Fūten rōjin nikki* (1961–61).

19. "Dokutan" (1915), "Binan" (1916), "Hakuchū kigo" (1918), "Yanagiyu no jiken" (1918), "Norowareta gikyoku" (1919), *Manji* (1928–30), *Yoshino kuzu* (1931), *Ashikari* (1932), "Nirasaki-shi no kuchi yori Shupaiheru Shutain ga tobidasu hanashi" (1933).

20. "Sannin hōshi" (1929), "Kakukai shōnin tengu ni naru koto" (1931), *Bushūkō hiwa* (1931–32), *Shunkin shō* (1933), *Kikigaki shō* (1935), *Shōshō Shigemoto no haha* (1949–50), "Ono no Takamura imōto ni koisuru koto" (1951), "Chino monogatari" (1951).

21. Translated by Howard Hibbett as "The Thief" in Tanizaki, *Seven Japanese Tales*, p. 113.

22. Ibid., pp. 115–16.

23. Itō, "Kaisetsu," pp. 294–95.

24. For the influence of Poe on Tanizaki, see Inoue Ken. Drawing on the memoirs of Satō Haruo and Akutagawa, Inoue suggests that Tanizaki became seriously interested in Poe from 1914. Inoue argues that, among Poe's works, "The Domain of Arnheim," with its theme of "second nature," had the deepest impact on Tanizaki. See also Lippit, pp. 82–103.

25. In fact, Tanizaki was not alone in paying attention to and experimenting with the performative aspect of a dramatized first-person, confessional narration in this period. See, e.g., Uno Kōji's early works such as "Kura no naka" (1918), which was modeled on the life and speech of the writer Chikamatsu Shūkō, and "Ku no sekai" (1919–20). Uno, who was later considered a typical I-novelist, was apparently inspired by Gogol's short stories. Significantly, Tanizaki enthusiastically praised Chikamatsu Shūkō's "Kurokami" (Jan. 1922), a first-person confessional narrative, not so much for its autobiographical interest but for the protagonist's self-revealing narration (Tanizaki, "Kurokami jo" [July 1924], in *Zenshū*, 23: 81–82).

26. For the influence of Western writers on young Tanizaki, see Ōshima, pp. 158–75; and Imura, pp. 215–55.

27. Praz, p. 207.

28. Kinoshita Mokutarō, "Pan no kai to Okujō teien" (1934), cited in Hashimoto Yoshiichirō, p. 33.

29. Noguchi Takehiko, *Tanizaki Jun'ichirō ron*, pp. 21–22.

30. See my discussion in Chapter 4 of this study.

31. When the Great Kantō Earthquake occurred on September 1, 1923, Tanizaki was staying at Hakone, a hot-springs resort west of Tokyo. Since his house in Yokohama was destroyed by the earthquake, he moved to Kansai (the Kyoto-Osaka-Kobe area) with his family. Being a genuine Tokyoite, born and raised in Tokyo, Tanizaki did not expect to stay long in Kansai, but he eventually married an Osaka woman and continued to live in Kansai for another thirty years. *Chijin no ai* is the first work that Tanizaki published after moving to Kansai.

32. Imai; Maeda Ai, "Taishō kōki tsūzoku shōsetsu no tenkai," in idem, *Kindai dokusha no seiritsu*, pp. 168–228.

33. Nomura, *Denki Tanizaki Jun'ichirō*, p. 297.

34. Imai, pp. 110–35; Hiratsuka Raichō.

35. Nakamura Mitsuo, "Tanizaki Jun'ichirō ron," *Nakamura Mitsuo zenshū*, 4: 287.

36. Nomura, *Denki Tanizaki Jun'ichirō*, pp. 235–41, 272–79.

37. Freud, "Fetishism" (1927), in *Standard Edition*, 21: 152–55. For a discussion of Freud's fetishisim in relation to fin de siècle European exoticism, see Bongie, p. 76.

Epilogue

1 As in the previous chapter, all citations of Tanizaki's works are from the 28-volume *Tanizaki Jun'ichirō zenshū*, hereafter referred to as *Zenshū*. All translations are mine.

2. Akutagawa, *Bungeitekina amarini bungeitekina*, pp. 18–19.

3. Kawabata, pp. 24–25.

4. Hata, pp. 77–126.

5. Paul Ricoeur, "The Creativity of Language" (1984), reprinted in *A Ricoeur Reader*, pp. 463–81.

Bibliography

Unless otherwise noted, the place of publication of Japanese-language items is Tokyo. The abbreviation KBHT is used for Yoshida Seiichi, Inagaki Tatsurō, et al., eds., *Kindai bungaku hyōron taikei*; and the abbreviation NBKSS for the series *Nihon bungaku kenkyū shiryō sōsho*, ed. Nihon bungaku kenkyū shiryō kankōkai.

Abe Jirō. "Byōsha no daizai to byōsha no taido." In KBHT, vol. 3, ed. Yoshida Seiichi and Wada Kingo. Kadokawa shoten, 1972.

———. "Jinsei hihyō no genri to shite no jinkakushugiteki kenchi." In KBHT, vol. 5, ed. Endō Tasuku and Sofue Shōji. Kadokawa shoten, 1972.

Abe Nōzei. "Jiko no mondai to shite mitaru shizenshugiteki shisō." In KBHT, vol. 3, ed.Yoshida Seiichi and Wada Kingo. Kadokawa shoten, 1972.

———. "Shizenshugi ni okeru shukan no ichi." In KBHT, vol. 3, ed. Yoshida Seiichi and Wada Kingo. Kadokawa shoten, 1972.

Akase Masako. *Nagai Kafū to Furansu bungaku*. Aratake shuppan, 1976.

Akutagawa Ryūnosuke. *Akutagawa Ryūnosuke zenshū*. Chikuma shobō, 1971.

———. *Bungeitekina amarini bungeitekina*. Kōdansha bunko. Kōdansha, 1972 [1927].

Anderson, Benedict. *Imagined Communities*. London: Verso, 1983.

Aono Suekichi. "*An'ya kōro* ni tsuite." In *Shiga Naoya*. NBKSS. Yūseidō, 1970.

Ara Masahito. "Watakushi shōsetsu ron." *Bungakukai* 6 (Sept. 1952): 23–30.

Ara Masahito, ed. *Tanizaki Jun'ichirō kenkyū*. Yagi shoten,1972.

Arishima Takeo. "Sengen hitotsu." In KBHT, vol. 5, ed. Endō Tasuku and Sofue Shōji. Kadokawa shoten, 1972.

Auerbach, Erich. *Mimesis: The Representation of Reality in Western Literature*. Trans. Willard R. Trask. Princeton: Princeton University Press, 1968.

Austin, J. L. *How to Do Things with Words*. 2d ed. Cambridge, Mass.: Harvard University Press, 1975.

Bakhtin, Mikhail. *The Dialogic Imagination: Four Essays*. Trans. Cary Emerson and Michael Holquist. Austin: University of Texas Press, 1981.

———. *Problems of Dostoevsky's Poetics.* Trans. Cary Emerson. Minneapolis: University of Minnesota Press, 1984.

Barthes, Roland. *Le degré zéro de l'écriture.* Paris: Seuil, 1972 [1953].

———. "L'effet de réel." *Communications* 11 (1968).

———. *The Grain of the Voice.* Trans. Linda Coverdale. New York: Hill and Wang, 1985.

———. *Image, Music, Text.* Trans. Stephen Heath. New York: Hill and Wang, 1977.

———. "Introduction à l'analyse structurale des récits." *Communications* 8 (1966): 1–27.

———. *The Responsibility of Forms.* Trans. Richard Howard. New York: Hill and Wang, 1985.

———. *The Rustle of Language.* Trans. Richard Howard. New York: Hill and Wang, 1986.

———. *S/Z.* Paris: Seuil, 1970.

Barthes, Roland, et al. *Poétique du récit.* Paris: Seuil, 1977.

Benveniste, Emile. *Problèmes de linguistique générale.* Paris: Gallimard, 1966.

———. *Problems in General Linguistics.* Trans. Mary Elizabeth Meek. Coral Gables, Fla.: University of Miami Press, 1971.

Bongie, Chris. *Exotic Memories: Literature, Colonialism, and the Fin de Siècle.* Stanford: Stanford University Press, 1991.

Booth, Wayne. *The Rhetoric of Fiction.* Chicago: University of Chicago Press, 1961.

Brooks, Peter. *Reading for the Plot.* Vintage Books. New York: Random House, 1985.

Cadava, Eduardo, et. al. eds. *Who Comes After the Subject?* New York: Routledge, 1991.

Chatman, Seymour. *Story and Discourse: Narrative Structure in Fiction and Film.* Ithaca, N.Y.: Cornell University Press, 1978.

Chiba Kameo. "Shinkankaku-ha no tanjō." In KBHT, vol. 5, ed. Endō Tasuku and Sofue Shōji. Kadokawa shoten, 1972.

Chikamatsu Shūkō (Tokuda Shūkō). "Shimamura Hōgetsu-shi no 'Kanshō soku jinsei no tame nari' o zeseisu." In KBHT, vol. 3, ed. Yoshida Seiichi and Wada Kingo. Kadokawa shoten, 1972.

Culler, Jonathan. *On Deconstruction: Theory and Criticism After Structuralism.* Ithaca, N.Y.: Cornell University Press,1982.

———. *The Pursuit of Signs: Semiotics, Literature, Deconstruction.* London: Routledge and Kegan Paul, 1981.

———. *Structuralist Poetics.* Ithaca, N.Y.: Cornell University Press, 1975.

Dazai Osamu. "Nyozegamon." In *Dazai Osamu zenshū,* vol. 10. Chikuma shobō, 1967.

de Man, Paul. *Allegories of Reading.* New Haven: Yale University Press, 1979.

———. "Autobiography as De-facement." *MLN* 94 (1979): 919–30.

———. *Blindness and Insight.* 2d ed. Minneapolis: University of Minnesota Press, 1983.

Derrida, Jacques. *De la grammatologie.* Paris: Minuit, 1967.

———. *La voix et le phénomène.* Paris: Presses Universitaires de France, 1967.

DeWoskin, "The Six Dynasties Chih-Kuai and the Birth of Fiction." In *Chinese Narrative: Critical and Theoretical Essays,* ed. Andrew Plaks. Princeton: Princeton University Press, 1977.

Doi Tadao. *Nihongo no rekishi.* Rev. ed. Shibundō, 1989.

Eagleton, Terry. *Literary Theory.* Minneapolis: University of Minnesota Press, 1983.

Eakin, Paul John. *Fictions in Autobiography*. Princeton: Princeton University Press, 1985.

Eguchi Kan. "Bundan no taisei to kaku sakka no ichi: 1918." In KBHT, vol. 5, ed. Endō Tasuku and Sofue Shōji. Kadokawa shoten, 1972.

Endō Shūsaku. "Kafū nikki ni tsuite." In *Kafū zenshū geppō*, no. 19 (Aug. 1972): 1–3. In vol. 19 of *Kafū zenshū*. Iwanami shoten, 1972.

Endō Tasuku. "Tokitō Kensaku kara *An'ya kōro* e." In *Shiga Naoya*. NBKSS. Yūseidō, 1970.

Etō Jun. "Nagai Kafū ron." 1959. In *Etō Jun chosaku shū*, vol. 2. Kōdansha, 1967.

Felman, Shoshana. *The Literary Speech Act*. Trans. Catherine Porter. Ithaca, N.Y.: Cornell University Press, 1983.

——. "Women and Madness: The Critical Phallacy." *Diacritics* 5, no. 4 (1975): 2–10.

Fish, Stanley. *Self-Consuming Artifacts: The Experience of Seventeenth-Century Literature*. Berkeley: University of California Press, 1972.

Foucault, Michel. *L'archéologie du savoir*. Paris: Gallimard, 1969.

——. *The Archaeology of Knowledge*. Trans. A. M. Sheridan Smith. London: Tavistock, 1972.

——. *The History of Sexuality*, vol. 1. Trans. Robert Hurley. New York: Vintage Books, 1980 [1978].

——. *Language, Counter-Memory, Practice: Selected Essays and Interviews by Michel Foucault*. Ed. and trans. Donald F. Bouchard. Ithaca, N.Y.: Cornell University Press, 1977.

——. *Les mots et les choses*. Paris: Gallimard, 1966.

——. *Power/Knowledge: Selected Interviews and Other Writings, 1972–1977*. Ed. Colin Gordon. Trans. Colin Gordon et al. New York: Pantheon Books, 1980.

Fowler, Edward. *The Rhetoric of Confession: Shishōsetsu in Early Twentieth-Century Japanese Fiction*. Berkeley: University of California Press, 1988.

Freud, Sigmund. *The Standard Edition of the Complete Psychological Works of Sigmund Freud*. 24 vols. Ed. James Strachey. London: Hogarth Press, 1953–74.

Fujita Shōzō. "Shōwa hachinen o chūshin to suru tenkō no jōkyō." In *Tenkō: jō*, ed. Shisō no kagaku kenkyū kai. Heibonsha, 1959.

Fukada Yasukazu (Ishūsei). "Shizenshugiteki keikō." In KBHT, vol. 2, ed. Inagaki Tatsurō and Satō Masaru. Kadokawa shoten, 1972.

Fukuda Tsuneari. "Shiga Naoya no kōzai." In *Shiga Naoya*. NBKSS. Yūseidō, 1970.

Futabatei Shimei. *Futabatei Shimei shū*. Nihon kindai bungaku taikei 4. Kadokawa shoten, 1971.

——. *Futabatei Shimei zenshū*. 9 vols. Iwanami shoten, 1964–65.

Genette, Gérard. "Discours du récit." In *Figure III*. Paris: Seuil, 1972.

——. "Frontières du récit." *Communications* 8 (1966): 152–63.

——. *Introduction à l'architexte*. Paris: Seuil, 1979.

——. *Narrative Discourse*. Trans. Jane Lewin. Ithaca, N.Y.: Cornell University Press, 1980.

——. *Nouveau discours du récit*. Paris: Seuil, 1983.

Gluck, Carol. *Japan's Modern Myths*. Princeton: Princeton University Press, 1985.

Harari, Josue, ed. *Textual Strategies: Perspectives in Post-Structuralist Criticism*. Ithaca, N.Y.: Cornell University Press, 1979.

Hasegawa Izumi. *Kindai Nihon bungaku hyōron shi.* Yūseidō, 1966.

Hasegawa Tenkei. "Futatabi shizenshugi no rikkyakuchi ni tsuite." In KBHT, vol. 3,. ed. Yoshida Seiichi and Wada Kingo. Kadokawa shoten, 1972.

———. "Genjitsu bakuro no hiai." In KBHT, vol. 3, ed. Yoshida Seiichi and Wada Kingo. Kadokawa shoten, 1972.

———. "Genjitsushugi no shosō." In KBHT, vol. 3, ed. Yoshida Seiichi and Wada Kingo. Kadokawa shoten, 1972.

———. "Genmetsu jidai no geijutsu." In KBHT, vol. 3, ed. Yoshida Seiichi and Wada Kingo. Kadokawa shoten, 1972.

———. "Mukaiketsu to kaiketsu." In KBHT, vol. 3, ed. Yoshida Seiichi and Wada Kingo. Kadokawa shoten, 1972.

———. "Niiche-shugi to biteki seikatsu." In KBHT, vol. 2, ed. Inagaki Tatsurō and Satō Masaru. Kadokawa shoten, 1972.

———. "Ronriteki yūgi o haisu." In KBHT, vol. 3, ed. Yoshida Seiichi and Wada Kingo. Kadokawa shoten, 1972.

———. "Shizenshugi ni tsuite." In KBHT, vol. 2, ed. Inagaki Tatsurō and Satō Masaru. Kadokawa shoten, 1972.

———. "Shizenshugi to wa nan zo ya." In KBHT, vol. 2, ed. Inagaki Tatsurō and Satō Masaru. Kadokawa shoten, 1972.

Hashimoto Minoru. *Tanizaki Jun'ichirō: sono mazohizumu.* Yagi shoten, 1974.

Hashimoto Yoshiichirō. *Tanizaki Jun'ichirō no bungaku.* Rev. ed. Ōfūsha, 1972.

Hasumi Shigehiko. *Monogatari hihan josetsu.* Chūōkōronsha, 1985.

———. *Natsume Sōseki ron.* Seitosha, 1978.

———. *"Shi-shōsetsu" o yomu.* Chūōkōronsha, 1979.

Hata Kōhei. *Tanizaki Jun'ichirō: "Genji monogatari" taiken.* Chikuma shobō, 1976.

Hattori Nankaku. *Nankaku sensei monjū.* In *Sorai gakuha.* Nihon shisō taikei 37. Iwanami shoten, 1972.

Hijiya-Kirschnereit, Irmela. *Selbstenblössungsrituale.* Wiesbaden: Franz Steiner, 1981.

———. *Shi-shōsetsu: jiko bakuro no gishiki.* Trans. Mishima Ken'ichi et al. Heibonsha, 1992.

Hirai Teiichi. "Nagai Kafū ron." 1937. In *Nagai Kafū.* NBKSS. Yūseidō, 1971.

Hirakawa Sukehiro. *Wakon yōsai no keifu: uchi to soto kara no Meiji Nihon.* Kawade shobō shinsha, 1971.

Hirano Ken. *Geijutsu to jisseikatsu.* Shinchō bunko. Shinchōsha, 1964 [1958].

———. "Nagai Kafū." 1954. In *Geijutsu to jisseikatsu.* Shinchō bunko. Shinchōsha, 1964 [1958].

———. "Tayama Katai." 1956–62. In *Geijutsu to jisseikatsu.* Shinchō bunko. Shinchōsha, 1964 [1958].

———. "Watakushi shōsetsu no niritsu haihan." 1951. In *Geijutsu to jisseikatsu.* Shinchō bunko. Shinchōsha, 1964 [1958].

Hirano Ken, Odagiri Hideo, and Yamamoto Kenkichi, eds. *Gendai Nihon bungaku ronsō shi.* 3 vols. Miraisha, 1956.

Hiraoka Tokuyoshi. *"An'ya kōro no sakusha."* In *Shiga Naoya zenshū geppō,* no. 12 (May 1974): 5–8; no. 13 (July 1974): 4–7. In vols. 8 and 13 of *Shiga Naoya zenshū.* Iwanami shoten, 1974.

———. *Meiro no shōsetsu ron.* Kawade shobō shinsha, 1974.

Hiraoka Toshio. *Nihon kindai bungaku no shuppatsu.* Kinokuniya shoten, 1973.

———. *Nihon kindai bungaku shi kenkyū.* Yūseidō, 1969.

Hiratsuka Raichō. *Genshi josei wa taiyō de atta.* Ōtsuki shoten, 1971–73.

Hirotsu Kazuo, Uno Kōji, and Kasai Zenzō. *Hirotsu Kazuo, Uno Kōji, Kasai Zenzō shū.* Nihon kindai bungaku taikei 40. Kadokawa shoten, 1970.

Hisamatsu Sen'ichi. "Nikki bungaku no honshitsu." In *Koten no mado.* Kadokawa shoten, 1960.

Hisamatsu Sen'ichi, Yoshida Seiichi, et al., eds. *Kindai I.* Zōho shinpan Nihon bungaku shi 6. Shibundō, 1975.

———. *Kindai II.* Zōho shinpan Nihon bungaku shi 7. Shibundō, 1975.

Honda Shūgo. "*An'ya kōro* no sōkō-rui." In *Shiga Naoya zenshū geppō,* no. 4 (Aug. 1974): 6–10. In vol. 6 of *Shiga Naoya zenshū.* Iwanami shoten, 1974.

———. *Shirakaba-ha no bungaku.* Shinchō bunko. Shinchōsha, 1960 [1951].

Imai Seiichi. *Taishō demokurashii.* Nihon no rekishi 23. Chūōkōronsha, 1974.

Imura Kimie. "Oscar Wilde." In *Ōbei sakka to Nihon kindai bungaku,* vol. 5. Kyōiku shuppan sentā, 1975.

Inazawa Hideo. *Tanizaki Jun'ichirō no sekai: seiyō to Nihon no kakawari.* Shichōsha, 1981.

Inoue Ken. "Tanizaki Jun'ichirō to E. A. Poe." *Hikaku bungaku kenkyū,* no. 32 (1977): 78–103.

Inoue Kiyoshi. *Meiji ishin.* Nihon no rekishi 20. Chūōkōronsha, 1974.

Inoue Yoshio. "Shiga Naoya to Akutagawa Ryūnosuke." In *Shiga Naoya.* NBKSS. Yūseidō, 1970.

Iriye Mitsuko. "Jigoku no hana ron." *Bungaku* (May 1972): 21–31.

Irokawa Daikichi. *Kindai kokka no shuppatsu.* Nihon no rekishi 21. Chūōkōronsha, 1974.

———. *Meiji no bunka.* Iwanami shoten. 1970.

———. *Meiji seishin shi.* Rev. ed. Chūōkōronsha, 1973.

Iser, Wolfgang. *The Implied Reader: Patterns of Communication in Prose Fiction from Bunyan to Beckett.* Baltimore: Johns Hopkins University Press, 1974.

Ishikawa Takuboku. "Jidai heisoku no genjō." In KBHT, vol. 3, ed. Yoshida Seiichi and Wada Kingo. Kadokawa shoten, 1972.

Isoda Kōichi. *Nagai Kafū.* Kōdansha, 1979.

Isogai Hideo. "Bunshōgo to shite no 'genbun-itchi.' " *Kokubungaku kaishaku to kyōzai no kenkyū* 25, no. 10 (1980): 50–56.

Itō Sei. "Kaisetsu." In *Tanizaki Junichirō zenshū,* vol. 10. Chūōkōronsha, 1959.

———. "Marcel Proust to James Joyce no bungaku-hōhō ni tsuite." In KBHT, vol. 7, ed. Takahashi Haruo and Yasumasa Masao. Kadokawa shoten, 1972.

———. *Shōsetsu no hōhō.* Shinchō bunko. Shinchōsha, 1957 [1948].

———. *Tanizaki Jun'ichirō no bungaku.* Chūōkōronsha, 1970.

Itō Sei, Saeki Shōichi, and Mishima Yukio. "Zadankai kindai bungaku no futatsu no nagare: Tanizaki-teki na mono to Shiga-teki na mono." In *Tanizaki Jun'ichirō.* NBKSS. Yūseidō, 1972.

Itō Sei, Usui Yoshimi, Kawamori Yoshizō, and Nakamura Mitsuo. "Zadankai Tanizaki Jun'ichirō ron: shisōsei to mushisōsei." In *Tanizaki Jun'ichirō.* NBKSS. Yūseidō, 1972.

Iwano Hōmei. "Gendai shōrai no shōsetsuteki hassō o isshin subeki boku no byōsha ron." In квнт, vol. 5, ed. Endō Tasuku and Sofue Shōji. Kadokawa shoten, 1972.
——. "Gendai shōsetsu no byōsha-hō." In квнт, vol. 3, ed. Yoshida Seiichi and Wada Kingo. Kadokawa shoten, 1972.

Jakobson, Roman. "On Realism in Art." In *Readings in Russian Poetics: Formalist and Structuralist Views*, ed. Ladislav Matejka and Krystyna Pomorska. Cambridge, Mass.: MIT Press, 1971.

Jay, Paul. *Being in the Text*. Ithaca, N.Y.: Cornell University Press, 1984.

Kamei Hideo. "Shaseibun no imisuru mono: bungaku ni okeru 'ishō' to 'rōdō' no jikaku." *Kokubungaku kaishaku to kyōzai no kenkyū* 25, no. 10 (1980): 64–71.

Karatani Kōjin. "Kindai Nihon no hihyō: Shōwa zenki I." *Kikan shichō* 5 (July 1989): 46–61.
——. *Nihon kindai bungaku no kigen*. Kōdansha, 1980.
——. *Origins of Modern Japanese Literature*. Trans. Brett de Bary. Durham, N.C.: Duke University Press, 1993.
——. "Shi-shōsetsu no keifugaku." *Kokubungaku kaishaku to kyōzai no kenkyū* 23, no. 16 (1978): 116–21.
——. "Shi-shōsetsu no ryōgisei: Shiga Naoya." In *Bungei dokuhon Shiga Naoya*, ed. Sudō Matsuo. Kawade shobō shinsha, 1976.

Katagami Tengen (Noboru). "*Futon* gappyō." In *Tōson, Katai*, ed. Yoshida Seiichi et al. Kokugo kokubungaku kenkyū shi taisei 13. Rev. ed. Sanseidō, 1978.
——. "Heibon shūakunaru jijitsu no kachi." In квнт, vol. 3, ed. Yoshida Seiichi and Wada Kingo. Kadokawa shoten, 1972.
——. "Jinseikan-jō no shizenshugi." In квнт, vol. 3, ed. Yoshida Seiichi and Wada Kingo. Kadokawa shoten, 1972.
——. "Mukaiketsu no bungaku." In квнт, vol. 3, ed. Yoshida Seiichi and Wada Kingo. Kadokawa shoten, 1972.
——. "Shizenshugi no shukanteki yōso." In квнт, vol. 3, ed. Yoshida Seiichi and Wada Kingo. Kadokawa shoten, 1972.
——. "Tayama Katai-shi no shizenshugi." In *Tōson, Katai*, ed. Yoshida Seiichi et al. Kokugo kokubungaku kenkyū shi taisei 13. Rev. ed. Sanseidō, 1978.

Katō Shūichi. "Mono to ningen to shakai." 1960–61. In *Nagai Kafū*. nbkss. Yūseidō, 1971.
——. *Nihon bungaku shi josetsu*, 2 vols. Chikuma shobō, 1980.

Katsuyama Isao. *Taishō shi-shōsetsu kenkyū*. Meiji shoin, 1980.

Kawabata Yasunari. *Shin bunshō dokuhon*. Shinchō bunko. Shinchōsha, 1954 [1950].

Kawachi Kiyoshi, ed. *Shizenshugi bungaku: kakkoku ni okeru tenkai*. Keisō shobō, 1962.

Kawasaki Yasuyuki, Naramoto Tatsuya, et al. eds. *Nihon bunka shi*. 3 vols. Yūhikaku, 1977.

Kawazoe Kunimoto. "Bungaku kakushin-ki to Eikoku no hyōron-zasshi." *Bungaku* 27 (Jan. 1959): 54–61.

Keene, Donald. *Dawn to the West: Japanese Literature in the Modern Era*. New York: Holt, Rinehart, and Winston, 1984.

Keene, Donald, ed. *Modern Japanese Literature*. New York: Grove Press, 1956.

Kindai bungaku hyōron taikei, see Yoshida Seiichi, Inagaki Tatsurō, et al.

Kinoshita Mokutarō. "Taiyō kisha Hasegawa Tenkei-shi ni tou." In KBHT, vol. 3, ed. Yoshida Seiichi and Wada Kingo. Kadokawa shoten, 1972.
Kitamura Tōkoku. *Jinsei ni aiwataru to wa nan no ii zo: Kitamura Tōkoku shū.* Ōbunsha bunko. Ōbunsha, 1979.
———. *Kitamura Tōkoku shū.* Meiji bungaku zenshū 29. Chikuma shobō, 1976.
Kitaoka Seiji. " 'Shōsetsu sōron' zaigen kō: Futabatei to Belinsky." *Kokugo to kokubungaku* (Sept. 1965). Reprinted in *Tsubouchi Shōyō, Futabatei Shimei.* NBKSS. Yūseidō, 1979.
Kobayashi Hideo. *Kobayashi Hideo zen hon'yaku.* Kōdansha, 1981.
———. *Kobayashi Hideo zenshū.* 12 vols. Shinchōsha, 1968.
Kobori Keiichirō. "Kaisetsu." In Mori Ōgai, *Ōgai senshū,* vol. 11.
———. *Wakaki hi no Mori Ōgai.* Tōkyō daigaku shuppankai, 1969.
Kōno Taeko. *Tanizaki bungaku to kōtei no yokubō.* Chūkō bunko. Chūōkōronsha, 1980 [1976].
Kōno Toshirō. "Kōki." In *Shiga Naoya zenshū,* vol. 1. Iwanami shoten, 1973.
———. "Tolstoy to Shirakaba-ha." In *Nihon kindai bungaku no hikaku bungakuteki kenkyū.* Shimizu kōbundō, 1971.
Kosugi Tengai. "Hayari uta jo." In KBHT, vol. 2, ed. Inagaki Tatsurō and Satō Masaru. Kadokawa shoten, 1972.
Kubo Tadao. "Tolstoy." In *Ōbei sakka to Nihon kindai bungaku,* vol. 3. Kyōiku shuppan sentā, 1976.
Kume Masao. "Junbungaku yogi setsu." In *Gendai Nihon bungaku ronsō shi,* vol. 1, ed. Hirano Ken, Odagiri Hideo, Yamomoto Kenkichi. Miraisha, 1956.
———. "Watakushi shōsetsu to shinkyō shōsetsu." In *Gendai Nihon bungaku ronsō shi,* vol. 1, ed. Hirano Ken, Odagiri Hideo, Yamomoto Kenkichi. Miraisha, 1956.
Kunikida Doppo. *Kunikida Doppo shū.* Meiji bungaku zenshū 66. Chikuma shobō, 1974.
Kuroda, S.-Y. "Réflexions sur les fondements de la théorie de la narration." In *Langue, Discours, Société: pour Emile Benveniste.* Ed. Julia Kristeva, Jean-Claude Milner, and Nicolas Ruwet. Paris: Seuil, 1975.
Kyokutei (Takizawa) Bakin. *Chinsetsu yumiharizuki.* Nihon koten bungaku taikei 61. Iwanami shoten, 1962.
———. *Kinsei mono no hon Edo sakusha burui.* Ed. Kimura Miyogo. Yagi shoten, 1988.
Lejeune, Philippe. *Je est un autre.* Paris: Seuil, 1980.
———.*Le pacte autobiographique.* Paris: Seuil, 1975. Citation is from a partial translation, "The Autobiographical Contract," in *French Literary Theory Today,* ed. Tzvetan Todorov. Cambridge, Eng.: Cambridge University Press, 1982.
Lemon, Lee T., and Marion J. Reis, eds. *Russian Formalist Criticism: Four Essays.* Lincoln: University of Nebraska Press, 1965.
Lippit, Noriko Mizuta. *Reality and Fiction in Modern Japanese Literature.* New York: M. E. Sharpe, 1980.
Maeda Ai. *Kindai dokusha no seiritsu.* Yūseidō, 1973.
———. "Meiji no hyōgen shisō to buntai: shōsetsu no 'katari' o meggute." *Kokubungaku kaishaku to kyōzai no kenkyū* 25, no. 10 (1980): 6–13.
Maruyama Masao. "From Carnal Literature to Carnal Politics." In *Thought and Be-*

havior in Modern Japanese Politics, ed. Ivan Morris. London: Oxford University Press, 1963.

Masamune Hakuchō. "Uchimura Kanzō" 1950. In *Masamune Hakuchō*. Nihon no bungaku 11. Chūōkōronsha, 1968.

Masaoka Shiki, "Joji-bun." 1900. In *Masaoka Shiki shū*, ed. Matsui Toshihiko. Kadokawa shoten, 1972.

Matejka, Ladislav, and Krystyna Pomorska, eds. *Readings in Russian Poetics*. Cambridge, Mass.: MIT Press, 1971.

Matsubara Shibun. "*Futon* gappyō." In *Tōson, Katai,* ed. Yoshida Seiichi et al. Kokugo kokubungaku kenkyū shi taisei 13. Rev. ed. Sanseidō, 1978.

McClellan, Edwin. "*An'ya kōro* ni tsuite." Trans. Fukuda Rikutarō. In *Shiga Naoya*. NBKSS. Yūseidō, 1970.

———. "Tōson and the Autobiographical Novel." In *Tradition and Modernization in Japanese Culture*, ed. Donald H. Shively. Princeton: Princeton University Press, 1971.

———. *Woman in the Crested Kimono: The Life of Shibue Io and Her Family Drawn from Mori Ōgai's "Shibue Chūsai."* New Haven: Yale University Press, 1985.

Mishima Yukio. *Sakka ron*. Chūkō bunko. Chūōkōronsha, 1974 [1970].

Miyagi Tatsurō. *Tanbi-ha kenkyū ronkō*. Ōfūsha, 1976.

Miyagi Tatsurō, ed. *Nagai Kafū no bungaku*. Ōfūsha, 1973.

Miyoshi, Masao. *Accomplices of Silence: The Modern Japanese Novel*. Berkeley: University of California Press, 1974.

———. "Against the Native Grain: The Japanese Novel and the 'Postmodern' West." *South Atlantic Quarterly* 87, no. 3 (Summer 1988): 525–50.

Miyoshi Yukio. *Sakuhin ron no kokoromi*. Shibunō, 1978.

Miyoshi Yukio, ed. *Kindai Nihon bungaku shi*. Yūhikaku, 1975.

Miyoshi Yukio and Takemori Tenyū, eds. *Kindai bungaku*. 10 vols. Yūhikaku, 1977–78.

Mori Ōgai. *Ōgai senshū*. 21 vols. Iwanami shoten, 1978–80.

Murayama Yoshihiro. "Kanbunmyaku no mondai: seiō no shōgeki no naka de." *Kokubungaku kaishaku to kyōzai no kenkyū* 25, no. 10 (1980): 40–45.

Mushakōji Saneatsu. "*An'ya kōro* to jiden shōsetsu." In KBHT, vol. 5, ed. Endō Tasuku and Sofue Shōji. Kadokawa shoten, 1972.

———. *Aru otoko*. Vol. 2 of *Mushakōji Saneatsu senshū*. Seidōsha, 1964.

———. "Bungaku to shakaishugiteki keikō." In KBHT, vol. 5, ed. Endō Tasuku and Sofue Shōji. Kadokawa shoten, 1972.

———. "Jibun no fude de suru shigoto." *Shirakaba* (Mar. 1911). In *Mushakōji Saneatsu zenshū*, vol. 23. Shinchōsha, 1956.

———. " 'Jiko no tame' oyobi sonota ni tsuite." *Shirakaba* (Feb. 1912). In KBHT, vol. 4, ed. Inagaki Tatsurō and Kōno Toshirō. Kadokawa shoten, 1971.

———. "Rokugō zakkan." *Shirakaba* (Dec. 1911). In *Mushakōji Saneatsu zenshū*, vol. 23. Shinchōsha, 1956.

———. "Shirakaba kankō no kotoba." In KBHT, vol. 4, ed. Inagaki Tatsurō and Kōno Toshirō. Kadokawa shoten, 1971.

Nagai Kafū. *Kafū zenshū*. 28 vols. Iwanami shoten, 1962–65.

Nagayo Michiyo (née Okada Michiyo). "*Futon, En*, oyobi watakushi." In *Tōson,*

Katai, ed. Yoshida Seiichi et al. Kokugo kokubungaku kenkyū shi taisei 13. Rev. ed. Sanseidō, 1978.

Nakamura Mitsuo. *Futabatei Shimei den.* Kōdansha bunko. Kōdansha, 1976 [1958].

———. *Fūzoku shōsetsu ron.* Shinchō bunko. Shinchōsha, 1958 [1950].

———. *Hyōron Nagai Kafū.* Chikuma shobō, 1979.

———. *Meiji bungaku shi.* Chikuma sōsho, no. 9. Chikuma shobō, 1963.

———. *Nakamura Mitsuo zenshū.* 16 vols. Chikuma shobō, 1971–73.

———. *Nihon no kindai shōsetsu.* Iwanami shoten, 1954.

———. *Shiga Naoya ron.* Chikuma sōsho, no. 50. Chikuma shobō, 1966 [1954].

Nakamura Murao. "Honkaku shōsetsu to shinkyō shōsetsu to." In *Gendai Nihon bungaku ronsō shi,* vol. 1, ed. Hirano Ken, Odagiri Hideo, Yamamoto Kenkichi. Miraisha, 1956.

Nakamura Shin'ichirō. "Kafū nikki ni tsuite." In *Kafū zenshū geppō,* no. 13 (Feb. 1972): 9–11. In vol. 13 of *Kafū zenshū.* Iwanami shoten, 1972.

Nakamura Yukihiko. *Kinsei bungei shichō kō.* Iwanami shoten, 1975.

———. *Kinsei sakka kenkyū.* San'ichi shobō, 1961.

———. *Kinsei shōsetsu shi no kenkyū.* Ōfūsha shuppan, 1961.

Nakano Shigeharu. "*An'ya kōro* zōdan." In *Shiga Naoya.* NBKSS. Yūseidō, 1970.

Naruse Masakatsu. "Kafū no nikki." 1965. In *Nagai Kafū.* NBKSS. Yūseidō, 1971.

Natsume Sōseki. *Sōseki zenshū.* 17 vols. Iwanami shoten, 1965–67.

Nihon bungaku kenkyū shiryō kankōkai, ed. *Nagai Kafū.* NBKSS. Yūseidō, 1971.

———. *Shiga Naoya.* NBKSS. Yūseidō, 1970.

———. *Shiga Naoya II.* NBKSS. Yūseidō, 1978.

———. *Shirakaba-ha bungaku: Arishima Takeo, Mushakōji Saneatsu.* NBKSS. Yūseidō, 1974.

———. *Shizenshugi bungaku: Kunikida Doppo, Tayama Katai, Tokuda Shūsei.* NBKSS. Yūseidō, 1975.

———. *Tanizaki Jun'ichirō.* NBKSS. Yūseidō, 1972.

———. *Tsubouchi Shōyō, Futabatei Shimei.* NBKSS. Yūseidō, 1979.

———. *Watakushi shōsetsu: Hirotsu Kazuo, Uno Kōji, Kasai Zenzō, Kamura Isota.* NBKSS. Yūseidō, 1983.

Noguchi Fujio. "*Bokutō kidan* o megutte." 1975. In *Bungei dokuhon Nagai Kafū.* Kawade shobō shinsha, 1981.

Noguchi Takehiko. *Shōsetsu no Nihongo.* Nihongo no sekai 13. Chūōkōronsha, 1980.

———. *Tanizaki Jun'ichirō ron.* Chūōkōronsha, 1973.

Nomura Shōgo. *Denki Tanizaki Jun'ichirō.* Rokkō shuppan, 1972.

———. *Tanizaki Jun'ichirō no sakuhin.* Rokkō shuppan, 1974.

Ochi Haruo. *Kindai bungaku no tanjō.* Kōdansha, 1975.

———. "*Shōsetsu shinzui* no botai." 1956. In *Tsubouchi Shōyō, Futabatei Shimei,* ed. Nihon bungaku kenkyūshiryō kankōkai. NBKSS.. Yūseidō, 1979.

———. "*Ukigumo* no yukue." In *Tsubouchi Shōyō, Futabatei Shimei.* NBKSS. Yūseidō, 1979.

Ochi Haruo, Kōno Toshirō, et al. "Shinpoziumu *An'ya kōro* o megutte." *Kokubungaku kaishaku to kyōzai no kenkyū* 21, no. 4 (1976): 6–39.

Oda Jun'ichirō, trans. "Karyū shunwa." In *Meiji honyaku bungaku shū.* Meiji bungaku zenshū 7. Chikuma shobō, 1972.

Oda Sakunosuke. "Kanōsei no bungaku." In *Shiga Naoya.* NBKSS. Yūseidō, 1970.

Oguri Fūyō. "*Futon* gappyō." In *Tōson, Katai*, ed. Yoshida Seiichi et al. Kokugo kokubungaku kenkyū shi taisei 13. Rev. ed. Sanseidō, 1978.

Ojima Kenji. "*Shōsetsu shinzui* to Bain no shūji-sho." *Kokubungaku kenkyū* 46 (June 1970): 22–33.

Okutsu Keiichirō. "Shugo to wa nani ka." *Gengo* 4, no. 3 (1975): 203–11.

Ōoka Shōhei. "Nikki bungaku no miryoku." In *Kafū zenshū geppō*, no. 7 (Aug. 1971): 3–5. In vol. 7 of *Kafū zenshū*. Iwanami shoten, 1971.

Ōshima Maki. "Tanizaki Jun'ichirō no debyū to Anatole France." In *Tanizaki Jun'ichirō*. NBKSS. Yūseidō, 1972.

Ōuchi Kazuko. "Kobayashi Hideo no shoki-sakuhin to Baudelaire." In *Hikaku bungaku kenkyū*, no. 37 (1980): 20–40.

Ozaki Yukio. "Preface to the Second Volume of *Setchū-bai*." In *Meiji seiji shōsetsu shū II*. Meiji bungaku zenshū 6. Chikuma shobō, 1967.

Plaks, Andrew. "Towards a Critical Theory of Chinese Narrative." In *Chinese Narrative: Critical and Theoretical Essays*, ed. A. Plaks. Princeton: Princeton University Press, 1977.

Praz, Mario. *The Romantic Agony*. London: Oxford University Press, 1970 [1st English ed. 1933].

Prince, Gerald. "Introduction à l'étude du narrataire." *Poetique* 14 (1973): 178–96.

Ricoeur, Paul. *A Ricoeur Reader: Reflection and Imagination*. Ed. Mario Valdes. Toronto: University of Toronto Press, 1991.

———. *Time and Narrative*, vol. 1 and 2. Trans. Kathleen McLaughlin and David Pellauer. Chicago: University of Chicago Press, 1984, 1985.

Rimmon-Kenan, Shlomith. *Narrative Fiction: Contemporary Poetics*. London: Methuen, 1983.

Robert, Marthe. *Roman des origines, origines du roman*. Paris: Grasset, 1972.

Rousseau, Jean-Jacques. *Les Confessions I*. Paris: Garnier-Flammarion, 1968.

Saeki Shōichi. *Denki to bunseki no aida*. Nanbokusha, 1967.

———. *Kindai Nihon no jiden*. Kōdansha, 1981.

———. *Monogatari geijutsu ron: Tanizaki, Akutagawa, Mishima*. Kōdansha, 1979.

———. *Nihonjin no jiden*. Kōdansha bunko. Kōdansha, 1979 [1974].

———. *Nihon no "watakushi" o motomete*. Kawade shobō shinsha, 1974.

———. "Shiga Naoya no shinpiteki jigen." *Bungei*, Jan. 1974, 278–89.

Saganoya Omuro (Hokubō Sanshi). "Shōsetsuka no sekinin." In KBHT, vol. 1, ed. Yoshida Seiichi and Asai Kiyoshi. Kadokawa shoten, 1971.

Said, Edward. *Orientalism*. Vintage Books. New York: Random House, 1979.

Sakagami Hiroichi. *Nagai Kafū nooto*. Ōfūsha, 1978.

Sakai Toshihiko. "Ren'ai-bungaku to shakaishugi." In KBHT, vol. 3, ed. Yoshida Seiichi and Wada Kingo. Kadokawa shoten, 1972.

Sasabuchi Tomoichi. *Nagai Kafū: daraku no bigakusha*. Meiji shoin, 1976.

Sasaki Hideaki. "Shiga Naoya ni okeru 'seishun' to 'bungaku.' " *Hikaku bungaku kenkyū*, no. 43 (1983): 46–74.

Sasaki Yukitsuna. "Myōjō no romantisizumu." In *Gendai bungaku kōza: Meiji no bungaku II*. Bessatsu Kokubungaku kaishaku to kanshō, 1975.

Satō Haruo. "*Bokutō kidan* o yomu." 1937. In *Bungei dokuhon Nagai Kafū*. Kawade shobō shinsha, 1981.

——. "Ich Roman no koto." In *Gendai Nihon bungaku ronsō shi*, vol. 1, ed. Hirano Ken, Odagiri Hideo, Yamamoto Kenkichi. Miraisha, 1956.

——. *Satō Haruo bungei ronshū*. Ed. Shimada Kinji. Sōshisha, 1963.

Seidensticker, Edward. *Kafū the Scribbler*. Stanford: Stanford University Press, 1965.

Seki Ryōichi. "*An'ya kōro*." In *Shiga Naoya*. NBKSS. Yūseidō, 1970.

——. *Shōyō, Ōgai: kōshō to shiron*. Yūseidō, 1971.

Sekiya Ichirō. "*Wakai* shidoku." In *Shiga Naoya: jiga no kiseki*, ed. Ikeuchi Teruo. Yūseidō, 1992.

Senuma Shigeki. "Taishō demokurasii to bungaku." In *Iwanami kōza Nihon bungaku shi*, vol. 15. Iwanami shoten, 1959.

Shiga Naoya. *A Dark Night's Passing*. Trans. Edwin McClellan. Kōdansha International, 1976.

——. *Shiga Naoya zenshū*. 16 vols. Iwanami shoten, 1973–74, 1984.

Shigetomo Ki, ed. "*Bokutō kidan*" no sekai. Kasama shoin, 1976.

Shikitei Sanba. *Ukiyo buro*. Nihon koten bungaku taikei 63. Iwanami shoten, 1957.

Shimamura Hōgetsu. "Bungei-jō no shizenshugi." In KBHT, vol. 3, ed. Yoshida Seiichi and Wada Kingo. Kadokawa shoten, 1972.

——. "*Futon* gappyō." In *Tōson, Katai*, ed. Yoshida Seiichi et al. Kokugo kokubungaku kenkyū shi taisei 13. Rev. ed. Sanseidō, 1978.

——. "Geijutsu to jisseikatsu no sakai ni yokotawaru issen." In KBHT, vol. 3, ed. Yoshida Seiichi and Wada Kingo. Kadokawa shoten, 1972.

——. "Ima no bundan to shin-shizenshugi." In KBHT, vol. 3, ed. Yoshida Seiichi and Wada Kingo. Kadokawa shoten, 1972.

——. "Kaigi to kokuhaku." In KBHT, vol. 3, ed. Yoshida Seiichi and Wada Kingo. Kadokawa shoten, 1972.

——. "Kanshō soku jinsei no tame nari." In KBHT, vol. 3, ed. Yoshida Seiichi and Wada Kingo. Kadokawa shoten, 1972.

——. "Shizenshugi no kachi." In KBHT, vol. 3, ed. Yoshida Seiichi and Wada Kingo. Kadokawa shoten, 1972.

——. "Torawaretaru bungei." In KBHT, vol. 3, ed. Yoshida Seiichi and Wada Kingo. Kadokawa shoten, 1972.

Shimamura Hōgetsu and Nakamura Seiko. "Moderu mondai no imi oyobi sono kaiketsu." In KBHT, vol. 3, ed. Yoshida Seiichi and Wada Kingo. Kadokawa shoten, 1972.

Shimazaki Tōson. *Tōson shishū*. Nihon kindai bungaku taikei 15. Kadokawa shoten, 1971.

——. *Tōson zenshū*. 18 vols. Chikuma shobō, 1966–71.

Shimizu Tōru. "Bunmei to bungaku no aida: Tanizaki Jun'ichirō no saihyōka o megutte." *Chūō kōron*, Nov. 1976, 326–38.

Shimonaka Kunihiko, ed. *Atarashii kokugo e no ayumi*. 2d ed. Vol. 6 of *Nihongo no rekishi*. Heibonsha, 1976.

Shinoda Kōichirō. *Shōsetsu wa ika ni kakareta ka*. Iwanami shoten, 1982.

Shioda Ryōhei. "Zuihitsu bungaku ron." *Kokubungaku kaishaku to kyōzai no kenkyū* 10, no. 9 (1965): 8–11.

Sibley, William. "Naturalism in Japanese Literature." *Harvard Journal of Asiatic Studies* 28 (1968): 157–69.

——. *The Shiga Hero*. Chicago: University of Chicago Press, 1979.

Sōma Gyofū. "Bungei-jō shukaku ryōtai no yūgō." In KBHT, vol. 3, ed. Yoshida Seiichi and Wada Kingo. Kadokawa shoten, 1972.

——. "*Futon* gappyō." In *Tōson, Katai*, ed. Yoshida Seiichi et al. Kokugo kokubungaku kenkyū shi taisei 13. Rev. ed. Sanseidō, 1978.

——. "Kokuhaku to kyakkan-ka." In KBHT, vol. 3, ed. Yoshida Seiichi and Wada Kingo. Kadokawa shoten, 1972.

Sudō Matsuo. *Shiga Naoya no bungaku*. Ōfūsha, 1963.

Sugimoto Hidetarō. *Sanbun no Nihongo*. Nihongo no sekai 14. Chūōkōronsha, 1981.

Sugiyama Yasuhiko. "Hasegawa Futabatei ni okeru genbun-itchi." In *Tsubouchi Shōyō, Futabatei Shimei*. NBKSS. Yūseidō, 1979.

——. "Shiga Naoya ni okeru shisō to buntai." 1970. In *Shiga Naoya II*. NBKSS. Yūseidō, 1978.

Sumiya Mikio. *Kindai Nihon no keisei to kirisutokyō*. Shinkyō shuppansha, 1950.

——. *Nihon no shakai shisō: kindaika to kirisutokyō*. Tōkyō daigaku shuppankai, 1968.

Takabatake Setsuko. "*An'ya kōro* kōsei-jō ni mirareru ichi mondai." In *Shiga Naoya*. NBKSS. Yūseidō, 1970.

Takada Mizuho. "Kindai no zuihitsu." *Kokubungaku kaishaku to kyōzai no kenkyū* 10, no. 9 (1965): 116–22.

Takahashi Hideo. *Shiga Naoya: kindai to shinwa*. Bungei shunjū, 1981.

Takahashi Toshio. *Kafū bungaku no chiteki haikei*. Kasama shoin, 1975.

Takayama Chogyū. *Takayama Chogyū, Saitō Nonohito, Anesaki Chōfū, Tobari Chikufū*. Meiji bungaku zenshū 40. Chikuma shobō, 1970.

Takemori Tenyū. "*An'ya kōro* sobyō." In *Shiga Naoya*. NBKSS. Yūseidō, 1970.

——. "Shiga Naoya ni okeru chichi to ko." 1970. In *Shiga Naoya II*. NBKSS. Yūseidō, 1978.

Takeuchi Ryōchi. "Shi-shōsetsu ni tsuite." *Bungaku* 21 (Dec. 1953): 66–69.

Tamiya Torahiko. "Shi-shōsetsu no unmei." *Bungaku* 21 (Dec. 1953): 59–62.

Tanigawa Tetsuzō. "*An'ya kōro* oboegaki." In *Shiga Naoya*. NBKSS. Yūseidō, 1970.

——. "Watakushi no mita Shiga-san." In *Shiga Naoya*. NBKSS. Yūseidō, 1970.

Tanizaki Jun'ichirō. *Naomi*. Trans. Anthony Chambers. New York: Alfred Knopf, 1985.

——. *Seven Japanese Tales*. Trans. Howard Hibbett. New York: Berkeley, 1965.

——. *Tanizaki Jun'ichirō zenshū*. 28 vols. Chūōkōronsha, 1966–70.

Tayama Katai. "Byōsha ron." In *Tōson, Katai*, ed. Yoshida Seiichi et al. Kokugo kokubungaku kenkyū shi taisei 13. Rev. ed. Sanseidō, 1978.

——. "*No no hana* jo." In KBHT, vol. 2, ed. Inagaki Tatsurō and Satō Masaru. Kadokawa shoten, 1972.

——. *The Quilt and Other Stories by Tayama Katai*. Trans. Kenneth G. Henshall. University of Tokyo Press, 1981.

——. "Rokotsu naru byōsha." In KBHT, vol. 2, ed. Inagaki Tatsurō and Satō Masaru. Kadokawa shoten, 1972.

——. "Sakusha no shukan." In KBHT, vol. 2, ed. Inagaki Tatsurō and Satō Masaru. Kadokawa shoten, 1972.

———. "*Sei* ni okeru kokoromi." In квнт, vol. 3, ed. Yoshida Seiichi and Wada Kingo. Kadokawa shoten, 1972.

———. "Shukan kyakkan no ben." In квнт, vol. 2, ed. Inagaki Tatsurō and Satō Masaru. Kadokawa shoten, 1972.

———. *Tayama Katai shū.* Nihon kindai bungaku taikei 19. Kadokawa shoten, 1972.

———. *Tayama Katai zenshū.* 17 vols. Bunsendō shoten, 1973–74.

———. *Tōkyō no sanjūnen.* Iwanami bunko. Iwanami shoten, 1981 [1917].

Terada Tōru. *Bungaku sono naimen to gaikai.* Rev. ed. Shimizu Kōbundō, 1970.

———. "Henki-sei kanbō." 1946. In *Bungei dokuhon Nagai Kafū.* Kawade shobō shinsha, 1981.

Tobari Chikufū. "Biteki seikatsu ron to Nietzsche." In квнт, vol. 2, ed. Inagaki Tatsurō and Satō Masaru. Kadokawa shoten, 1972.

Todorov, Tzvetan. "Les catégories du récit littéraire." *Communications* 8 (1966): 125–51.

———. "The Origins of Genres." *New Literary History* 8, no. 1 (1976): 159–69.

———. *Poetique de la prose.* Paris: Seuil, 1971.

Todorov, Tzvetan, ed. *French Literary Theory Today.* Cambridge, Eng.: Cambridge University Press, 1982.

Togawa Shūkotsu. "Henchō ron." In *Jogaku zasshi, Bungakukai shū.* Meiji bungaku zenshū 32. Chikuma shobō, 1973.

———. "Katsudō ron." In *Jogaku zasshi, Bungakukai shū.* Meiji bungaku zenshū 32. Chikuma shobō, 1973.

Tōkai Sanshi. *Kajin no kigū.* In *Meiji seiji shōsetsu shū,* II, ed. Yanagida Izumi. Meiji bungaku zenshū 6. Chikuma shobō, 1967.

Toyama Shigehiko. "Koe no buntai." *Kokubungaku kaishaku to kyōzai no kenkyū,* 25, no. 10 (1980): 36–39.

Tsubouchi Shōyō. "Ryūtei Tanehiko no hyōban." In квнт, vol. 1, ed. Yoshida Seiichi and Asai Kiyoshi. Kadokawa shoten, 1971.

———. "Shakespeare kyakuhon hyōchū." In квнт, vol. 1, ed. Yoshida Seiichi and Asai Kiyoshi. Kadokawa shoten, 1971.

———. *Shōsetsu shinzui.* In *Tsubouchi Shōyō shuū.*

———. *Tamenaga Shunsui no hihyō.* In квнт, vol. 1, ed. Yoshida Seiichi and Asai Kiyoshi. Kadokawa shoten, 1971.

———. *Tōsei Shosei katagi.* In *Tsubouchi Shōyō shū.*

———. *Tsubouchi Shōyō shū.* Nihon kindai bungaku taikei 3. Kadokawa shoten, 1974.

Uchida Roan. *Meiji no sakka.* Chikuma shobō, 1941.

Ueda Bin. "Shizenshugi." In кънт, vol. 3, ed. Yoshida Seiichi and Wada Kingo. Kadokawa shoten, 1972.

Uemura Masahisa. *Uemura Masahisa chosaku shū,* vols. 3 and 4. Shinkyō shuppansha, 1966.

Uno Kōji. *Uno Kōji zenshū,* 12 vols. Chūōkōronsha, 1972.

———. " 'Watakushi shōsetsu' shiken." In *Gendai Nihon bungaku ronsō shi,* vol. 1, ed. Hirano Ken, Odagiri Hideo, Yamamoto Kenkichi. Miraisha, 1956.

Wada Kingo. *Byōsha no jidai.* Sapporo: Hokkaidō daigaku tosho kankōkai, 1975.

Wada Kingo and Sōma Tsuneo, eds. *Tayama Katai shū.* Kindai bungaku taikei 19. Kadokawa shoten, 1972.

Walker, Janet. *The Japanese Novel of the Meiji Period and the Ideal of Individualism.* Princeton: Princeton University Press. 1979.

Wellek, Rene. *Discriminations: Further Concepts of Criticism.* New Haven: Yale University Press, 1970.

Yamada Yūsaku. "*Wakai* no kōzō." In *Issatsu no kōza Shiga Naoya.* Yūseidō, 1982.

Yamaji Aizan. "Gendai Nihon kyōkai shi ron." In idem, *Shiron shū.* Misuzu shobō, 1958 [1905].

Yamamoto Kenkichi. *Watakushi shōsetsu sakka ron.* Shinbisha, 1966 [1943].

Yamamoto Masahide. *Genbun-itchi no rekishi ronkō.* Ōfūsha, 1971.

———. *Genbun-itchi no rekishi ronkō: zokuhen.* Ōfūsha, 1976.

———. *Kindai buntai hassei no shiteki kenkyū.* Iwanami shoten, 1965.

Yanabu Akira. *Hon'yakugo seiritsu jijō.* Iwanami shoten, 1982.

———. "Seiōteki hassō to hyōgen: hon'yaku de tsukurareta Nihon 'bun.'" *Kokubungaku kaishaku to kyōzai no kenkyū* 25, no. 10 (1980): 46–49.

Yanagida Izumi. "Gi Shuku-shi to Futabatei Shimei." *Kokubungaku kaishaku to kanshō* 23 (May 1963): 8–14.

———. *Seiji shōsetsu kenkyū: jō.* Shunjūsha, 1935.

———. *Seiyō bungaku no inyū.* Shunjūsha, 1974.

———. "*Shōsetsu shinzui*" *kenkyū.* Shunjūsha, 1966.

———. *Wakaki Tsubouchi Shōyō.* Shunjūsha, 1960.

Yanagida Izumi, Katsumoto Seiichirō, and Ino Kenji, eds. *Zadankai Meiji bungaku shi.* Iwanami shoten, 1961.

———. *Zadankai Taishō bungaku shi.* Iwanami shoten, 1965.

Yano Ryūkei. *Keikoku bidan.* In *Yano Ryūkei shū.* Meiji bungaku zenshū 15. Chikuma shobō, 1970.

Yasuoka Shōtarō. *Shiga Naoya shiron.* Kōdansha bunko. Kōdansha, 1983 [1968].

Yokomitsu Riichi. "Junsui shōsetsu ron." In квнт, vol. 7, ed. Takahashi Haruo and Yasumasa Masao. Kadokawa shoten, 1972.

———. "Kankaku katsudō." In квнт, vol. 6, ed. Miyoshi Yukio and Sofue Shōji. Kadokawa shoten, 1973.

Yosano Tekkan. *Yosano Tekkan, Yosano Akiko shū.* Meiji bungaku zenshū 51. Chikuma shobō, 1968.

Yoshida Seiichi. *Nagai Kafū.* Vol. 5 of *Yoshida Seiichi chosakushū.* Ōfūsha, 1979.

———. *Rōmanshugi no kenkyū.* Tōkyōdō shuppan, 1970.

———. *Shizenshugi no kenkyū: gekan.* Tōkyōdō shuppan, 1955.

———. *Zuihitsu nyūmon.* Shinchō bunko. Shinchōsha, 1965 [1961].

Yoshida Seiichi et al. eds. *Tōson, Katai.* Kokugo kokubungaku kenkyū shi taisei 13. Rev. ed. Sanseidō, 1978.

Yoshida Seiichi, Inagaki Tatsurō, et al. eds. *Kindai bungaku hyōron taikei.* 10 vols. Kodokawa shoten, 1971–75.

Zola, Emile. *La fortune des Rougon.* Paris: Garnier-Flammarion, 1969.

———. *Le roman expérimental.* Paris: Garnier-Flammarion, 1971.

Index

In this index an "f" after a number indicates a separate reference on the next page, and an "ff" indicates separate references on the next two pages. A continuous discussion over two or more pages is indicated by a span of page numbers, e.g., "57-59." *Passim* is used for a cluster of references in close but not consecutive sequence.

Browning, Robert, 201
Buddhism, 192–93, 194
Bulwer-Lytton, Edward George, 192
Bundan (literary circle): I-novel and, 8, 55, 59–60, 203
Bungaku (literature), 25f, 195–96. *See also* Literature
Bungaku gokusui ronsō (Debate over the rise or decline of literature), 25–26
Bungakukai (magazine), 29, 36–42 *passim*, 75
Bungakushi (history of literature), 196. *See also* Bungaku; Literary history; Literature
Bungei jidai (magazine), 178
Bungei sensen (magazine), 205
Bungei shunjū (magazine), 54, 206
Bunko (magazine), 196
Bunraku (puppet theater), 16, 181
Byron, George Gordon, 40, 75, 201

Carlyle, Thomas, 36, 47, 192, 201
Chekhov, Anton, 49
Chijin no ai (A fool's love; Naomi), *see under* Tanizaki Jun'ichirō
Chikamatsu Monzaemon, 196
Chikamatsu Shūkō, 49–50, 62, 203, 218; "Kurokami" (Black hair), 218
Chin Sheng-t'an, 191
Chinese narrative tradition, 16ff
Chinese vernacular fiction: and *shōsetsu*, 16, 25–26, 31, 190–91, 199
Christianity: and notion of independent moral subject, 33–39; and notions of self, 33–39 *passim*, 201–2; Freedom and People's Rights movement and, 33ff, 199–200; and ideal of love, 34, 37, 74–76, 104–12 *passim*; in early Meiji period, 34–36, 200; and Western literature, 35–36, 200f; in Shiga Naoya's texts, 103–12 *passim*. *See also* Protestantism
Chūō kōron (magazine), 95, 103, 154
Classical literature, Japanese: in I-novel discourse, 3, 51, 120–21, 131, 178, 183–84, 189–90, 196, 204, 210. *See also* Japanese tradition
Confession: Tayama Katai's *Futon* and, 70–71, 91–92; Tanizaki Jun'ichirō and, 151–59. *See also* Autobiography; I-novel; I-novel discourse; Narration

Confucianism: and *shōsetsu*, 17f, 21, 191. *See also* Neo-Confucianism
Constant, Benjamin, 57

Dadaism, 97, 177
D'Annunzio, Gabriele, 162
Dante, Alighieri, 162, 201
Dazai Osamu, 62f, 93, 96
Decadence, European, 154, 161–65 *passim*, 169, 173f
Degas, Edgar, 163
Derrida, Jacques, 3
Discourse, 185f, 212; definitions of, 11–12; on new notion of *shōsetsu*, 24–25, 36, 194n46, 196; direct vs. indirect, 71–72. *See also* Enunciation; I-novel discourse; Narration
Disraeli, Benjamin, 18; *Contarini Fleming*, 36, 200
Don Quixote (Cervantes), 85
Doppo, *see* Kunikida Doppo
Dostoyevsky, Feodor Mikhailovich, 31, 217; *Crime and Punishment*, 51, 56
Dumas, Alexandre, 18, 197

Eagleton, Terry, 192
Eliot, George, 192
Emerson, Ralph Waldo, 36
Emperor: and the subject, 33, 38, 199
Enunciation, 11–12, 158, 180–85. *See also* Discourse; Narration; Subject
Etō Jun, 141, 149, 216
Evolutionism: *shōsetsu* and, 20–23 *passim*
Exoticism, 143, 162–65, 169, 173ff, 181–86 *passim*, 219
Expressionism, 97, 177

Fact: and historical sources, 19, 191f; Tayama Katai's *Futon* and, 69, 79, 89–92 *passim*; and I-novel discourse, 89–92 *passim*, 99; as ideology, 89–90, 169. *See also* Fiction; Reality; Referentiality; Representation; Shiga Naoya
Fatal Woman, *see* Femme fatale
Femme fatale, 160–63 *passim*, 169–74 *passim*
Fetishism, 162, 173–74
Fiction: vs. fact, 3ff, 90, 99, 142–50 *passim*, 176, 184ff, 191; and social reality, 54, 205; Western novelists and, 4f, 59f, 65; and truth, 22–25 *passim*, 142–50 *passim*.

in, 1–2, 62, 79, 209; Tayama Katai's
Futon in, 65, 69, 71; and tradition, 189–
90. *See also* Evolutionism; Literature
Literature: modernization and, 7, 185f;
changing notions of, 25, 28, 40, 185f,
189, 195–96; ideology of, 40, 74–76,
89–90, 162, 165, 192. *See also Bungaku*;
Novel; *Shōsetsu*
Loti, Pierre: *Madame Chrysanthemum*, 143
Love, ideal of, 10, 208ff; and *shōsetsu*, 21f;
and Western literature, 21f, 37, 39, 73–
76 *passim*, 85, 88, 106; and Christianity,
34, 37, 74–76, 104–12 *passim*; and notions of self, 37, 39, 75–76, 88, 104–12
passim, 167, 209f; in Tayama Katai's
Futon, 73–76 *passim*, 85–86, 88, 168;
and sexuality, 73–76, 81–88 *passim*,
105–12 *passim*, 210; and narcissism, 76,
168–69; and marriage, 85–86, 105–12
passim, 209; in Shiga Naoya's texts, 104–
12 *passim*

Maeterlinck, Maurice, 94, 195
Makino Shin'ichi, 7, 204
Mao Tsung-kang, 191
Maruyama Masao, 4,
Marxism, 8, 53–58 *passim*, 136, 206
Masamune Hakuchō, 49, 62, 78f, 201
Masaoka Shiki, 10, 29, 46, 77–78, 203,
208–9
Mass society: and I-novel, 8, 54f
Matsuo Bashō, 51, 204
Maupassant, Guy de, 57f, 78, 85, 135, 150,
195, 217
Merimée, Prosper, 163
Mill, John Stewart: *On Liberty*, 27
Minpon shugi (popular polity), 52
Minshū geijutsu (popular art), 54, 205
Miyako no hana (magazine), 24
Miyazaki Muryū, 197
Modern Girl (*modan gāru*), 166–69
Modernism, 8, 57f, 60, 97, 136, 177–78,
206
Modernity, 2–5 *passim*, 10ff, 63, 65, 150,
168–72 *passim*, 185f
Modernization, of Japan, 7–11 *passim*, 20f,
27, 33, 149f; and language, 7, 31, 42–47,
176–80, 184–86, 202
Monet, Claude, 163
Monogatari (narrative fiction), 153
Moore, George, 153

Mori Ōgai, 24f, 44–45, 57, 79f, 194f, 203,
208, 215
Morley, John, 192
Motoori Norinaga, 192
Mozume Takami, 43–44
Murasaki Shikibu: *Genji monogatari* (The
tale of Genji), 183–84, 192, 198
Murō Saisei, 49, 178
Mushakōji Saneatsu, 48–53 *passim*, 201,
205; *Omedetaki hito* (A blessed person),
48; on notion of self, 94–95, 112; and
genbun-itchi, 97, 177f
Musset, Alfred de, 135
Myōjō (magazine), 39

Nagai Kafū, 11, 49, 80, 157; and Zola, 80–
81, 135, 209, 214; literary career of,
135–36, 215; postwar reception of, 136,
141, 149; and individualism, 136, 149
—*Bokutō kidan* (A strange tale from east of
the river), 11, 215; contemporary reception of, 135, 141; and I-novel discourse, 136, 141, 145, 150; identity of
first-person narrator in, 137–50; genre
distinctions and, 137–48 *passim*; fiction
writing in, 138–50 *passim*; narrative levels in, 139–50 *passim*; narrator and author in, 139–44, 148, 150, 216; and
"Postscript" ("Sakugo zeigen"), 140,
143–44, 149, 215–16; referentiality in,
140–45 *passim*; identity and proper
names in, 140–42; enunciating subject
and enunciated subject, 142, 145; fiction, facts, and truth, 142–50, 216;
transformation of life into art, 142–45;
reality and literary mediation in, 143,
147–50; and Kafū's literary diary (*Danchōtei nichijō*), 144–45; verisimilitude vs.
experiential truth, 146–47, 148; Great
Kantō Earthquake in, 148ff; double vision in, 148–50; on modernization, 149f
—Other texts: *Amerika monogatari* (Tales of
America), 135; *Danchōtei nichijō* (Kafū's
literary diary), 144–45; *Furansu monogatari* (Tales of France), 135; *Jigoku no hana*
(A flower in hell), 80–81, 135, 209;
Kanraku (Pleasure), 135; *Kichōsha no
nikki* (Diary of a returnee), 135; *Reishō*
(Sneers), 135; "Saiyū nisshi shō" (Excerpts from journal kept while wandering in the West), 215f; *Sango-shū* (Coral

Sakurada Momoe, 197

Sanba, *see* Shikitei Sanba

Santō Kyōden, 196

San'yūtei Enchō, 31

Sasaki Yukitsuna, 202

Satō Haruo, 49, 55, 97, 141, 177f; and Tanizaki Jun'ichirō, 155–56, 217f

—Other texts: "Bokura no kekkon" (Our marriage), 156; *Junjō shishū* (Lyrical poems), 155; *Kono mittsu no mono* (These three things), 156; *Kozo no yuki ima izuko* (Where are the snows of yesteryear), 156; "Sanma no uta" (A song of mackerel), 155

Satomi Ton, 205

Seidensticker, Edward, 215f

Seiji shōsetsu (political fiction): notion of *shōsetsu* in, 18f; and Freedom and People's Rights movement, 18ff, 28, 30, 197–98

Seishi (official, orthodox history): vs. *shōsetsu*, 17ff, 191f. *See also Haishi*; *Shōsetsu.*

Seitō (magazine), 167

Seki Ryōichi, 192

Sekiya Ichirō, 130

Self: and I-novel discourse, 2f, 8, 11, 15–16, 51–65 *passim*, 184–86, 205; modernization and, 7, 11, 33; language and, 7–11 *passim*, 40–47 *passim*, 185; Taishō Democracy and, 8, 52–55, 206; and Marxism, 8, 53–58 *passim*, 206; as privileged signifier, 10, 40, 53, 55, 186, 190, 201; preoccupation with notion of, 11, 15f, 37–42, 46–47, 51–65, 90–91, 136, 141, 150, 184–86, 190, 201, 205; and novel writing, 11, 40, 51–65 *passim*, 93–96, 109, 113, 117, 119, 184–86, 190; nation-state and, 33, 39, 199; as political subject, 33, 199; and Christianity, 33–39 *passim*, 201–2; and ideal of love, 37, 39, 75–76, 88, 104–12 *passim*, 167, 209f; art and, 39, 51–55 *passim*, 94–95, 184–86; mediation of Western literature and, 40–47 *passim*, 73–76 *passim*, 84–90 *passim*, 106, 163, 200; Shirakaba group and, 94–95, 110, 112, 167. *See also* Individual; Subject; *and specific authors by name*

Sexuality, 10, 160; love and, 73–76, 81–88 *passim*, 105–12 *passim*, 210; in Japanese Naturalism, 79–88, 112, 165, 169, 210;

and truth, 86–88, 165, 210; Michel Foucault on, 87; and European Decadence, 154, 161–65, 169, 217. *See also* Shiga Naoya; Tanizaki Jun'ichirō; Tayama Katai

Shakespeare, William, 24, 51

Sharebon (books on refined manners in pleasure quarters), 20

Shasei (sketch, literary *dessin*), 9–10, 46, 77–78, 208–9

Shaseibun (sketch prose, literary *dessin*), 46, 77

Shelley, Percy Bysshe, 36

Shiga Naoya, 5, 11, 49, 62, 185, 201; Kobayashi Hideo on, 93, 120, 213; and I-novel discourse, 93f, 99–105 *passim*, 109, 124–25, 131, 204, 212; critics' descriptions of, 93–96 *passim*, 120–21, 210; Akutagawa Ryūnosuke on, 93, 95–96, 152f; protagonist and author in texts of, 93–103 *passim*, 108f, 125, 128–29, 212, 214; and respect for self, 95, 110, 112; and *genbun-itchi*, 96–97, 177; and genre distinctions, 97–99; on factuality of his works, 99, 103, 211, 214; recurrent characters in texts of, 100; recurrent motifs in texts of, 100, 127; and narrative shaping of life, 100–102, 109–13 *passim*, 123–29 *passim*, 211; first-person recollection in texts of, 101f, 113; on author and his works, 101–2, 211–12; moods (*kibun*) in texts of, 103–4, 127; Christianity in texts of, 103–12 *passim*; love in texts of, 104–12 *passim*; sin of fornication and sexual desire in texts of, 105–12 *passim*; identity of self in texts of, 108–12 *passim*, 121–22, 129–30, 212ff; and autobiographical framing, 109, 123–25, 214; spontaneity in texts of, 110–12, 122; and Japanese literary tradition, 120–21, 131; metaphor in texts of, 123, 127–31 *passim*; nature in texts of, 123, 127–31 *passim*, 213f; and third-person autobiographical novel, 123–25; on *An'ya kōro* (A dark night's passing), 125–27; family romance in texts of, 126–27

—*An'ya kōro* (A dark night's passing), 100, 190; protagonist and author in, 5, 99, 125; fictional scenario in, 126–28; and nature, 127–31 *passim*

Library of Congress Cataloging-in-Publication Data

Suzuki, Tomi, 1951–
Narrating the self : fictions of Japanese modernity / Tomi Suzuki.
p.   cm.
Includes bibliographical references and index.
ISBN 0-8047-2552-7 (cl.) : ISBN 0-8047-3162-4 (pbk.)
1. Japanese fiction—1868– —History and criticism.
2. Autobiographical fiction, Japanese—History and criticism.
3. Shiga, Naoya, 1883-1971—Criticism and interpretation.
4. Tanizaki, Jun'icherō, 1886-1965—Criticism and interpretation.
5. Literature, comparative—Japanese and Western.
6. Literature, comparative—Western and Japanese.
I. Title.
PL747.57.A85S89   1996
895.6'3009—dc20   95-11917
                                                         CIP

Original printing 1995

Last figure below indicates year of this printing:

05   04   03   02   01   00   99   98   97